THE POWER OF EMOTIONS

Emotions make history and have their own history. Exploring the emotional worlds of the German people, this book tells a very different story of the twentieth century. Ute Frevert reveals how emotions have shaped and influenced not only individuals but entire societies. Politicians use emotions, and institutions frame them, while social movements work with and through them. Ute Frevert's engaging analysis of twenty essential and powerful emotions – including anger, grief, hate, love, pride, shame and trust – explores how emotions coloured major events and developments from the German Empire to the Federal Republic until this very day.

Emotions also have a history, illustrated by the changing forms, meanings and atmosphere of various emotions in twentieth-century Germany: for example, hate was a driving force behind National Socialism but is out of place in a democracy. Around 1900, people associated practices with love or nostalgia that do not resonate with us today. Showcasing why Germans were enthusiastic about the war in 1914 and proud of their national football team in 2006, this book highlights the historical power of emotions as much as their own historicity.

UTE FREVERT is Director of the Max Planck Institute for Human Development, Berlin, and President of the Max Weber Foundation. Until 2007, she was Professor of German history at Yale University. She is a Corresponding Fellow of the British Academy and has been awarded the German Order of Merit for her international contribution to modern social, cultural and political history.

T0384653

THE POWER OF EMOTIONS

A History of Germany from 1900 to the Present

UTE FREVERT

Max Planck Institute for Human Development, Berlin

Translated by Emma C. Lawson and Daniela Petrosino

CAMBRIDGE
UNIVERSITY PRESS

Shaftesbury Road, Cambridge CB2 8EA, United Kingdom

One Liberty Plaza, 20th Floor, New York, NY 10006, USA

477 Williamstown Road, Port Melbourne, VIC 3207, Australia

314–321, 3rd Floor, Plot 3, Splendor Forum, Jasola District Centre, New Delhi – 110025, India

103 Penang Road, #05–06/07, Visioncrest Commercial, Singapore 238467

Cambridge University Press is part of Cambridge University Press & Assessment, a department of the University of Cambridge.

We share the University's mission to contribute to society through the pursuit of education, learning and research at the highest international levels of excellence.

www.cambridge.org
Information on this title: www.cambridge.org/9781009376839

DOI: 10.1017/9781009376792

Originally published as *Mächtige Gefühle: Von A wie Angst bis Z wie Zuneigung – Deutsche Geschichte seit 1900* by Ute Frevert. Copyright © 2019 S. Fischer Verlag GmbH, Frankfurt am Main.

First English edition published 2023

© Ute Frevert 2023

Printed in the United Kingdom by TJ Books Limited, Padstow Cornwall

A catalogue record for this publication is available from the British Library.

Library of Congress Cataloging-in-Publication Data
Names: Frevert, Ute, author.
Title: The power of emotions : a history of Germany from 1900 to the present / Ute Frevert, Max Planck Institute for Human Development.
Other titles: Mächtige gefühle. English | History of Germany from 1900 to the present
Description: First English edition. | Cambridge, United Kingdom ; New York, NY : Cambridge University Press, 2023. | "Originally published as Mächtige Gefühle: Von A wie Angst bis Z wie Zuneigung–Deutsche Geschichte seit 1900 by Ute Frevert. Copyright © 2019 S. Fischer Verlag GmbH, Frankfurt am Main." | Includes bibliographical references and index.
Identifiers: LCCN 2023003370 (print) | LCCN 2023003371 (ebook) | ISBN 9781009376839 (hardback) | ISBN 9781009376822 (paperback) | ISBN 9781009376792 (epub)
Subjects: LCSH: Germany–History–20th century. | Germany–History–21st century. | Emotions. | History–Psychological aspects.
Classification: LCC DD232 .F7413 2023 (print) | LCC DD232 (ebook) | DDC 943.08/4–dc23/eng/20230125
LC record available at https://lccn.loc.gov/2023003370
LC ebook record available at https://lccn.loc.gov/2023003371

ISBN 978-1-009-37683-9 Hardback
ISBN 978-1-009-37682-2 Paperback

CONTENTS

FIGURES

ACKNOWLEDGEMENTS

I thank my daughter Bettina for collaborating with me on the exhibition and for giving her critical input on this book. As always, Uli Schreiterer was my biggest critic, pushing me to write several versions of the text. It is not only for this that I am grateful to him.

My thanks also go to Lena Herenz and Philine Höhn who assisted me with the research, and to Kerstin Singer who set me on the trail of images I would not otherwise have found. In addition to her and my German editor Tanja Hommen, Philipp Nielsen and Kerstin Pahl read the manuscript in its entirety and provided generous feedback that improved the work. Close collaboration with Emma C. Lawson and Daniela Petrosino (and, in part, with Kate Davison) made the text as correct and smooth as could be. The book differs from the German original in many ways, as I have adjusted it for non-German audiences.

GERMAN ABBREVIATIONS

AfD   Alternative für Deutschland (Alternative for Germany)
APO   Außerparlamentarische Opposition (extra-parliamentary opposition, a German protest movement)
BRD   Bundesrepublik Deutschland (Federal Republic of Germany, FRG)
CDU   Christlich Demokratische Union Deutschlands (Christian Democratic Union of Germany)
CSU   Christlich-Soziale Union in Bayern (Christian Social Union in Bavaria)
DDP   Deutsche Demokratische Partei (German Democratic Party)
DDR   Deutsche Demokratische Republik (German Democratic Republic, GDR)
DNVP   Deutschnationale Volkspartei (German National People's Party)
DSF   Deutsch-Sowjetische Freundschaft (Society for German-Soviet Friendship)
DVP   Deutsche Volkspartei (German People's Party)
FDGB   Freier Deutscher Gewerkschaftsbund (Free German Trade Union Confederation)
FDJ   Freie Deutsche Jugend (Free German Youth)
FDP   Freie Demokratische Partei (Free Democratic Party)
KdF   Kraft durch Freude (Strength through Joy)
KPD   Kommunistische Partei Deutschlands (Communist Party of Germany)
NPD   Nationaldemokratische Partei Deutschlands (National Democratic Party of Germany)
NSDAP   Nationalsozialistische Deutsche Arbeiterpartei (National Socialist German Workers' Party)
PDS   Partei des Demokratischen Sozialismus (Party of Democratic Socialism)
PEGIDA   Patriotische Europäer gegen die Islamisierung des Abendlandes (Patriotic Europeans Against the Islamization of the West)
RAF   Rote Armee Fraktion (Red Army Faction)
RIAS   Rundfunk im amerikanischen Sektor (Radio in the American Sector of Berlin)

SA   Sturmabteilung (literally 'Storm Detachment', Stormtroopers)
SED   Sozialistische Einheitspartei Deutschands (Socialist Unity Party
         of Germany)
SPD   Sozialdemokratische Partei Deutschlands (Social Democratic Party of
         Germany)
SS   Schutzstaffel (literally 'Protection Squadron')

~

Introduction
Powerful Emotions in German History

Everyone knows from experience that emotions are powerful. They motivate us, colour our relationships and views, determine what is important for us and what is not. But it is less clear how they affect history beyond individual lives and interpersonal relationships: how do they make history, and how are they themselves shaped by history? This book explores these questions.

Why? Does paying attention to emotions and analysing what they do promise to give us a better understanding of the world? Can this perspective foster new insights into history? Can it shine a different light on the past and present?

Even a fleeting glance at contemporary developments reveals that emotions make the world go round. In January 2019, sixteen-year-old Greta Thunberg gave a passionate speech at the World Economic Forum in Davos, Switzerland: 'I want you to panic. I want you to act as if your house was on fire.' The threat posed by climate change, the Swedish activist argued, demanded immediate action from politicians and economic leaders. Her appeal resonated forcefully among young people all over the globe who, through the Fridays for Future movement, were applying pressure to national governments and international organizations. Invoking emotions like fear, empathy, solidarity and indignation helped sustain the movement, render it visible and emphasize its urgency.

A year later, the world faced another crisis that confronted states, societies, scientific communities and economies with unprecedented challenges. The COVID-19 pandemic caused widespread fear among citizens, and they turned to the authorities for protection. Trust alternated with distrust, and many countries soon experienced waves of passionate resistance to policies meant to contain the risk of infection. Angry protests left their mark on governments and parties that sought re-election, with the result that they tended to avoid more drastic yet necessary measures. The crisis encapsulates how emotions shape individual and collective behaviour, feed conflicts and struggles, and influence politics in the streets and in the chambers of power.

This could be witnessed across the world, albeit with stark national differences and peculiarities. In Germany, the crisis triggered a resurgence of resentment and animosity between town and country, native-born and

1

migrant, East and West. These fracture lines often translated into political cleavages that further polarized society, calling into question the idea of national solidarity that had, at the beginning of the pandemic, been strongly felt and celebrated.

Germany's recent history has known a great many challenges and ruptures. During the twentieth century, the nation experienced five different political regimes, with borders, territories and populations constantly changing. There was no shortage of dramatic events and upheavals in the lives of each and every citizen. This makes the country an ideal case study for examining history through the lens of feelings, passions and affects.[1]

Emotions Make History

The power of emotions is, above all, motivational. Emotions move and spur people to do certain things while refraining from doing others – decisions that alter the course of history. This holds for the man who attacked a synagogue in Halle in October 2019, killing two people out of hatred for Jews, migrants and women, just as it does for the right-wing extremist who, in February 2020, murdered nine people of non-German descent in the city of Hanau. It is true of citizens who are enraged by such crimes and who bring different emotions into play: grief, anger, empathy, solidarity, shame, fondness. It applies to politicians who respond with practical measures, ordering better protection for Jewish and Muslim places of community and worship, combating hate on the internet and pushing the police to more closely surveil right-wing fanatics. At all levels of society, people translate emotions into concrete actions and practices.

The power of emotions to mobilize individuals and social groups was particularly apparent in 2015, at the height of the so-called refugee crisis. Many Germans were shocked and enraged by images from camps along the Balkan route. Hungary's brutal treatment of refugees was considered, as the 6 September 2015 issue of the tabloid *Bild am Sonntag* wrote, a 'scandal'. When Chancellor Angela Merkel put an end to this scandal by allowing the refugees into Germany, she acted on a reasonable supposition: the people coming through Turkey to Europe on their March of Hope were determined, and nothing short of physical violence would break that determination. The German public, whose sympathies had already been sparked by the photo of a

---

[1] Emotions, affects, feelings and passions are used interchangeably in this book – even though the author is well aware of their different meanings across time and space. See Ute Frevert et al., *Emotional Lexicons: Continuity and Change in the Vocabulary of Feeling 1700–2000* (Oxford: Oxford University Press, 2014); focusing on English-language sources: Thomas Dixon, *From Passions to Emotions: The Creation of a Secular Psychological Category* (Cambridge: Cambridge University Press, 2003).

three-year-old Syrian child who had drowned in the Mediterranean, refused to accept the sight of more pain and hardship. Given this context, the chancellor's decision to keep the borders open seemed both logical and without alternative.

That it was the right decision was confirmed when countless citizens stepped up to greet the new arrivals and supply them with the basics. Volunteers organized bazaars and buffets, children donated soft toys, churches provided beds. The empathy of many had inspired the order not to close the borders. The experience was repeated five years later on a smaller scale. Pressure from below built up until the German government felt compelled to accept a few children from the disastrously overfilled refugee camps in Greece.

But emotions like empathy and compassion are not forces of nature. They do not run without rules, rob people of their senses and induce them to act in ways they never would have permitted themselves in a more sober state of mind. Yes, this conception of emotions has a long philosophical and medical tradition. Yet that makes it neither true nor valid. As recent scholarship from anthropology and cultural studies has elucidated, emotions are shaped by culture as well as by personal and collective experience. They feed on socio-cultural repertoires that invest them with nuance and meaning. How and what people feel always depends on what they have learnt about emotions.

Neuroscience confirms this view. Studies in the field have shown that the classic binary of reason and emotion is untenable. Emotions are tightly interwoven with cognitive operations in which the entire brain is involved. These neural connections are the end result of lifelong learning processes that vary across space, time and societies. American psychologist Lisa Feldman Barrett calls them 'constructed emotions' and emphasizes that people themselves shape and model how they feel.[2]

Historical experiences play a significant part in the construction of emotions. In Germany, images of desperate people fleeing their war-torn home in 2015 evoked memories of the flight and forced migration that millions of families had gone through after the Second World War (Figure 1). At the same time, the sight of tall fences intended to keep refugees away from the Hungarian border struck a dissonant chord with the unforgettable euphoria felt when the Austria–Hungary border – part of the Iron Curtain – opened in the summer of 1989, allowing vacationing GDR citizens to cross in large numbers (Figure 2).

Alongside personal experiences and collective memories, social institutions and the media influence how and which emotions are felt and expressed. Without the constant stream of images that filled German television screens in

---

[2] Lisa Feldman Barrett, *How Emotions Are Made: The Secret Life of the Brain* (Boston: Houghton Mifflin Harcourt, 2017).

Figure 1   1948: Refugees wait to cross the Russo-British frontier at Helmstedt (Photo by Keystone-France/Gamma-Keystone via Getty Images)

Figure 2   1989: Refugees from the GDR reach the Austria–Hungary border (Photo by Votava/brandstaetter images via Getty Images)

2015, people's sensitivity towards what was happening and their willingness to help would hardly have been so great. Families, schools and religion also leave an imprint on how people feel and handle those feelings. The same goes for the workplace, the football stadium and the concert hall, as well as for choirs, civic associations, social movements and political parties. Everywhere, people encounter rules and practices that encourage some emotions but label others taboo, and those rules are further differentiated by gender and age. What applies to men might not apply to women and vice versa; society expects different emotional behaviour from children and adolescents compared to adults. In earlier centuries, when religion and the church dominated how life was lived more than any other institution, Protestants, Catholics and Jews were raised to feel distinct emotions. Love, humility, sympathy, jealousy, hope and longing meant different things for different religions and denominations.

Emotions Have a History

Emotions not only *make* history. They are also *made by* history. They are transformed by social institutions and events that differ across time and place. Emotions *have* a history, and it is complex. For one thing, the occasions and contexts that summon certain emotions change. The all-pervasive fear of war and violence that followed the two world wars was unknown before 1914, particularly because people remembered the battles of 1870/1871 as ones with minimal casualties and huge financial gains. At the start of the twentieth century, nobody was afraid of terrorist attacks and climate change; instead they were fearful of epidemics like cholera and typhus. But as modern medicine and hygiene began to defeat infectious diseases, the fear of them waned. By the time the COVID-19 pandemic hit Europe in early 2020, many people no longer knew what it felt like to be frightened of plagues. While case numbers were climbing rapidly and people in Italy and France were barely allowed to leave their homes, only half of those surveyed in Germany stated that they were trying to avoid public spaces and transport. And only four out of ten had limited their contact with others, while a quarter judged the fear to be 'totally exaggerated'.

At the same time, fears that are still with us felt different in the past to how they do now. Towards the end of the nineteenth century, many people suffered and died from cancer. Nevertheless, patients had to contend with different rules and prohibitions, other interpretations and social perceptions of their illness from those existing today. This clearly affected their emotions. Even when they were facing death, they did not openly admit their fear as is now both common and encouraged.[3] Here, too, faith played a decisive role. Those

---

[3] Bettina Hitzer, *The History of Cancer and Emotions in Twentieth-Century Germany*, trans. Adam Bresnahan (Oxford: Oxford University Press, 2022), esp. ch. 4.

who firmly believed in life after death and the community of the living and dead could pass away with more serenity than those gazing into the void.

The social and cultural framing of emotions becomes further apparent when we study the ups and downs of 'affective-expressive emphasis'.[4] Some anthropologists distinguish between 'hot' and 'cold' cultures: while the former celebrate innovation and creativity, the latter permit little change. But hot and cold can also serve as measures of how intensely emotions and passions are experienced and expressed in a particular society. It was not for nothing that the political style of West Germany's early years was defined by appeals for sobriety and objectivity, which were supposed to supplant the mad emotionality of the 'Third Reich'. The first federal president, Theodor Heuss, admonished his fellow citizens every year to remain 'sober' and 'without illusion' and to liberate themselves from the 'shackles of buzzwords and ideologies' that 'recalled the bad time when the din, the noisy music suppressed the rational exchange of arguments and counterarguments'.[5]

Such reminders are one component of a politics of emotions that attempts to regulate a society's emotional economy. Another is formed by statements about which emotions are good and acceptable and which are not. How much national pride should be tolerated before things go too far? How much solidarity and empathy are needed to keep a society from freezing over? Who is deserving of these emotions, and who does not qualify, and on what grounds? How should people deal with envy and jealousy? When and for whom is fear – of whom or of what – justified? The answers to these questions are neither simple nor readily agreed. Democracies do not make things easy for themselves on this front, because they cannot dictate emotional politics from above. Citizens do listen, more or less attentively, to what presidents or chancellors tell them at Christmas, on New Year's Eve and on other occasions throughout the year. But they also pursue their own aims, both alone and with others, that are bound up with their place of residence, social status, gender, age, religion and worldview. They reject prescriptions about how they should feel in a given situation and react defiantly when they sense that attempts at manipulation are afoot. The greater value people place on their own individuality and uniqueness, the more they prioritize emotional autonomy and independence.

This emphasis is part of the culture that defines the contemporary 'society of singularities'.[6] But it neglects and overlooks a crucial fact. Certainly,

[4] Talcott Parsons, 'Religion in Postindustrial America: The Problem of Secularization', *Social Research* 41, no. 2 (1974): 193–225, quote 221.

[5] Reinhard Kiehl, ed., *Alle Jahre wieder* (Düsseldorf: My favourite book, 2001), 84, 93, 110 (the book contains all Christmas and New Year's Eve speeches by West German presidents and chancellors between 1949 and 2000).

[6] Andreas Reckwitz, *The Society of Singularities* (Cambridge: Polity Press, 2020).

everyone has, and for the most part knows, their own feelings. However, emotions are not just subjective, private phenomena. If they were, people would not be able to communicate about them and through them. The language of emotions, which comprises words as well as gestures, would be incomprehensible if emotions could not be discussed and shared during conversations, concerts, football matches, public screenings or political demonstrations. Such events provide platforms for the constitution of felt communities of varying duration, and some remain lifelong memories.

Still, just because emotions have a language and can be communicated does not necessarily mean they actually get spoken about. Not everyone wears their heart on their sleeve, keeps a diary or has friends to whom they disclose their most intimate feelings. Not everyone reads novels to learn about emotions they might otherwise never have felt. Who downloads mindfulness apps, and who subscribes to hygge or wokeness? All these practices have a historical and social specificity; not every culture, era or milieu observes them.

Emotional Signatures of the Twentieth Century

In hindsight, the twentieth century was a time of intense emotions that were spoken about more than ever before. It kicked off with celebrations and grand hopes. In 1900, the general sentiment was that people (in Western and Central Europe, at least) had never had it so good. The past had brought wonderful things and inspired expectations that the future would be even better. People were meant to feel proud of what had been accomplished. The melancholic tenor of the *fin de siècle* seemed to be over; tension and conflict, at least according to editorials and public speeches, were forgotten.[7]

Fourteen years later, the First World War broke out. At the time nobody knew that it would be the first of two. Quite a few people greeted it with enthusiasm and had glorious hopes for it, which, as we now know, went nowhere. All over Europe, the war turned things upside down, drew new borders, saw the downfall of old empires and ushered in the birth of new states. For Germany, its end was a devastating shock. Most people were unprepared for defeat, since high-ranking generals had remained confident of the coming victory until the very last. Many found the Allies' conditions of peace unfair and humiliating, while others viewed the 1918 Revolution as a dishonourable betrayal and a 'stab in the back' of the brave military. They fanned the flames of fanatic hatred against the socialists they blamed for it all. Political polarization and the unrelenting enmity between right and left was the heaviest burden borne by the fledgling Weimar Republic.

---

[7] Ute Frevert, ed., *Das Neue Jahrhundert: Europäische Zeitdiagnosen und Zukunftsentwürfe um 1900* (Göttingen: Vandenhoeck & Ruprecht, 2000).

Nevertheless, the republic started 1919 with optimism and pluckily undertook political and social reforms. Women gained suffrage and the right to hold political office. They entered parliament, where they engaged with social issues and combated destructive passions. Democratic ideals flowed into educational politics and welfare policy; urban planners experimented with spacious housing projects; cultural creativity blossomed. Young women mothballed their long dresses, cut their hair short, played sports and looked for role models on the cinema screen. In cities, bars for homosexuals opened up, as did sexual counselling centres for the 'modern marriage'. Situated between Paris and Moscow, Berlin became the capital city of the avant-garde, where *tout le monde* rushed to meet.

But Berlin was also home to racist, extreme right-wing politicians such as Joseph Goebbels, who became a regional leader of the Nazi Party in 1926, an MP in 1928 and the party's national head of propaganda in 1930. His vicious and insulting diatribes made him notorious in parliament, but the most important fights against communists, social democrats and the police took place out on the street. After the stock market crash of 1929, the National Socialists swiftly grew in popularity. In July 1932, they received 37 per cent of the vote and became the biggest party in the Reichstag. Forces that could counter their ascent were nowhere in sight. Although the Social Democrats and Communists together won about 36 per cent, their animosity towards one another snuffed out any possibility of cooperation.

Meanwhile, the bourgeois centre disintegrated. It had always held ambiguous feelings about the Weimar Republic. Some centrists did turn into 'republicans in mind', all the while secretly remaining 'monarchists at heart'.[8] Others drifted into the rightist-nationalist constellation. When foreign minister Gustav Stresemann died in 1929, the fault lines could no longer be ignored. Hundreds of thousands attended his wake, and the funeral procession in Berlin was, in the words of liberal publicist Harry Graf Kessler, 'endless': 'Reichsbanner [an association of republican veterans] cordoned off the procession left and right . . . The procession stopped in front of the Foreign Office. Black drapes covered the window of Stresemann's office and a basket with white lilies decorated the window sill; it was truly the most intense, most human sight.' On the other side, though, bitter struggles over Stresemann's political legacy ignited the day after the public burial. Even Stresemann's own party tried everything in its power to pervert his image 'into that of an anti-republican chauvinist, in order to capture for the right wing the moral capital

---

[8] Friedrich Meinecke, 'Verfassung und Verwaltung der deutschen Republik [1918/19]', in Friedrich Meinecke, *Politische Schriften und Reden*, ed. Georg Kotowski (Darmstadt: Toeche-Mittler, 1958), 280–98, here 281. See Andreas Wirsching and Jürgen Eder, eds, *Vernunftrepublikanismus in der Weimarer Republik* (Stuttgart: Steiner, 2008).

that he had left behind'.[9] Whereas the National Socialists bolstered their strength, the liberal-conservative parties withered away. In 1920, they had claimed about a quarter of the votes; twelve years later, they won less than 3 per cent.[10]

After 1933, only one party set the tone, and it was an emotionally loaded one. For those who conformed politically and racially, the Nazis promised economic boons, international importance and a happily unified populace replenished by 'Strength through Joy'. National honour and pride were prized as emotions of utmost significance, and those who betrayed them in the eyes of the regime were forced into concentration camps or to the gallows. The hateful ideology of antisemitism became state doctrine, culminating in the cold-blooded murder of millions of Jewish men, women and children throughout Europe. The Wehrmacht and SS conducted a war of extermination in Eastern Europe with unprecedented brutality, and in Western and Southern Europe, too, German occupiers inflicted pain and suffering on local populations. Even though the number of soldiers who died for 'Führer, *Volk* and *Vaterland*' rapidly escalated after 1941, many Germans continued to believe in the approaching 'final victory' until the very end, a delusion captured best in the words of film star Zarah Leander: 'I know that someday a miracle will happen.'

Instead of a miraculous final victory came unconditional surrender. Germany's borders were redrawn, particularly in the east, and the remaining territory was occupied and divided up into four zones. The two states that arose out of them in 1949 were not sovereign, nor did they have their own militaries. Jammed between blocs dominated by superpowers armed to the teeth, each German state developed its own social forms, institutions and emotional styles. Even after East German citizens brought about the fall of their government in 1989 in Germany's first ever peaceful revolution and Germans celebrated reunification a year later, it was no stretch of the imagination to view East and West Germans as two different species. Their comportment, language and clothing; their relationships, consumption habits and political preferences – everything was different. Those are just a few of the reasons why people who belong together – a sentiment shared by many,

---

[9] *Harry Graf Kessler, Tagebücher 1918–1937*, ed. Wolfgang Pfeiffer-Belli (Frankfurt: Insel-Verlag, 1982), 631–32. The German edition was used to refer to entries unavailable in the abridged English edition.

[10] Between 1928 and 1932 alone, the right-wing liberal German People's Party (DVP) lost over 2.2 million votes, sinking from 8.7 to 1.1 per cent of the total. The centre-left, socially liberal German Democratic Party (DDP) – which counted future president of West Germany Theodor Heuss among its founding members – lost 1.1 million votes in the same period and shrank from 4.9 to 1 per cent. The explicitly anti-republican and antisemitic German National People's Party (DNVP), which gained 20 per cent of the votes in 1924, moved so far into the ethnonationalist camp after 1930 that its MPs had no reservations in joining the NSDAP in 1933.

including former chancellor Willy Brandt – grew and grow together only slowly and in fits and starts. Both sides have felt disappointment and resentment about the process of unification, and such resentment finds ample representation in people's political leanings and choices.

A New Narrative?

The facts and figures of twentieth-century German history are well known, but interpretations vary with the perspective one takes. Those interested in economic matters and social cohesion will notice different developments, entanglements and caesuras to those engaged with the history of politics or culture. What new knowledge can we uncover by analysing the history of emotions? Answering the question at this point would necessitate squeezing in the following twenty chapters here. But a few gestures of what we stand to gain from taking a historical view of emotions are in order:

- The expression 'German Angst' has become rather common. Why has 'angst', like kindergarten, blitzkrieg and schadenfreude, found its way into the English language? Is angst a specifically German emotion? Are Germans particularly susceptible to angst and fear, and if so, of which sort? One may think of the proverbial German fear of inflation or the fear of acid rain and dying forests that concerned many people in the 1980s. One wonders where such fears originated and what they led to – and who coined the term 'German Angst' and for what reason.
- Since 2010, the authoritative *Duden* dictionary has contained an entry for the word *Wutbürger*, or 'angry citizen'. In the same year, Stéphane Hessel – born in Berlin in 1917 – published the manifesto *Time for Outrage: Indignez-vous!* Millions of people bought and read it. Were they all angry citizens? That depends on how one understands the term and what significance one ascribes to it. Some people proudly self-identify with it while others utter it as an insult. Normally anger is not the first trait that comes to mind when one thinks of an even-tempered, rational adult. After all, since the nineteenth century, the ability to control one's anger has been a cornerstone of a middle-class upbringing. But what about anger towards the powerful and the quiet grumblings of the powerless? And at what historical junctures have these grumblings grown loud and impossible to ignore?
- Over the last few years, envy has been a topic of heated political debate. But that is nothing new. In the 1920s, right-wing parties accused those on the left of being jealous and denying people the comforts they had inherited or earned. In 1994, Christian Democrat (CDU) politicians countered 'jealous socialist chants' with a 'categorical Yes to merit'.[11] In these instances, the

---

[11] *CDU-Informationsdienst Union in Deutschland* 11 (1994): 4–7.

charge of envy or jealousy served to defame a political opponent – a function it continues to have. Envious people, it is said, are unwilling to exert themselves and prefer to pilfer from others' pockets. But this obscures the more fundamental question about the relationship between envy and competition, a keystone of the economic and social system. It also calls for a re-examination of the concepts of merit and performance and the ways in which they are measured. How do people grapple with disparities in individual performance and competitive disadvantages, and what precedents and experiences do they draw on? How does envy relate to solidarity and the expectation that the well-off should support the less affluent?

- In recent times, politicians have started to claim humility for themselves. They 'humbly' accept disastrous election results and 'humbly' celebrate victories; they pretend to put their egos in the backseat and bow to the will of the voters. This is surprising, since the word humility, once closely tied to religious language and practice, had long left the active vocabulary. Now it has, somewhat miraculously, returned, and occupies a space beyond the religious sphere, with career guides advising readers on how to become more humble in order to gain others' sympathy and better reach one's aims. Unlike humility, humiliation has remained a word on everyone's lips. East Germans feel humiliated by West Germans, women by men, pupils by teachers, employees by managers. In international relations, too, humiliation plays an outsized role, as in the long chain of intentional and perceived disparagements exchanged by Germany and France between 1870 and 1945. How did humility as an individual emotional disposition and humiliation as a political strategy unfold during a century in which positions of power and powerlessness were flipped so often and so rapidly?

- Love is doubtless one of the most powerful emotion words. But love is not just a word. It is lived, experienced and negotiated. It forges the most important relationships that people enter into in their lives, and its quality changes over a person's life span. On the one hand, the transformation occurs in its own unique way, for every couple, in every child–parent relationship, in every friendship. On the other hand, these deeply personal emotions are not only observed, commented on and evaluated by others. They are also defined and framed from the outside. People in the twentieth and twenty-first centuries lived and live in a world permeated by media. Advice columns, films, novels and advertisements evoke expectations of what relationships are supposed to look like and offer consumers products and techniques to optimize them. At the same time, laws impose more or less restrictive rules on who can be in a romantic relationship and what this means in terms of rights and obligations. Only since 2017 have same-sex couples in Germany been able to consecrate their love in marriage under the protection of the law. The Catholic Church continues to refuse to marry them, while some Protestant churches have come around. In the 1950s, both churches resisted what they deemed 'mixed marriages' between Catholics and Protestants. In 1935, the National Socialist state had prohibited marriages between Jewish and non-Jewish Germans. But church and state not only controlled the behaviour of wives and husbands. They also sanctioned extramarital love. Up until the 1970s, unmarried couples were not allowed to share a hotel room in many places on the grounds that they were living in 'wild marriages' rooted in 'fornication'. People who felt suffocated by the tight corset of bourgeois morality fought for the loosening of such prohibitions and restrictions. They won the support of a public that was gradually becoming more liberal and chose to define love and sexuality between consenting adults as a strictly private matter. New gender roles played their part in making the bonds and pleasures of love more dynamic, diverse and colourful.

- Thus even seemingly private emotions are socially framed. They change over the course of an individual's life just as they do over the course of history. Conversely, public and official relations depend upon personal preferences and distastes. On the international political stage, the ability of politicians to get along with one another and trust each other is significant. When Social Democrat (SPD) politician Egon Bahr died in 2015 at the age of ninety-three, the former US secretary of state Henry Kissinger – only a year younger – did not pass up the chance to travel to the funeral of his 'lifelong friend' in Berlin. Their friendship had got off to a rocky start, and their political goals and the paths they took to reach them diverged widely. As national security advisor to President Richard Nixon, Kissinger was bothered that the architect of West Germany's Ostpolitik seemed to be 'free of any sentimental attachment to the United States'. He thought that Bahr 'was obviously not as unquestioningly dedicated to Western unity as the people we had known in the previous government' and that he placed too much weight on 'friendship with the East'. Only years later did Kissinger's distrust turn into admiration and personal friendship, which, Kissinger stated in his eulogy, was reflected in 'American-German relations today'. He proclaimed that 'our ultimate task is to eventually tame suspicions and submerge ambivalence in friendship', and that only then could serious diplomacy take place.[12]

This handful of examples reveals some of the multifarious ways in which emotions are interwoven into history. They shape human relationships, whether in the family or political life. They alternately enable and inhibit understanding and collaboration. They are deciding factors in whether

---

[12] Henry A. Kissinger, *White House Years* (Boston: Little, Brown & Co, 1979), 409–11; Henry A. Kissinger, 'Memorial Remarks for Egon Bahr', 17 September 2015, www.henryakissinger .com/remembrances/memorial-remarks-for-egon-bahr/, accessed 17 December 2021.

something is considered significant or insignificant. People who feel strongly about an issue act differently from those who are apathetic about it. But emotions are not simply present or absent. They live on in memories and influence future behaviour. The kind of 'sentimental attachment' to a country that Kissinger thought Bahr lacked usually begins with a personal experience: one spends time there, meets friends and becomes acquainted with a different way of living. All that gives rise to sympathy and affection, which then moulds the visitor's future perspectives.

Emotional Styles, Emotional Techniques, Emotional Politics

Emotions are not exclusively singular, subjective or individual. They adhere to social conventions and rules, both explicit and implicit. Every community, whether a long-standing institution or a short-term coalition, demands some degree of conformity in the emotions members can feel and the intensity with which they can feel them. Achieving that conformity necessitates practice, including sanctions for what is perceived as deviant and unacceptable. If you expressed favourable feelings for the Soviet Union in 1950s West Germany, you had a problem – even if it was not quite as severe as that of East Germans who celebrated their enthusiasm for rock music or the American way of life. Whatever their object might be, how emotions are expressed and lived out has always been subject to social scrutiny.

Young people in particular experiment with alternative emotional styles in their peer groups. After these styles become the norm, the next generation, or at least some cohort of it, discards them in favour of its own. In the 1970s, feminism paved the way for a culture of concern (*Betroffenheit*), of being affected by the world's ills and injustices and showing empathy for those who suffer. The 1990s ushered in the more masculine cult of coolness, a rehashing of an emotional style that had already crested in the 1920s and 1950s.[13] Modelling one's own behaviour on it meant engaging in a sort of detached irony, acting as if one were not moved by things. Emotional exuberance was made taboo, distance rewarded, nonchalance celebrated. The more a person sought to embody these styles, the more the styles influenced that person's own feelings and actions.

As early as 1877, Wilhelm Wundt, the founder of experimental psychology, discovered that emotional styles and the feelings experienced by their

---

[13] Cora Stephan, *Der Betroffenheitskult* (Reinbek: Rowohlt, 1994); Klaus Neumann-Braun and Birgit Richard, eds, *Coolhunters: Jugendkulturen zwischen Medien und Markt* (Frankfurt: Suhrkamp, 2005). On the broader development of this emotional style, see Peter N. Stearns, *American Cool: Constructing a Twentieth-Century Emotional Style* (New York: New York University Press, 1994); Helmut Lethen, *Cool Conduct: The Culture of Distance in Weimar Germany* (Berkeley: University of California Press, 2002).

adherents mutually affect one another. His primary examples were the famed professional mourners in Mediterranean societies, for whom 'the expression itself elicits the emotion'.[14] Laughter yoga works similarly. I remember an experiment that I only reluctantly participated in at first. It involved a large group of people who hardly knew one another. A coach led us through a series of stretches and breathing exercises, finally having us act as if we were laughing. The effect was stunning, and not just for me. At the end of the session, I felt happier, more joyful, more relaxed – and my interactions with the others showed it.

The professionally guided experiment followed a principle developed by psychologists around 1900: 'We don't laugh because we're happy; we're happy because we laugh.'[15] Around the world, there are thousands of groups whose members get together just to laugh. Schools, daycares, clinics, senior centres, businesses and fitness clubs have all adopted the exercise. Some people claim that laughter has healing properties and that they want to cultivate harmony and amity, while others do it to become better adjusted and more productive.

Whatever people's motivations and goals, laughter yoga illustrates how emotions can be consciously evoked and stabilized. There are techniques that bring body and mind in tune and synchronize them with others. In earlier times, religious institutions excelled in creating such techniques and environments. During the twentieth century, media, and film in particular, took over. Advertising, too, employs bodily and psychological knowledge to nudge consumers to purchase certain commodities and services. Last but not least, politicians and governments engage architecture, lighting, music and other devices to create emotional atmospheres that make people more receptive to highly affective messages.

National Socialism was by no means the only political system that sought to captivate the population by manipulating their emotions with overpowering theatrics. East Germany's 'actually existing socialism' also showed great interest in shaping and controlling the emotions of its citizens. Even democratic societies manage people's emotions, if by less martial, grandiose means. From the family to the school, the military to the welfare state, sports teams to fan clubs, institutions seek to rein in hate, envy and resentment while fostering trust, empathy and solidarity. But there is no guarantee that those efforts will succeed. Liberal societies cannot steer the media and bring institutions into line; their members seldom, if ever, march in lockstep. Though they establish

---

[14] Wilhelm Wundt, 'Ueber den Ausdruck der Gemüthsbewegungen', *Deutsche Rundschau* 11 (1877): 120–33. See also Wilhelm Wundt, *Outlines of Psychology*, trans. Charles Hubbard Judd (Leipzig: Engelmann, 1897), 169–84 (§ 13, Emotions).

[15] William James, 'What Is an Emotion?', *Mind* 9, no. 34 (1884): 188–205. See Maria Gendron and Lisa Feldman Barrett, 'Reconstructing the Past: A Century of Ideas about Emotion in Psychology', *Emotion Review* 1, no. 4 (2009): 316–39.

general guidelines, individuals are free to decide which advice and conventions they want to follow.

The Book and Its Structure

This book explores the economy and politics of emotions in Germany since the turn of the twentieth century, analysing which emotions were mobilized by whom to what ends. The politics of emotions was by no means the exclusive domain of government, parties, the media and commerce. It played out wherever people addressed their feelings, pursued their passions and were emotionally moved, whether inwardly, in peace and quiet, or outwardly, in public.

The economy and politics of emotions left traces that the historian can uncover in a wealth of sources: personal letters and diaries, court records and judicial decisions, (war) poems and song lyrics, graffiti, newspapers, posters and advertisements. Speeches by monarchs, state presidents and prime ministers constituted one part of the emotionally charged communications that defined the modern era of mass politics and mass participation. On the other side, citizens began to speak for themselves. Many wrote to the authorities telling of their grievances, desires, hopes and fears. Public archives contain countless letters from people from all social strata, men and women, old and young. They clearly felt the need to pour their hearts out to their leaders and articulate their joyful feelings as well as their anger and indignation. In 1949, Federal President Heuss received 'a few hundred letters' a day; five years later, it was 'hundreds, if not thousands' that he 'at least fleetingly' looked over and, when they had 'a personal character', personally responded to.[16]

Not all such letters have been preserved. After 1933, the Chancellery of the Führer tended to only save 'nice' letters.[17] Despite these filters, the writings that have been retained are a rich resource. They give a voice to those who are often muted in the official memory of the nation. The same is true of private papers and collections, some of which serendipitously ended up in my possession. Among them were a mother's handwritten recollections of her son who had died in the First World War, as well as letters sent between former classmates who were called to the front in 1941. They attest to the valence and binding power of enthusiasm, honour, love, grief and hate.

[16] Theodor Heuss, *Hochverehrter Herr Bundespräsident! Der Briefwechsel mit der Bevölkerung 1949–1959*, ed. Wolfram Werner (Berlin: De Gruyter, 2010), 97, 353.

[17] Federal Archive Berlin, NS 51, no. 71. Red notes in the margins evaluated a letter from one woman, who stated she would sacrifice her husband to the war and continue to raise her children (aged eleven and thirteen) in Hitler's spirit, as one of 'the nice letters' (27 September 1938). This indicates there must have also been not-so-nice letters, which were rarely preserved (or which are located somewhere I could not find them).

None of these sources ever talked of just one single emotion. As in everyday life, emotions in the source material appear in mixed form. Anger, hate and fear are often knotted together, as are nostalgia (for the past) and hope (for the future), love and empathy, pride and exaltation. Still, this book analyses emotions individually, in themselves, not as an entangled mass. The alphabetical order lends it the character of a (truncated) dictionary, starting with 'Anger' and ending with 'Trust'. The connections between the emotions are marked in the text so that readers can move back and forth through the pages.

Why did I decide on a lexicon of emotions rather than a chronologically ordered narrative that might identify moments in German history when emotional styles and dominant patterns shifted? Plausible, too, would have been a thematic history that investigated events and developments in order to dissect which emotions were in play and how they mutually reinforced, weakened or neutralized one another. One could write a history of the emotions of wars and revolutions, economic crises and social movements, the founding and collapse of states, all represented on a barometer tracking the rise and fall of collective feelings.

But then the historicity of emotions, their malleability over time and space, would have disappeared and fallen prey to the assumption, supported by many psychological theories, that emotions are substantially stable entities that share the same phenomenology and physiology. Love is love and has been love since early humanity. Anger is anger and has been so even before the time of Achilles, the ill-tempered Greek hero. But how do we know that? And why should we take this assumption for granted? If emotions are deeply embedded in social, economic, political and cultural environments, they also change with those environments. In this vein, love did not mean the same thing and was not felt alike in 1900 and 2020. Hate and disgust underwent many metamorphoses during the long twentieth century, as did the manifold forms and functions of fear, honour, humility and pride. Such changes in the experience and meaning of emotions would be lost in a narrative that closely followed the chronology of historical events and processes.

That is why I decided in favour of the lexical format. It showcases both how and where emotions influenced history *and* the degree to which they were themselves shaped by specific developments and circumstances. Another benefit is that readers can pick up the book and read at their leisure. They do not have to go from the first page to the last but can be led along by their personal curiosity. Every chapter is self-contained.

Speaking of curiosity: perhaps it seems strange that my emotional lexicon contains curiosity. Some might disagree that curiosity or honour or humility are even emotions. Contemporary psychology textbooks do not list them as such. Instead, they are generally concerned with the so-called basic emotions, six or seven in number, among them anger, happiness, surprise, disgust, sadness, fear and contempt.[18] Yet history knows a far more colourful and diverse palette of emotions. Empathy, hope, hate, belonging, trust and love, shame and pride, and even curiosity, honour and humility: all these and many others are classified and documented in the history of culture and knowledge. German encyclopaedias and dictionaries of the nineteenth and early twentieth centuries did not call them emotions but *Gemütsbewegungen*, movements of the soul or mind. *Emotion* as the all-encompassing general term only entered the German language far later, in the footsteps of Anglo-Saxon psychology.

Such scientific import not only contributed to the shrinking of emotion words and concepts in academic discourse as well as in everyday communi-cation. It also highlights the problem of translation. The German term *Gemüt* is synonymous neither with 'soul' nor with 'mind', as it is often translated. Legions of writers have spilled ink explaining what it meant, how it defined Germans in contrast to, say, French people, and why this was utterly import-ant. Having a proper and deep *Gemüt* characterized a true German and distinguished him or her from non-Germans. The *Gemüt* was formed through social interaction and culture: songs and prayers, poems and novels left their mark, especially during childhood and adolescence. The *Gemüt* hosted all kinds of feelings and brought them into order, elevating some over others. It was, in short, equivalent to and in charge of a person's emotional economy.

Gemüt thus comes with a cultural and historical baggage that is very difficult to capture in translation. The same holds true for many other German emotion words. Take *Geborgenheit*, the subject of the second chapter. The English noun 'belonging' does not do justice to the complexity of meaning inherent in the German original. The verb *bergen* connotes to salvage, to rescue, to harbour, to retrieve, to save. Someone who is *geborgen* feels secure, protected, warmly embraced. 'Belonging' only fleetingly touches upon these feelings, which have a physical as well as mental substance. But there is no better solution, and we will have to make do with the translation that comes closest.

This said, there is a lesson to be learnt. When emotion words do not map onto each other in different languages, they prove that feelings themselves are culturally specific. This sets limits on the universalistic approach to emotions as promulgated by most psychologists. It also invites us to keep an eye on chronology. If there is synchronic difference, we might expect diachronic difference as well. Again, language drops crucial clues. Even when it appears to remain unchanged and people continue to speak of love and hatred, envy and trust, they might refer to different feelings from those former generations

---

[18] The concept of basic emotions has been propagated by the influential psychologist Paul Ekman since the 1960s: Paul Ekman, 'Basic Emotions', in *Handbook of Cognition and Emotion*, ed. Tim Dalgleish and Mick J. Power (Chichester: Wiley, 1999), 45–60.

had experienced under the same name. It is therefore of utmost importance to dissect the semantics and references of such language and to put them in historical context.

Certain emotion words, however, have virtually disappeared in recent decades. What do we make of this? Can emotions be nameless? Can they endure without being addressed, in private or in public? Reflective minds usually strive to find a word for what they see and feel. Words are semantic units that convey meanings and connect a feeling to other experiences and expectations. Without words, feelings would remain unintelligible and non-negotiable. Spoken and written language thus serves as a treasure trove of human emotions – notwithstanding the added value of nonverbal, bodily means of communication.

What distinguishes emotions from perceptions, thoughts and opinions is the high degree of bodily stimulation they elicit. A person who loves or hates, or feels curious or humiliated, senses it viscerally and expresses it through body language. Even trust – a milder, less exciting emotion – causes corporeal vibrations and a certain posture, comportment and tone of voice. The German word for the kind of affection lived out in a friendship – *Zuneigung* – has a bodily gesture written into its very name. One inclines (*neigt*) oneself towards another person; one seeks nearness and physical contact. Though frowned upon during the COVID-19 pandemic, this is a common emotional expression that involves the entire body.

The forms these movements and dispositions take vary among cultures and across history. Who is allowed to come close to whom is a matter of social convention. That men and women – politicians included – greet each other with a hug and a kiss is a relatively new phenomenon and is by no means standard practice in every part of the world. The number of kisses and the tightness of the hug differ from country to country, from region to region. Physical actions and reactions depend on how a person relates to their own body. Some view it as a highly efficient machine, while others would prefer to protect it in a bubble. Cultural scripts and stereotypes exist for both. Societies and social groups construct images of the body and disseminate them through media. This has immediate consequences for how emotions are perceived and expressed. Conceptualizing the body as hard or soft, permeable or steely, resilient or fragile, all influences the intensity and quality of what people feel.

Over the course of the twentieth century, the mechanization of industrial labour increased, only to be pushed aside by digitalization and the expansion of the service economy. These shifts contributed to the coming and going of a plurality of emotional and bodily regimes, as did new forms of motorized movement and broader participation in competitive sports. The medicalization of almost every aspect of life, along with the growing popularity of therapy, have also done their bit in altering our approaches to our bodies and emotions. How shifts in bodily regimes affected emotional practices is still widely unknown and needs far more research.

At the same time, emotions are not exclusively a corporeal matter. They also have a cognitive component and are bound up with evaluations and the lessons of experience. Compared to purely intellectual ruminations, however, their practical import is exponentially greater. They spur action, lift people out of their seats, give them pause, and change their orientation towards life and the world. This is what lends emotions their historical force.

This book demonstrates how twenty different emotions helped shape German history in the last century. Fear and anger fuelled protest, but so did grief and empathy. Belonging was often associated with conceptions of home and homeland that have, since the 1920s, been a matter of conflict and controversy. Curiosity pushed education and science forward, while also inspiring the wanderlust that, for many years, led Germans to undertake more travel abroad than any other nationality. Solidarity – the feeling of camaraderie and mutual care shared by members of labour unions and cooperatives – was the godfather of the welfare state. Without friendly affection, there would be no multi-layered process of European unification with countless protagonists.

Why did I pick twenty emotions, instead of, say, eighteen or twenty-five? Certainly, more or less would have been conceivable and perhaps desirable. Everyone will find one or another emotion missing. But the number twenty is not purely random, either. After all, the book is about the twentieth century, as was the exhibition that it grew out of: *The Power of Emotions: Germany 19/19*. It featured twenty posters on different emotions, illustrating their significance in German history from the Weimar Republic to today. Together with my daughter Bettina, I curated the exhibition, which travelled to 2,500 locations around the world: to schools, community colleges, town halls, city libraries, universities and Goethe Institutes.[19] It was met with praise and drew crowds, but its form only allowed for brief texts and captions. Many visitors wanted more context and more nuance. This book seeks to accommodate that wish.

---

[19] The exhibition was made possible by the patronage of the federal foreign minister and was organized by the Foundation 'Remembrance, Responsibility and Future' and the Federal Foundation for the Study of the Communist Dictatorship in Germany: www .machtdergefuehle.de/?lang=en, accessed 7 April 2022.

Anger

Jacques Tilly's political floats in Düsseldorf's annual carnival parade almost always cause a furore. Routinely, someone or other feels insulted by his biting satire and voices their protest. In 2017, however, everybody seemed content. No one had a problem with either the text or the visual depiction of the slogan, 'With too much rage in the belly, democracy is on its arse'. Evidently, the artist had struck the right chord and articulated exactly how many were feeling (Figure 3).

The reference was unmistakable: on 3 October 2016, during an official celebration of German reunification in Dresden, right-wing demonstrators had shouted down the chancellor and president as 'traitors' and a 'pack of liars'. A prominent Alternative für Deutschland (AfD) politician defended the heckling as an instance of 'lived democracy', citing the fundamental right to freedom of expression: the hecklers were angry and had carried their legitimate feelings to the streets. To do so was their proper and legal right.

This was only partly true. Freedom of expression, as protected by the constitution, has limits. Anyone who maliciously slanders another person and knowingly lies in public can be prosecuted for this. Yet politicians often forego pressing charges, preferring to tune out dissent and do what the AfD representative cynically and sneeringly recommended: 'You just have to cope with it.'[1] Those who cannot cope or who get fed up with personal insults from angry citizens either withdraw and quit, or attempt, as Green Party politician Renate Künast did in 2016, to personally confront them and open a dialogue.

Nobody disputes that anger, rage and outrage have their place in democracy. As Tilly's carnival float suggested, it is about the degree ('too much') and form in which they are expressed. Should citizens with 'rage in their belly' not also be required to enter into dialogue, give reasons for their anger and be open to counter-arguments? Those who cannot contain their proverbial bile, who 'see red' and are neither willing nor able to engage in argument, opt out of democratic society.

[1] Jan Schumann, 'TV-Kritik "Hart aber fair": AfD-Chef sieht Volksverräter-Rufe als gelebte Demokratie', *Berliner Zeitung*, 11 October 2016, https://bit.ly/3ZTNipU, accessed 21 December 2021.

Figure 3   Rage in the belly: 2017 carnival parade, Düsseldorf (Jacques Tilly)

Anger, Rage and Fury

Rage or fury (*Wut*), according to the *Brockhaus* encyclopaedia of 1974, is a 'state of high emotional excitement'. It develops 'in response to an impairment of the personality or vital sphere' and is accompanied by 'motor and vegetative phenomena'. It can 'unload itself in the form of an act aimed at destruction'. In contrast to anger (*Zorn*), it leaves no room for 'reflection and reconsideration'. The borderlines of pathological fury, as described in earlier lexicon entries, were seen as fluid. In 1895, under the heading '*Wut*', the description referred only to 'mania and rabies' (*Hundswut*, literally 'dog rage'); in the 1957 edition, the reference to 'rabies' stood next to 'excessive anger'. It included the violent outbursts of toddlers in their 'terrible twos', whereas adults were expected to control themselves and curb their rage.[2]

Rage, as is clear from such definitions, was not and is not seen as a positive feeling. An enraged person is considered aggressive, destructive and uncontrolled; they say and do things that they would not say or do in a calm state or

---

[2] *Brockhaus' Konversations-Lexikon*, 14th ed., vol. 16 (Leipzig: Brockhaus, 1895), 881; *Der Große Brockhaus*, 16th ed., vol. 12 (Wiesbaden: Brockhaus, 1957), 618; *Brockhaus Enzyklopädie*, 17th ed., vol. 20 (Wiesbaden: Brockhaus, 1974), 522; ibid., 19th ed., vol. 24 (Mannheim: Brockhaus, 1994), 379.

with deliberation. Anger, by contrast, lacks this excess; according to the 2006 *Brockhaus*, it has a 'rational and in the broadest sense ethical component'. It also expresses a 'passionate and vehement indignation' about something that 'is felt to be wrong or contradicts one's own intentions and wishes'. If this indignation remains appropriate to the occasion and corresponds to civilized manners, 'manly' and 'justified anger' even has dignity and legitimacy.[3]

In former times, anger was primarily an attribute of the powerful, akin to the wrath of God or the wrath of Achilles, the godlike hero from the *Iliad*. Not everyone could afford anger, nor could everyone be angry. In fact, powerful men and women were compelled to show anger when the need arose, otherwise their power was hardly worth much. This was the argument made in October 1918 by Admiral Adolf von Trotha, head of the German Imperial Naval Cabinet. Outraged by President Woodrow Wilson's call for an immediate end to submarine warfare, he advocated that the German people be called to 'national unity and the organization of all forces'. In the name of national > honour, the war should be continued. Otherwise, the enemy would 'lose all respect for us and treat us with perfidious malice because he sees that we are no longer capable of anger'. Those who expressed their anger thus demonstrated power and protected their honour.[4] General Erich Ludendorff, who headed the Supreme Army Command alongside Paul von Hindenburg, saw it the same way. Accordingly, in an act of powerful and empowering anger, the naval command ordered the deployment of the High Seas Fleet. When sailors defied the order, the revolution began.

1918 Revolution

The mutineers were likewise furious, outraged, angry. If they had been asked about these feelings at the time, they would have had difficulty drawing a distinction, because in everyday language rage, anger and indignation were interchangeable and overlapping. But they were clear about wanting to discontinue the hopeless war and avoid certain death. As more and more people joined them, impotence turned into power, and rage into anger (Figure 4).

In December 1918, delegates from local workers' and soldiers' councils across Germany met in Berlin to mould the political power they had gained since the kaiser's abdication into a new shape based on the rule of law. Wilhelm Dittmann, member of the Council of People's Deputies, ended his fiery speech with the 'glorious words of Ferdinand Freiligrath': 'We hammer anew the old rotten thing, the state; We, who share in God's wrath, hitherto

---

[3] *Brockhaus Enzyklopädie*, 21st ed., vol. 30 (Leipzig: Brockhaus, 2006), 675.
[4] Adolf von Trotha, *Volkstum und Staatsführung* (Berlin: Großdeutsche Verlagsanstalt, 1928), 150.

Figure 4   Socialist Karl Liebknecht addresses Berliners at the outbreak of the German
Revolution, 1918 (Photo by Boury/Three Lions/Hulton Archive/Getty Images)

the proletariat!' For this he earned 'boisterous cheers and applause from the
whole congregation'.

In Freiligrath's 1840s verses, the proletariat succeeded the wrathful God in the
guise of a ship's boilerman who turned anger into action in order to rebuild and
reinvigorate the worn-out state. In late 1918, the delegates in Berlin, 488 men
and two women, had a similar vision. They directed their anger against 'the old,
guilt-laden, defeated government' as well as 'the Prussian junkers and barons'
who had put 'the German people in fetters' and waged a murderous war.
Empowered by the revolution, such anger would hopefully lead to a political
order committed to democratic processes and system change.[5]

Mixed feelings – anger and shame, grief and outrage – had prompted Mrs
C. Reinhardt of Ludwigshafen to write to the Munich Workers' and Soldiers'
Council on 9 November 1918 and give her 'joyful approval' of the proclam-
ation of the Bavarian Republic. Her twenty-four-year-old son had died at the
Somme in 1916, and she was troubled by the question of why millions of
families had accepted the death of their loved ones in the war rather than being
outraged by it. Her answer: 'Because we were gagged by the censor. Because
the old authorities put those of us with an honest word on our lips under

---

[5] *Allgemeiner Kongreß der Arbeiter- und Soldatenräte Deutschlands: Stenographische
Berichte, Berlin 1919* (Berlin: Olle & Wolter, 1973), 1–2, 24.

police supervision and sent the best of us to prison.' The time had come to convert silent, powerless anger into a courageous, energetic policy of peace: 'The foundation must be laid in the nursery and built up in the school: away with the glorification of battle, away with the heroic songs.'[6]

Reactionary Rage

Others, however, were outraged by 'treason and mutiny' and welcomed the political murders with which right-wing circles sought to destabilize the young republic. 'It is good that Erzberger the pig is dead, hopefully you and the whole clique will soon follow', wrote a Berliner, who did not give his name, to President Friedrich Ebert in 1921. 'I could write more, but would soon choke on the rage. Anyway, I wish you comrades a happy ascension soon, so that we can get a kaiser again, and me and my pals will earnestly help.'[7]

The image of choking on rage that could not get out was a common one that could also be found in legal texts and practices. Anyone who was 'incited to rage' or was 'under the immediate influence of feelings of anger that made calm deliberation impossible' during the planning and execution of a crime could claim extenuating circumstances, which considerably reduced the sentence. This is what happened in 1922 when a Berlin court ruled against the thirty-year-old businessman Robert Rauth. A lieutenant of the reserve during the war, Rauth had called Ebert a 'boor' and defiantly stood by the disrespectful slur: 'I am an officer and feel offended in my > honour that the president has been so bold as to forbid me to wear the uniform'; he was referring to the ban on uniforms for former officers who were no longer part of the post-war army. The court regarded the expression as 'an indecency', but not as 'malicious slander. It does not spring from a dishonourable, mean disposition, but, as one must believe the accused, from a momentary surge of rage and displeasure.' Having been wounded four times in battle, Rauth's feelings were 'humanly explicable'. Therefore, although the prosecutor's office had demanded two weeks in prison, the judge imposed only a fine.[8]

The argument that one had been 'incited to rage' and had acted under the influence of 'justified emotion' was most frequently used in murder and

---

[6] Bavarian State Archive Munich, II, MA no. 102378: C. Reinhardt, 9 November 1918.

[7] Federal Archive Berlin, R 601, no. 17: anonymous, 1 September 1921. Matthias Erzberger, a member of the Catholic Centre Party, had signed the armistice agreement on 11 November 1918 and later served the republic as minister of finance. He was murdered by right-wing terrorists in 1921.

[8] Ludwig Ebermayer et al., *Reichs-Strafgesetzbuch mit besonderer Berücksichtigung der Rechtsprechung des Reichsgerichts*, 3rd ed. (Berlin: De Gruyter, 1925), 638; Federal Archive Berlin, R 601, no. 19: court record, 11 February 1922.

manslaughter trials. In most cases, it was invoked by a husband who had killed his unfaithful wife or her lover and defended his actions on these grounds in the hope of a reduced sentence. In the 1920s, judges in the predominantly conservative judiciary willingly conceded the motive to far-right nationalists who murdered liberal or left-wing citizens and politicians. Of the 376 political murders committed between 1919 and 1922, 354 were attributed to right-wing extremists. Not one of them was executed, unlike left-wing perpetrators, who in ten out of twenty-two cases were sentenced to death. The average right-wing offender was detained for four months, and many murders went unpunished. This was carefully documented by the statistician Emil Julius Gumbel, who, as a socialist and pacifist, was himself in the crosshairs of right-wing terrorists.[9]

Fortunately, not everyone who was dissatisfied with national politics took up arms. Most men talked off their grudges in the tavern, like August Brehmer, a fifty-eight-year-old retired street maintenance overseer, in 1921. He called Friedrich Ebert a 'blackguard' and ranted loudly that it was 'good that Erzberger, that swine, is dead, so that Wirth [chancellor and centrist politician] can have his turn, and President Ebert can rack off to France like a breeding boar with his breeding sow daughter'. Such talk outraged the invalid Schwarz, a leftist, who was sitting with him. The innkeeper, though, reminded Schwarz of 'how often he would have called Kaiser Wilhelm a blackguard, scoundrel and coward', whereupon Schwarz calmed down and continued drinking with Brehmer.[10] Letting off steam with mates over a drink, getting worked up over anything and everything under the influence of alcohol, was a custom that hardly anyone took exception to. Some even viewed it as a tried-and-tested means of de-escalation, a safety valve for political anger that might otherwise find some other, more severe outlet.

But the reverse could also happen. In the tavern, men found like-minded spirits, egged each other on and saw their political feelings confirmed. In the 1890s, the political police had therefore dispatched officers disguised as workers to pubs and beer halls to eavesdrop on conversations and generate surveillance reports.[11] During the Weimar period, especially from 1929 onwards, it was primarily urban streets on which anger, outrage and > hate

---

[9] Emil Julius Gumbel, *Vier Jahre politischer Mord* (Berlin: Neue Gesellschaft, 1922). See also Arthur David Brenner, *Emil J. Gumbel: Weimar German Pacifist and Professor* (Boston, MA: Brill, 2001).

[10] Federal Archive Berlin, R 601, no. 19: letter of indictment from the chief public prosecutor, 30 October 1921.

[11] Richard J. Evans, *Proletarians and Politics: Socialism, Protest and the Working Class in Germany before the First World War* (New York: Harvester Wheatsheaf, 1990), esp. 124–91.

ran riot and found fuel. Communists and Nazis fought on and for the streets, sometimes against the police, with ever-greater frequency against one another. Every clash increased the rage and welded each of the battle sides closer together.[12]

More than a few admired the idea of 'sacred anger' and dreamt of actively joining the 'fighters' front'. They also gave advice on how to win the fight. 'Legally, due to a majority in the gossip chamber [parliament] in Berlin, we will never succeed', Wuppertal merchant Heinrich Riepenberg wrote to Adolf Hitler in 1930. Only 'fist and sword' could help, and for him, the fist was loose: 'Often, when I read that Dortmund spite rag, the *General-Anzeiger*, for the sake of information, I am seized by anger; I just want to get inside the editorial office and, with a dog whip, left and right, strike the faces of these wretches who every day breathe their poison gas into a quarter of a million souls.' Only his duties as a family man prevented Riepenberg from doing so.[13]

People's Anger in the 'Third Reich'

When the Nazis finally (and legally) came to power in 1933, they immediately extinguished any possibility for people to publicly express anger, rage and outrage at their politics. Internally and externally, the regime was keen to convey the image of a happy, pacified population who had no reason to be 'restless, hateful and distrustful'.[14] From time to time, though, 'people's anger' (*Volkszorn*) was deliberately invoked and mobilized in order to strengthen the regime and justify its political decisions to the world.

So it was in early November 1938, when a young Polish Jew shot a German diplomat in Paris. According to Nazi press directives, the assassination deserved the greatest attention and had to 'completely dominate the front pages'. Editorials were to make it clear that 'it must have the most serious consequences for the Jews in Germany'. Stormtroopers and NSDAP members subsequently attacked Jewish shops and synagogues across the country. When the diplomat succumbed to his injuries on 9 November, the minister of propaganda delivered a thirty-minute hate speech to party leaders, who had gathered in Munich for an evening of merriment to mark the fifteenth

---

[12] Eve Rosenhaft, *Beating the Fascists? The German Communists and Political Violence, 1929–1933* (Cambridge: Cambridge University Press, 1983); Sven Reichardt, *Faschistische Kampfbünde* (Cologne: Böhlau, 2002); Sven Reichardt, 'Violence and Community: A Micro-Study on Nazi Storm Troopers', *Central European History* 46, no. 2 (2013): 275–97; Pamela E. Swett, *Neighbors and Enemies: The Culture of Radicalism in Berlin, 1929–1933* (Cambridge: Cambridge University Press, 2004); Molly Loberg, *The Struggle for the Streets of Berlin: Politics, Consumption, and Urban Space, 1914–1945* (Cambridge: Cambridge University Press, 2018).

[13] Federal Archive Berlin, NS 51, no. 51/1: Heinrich Riepenberg, 26 September 1930.

[14] *Reden des Führers am Parteitag der Ehre* (Munich: Eher, 1936), 14.

Figure 5   Frankfurt's synagogue in flames on 10 November 1938 (Photo by Pictures from History/Universal Images Group via Getty Images)

anniversary of the failed 1923 coup. 'Spirited applause. Everybody dashed off to the telephones. Now the people will act', Joseph Goebbels noted happily in his diary (Figure 5).

Those who acted, however, were the usual suspects: Stormtroopers and party members. In Munich, Goebbels reported that the militia 'Adolf Hitler' did a 'thorough job': 'A synagogue is smashed to pieces', its windowpanes 'tinkle'. For Berlin, he himself gave the order to destroy the synagogue in upper-class Fasanenstrasse: 'Now the people's anger rages.' That night, 1,400 synagogues burnt down across 'Greater Germany' (which by this time included Austria); countless shops, apartments and cemeteries were devastated; tens of thousands of Jewish men were arrested, abused and sent to concentration camps. Though the 'terrible work' was organized and carried out by the party, its role 'as the author' was not to be publicly known.[15]

[15] Joseph Goebbels, *Die Tagebücher*, ed. Elke Fröhlich, part 1, vol. 6 (Munich: Saur, 1998), 178–83; *NS-Presseanweisungen der Vorkriegszeit*, vol. 6/III (Munich: Saur, 1999), 1050; *Nuremberg Trial Proceedings*, vol. 4, 66, https://avalon.law.yale.edu/imt/12-18-45.asp, accessed 21 December 2021; Uta Gerhardt and Thomas Karlauf, eds, *The Night of Broken Glass: Eyewitness Accounts of Kristallnacht*, trans. Robet Simmons and Nick Somers (Cambridge: Polity Press, 2012), esp. 3–6.

Propagandistically, Goebbels had hit the mark with the term *Volkszorn*, people's anger. It sounded powerful, spontaneous, just and reminiscent of God's wrath. It thus took on an almost holy character, something not to be doubted or questioned. If the people felt assaulted and therefore became angry, they were allowed, even compelled, to strike back and teach their attacker a lasting lesson. Nobody should be surprised or get worked up about that. Popular anger testified to Germany's strength and determination to no longer accept 'foreign' provocations such as the Paris assassination, which was supposedly motivated by Jewish resentment against the potent superiority of the 'master race'.

Resentment

Friedrich Nietzsche, who was idolized by many Nazis and non-Nazis alike, described resentment in 1887 as an expression of 'slave morality' directed against the 'aristocratic mode of evaluation' with its triumphant affirmation of 'life and passion'. 'Men of resentment' cultivated 'poisonous and hostile feelings'; they had 'a perfect understanding of how to keep silent, how not to forget, how to wait, how to make [themselves] provisionally small and submissive'.[16] An entry in the 1929 edition of *Meyers Lexikon* reveals the extent to which this description had become common knowledge: it defined resentment as a 'feeling, especially of revenge, and, as Nietzsche had it, of impotent hatred felt by the socially and spiritually inferior person against the noble and powerful'. The Nazi edition of 1942 upped the ante: > hate was no longer impotent, but 'cowardly'. It belonged to 'inferior and inefficient' people and was 'a tactic of Jews and the (Christian) priesthood' to weaken 'the strong and efficient'.[17]

It was obvious that National Socialists, who proudly recognized themselves in Nietzsche's 'master race', wanted nothing to do with the resentment of weaklings and cowards and instead celebrated the honest, unconcealed anger of the strong and brave. Yet the negative connotation of the term did not disappear in 1945. When Federal President Theodor Heuss received a letter of

---

[16] Friedrich Nietzsche, *On the Genealogy of Morals*, trans. Douglas Smith (Oxford: Oxford University Press, 1996), 22–24. In 1912 Max Scheler had translated '*Ressentiment*' as '*Grollen*', or rancour, which 'comes closest to the essential meaning of the term ... a suppressed wrath, independent of the ego's activity, which moves obscurely through the mind. It finally takes shape through the repeated reliving of intentionalities of hatred or other hostile emotions. In itself it does not contain a specific hostile intention, but it nourishes any number of such intentions' (Max Scheler, *Ressentiment*, trans. Lewis B. Coser and William W. Holdheim, new ed. (Milwaukee, WI: Marquette University Press, 1994), 27).

[17] *Meyers Lexikon*, 7th ed., vol. 10 (Leipzig: Bibliografisches Institut, 1929), 223; ibid., 8th ed., vol. 9 (1942), 337.

complaint in 1951 from a retired school principal who alleged he was not allowed to publicly question the government's decisions, Heuss replied that his interlocuter was apparently motivated by a 'rather cheap resentment' that lacked any empirical evidence.

The teacher would certainly have denied this. All he wanted was to voice his concern about the influence of the Catholic Church and Chancellor Konrad Adenauer's re-armament policy. Heuss was less harsh in 1952, incidentally, when he conversed with a former officer who also expressed his 'mental reservation' against this policy, albeit for other reasons. Like every 'fair think-ing' man, he was outraged over the fact that 'even today, our fallen comrades are dishonoured through lack of respect and remembrance, and those who lost their health and livelihood in service to the fatherland are defamed'. The president firmly rejected the argument and informed 'dear Mr Neunhoeffer' that he had 'taken the wrong tone'. At the same time, he understood Neunhoeffer's 'individual bitterness' and emphasized that he himself had repeatedly defended German officers from insults after the war (> Honour).[18]

Heuss thus distinguished between what he considered to be unjustified resentment and legitimate disappointment and anger, whose motives and impetus he could agree with. Resentment remained where it had been before: among the set of 'bad' feelings not valued by society. In 1956, the *Brockhaus* defined resentment literally as the 'reliving of an earlier feeling, in particular an insult suffered and the grudge associated with it'. In practice, however, it was 'often used in the sense of unacknowledged envy and hatred towards a person due to a feeling of being worse off than them, neglected, or disadvantaged by fate'. The equation with > hate and > envy intensified its unpleasant overtones. These receded only in the 1990s, when resentment came to mean 'a negative attitude towards a person, a group or an issue based on feelings, certain experiences or prejudices'.[19]

Outrage

Such neutrality speaks to a more general trend of affirming emotions that signal discontent and opposition. Throughout the twentieth century, German encyclopaedias kept completely silent about outrage, *Empörung*, which did not have a single entry. In recent years, the term has seen a mighty upswing. According to Google, outrage is, on the one hand, synonymous with insurrection, rebellion and mutiny, while on the other hand it describes the

---

[18] Theodor Heuss, *Hochverehrter Herr Bundespräsident! Der Briefwechsel mit der Bevölkerung 1949–1959*, ed. Wolfram Werner (Berlin: De Gruyter, 2010), 184–86, 190–92.

[19] *Der Große Brockhaus*, 16th ed., vol. 9 (Wiesbaden: Brockhaus, 1956), 691; *Brockhaus Enzyklopädie*, 19th ed., vol. 18 (Mannheim: Brockhaus, 1992), 320.

'indignation accompanied by strong emotions as a reaction to the violation of moral conventions'. This is partly tautological (outrage equals indignation). But it also lays the groundwork for a reading that justifies outrage as ethically based, similar to anger. Those who are outraged clearly have good reasons: they oppose circumstances, decisions or conditions that contradict their sense of justice. 'Time for outrage! Indignez-vous!' This was the ninety-three-year-old Stéphane Hessel's 2010 appeal to a new generation. His short book was immediately translated into thirty languages and sold three million copies. Hessel, who had fought in the French Resistance, mentioned outrage as his primary motive, and he called on the young ones to look around for topics of indignation. He saw plenty: the violation of human rights, the wide gap between rich and poor, the destruction of the environment.[20]

The concept of justice and the grounds for outrage have changed over the past hundred years. Between 1914 and 1918, many found it unfair that the losses and profits of the war were unequally distributed among the population and that some were starving while others were feasting. Food riots and crusades against 'shirkers' and 'war profiteers' were the result. After the defeat, compressed outrage was directed against the victorious powers' peace terms, which were perceived as heavily biased.

The communist camp was outraged by the SPD's 'betrayal' following the 1918 Revolution, when Social Democrats had opposed a Soviet-style system of workers' and soldiers' councils and advocated a national assembly representing all popular opinions. Monarchists were outraged at the forced abdication of kaiser and kings. Socialists were outraged at the persistence of a class-based justice system that left the brazen denigration of the republic and its representatives mostly unpunished. All their outrage found room and air: it was not kept a secret grudge or simmering resentment but surged into the public realm and ultimately determined the political agenda of the Weimar Republic.

Totalitarian and dictatorial regimes were far less inclined to give outrage free rein. Neither National Socialism nor the German Democratic Republic permitted angry citizens to speak out in public. Instead, the GDR cultivated the tradition of individual petitions to state organs or the ruling party. They allowed citizens to express their dissatisfaction with everyday socialist life and draw attention to problems that the Socialist Unity Party (SED) then promised to solve. Collective protests or even demonstrations, however, were strictly forbidden, except when the state commissioned them. In such cases, outrage was prescribed from above and directed towards the 'imperialist and revanchist' politics of the capitalist West. In language reminiscent of Goebbels, the

---

[20] Stéphane Hessel, *Time for Outrage: Indignez-vous!*, trans. Damion Searls and Alba Arrikha (London: Quartet Books, 2011). The French original appeared in 2010 and sold over a million copies within the first four months.

GDR also deliberately kept alive the outrage over 'Anglo-American terror bombers', who had reduced Dresden and many other German cities to rubble in the final years of the war.

Other types of indignation, though, went completely unacknowledged. The regime did not care about outraged citizens who, in 1975, watched in disbelief as a child who had fallen into the Spree river from its West Berlin bank drowned under the eyes of GDR border guards, who did not permit his rescue by Western authorities. Angry protests against the singer Wolf Biermann's expatriation in 1976 likewise failed to have an impact on the state leadership. In June 1987, it haughtily ignored the outrage of 'youngsters' who sharply criticized the 'ruthless and brutal action of the Stasi against peaceful teenagers in Berlin who only wanted to listen to rock music'.

Even > grief, itself a rather introverted feeling, could develop into outrage, as illustrated by a letter sent to Erich Honecker from an East Berlin family in February 1989, with full particulars of all its signatories: 'We hereby express our grief and dismay over the violent death of Chris Gueffroy. For us, the death of this young man at the Berlin Wall stands in complete contradiction to statements that there is no order to shoot. We hold it to be a scandal for this country that a quest for personal freedom ended in death.' The family never received an answer. Eight months later, when popular outrage had become so great that the government opened the border, shots ceased to be fired.[21]

West German Demonstrations and Protest Movements

The ways in which widespread dissatisfaction was articulated in the period leading up to the revolution of 1989 have been well-documented. Overall, the civil rights movement proceeded cautiously so as not to provoke a 'Chinese solution' from the regime. As late as September 1989, Egon Krenz, Honecker's deputy and soon-to-be successor, had praised the Beijing government for the massacre in its capital, promised class solidarity and reaffirmed that 'on the barricades of socialist revolution' the GDR was facing the same opponent. To resist such intimidation and take to the streets in spite of imminent threats demanded more courage than even the most seasoned West German demonstrators could imagine. In their country they generally had – and used – the opportunity to make their outrage public without expecting any risk or danger. Whether during the Easter marches and protests against re-armament in the 1950s, against the Vietnam War in the 1960s and early 1970s, or against

---

[21] Siegfried Suckut, *Volkes Stimmen: 'Ehrlich, aber deutlich' – Privatbriefe an die DDR-Regierung* (Munich: dtv, 2015), 194, 207 ff., 361, 414. A similar range of reactions spanning grief and rage were triggered by the self-immolation of Pastor Brüsewitz in 1976 (> Grief).

the deployment of new nuclear missiles from 1981 onwards, personal courage was never a prerequisite for participation.

Violent attacks by police units did occur now and again. During the rallies against the visit of the Shah of Iran in 1967, the West Berlin police acted aggressively, making generous use of their truncheons and shooting Benno Ohnesorg, a university student. But this sparked an immediate hail of public criticism, especially from liberal and left-wing quarters.[22] When the Hamburg police used a kettling technique against a small and unregistered demonstration in 1986, another protest march was promptly called, with tens of thousands of participants. The police leadership subsequently faced legal action, and those affected received compensation.

That demonstrations were a legal and legitimate means of venting anger and outrage was never a matter for debate in the Federal Republic. In contrast to the GDR, political criticism, whether from the left or the right, was protected under the law. In the early 1970s, incensed citizens (many of them post-1945 expellees and refugees) as well as neo-Nazis railed against the social-liberal coalition government's 'new eastern policy'. Unhindered, they called the chancellor a 'traitor of the people' and chanted 'Brandt against the wall!' While the opposition to Ostpolitik engaged predominantly older and middle-aged men (and far fewer women), the vast majority of demonstrations drew young protesters of both genders. 'Going to the demo' became part of a youthful, left-wing urban lifestyle and attitude.[23]

The fact that the number of people taking to the streets increased exponentially from the 1960s did not automatically mean that they had more reasons than former generations to be angry and outraged. Rather, they allowed themselves to openly express feelings of discontent, fuelled by the hope that such publicity would leave its mark on political institutions and personnel. Sidestepping traditional venues of engagement like political parties, they formed new social movements and invented unorthodox tactics and practices to make their worries and concerns known. Women's emancipation, environmental protection, anti-nuclear power, disarmament: these were post-material issues that did not find much resonance among established parties or trade unions, but to which large sections of the younger, better-educated generation felt deeply committed. Within that generation, it was no longer just 'angry young men' who spoke up. Young women also discovered and came to value anger as a mobilizing force. In 1986, following the devastating Chernobyl

[22] Kai Hermann, 'Die Polizeischlacht von Berlin', *Die Zeit*, 9 June 1967, www.zeit.de/1967/23/die-polizeischlacht-von-berlin/komplettansicht; 'Nicht zu fett', *Der Spiegel*, 16 June 1967, www.spiegel.de/spiegel/print/d-46409207.html, both accessed 21 December 2021.

[23] Ute Frevert, 'Feeling Political in Demonstrations: Street Politics in Germany, 1832–2018', in Ute Frevert et al., *Feeling Political: Emotions and Institutions since 1789* (Cham: Palgrave Macmillan, 2022), 341–71.

reactor catastrophe, mothers in particular used their 'rage as an impetus for action' to organize and initiate a campaign 'against this policy of cornucopian madness'.[24] Some women even took up leadership positions and became highly visible in politics, such as Petra Kelly as head of the Green Party in 1980.

The history of this party, which first entered the Bundestag in 1983, assumed governmental responsibility in 1998 and collected a fifth of all votes cast in the European elections of 2019, provides an impressive record of the successes and failures of the Federal Republic's culture of outrage. The Greens were successful as a political melting pot for those active in the new social movements. They were also successful in making their concerns acceptable to other parties and the broader population. But there are limits. The Greens fare best in the urban milieus of the educated middle classes, who earn decent incomes. Their election results are highest in university cities, such as Tübingen or Freiburg, and poorest in the Rhine and Ruhr areas and in the east. Cooperation between environmentalists and coal miners rarely occurs, and trade unionists who protest against pit closures and job losses usually find little > empathy and > solidarity among Green supporters with comparatively safe service occupations.

Approval ratings have been exceptionally low in the new states that joined the Federal Republic in October 1990, eleven months after the fall of the Berlin Wall. When the first free GDR elections were held in March 1990, the Alliance 90 – composed of those groups that had spearheaded the oppositional movement of 1989 – failed to reap the benefits and received only 2.9 per cent of the vote. Joining forces with the Greens in 1993 did not help much. On websites, blogs and social media, the party has regularly been accused of moral conceit, perpetual outrage and denying reality. Above all, critics claim, Alliance 90/The Greens have never understood the East.

Such understanding has instead been provided by Die Linke (The Left), and the far-right AfD, founded in 2013.[25] Both parties intentionally compete for votes from citizens who feel they bore the brunt of reunification and who angrily reject the new Germany. The AfD, in particular, cultivates what its more intellectual proponents call *thymos*, the Greek word for anger. Drawing on the ideas of the philosopher Peter Sloterdijk, they argue that the Federal Republic suffers from a 'thymotic undersupply'. The state as well as the 'old parties' allegedly silence citizens, operate above their heads and rob them of courage, spirit and rebellious energy. In contrast, those 'fighting for the

---

[24] Quoted in Ulrike Röhr, ed., *Frauen aktiv gegen Atomenergie – Wenn aus Wut Visionen werden: 20 Jahre Tschernobyl* (Norderstedt: Books on Demand, 2006), 73, 89.

[25] Die Linke was founded in 2007, when the Party of Democratic Socialism (PDS), successor to the GDR's ruling SED party, merged with the far smaller West German Labour and Social Justice alliance.

preservation of Germany's ethno-cultural identity' promote 'everything that serves to raise and harness thymic tension, that great sense of anger towards anti-German political forces'. It goes without saying that this anger is 'defensive', and therefore viewed as just. Right-wing ideologues thus claim for themselves the tradition of 'noble anger' dating back to antiquity, without, however, drawing a clear distinction between such anger and rage, as was still done in the 1950s.[26]

Wutbürger

Meanwhile, even rage has turned into a valued, accepted and legitimate feeling, and is no longer considered excessive or misguided. Over the years, it has been self-confidently reclaimed by people on both the right and the left. 'Too much anger, too little rage!' cried a piece of graffiti in one of Berlin's less gentrified districts in 2017, announcing an upcoming 'anti-capitalist' protest against rent increases and luxury renovations. Such rage was fully justified from the perspective of those who felt it. They would not, however, have described themselves as *Wutbürger* – 'angry citizens' or 'citizens of rage'. Nor did the neologism appeal to right-wing male demonstrators who preferred black bomber jackets and combat boots to standard civilian attire.

The term *Wutbürger*, coined by a *Spiegel* journalist in 2010 and immediately named Word of the Year, was in fact directed at people who embodied the mainstream in how they dressed, lived and behaved. Even among them rage stirred, as the protests against a major urban development project in the city of Stuttgart illustrated. According to the Association for the German Language, the term *Wutbürger* articulated a sense of 'people's outrage that political decisions are being made over their heads'. It thus reflected 'citizens' great need to have a say in socially and politically relevant matters beyond the ballot box'.[27]

This was neutrally worded, but not without sympathy. Yet the journalist had not meant it that way at all. For him, *Wutbürger* were comfortable senior citizens unconcerned with the future, who had only personal convenience in mind and were oblivious to younger generations and their needs. This was only partly true of the Stuttgart protestors, though. Tens of thousands

---

[26] Peter Sloterdijk, *Rage and Time: A Psychopolitical Investigation*, trans. Mario Wenning (New York: Columbia University Press, 2010); Götz Kubitschek, 'Hygienefimmel und Thymos-Regulierung', *Sezession* 70 (2016): 10–13; interview with Marc Jongen, *Frankfurter Allgemeine Sonntagszeitung*, 10 January 2016; Uffa Jensen, *Zornpolitik* (Berlin: Suhrkamp, 2017), 118–25.

[27] Dirk Kurbjuweit, 'Der Wutbürger', *Der Spiegel*, 11 October 2010, www.spiegel.de/spiegel/a-724587.html; https://gfds.de/wutbuerger-zum-wort-des-jahres-2010-gewaehlt/, both accessed 21 December 2021.

participated, from all age groups and social classes. After many people were injured in a police operation against demonstrators and park protectors in 2010, conciliation talks were held between supporters and opponents. To veteran Christian Democrat Heiner Geißler, who moderated the dialogue, critics of Stuttgart 21 were neither 'old communists' nor '*Wutbürger*'. He voiced understanding for their complaints and called on the politicians responsible to better inform citizens and take their worries seriously. The newly elected state government, a coalition of Greens and Social Democrats, took the advice to heart and put the matter to a people's vote. Since then, the level of rage has dropped significantly. As of 2023, only a handful of citizens still attended the vigils and Monday demonstrations, thus invoking the memory of the Peaceful Revolution in the GDR.[28]

Monday demonstrations have also been occurring in Dresden since 2014. At their peak, the organizing group Patriotic Europeans Against the Islamization of the West (abbreviated as PEGIDA) could boast 25,000 participants, mostly male and of advanced age, accompanied by younger neo-Nazis and hooligans only too willing to resort to violence. Their numbers swelled with the 'refugee crisis' of 2015. In choosing Monday for their weekly protests, they hijacked what is almost universally regarded as a positive tradition of resistance from 1989. Banners bearing the historic slogan 'We are the people' (*Wir sind das Volk)* explicitly asserted this connection. At the same time, they claimed to be protecting Germans from 'ethnic replacement' (*Umvolkung*) as a result of 'mass immigration'. The AfD quickly seized on these catchphrases and honed them for its own purposes. The party fuelled the rage of its supporters towards those it blamed for their perceived misery ('Merkel must go!') and called on them to 'resist the elites' who allegedly lied and cheated the people, just as GDR officials had done back in the day. 'Complete the transformation' was the 2019 party slogan in several eastern state elections, where the AfD enjoyed notable gains.

As ample historical evidence shows, anger and outrage can effectively be fed and nourished with propaganda that directs them towards certain groups and uses them for populist mobilization. Yet they are difficult to stabilize, perpetuate and shield from implosion. Permanent outrage, incessant rage, eternal anger: even in times of digital communication, they are impossible to maintain. It is true that the internet is helping to rapidly spread and radicalize the language of anger and > hate. This inevitably creates the impression that the number of angry and hateful people is increasing exponentially. But is this impression really accurate? Undoubtedly, it takes far less time and effort to send a hate tweet at the click of a mouse than to write a letter to the editor and send it in the post. Nevertheless, in both cases it is difficult to keep the rage

---

[28] *Frankfurter Allgemeine Zeitung*, 13 October 2010, 4.

burning and to perpetually widen the circle of enraged people. Few citizens find the time and energy for this. While resentment, that secret grudge, can simmer away for a long while, anger, outrage and indignation need fresh fuel and fast rhythms. Even Joseph Goebbels knew that *Volkszorn* would soon ebb, and rage burn out quickly, if not rekindled again and again.

Productive and Destructive Anger

Anger, rage and resentment are highly ambivalent feelings for democracies. On the one hand, they signal that people are dissatisfied and feel disappointed. As Max Scheler observed in 1912, such discontent must be particularly widespread in societies that tolerate 'wide factual differences in power, property, and education', while at the same time granting citizens equal rights and inviting respective expectations. They thus inevitably breed and carry 'a potent charge of resentment'.[29] If the resentment felt by those losing the game turns into outrage, this can, however, prompt the winners to pay more attention to previously overlooked interests and needs. In this respect, anger can be politically productive and have a positive effect.

On the other hand, anger can be extremely destructive when those feeling it refuse to engage in dialogue and reject basic democratic rules. In this case, anger not only renders a person impervious to the opinions and feelings of others. It also undermines the conditions for a political order that, for all impassioned struggles and conflicts, demands and provides procedures for negotiation and settlement.

This political order is of little value to extremist groups. In the 1970s and 1980s, members of the Red Army Faction (RAF) were not interested in talking or negotiating with representatives of the 'pig system', which they rigorously fought with terrorist means. Though their outrage was partially understandable, they found no outlet other than assassination attacks on high-ranking politicians, officials and 'capitalists'.[30] Similar modes of thinking and feeling apply to the new 'angry men' of the far right who happily follow their intellectual guru Götz Kubitschek's 2016 directive: 'No compromises, no reconciliation with the establishment.' Instead, 'the rift must be deepened'.[31] Those thymic tones have echoed throughout society and find considerable resonance. Jacques Tilly's political carnival float is not the only warning signal pointing to the consequences for democracy.

[29] Scheler, *Ressentiment*, 33.
[30] Karrin Hanshew, *Terror and Democracy in West Germany* (Cambridge: Cambridge University Press, 2012).
[31] Kubitschek, 'Hygienefimmel', 13.

~

Belonging

In an international competition held by, among others, the Goethe Institute in 2004, the word *Geborgenheit* – that deep and infinitely warm sense of safety and security, comfort and trust, loving protection and being taken care of – was chosen as the second most beautiful in the German language. It is one of the most powerful emotions, albeit one difficult to translate into other languages (except Dutch and Afrikaans).[1] *Geborgenheit* is primarily formed in private spaces, especially within the family. Some also find it in language, literature or nature. Others simply associate it with *Heimat*, home, another emotionally laden concept.

Geborgenheit and *Heimat* are not merely private matters. Their political dimension has been repeatedly demonstrated, as in 2018, when the German government created a special *Heimat* Ministry tasked with ensuring feelings of belonging among citizens. In times of global upheaval and ever-accelerating rates of societal transformation, the state was eager to offer Germans a sense of togetherness and cohesion. Expanding the former Ministry of the Interior with these new responsibilities seemed therefore immensely important. When asked what he understood by *Heimat* – a word encompassing both 'home' and 'homeland' in English – the minister answered pithily: 'Home is the place where we feel safe and that we belong.' He added that it was perfectly fine for people to have more than one.[2]

With this postscript, Horst Seehofer hoped to end the debate triggered by the renaming of the ministry. Critics had taken offence at the concept, suspecting it might signal a return to the archetypal German navel-gazing from which immigrants were automatically excluded. The minister corrected this 'misunderstanding' and emphasized that '*Heimat* is not about folklore, custom or > nostalgia. Anyone who understands it that way has not

---

[1] Jutta Limbach, ed., *'Das schönste deutsche Wort'* (Ismaning: Hueber, 2005), 153. *Geborgenheit* was surpassed only by *Habseligkeiten* – the meagre belongings of a person who has few, if any, other possessions. See also http://bit.ly/3T1nbde, accessed 31 March 2022.

[2] Ferdinand Otto, 'Heimat, wie er sie sieht', *Zeit online*, 3 May 2018, http://bit.ly/40p9AA0, accessed 17 December 2021.

recognized the signs of the times. *Heimat* is about anchoring and rootedness, a culturally ancestral locus in a globalized world. It is simply about cohesion, about belonging, about the support that every person in our country needs.'[3]

Geborgenheit and *Heimat* – 'belonging' and 'homeland' – were thus ministerially linked and politically charged. Both words convey multiple layers of meaning that are deeply embedded in German history. For a time, it appeared as though these layers had been stripped away. *Geborgenheit*, argued the sociologist Franz-Xaver Kaufmann in 1970, corresponds to the 'socio-cultural conditions of archaic cultures'. By the time he was writing, such conditions and their 'states of consciousness' were only still to be found in 'rural areas'.[4] In 1977, the federal president Walter Scheel admitted that the word *Geborgenheit* might sound 'a little strange to some people'. Current debates, however, prove that it has stood the test of time. The feeling associated with it has not disappeared either, even though it has changed and shifted noticeably.

Family, *Heimat* and Nation during the First World War

This feeling became an issue whenever a threat appeared, as during the First World War. Soldiers went into the field under the banner of their endangered homeland and sought to protect the place and social context to which they felt they belonged. *Heimat* referred primarily to the narrow horizon of each individual, that is, the region, family and cultural environment in which they had grown up. But *Heimat* was also the fatherland, the nation that the soldier was part of and whose > honour he defended on the battlefield.

This nation, to which all Germans belonged, had been a topic of increasing conversation during the nineteenth century. In 1871, it found territorial form in the German Empire. Although regional ties and dynastic attachments were maintained in Mecklenburg and Württemberg, Bavaria and Saxony, Hesse and Prussia, among other lands, they were now accompanied by an overarching sense of belonging to the new imperial state. This was not an automatic process and required the assistance of a great many institutions: a common flag, a kaiser, an imperial chancellor, a national fleet, a central parliament, and a unified legal system across all federal states. When Kaiser Wilhelm II called the nation to war in August 1914, it seemed as though all 'tribal differences' had been overcome and that the German people stood united against the 'ill will' and 'onslaught of hostile forces'.[5]

---

[3] http://bit.ly/3JA46fD, accessed 17 December 2021.

[4] Franz-Xaver Kaufmann, *Sicherheit als soziologisches und sozialpolitisches Problem* (Stuttgart: Enke, 1970), 155; Reinhard Kiehl, ed., *Alle Jahre wieder* (Düsseldorf: My favourite book, 2001), 325.

[5] In his speech from the throne on 4 August 1914, Wilhelm II had the members of the Reichstag pledge that they would 'stand with me through thick and thin, through hardship

Before the enemies could begin their onslaught, the German armies marched out to invade neighbouring countries. The four-year battle on the Eastern and Western Fronts took place almost exclusively on foreign soil: in France, Belgium, the Baltic countries and Russian Poland. Although far away, the homeland remained ever-present for the soldiers tasked with its protection, not least through letters, pictures, poems, stories and regular visits home while on leave (Figure 6). Since the Romantic period, *Heimat* had been associated in visual art and literature with nature, landscape, village and small-town idylls, church buildings, local dialects, tales and legends. In 1914 it also took on a decidedly feminine character, as mothers, brides and wives waited 'at home' for the soldiers to return. *Heimat* was the women whose 'honour' was threatened by the enemy and who therefore needed male military protection.

Of countless war poems, one entitled 'Farewell' and published on 4 August 1914 exclaimed, 'Farewell, dear homeland! Farewell you sacred hearth! We go forth to defend our sweetest possessions in the war nefariously forced upon us. Weep not, you good-hearted German women, weep not, you brides and sisters! We will save your honour with our heart's blood!'[6] Here, homeland, fatherland, mothers, brides and sisters merged into an inextricable bond of identification. This was nothing new in principle. But four long years of war turned it into a heartfelt experience for millions of men, giving it an urgency that earlier generations could scarcely have imagined.

Not everyone suffered from the absence of *Heimat*, though. Ernst Jünger, who in 1914 at the age of nineteen volunteered to join the armed forces out of a sense of 'adventure' and fought on the Western Front, felt anything but uncomfortable there. His visits home while on leave did not feature strongly in the diary he kept during the war, nor in his subsequent memoir *The Storm of Steel*, first published in 1920. Only once, as he lay wounded on a hospital train to Heidelberg in the spring of 1915, was he seized by peculiar feelings: 'As I saw the slopes above the Neckar wreathed in cherry blossom I felt a vivid pang of home-sickness. How beautiful a country, worth bleeding and dying for! I had never felt its magic so strongly.' A year later, when he was admitted to a garrison hospital in Gera with another injury, he was immune to the magic, but irritated by the 'nosy gawping of rubbernecked voyeurs'. 'Eager not to fritter away too much time in Germany', he complained that the wound was

and death, without party differences, without tribal differences, without denominational differences' (www.reichstagsprotokolle.de/Blatt_k13_bsb00003402_00012.html, accessed 17 December 2021).

[6] The anonymously published poem was printed in the *Ingolstädter Tagblatt* and came from the local secondary school teacher and reserve lieutenant Fritz Schmidt, who sent two 'patriotic outpourings' to the Bavarian king, Ludwig III, on 4 August 1914 (Bavarian State Archive Munich, III Geh. Hausarchiv, Cabinet Files Ludwig III, no. 71).

Figure 6   WW1 propaganda: a steamy dumpling symbolizes the soldiers' return to the *Heimat* (Photo by Imagno/Getty Images)

'not healing as quickly as I would like', and impatiently concluded 'after a few days in Hanover and at home, I can bear it out there for another year'. 'Out there' was the community of comrades: 'It was like coming back to a family circle.' Though this family lacked a mother's protection, it offered a ring of brothers united in duty and battle who would defend one another with their lives. It was a home away from home, emotionally intense and necessary for survival.[7]

Home and Belonging on the Left and Right

Heimat, by whatever definition, was for soldiers far more important and concrete than state and nation. In contrast to such 'hazy concepts', noted Jünger in 1922, everyone knew what home meant: 'Home is a feeling.'[8] It could be felt by all, whether on the left or the right. In 1929, Kurt Tucholsky described his love for home and homeland as an emotion 'separate from all politics'. It honoured neither state nor fatherland, but his own 'private Germany' that had been formed and enriched through childhood impressions. This private homeland could be in the mountains for one person, by the sea for another or somewhere in between for a third. But the famously belligerent journalist did not leave it at that. He self-confidently claimed the whole country as his homeland on the grounds that it was his birthplace and he spoke the language.

At this point, Tucholsky's *Heimatliebe* did become eminently political. He vigorously repudiated those 'who call themselves "nationalist"' and claimed 'an exclusive lease on this land and its language'. Among them were the supporters of the German National People's Party and its kindred veterans' association, The Steel Helmet. Strikingly, he made no mention of the National Socialists, whose enormous electoral successes still lay ahead.

In refusing to surrender his love for homeland, despite his immunity to all things patriotic and 'fatherland-ish' such as flags, Tucholsky was not only speaking for himself. He also spoke on behalf of 'the communists, the young socialists, the pacifists, and the lovers of freedom of all degrees' who held fast to their homeland without a need to rattle any sabres. He could have included Jews as well. Although he had left Judaism in 1911, as the son of Jewish parents he was certainly sensitized to the racist hostility faced by Jews long before

---

[7] Ernst Jünger, *Kriegstagebuch 1914–1918*, ed. Helmuth Kiesel (Stuttgart: Klett-Cotta, 2010), 186; Ernst Jünger, *In Stahlgewittern: Ein Kriegstagebuch*, 21st ed. (Berlin: Mittler, 1941), 31, 284. (Ernst Jünger, *The Storm of Steel*, intro. R. H. Mottram (London: Chatto & Windus, 1929), 29–30, 281. The last sentence of the first quote was missing in the English translation.)

[8] Ernst Jünger, 'Der Kampf als inneres Erlebnis', in Ernst Jünger, *Sämtliche Werke*, vol. 7 (Stuttgart: Klett-Cotta, 1980), 9–103, here 83.

1933.[9] During the First World War, doubts about their civic loyalty had been sown by *völkisch*-nationalist groups. Antisemitic sentiment continued into the 1920s and found great resonance among those on the political right.

In 1923, a craftsman from Nuremberg approached the Bavarian government with three proposals on how 'to save our poor afflicted people from even more mischief and injustice'. Besides expelling foreigners and taking action against usury – a behaviour typically imputed to Jews – he urged that 'all Jews be shown the road to where they belong: to "Jerusalem". That is their true homeland and it is also where they belong.'[10] In 1924, the editor of *Unser Vaterland*, a 'monthly magazine for all Germans', published an article by a retired colonel in which the author made it very clear that not all Germans belonged to this fatherland. Rather, he noted a big difference between 'the German people' and those 'German citizens of un-German character and blood' who in 1919 had pursued an 'undignified policy of rapprochement and servile compliance'. They were, in the colonel's view, incapable of having an 'appreciation for homeland and fatherland and a love for both', let alone any sense of national or personal > honour.[11]

The Munich law student Hans Bloch saw things differently. Bloch, who came from a middle-class Jewish family, had gone to war for Germany in 1915 as a nineteen-year-old volunteer and had been awarded the Iron Cross 1st and 2nd Class. After the war, he described the 'House of the Germans' as follows:

> A German is one to whom his mother sang a German song. A German is one who speaks German and thinks in German words. Language creates a people and defines its perimeter. Once, in prehistoric times, there was race. This has long since become a chimera. Landscape, homeland is stronger. This is what creates colour and music. History is heavy with weight. It reveals limits and destinies.[12]

Similar words were used by the Bavarian Association of Israelite Communities in 1922. In a letter to their state premier, they expressed 'grave

---

[9] *Deutschland, Deutschland über alles! A Picture-book by Kurt Tucholsky and John Heartfield* [1929], trans. Anne Halley (Amherst: University of Massachusetts Press, 1972), 220–26, quotes 222, 225–26.

[10] Bavarian State Archive Munich, II, MA no. 102388: letter from 2 August 1923. On 5 December 1923, members of the Bavarian People's Party submitted the same proposal: 'Expulsion of foreign elements from Poland and Galicia' along with 'all troublesome foreigners': 'Bavaria belongs to the Bavarians' (ibid.).

[11] Oberst a.D. Zeiss, 'Volk und Vaterland', *Unser Vaterland*, 1 (October 1924): 9–10.

[12] Sinja Strangmann, 'Eduard und Hans Bloch – Zwei Generationen jüdischer Soldaten im Ersten Weltkrieg', in *Krieg! Juden zwischen den Fronten 1914/1918*, ed. Ulrike Heikaus and Julia B. Kohne (Munich: Hentrich & Hentrich, 2014), 253, 262. Nor did Hans Bloch surrender his 'position on Germany' to the Nazis; it was, he wrote on 9 August 1933, 'clearer, purer, more determined and more devoted than ever at this moment' (256).

concern'. They were worried about the upsurge of the *völkisch* movement within the armed forces and, above all, 'within the schools, among teachers and pupils'. In many places, Jewish children were being made 'martyrs for their faith and their descent': 'The concept of being German, the concept of national sentiment, formerly the common property of all Germans, is being taken over by *völkisch*-minded youth and reinterpreted in solely *völkisch* terms.' As a counterweight, the association spelled out its commitment to nation and homeland: 'It seems to us that the shared experience of joy and suffering, over many centuries, on the same soil and through a shared language and culture, is more important than mere shibboleths such as race and blood-kinship.' *Völkisch* efforts to dissolve this 'cultural community' placed a question mark over the continued existence of Jews in Germany.[13]

Exile as 'Unbelonging'

It took only another eleven years for the existence of Jewish Germans to be called into question. In 1933, it was not just right-wing youth groups, student fraternities and paramilitary associations that wanted them out. The state itself, with all its powerful institutions, made this happen. Many who left the country for good took the feeling of losing their homeland, or rather, being dispossessed of it, with them into exile. They made a point of speaking German even after emigration, founded German newspapers and maintained conventions such as sitting down to coffee and cake in the afternoon. When Alice Schwab, née Rosenthal, who had left her hometown of Heilbronn in 1937 to build a new life for herself in England, died in 2001 at the age of eighty-six, her wish was to return '*hoim*'. For her, 'home' was not what her children thought it was, namely London, where she had lived for more than sixty years, but Heilbronn, the place of her family roots, where she had spent her childhood and youth.[14]

Childhood memories, as Tucholsky had pointed out, were central to feelings of home. Smells, sounds, topographies, the effects of light, the familiar language or dialect, everyday family rituals and social habits combined to create a sense of belonging, from which negative experiences usually remained obscured. The fact that Alice Rosenthal had witnessed the antisemitic boycott of her father's local wine business in 1933 did not preclude her seeing the city as the true home to which she longed to return. By the end of her life, she had almost completely forgotten the English she had learnt and had reverted to speaking Swabian German, the dialect of her childhood. Home was indeed, as Jünger had put it, a feeling that had never left her, even though it was not until

---

[13] Bavarian State Archive Munich, II, MA no. 102386: letter from 30 April 1922.

[14] Joachim Schlör, *Escaping Nazi Germany: One Woman's Emigration from Heilbronn to England* (London: Bloomsbury, 2021), 6.

shortly before her death that she was able and willing to give it room for expression.

The writer Jean Améry had also come to know this feeling, albeit at an earlier point in life. Born Hans Mayer to a Jewish family in Vienna in 1912, he left Austria for Belgium with his wife at the end of 1938. Reflecting on his emigration experience in a 1966 essay, 'How Much Home Does a Person Need?', Améry described the emotion of 'homesickness, a nasty, gnawing sickness' he had felt for the first time at the beginning of 1939 and that had never again left him. Standing in line for weekly assistance from the Antwerp Jewish Aid Committee, he recalled feeling completely 'uprooted' and unprotected (*entborgen*). Unlike those who had found a 'mobile substitute for home' in their religion, wealth or fame where they could feel *geborgen* and secure, he perceived himself as completely 'lost'. He understood at that moment 'how much a person needs a home', especially when they no longer had one.

For Mayer/Améry, too, home was 'the land of one's childhood and youth'; there was 'no "new home"'. Yet the old one was gone as well once he realized that what he had thought was his homeland 'had never been ours'. He thus strictly ruled out a return to Austria, having been liberated from the Bergen-Belsen concentration camp in 1945, and instead resided in Brussels. Still, he chose Vienna as the place for his second wedding ceremony in 1955, and it was in Salzburg that he took his own life in 1978. He was given a grave of honour in Vienna's Central Cemetery.[15]

Another Kind of Expellee: *Heimat-Vertriebene*

Early on in his reflections on *Heimat*, Améry tried to distinguish his own loss of belonging from that of another group that enjoyed far greater attention at the time. The twelve to fourteen million German refugees and expellees who were forced to leave their homes in Poland, Czechoslovakia, Hungary, Romania or Yugoslavia as a result of post-war ethnic cleansing also 'lost their possessions, homestead, business, fortune, or perhaps only a modest job; beyond that, they lost the land, meadows and hills, a forest, a silhouette of a city, the church in which they had been confirmed'. But they lost them to and through strangers. The Jewish emigrants, on the other hand, had been expropriated and expatriated by their own fellow citizens: by 'the schoolmate from the same bench, the neighbour, the teacher', who had suddenly 'become

---

[15] Jean Améry, 'How Much Home Does a Person Need [1966]', in Jean Améry, *At the Mind's Limit*, trans. Sidney Rosenfeld and Stella P. Rosenfeld (Bloomington: Indiana University Press, 1980), 41–61, quotes 43–44, 46, 48, 50.

informers or bullies', or 'at best, embarrassed opportunists'. This is also why their homeland had no 'strongly expressed desire for our return' and, unlikely as it was, would have seen it as an 'embarrassment'.[16]

Améry was absolutely right. At the same time, though, he overestimated the homeland's desire to welcome those whose homes had been in Germany's former eastern territories or the Czech Sudetenland. They were by no means met or received with much enthusiasm. In the GDR, their stories of expulsion from countries under Soviet control were a political taboo and neutralized through terms such as 're-settler' and 'new citizen'. It was only in private, if at all, that one could mourn the loss of one's homeland, as in a self-penned, rhyming poem confidingly sent by sixty-one-year-old Gertrud Kober to President Wilhelm Pieck in 1950:

> Home, home, how beautiful you were.
> Oh! If only I could see you once more.
> That was my hometown, where my cradle lay,
> and it's been a long time since we said goodbye.
> But in my mind's eye the memory stays clear.
> I'll never forget my beautiful Silesian land, my Liegnitz, my dear.[17]

In the Federal Republic, a woman like Kober would have played into the hands of Cold War propagandists who brandished forced migration as evidence of communist brutality and contempt for humanity. The fact that the victims could be weaponized ideologically and politically did not, however, ease their actual integration. Repulsion, contempt and exclusion were frequent reactions of the host population to those 'Polacks', who often brought with them a different religion, different eating and drinking preferences and a different dialect. In his New Year's Eve presidential address of 1950, Theodor Heuss called it a 'disgrace' that 'an association or party of "natives" had formed against the refugees'. This remark provoked a deluge of critical letters, especially from Schleswig-Holstein, where there were three 'foreigners' to every four 'natives' and the discord was palpable. Since the 'foreigners' enjoyed powerful representation in the League of Expellees and Disfranchised – which won almost 24 per cent of votes in the 1950 state elections and was thus the second strongest party after the SPD – it seemed legitimate to the 'natives' for them to voice their concerns in a separate organization, the Schleswig-Holstein Society.[18]

---

[16] Ibid., 42, 51.

[17] Federal Archive Berlin, DA 4 (Presidential Office GDR, Pieck 1949–1960), no. 1134: letter from 12 December 1950.

[18] Kiehl, *Alle Jahre wieder*, 49; Theodor Heuss, *Hochverehrter Herr Bundespräsident! Der Briefwechsel mit der Bevölkerung 1949–1959*, ed. Wolfram Werner (Berlin: De Gruyter,

From the mid-1950s onwards the situation eased. In 1959, the *völkisch* journalist Max Boehm could attest to the newcomers' 'psychological acclimatization'. He also recognized 'a process of re-rooting' that necessarily led to a hybrid identity and consciousness. Regrettably, noted Boehm, this meant that 'the old homeland is in danger of falling more and more into the emotional background'.[19] Expellee associations and parties shared this regret, as they sought to preserve both the memory of their 'native land' and their claim to it. In 1950, the Charter of the German Expellees had demanded that 'the right to the homeland is recognized and carried out as one of the fundamental rights of mankind given by God'. At the same time, it urged the host society to feel a 'co-responsibility' for the fate of expellees and to ease their difficult lot (> Empathy, > Solidarity). The multi-billion Equalization of Burdens Act of 1952 and the Federal Expellees Act of 1953 granted material and legal form to this co-responsibility.

Nevertheless, expellee politicians stuck to their demands for 'living space in the West, right of homeland in the East', thus condensed in 1964 by right-winger Linus Kather.[20] Their concerns found widespread approval across party lines. In a 1963 telegram greeting to the annual Silesian convention in Cologne, the SPD executive – Willy Brandt, Herbert Wehner and Erich Ollenhauer – declared their unwavering support for people's right to self-determination: 'Abandonment is betrayal, nobody would dispute that.' The right to the homeland could not be 'hawked for a dish of lentils'.[21]

Politically, *Heimat* and associated feelings of belonging became fiercely contested in the Federal Republic around 1970. Whereas in the nineteenth century the 'right to the homeland' simply denoted the legal right to be supported in the case of poverty by one's community of origin, after 1945 it acquired a strong emotional charge that weighed heavily on the domestic political climate. In the wake of the Ostpolitik administered since 1969,

---

2010), 148–49. The League of Expellees and Disfranchised only catered to the special interests of expellees and was dissolved in 1961.

[19] Michael Schwartz, 'Assimilation versus Incorporation: Expellee Integration Policies in East and West Germany after 1945', in *Vertriebene and Pieds-Noirs in Postwar Germany and France*, ed. Manuel Borutta and Jan C. Jansen (Basingstoke: Palgrave Macmillan, 2016), 73–94, quotes 82.

[20] Andreas Kossert, *Kalte Heimat: Die Geschichte der deutschen Vertriebenen nach 1945* (Bonn: Bundeszentrale für politische Bildung, 2015), 151, 92 ff.; Linus Kather, *Die Entmachtung der Vertriebenen*, vol. 1 (Munich: Olzog, 1964), 19. Kather, who had initially been active in the CDU, later joined the League of Expellees and Disfranchised before moving further to the right and siding with the National Democratic Party (NPD). For a broader view also in terms of *Heimat*, homesickness and belonging, see Andrew Demshuk, *The Lost German East: Forced Migration and the Politics of Memory, 1945–1970* (Cambridge: Cambridge University Press, 2012).

[21] Kossert, *Kalte Heimat*, 165.

tensions rose. When Willy Brandt, now chancellor, recognized Poland's western border as inviolable and thereby ruled out any territorial claims, expellees
accused him of betrayal. In October 1970, at a rally of 3,000 people organized
by right-wing radicals in Würzburg, one banner depicted a gallows intended
for the chancellor. Protesters chanted 'Willy Brandt to the wall – Hang
the traitor – Germany will not be given up, Willy Brandt will be strung up'
(> Anger).[22]

Such hateful diatribes notwithstanding, most expellees and refugees had in
the meantime settled into their new homes. They no longer saw themselves
as 'homeless', like 'strangers on the face of the earth', as the 1950 charter had
described them; its pathos-soaked assertion that 'to separate man forcibly
from his native land means to kill him in his mind' did not reflect the reality
of their lives. They joined local sports and shooting clubs, and, if the
denomination suited, sang in the church choir. They also cultivated their
own cultural and folk traditions, keeping them alive through songs, cos-
tumes, souvenir books and *Heimat* festivals. By the 1960s, hardly anyone
dreamt of returning permanently to the old homeland, especially since –
quite apart from political circumstances – the economic conditions there
were anything but attractive.

Among young people and those born after 1945, the much-vaunted 'right to
the homeland' was a mere chimera anyway. They spoke the vernacular dialects
and learnt about where they lived in local history lessons (*Heimatkunde*) at
school. They could go to the cinema to see a *Heimatfilm* – a much-loved genre
in the 1950s – and witness the new hybridity of home on the screen. In one of
the most famous plotlines, a girl from Silesia overcomes a series of dramatic
conflicts to finally find her guy, a local gamekeeper in Lüneburg (*The Heath Is
Green / Grün ist die Heide*, 1951).[23] Such 'mixed marriages' were entered into
by three out of every four men and women who held an expellee identity card.
Over time, fewer and fewer of them applied for such cards for their children.[24]

Un-housed-ness

Around 1950, notions of homelessness and feelings of estrangement did not
solely circulate among refugees. In fact, the language used by the Charter bore
a striking resemblance to an intellectual discourse centred on the idea of
Unbehaustheit, or 'un-housed-ness'. It had been dug up by the poet and

---

[22] 'Würzburger Widersprüche', *Die Zeit*, 20 November 1970, www.zeit.de/1970/47/wuerz
burger-widersprueche/, accessed 17 December 2021.

[23] Susanne Scharnowski, *Heimat* (Darmstadt: wgb, 2019), 124–42.

[24] Matthias Stickler, *'Ostdeutsch heißt Gesamtdeutsch': Organisation, Selbstverständnis und
heimatpolitische Zielsetzungen der deutschen Vertriebenenverbände 1949–1972*
(Düsseldorf: Droste, 2004), 138.

literary critic Hans Egon Holthusen for the title of an essay collection in 1951. Born in 1913, Holthusen had joined the SS in 1933 and served in the army's signal corps during the war. After 1945, he remoulded the concept of 'un-housed-ness', known from Goethe's *Faust*, into the paradigmatic life-attitude of modern man in his 'uprootedness' and 'dizzying insecurity'.[25] Such tropes clearly appealed to the war generation. Wolfgang Borchert's drama *The Man Outside*, which from 1947 onwards enjoyed great success as a play for both radio and stage, told the story of Beckmann, a war returnee who had been cast out by God and his homeland (represented by his wife) and in whom many men apparently recognized themselves.[26]

The existentialist tenor of this literature suited the contemporary mood. Anyone with a guilty past as a Wehrmacht soldier or member of the SS could find helpful relief in Martin Heidegger's concept of *Geworfenheit*, or 'thrown-ness'. When Holthusen's SS past became public in 1966, he dismissed it as an experience of 'depoliticization', citing vanity, elitism and the 'chic' black uniforms as motives for joining.[27]

Yet even those who felt radically 'uprooted' and 'unhoused' – and cultivated such feelings as something special and distinctive – were usually not averse to finding a new home, getting a new job and putting down new roots. Holthusen himself made it to the presidency of the Bavarian Academy of Fine Arts and, in 1987, received the Federal Republic's Great Cross of Merit. For the eight million refugees who were not only figuratively but literally 'unhoused', the state built new flats at lightning speed and took steps to repair bomb damage (Figure 7). As early as 1950, Chancellor Adenauer proudly announced that over 330,000 'homesteads' had been built. Around the same time, the trade unions re-founded their own housing enterprise and eloquently named it Neue Heimat (new home).[28]

---

[25] Hans Egon Holthusen, *Der unbehauste Mensch: Motive und Probleme der modernen Literatur* (Munich: Piper, 1951), 10.

[26] Wolfgang Borchert, *The Man Outside: The Prose Works*, trans. David Porter (London: Calder & Boyars, 1966); Ulrike Weckel, 'Spielarten der Vergangenheitsbewältigung – Wolfgang Borcherts Heimkehrer und sein langer Weg durch die westdeutschen Medien', in *Medien – Politik – Geschichte*, ed. Moshe Zuckermann (Göttingen: Wallstein, 2003), 125–61.

[27] Martin Heidegger, *Kant and the Problem of Metaphysics*, trans. Richard Taft (Bloomington: Indiana University Press, 1990), 181; Hans Egon Holthusen, 'Freiwillig zur SS', *Merkur* 20, no. 223–224 (1966): 921–39, 1037–49, quote 958.

[28] Michael Mönninger, '*Neue Heime als Grundzellen eines gesunden Staates*': *Städte- und Wohnungsbau der Nachkriegsmoderne* (Berlin: DOM, 2018); Andres Lepik and Hilde Strobl, eds, *Die Neue Heimat (1950–1982): Eine sozialdemokratische Utopie und ihre Bauten* (Munich: Detail, 2019). 'Neue Heimat' was actually the name the Nazi organization German Labour Front had given to the housing association founded by and seized from the (abolished) trade unions.

Figure 7 Model of a settlement for displaced persons in Westphalia, 1956 (Photo by ullstein bild/ullstein bild via Getty Images)

The republic also provided the social and economic security that was especially longed for by those who had lost house and home and wanted to get back on their feet as quickly as possible. From the very beginning, the economy occupied a prominent place in annual speeches by successive chancellors and presidents, who reported on the strength of national outputs and the number of jobs created in the preceding year. They also noted the increase in pensions, the rise in purchasing power and the expansion of consumer choice.

'Belonging through Assured Progress'

By contrast, *Heimat* was less and less a focus for discussion once the expellees had been integrated and the last prisoners of war had returned from the Soviet Union. Instead, from the 1960s the word *Geborgenheit* began doing the rounds. In 1964 Chancellor Ludwig Erhard still used it exclusively with reference to 'family and home', thus promoting an idea of belonging that was limited to the private sphere. By the end of 1970, though, Willy Brandt expressed the wish that his fellow citizens would gain a sense of 'belonging through assured progress' (*Geborgenheit im gesicherten Fortschritt*).

The slogan was hard to beat for its suggestive power: *Geborgenheit* touched on deep psychological layers and spoke to the individual's need to be in good and safe hands. One felt *geborgen* either in the 'earth's womb', with one's own mother and family, or with God. Brandt offered a fourth option, albeit one that represented a contradiction in terms. As a general rule, 'progress' was not in harmony with 'belonging'. To take the path of progress usually meant to pursue an uncertain and open-ended path and leave behind the sense of security and safety offered by the familiar. Here, the adjective 'assured' promised a solution. It could be read in two ways: either progress was a sure thing and not at all in question, or one might feel secure even on fundamentally insecure terrain. Brandt let both meanings hover in the air. In this vein, he could accommodate the planning and 'can-do' euphoria that prevailed at the time, as well as the idea already laid down in the Basic Law: that social security and social policy were the key prerequisites for realizing democracy's quest for freedom.[29]

In late 1975, in the face of growing economic problems and high inflation rates, Chancellor Helmut Schmidt picked up Brandt's thread when he drew a direct causal link from the 'social security safety net' and other welfare benefits to the 'social belonging of the individual' and the 'inner stability' of society and state. Yet he was also aware that many citizens found society too cold, rational, bereft of 'human warmth' and that they missed feeling a sense of 'belonging'. In 1977, Federal President Walter Scheel cited studies showing the number of happy people in the Federal Republic was decreasing; as he saw it, this related to a lack of belonging.[30] He himself had made a major contribution to cheerfulness in 1973 when, while still foreign minister, he entered the music charts with his rendition of the folk song 'Hoch auf dem gelben Wagen' (High on the yellow wagon), supported by the Düsseldorf Men's Choral Society.

Like all folk and homeland poetry, however, the song was not without melancholic tones. On life's journey through meadows, fields and pastures, accompanied by dancing, music and smiling faces, there was no standing still, no lingering, no holding on. In the end, though, death was always waiting (Scheel wisely omitted that final verse). Darker and brighter colours also blended in Edgar Reitz's epic *Heimat* film series that opened in cinemas in 1984. Despite its title, Reitz certainly did not depict the fictional village of Schabbach and its inhabitants through a rose-tinted lens. What took place between 1919 and 1982 in this ostensibly godforsaken region near the French border was anything but idyllic and harmonious. As a 'German chronicle', the multi-award-winning series was steeped in the drama and dynamics of the

---

[29] Kiehl, *Alle Jahre wieder*, 203, 277; Gabriele Metzler, '"Geborgenheit im gesicherten Fortschritt": Das Jahrzehnt von Planbarkeit und Machbarkeit', in *Demokratisierung und gesellschaftlicher Aufbruch*, ed. Matthias Frese et al. (Paderborn: Schöningh, 2005), 777–97.

[30] Kiehl, *Alle Jahre wieder*, 316, 324–25.

time and its plot richly peppered with personal disappointments and estrangements.[31]

In some ways, it fit the new *Heimat* movement that emerged in the late 1970s. No doubt, its supporters would have fiercely objected to this name, as they considered *Heimat* to be a cipher for backward folksiness, brass-band oompah music and the beer-swilling customs of local clubs and festivals. But in actual fact, the manifold environmental and anti-nuclear initiatives were modern movements for homeland protection. Unlike former associations that had carried *Heimat* and *Heimatschutz* in their names since 1904, these new groups no longer travelled in the slipstream of nationalist right-wingers. Instead, they mobilized liberal academics and left-wing students who despite their ideological leanings shared many conservatives' concern as to whether 'assured progress' was sufficiently safe. In view of the health and ecological hazards posed by nuclear power plants, air- and water-polluting industries and landscape-destroying autobahns and airports, appeals for preservation – in which environment and homeland merged – received a great deal of support. This was true not least of leftist alternative milieus, which, in rejecting what they perceived to be the cold and technocratic conditions of capitalist industrial society, created their own islands of 'warm community' and 'belonging'.[32]

'Social Belonging' in the GDR

Brandt's social democratic formula of 'belonging through assured progress' thus had only limited persuasive power, if any at all, and a very short half-life. The GDR did not fare much better. In the 1950s, the regime had initially relied on a broad notion of homeland – which still included the Federal Republic – with slightly socialist overtones. In 1954, for instance, an article in the *Berliner Zeitung* congratulated footballers 'from the west of our homeland' on winning the World Cup. And since 1951, children had been singing a popular song called 'Unsere Heimat' ('Our Homeland') in which everything, from animals, meadows and forests to villages and towns, belonged to 'the people', 'our people', and was therefore loved. Exactly who did or did not belong to this 'people' was deliberately left unclear.[33]

---

[31] Edgar Reitz and Peter Steinbach, *Heimat: Eine deutsche Chronik* (Nördlingen: Grenco, 1988); Eric L. Santaner, *Stranded Objects: Mourning, Memory, and Film in Postwar Germany* (Ithaca, NY: Cornell University Press, 1990), 57–102.

[32] Edeltraud Klueting, ed., *Antimodernismus und Reform: Zur Geschichte der deutschen Heimatbewegung* (Darmstadt: wbg, 1991); Sven Reichardt, 'Is "Warmth" a Mode of Social Behaviour? Considerations on a Cultural History of the Left-Alternative Milieu from the Late 1960s to the Mid 1980s', *Behemoth* 3, no. 2 (2010): 83–99.

[33] *Berliner Zeitung*, 6 July 1954, 4; Jan Palmowski, *Inventing a Socialist Nation: Heimat and the Politics of Everyday Life in the GDR 1945–1990* (Cambridge: Cambridge University

This changed during the Honecker era, when the regime propagated an image of itself as an independent socialist nation and narrowed the territorial definition of what the homeland encompassed. In this new concept of the nation, citizens were supposed to feel not only secure in socio-economic terms but also *geborgen*, that is, lovingly protected and taken care of. As the writer Günter de Bruyn recalled, *Geborgenheit* became 'the most effective agitational word' in the 1970s, while the laborious language of 'advancing and triumphing' receded into the background.[34] The country's Labour Code, adopted in 1977, sought to guarantee the 'social security and *Geborgenheit* of workers and their families'. The idea of social belonging was widely discussed within workplace brigades as well as in newspapers, guidebooks and political sessions. In 1976, the SED newspaper *Neues Deutschland* calculated for its readers the 'huge sums of money spent in the service of social *Geborgenheit*' to maintain 'stable consumer prices, favourable transport fares and low rents' through state subsidies. In 1985, it extolled 'social security, happiness and *Geborgenheit*' as the 'everyday stuff of our life'.[35]

Throughout the confrontational political competition with the Federal Republic, the GDR regime had always claimed social security as its decisive advantage (and falsely averred that it did not exist in the West). With the motif of *Geborgenheit*, it sought to add an appealing and easy-to-grasp emotional element to existing notions of material security that carried a promise of personal happiness and collective harmony. It also made clear that such happiness and harmony was owed above all to the socialist state and its ruling party, which could expect gratitude and compliance for its care.[36]

Whether or not GDR citizens actually felt a sense of belonging, comfort and safety is another matter. After the Wall was built in 1961, they had no choice but to settle into their socialist home. To be sure, they grumbled about the high prices of consumer goods, the gaps in supply chains, a lack of materials in the factories and the bloated administrative and party apparatus. In 1987, workers

Press, 2009), 186; Dorothee Wierling, 'Über die Liebe zum Staat – der Fall der DDR', *Historische Anthropologie* 8, no. 2 (2000): 236–63, here 238–40.

[34] Palmowski, *Inventing*, 118–19, 134–38, 149–85 (pointing out that local and regional homeland activities both intensified and shaped understandings of homeland for large sections of the population); Günter de Bruyn, *Vierzig Jahre: Ein Lebensbericht* (Frankfurt: Fischer, 1998), 186.

[35] *Neues Deutschland*, 22 September 1976, 3; ibid., 17 May 1985, 5; *Neue Zeit*, 9 October 1976, 3; *Berliner Zeitung*, 9/10 December 1978, 10.

[36] Hans Günter Hockerts, 'Soziale Errungenschaften? Zum sozialpolitischen Legitimitätsanspruch der zweiten deutschen Diktatur', in *Von der Arbeiterbewegung zum modernen Sozialstaat*, ed. Jürgen Kocka (Munich: Saur, 1994), 790–804, esp. 798.

from Merseburg communicated their dissatisfaction in an anonymous letter to the SED's district newspaper: 'This is no home for us, with all its slovenliness and parasitism. We love a homeland where one can elect one's own representatives and they then demonstrate through their performance what socialism is capable of, rather than making such a mess all the way down the line.' But even discontented critics appreciated the social security that their walled-in and immobilized country offered them.[37] The absence of a strong competitive economy – the necessary foundation for such security – and the dire situation of the 1980s, when social *Geborgenheit* could only be financed on credit from the Federal Republic, were not known to most.

Migration: Guest Workers, Contract Labourers and Fellow Citizens

Today people know. But that does not stop GDR nostalgists from glorifying a sense of belonging and security in retrospect and playing it off against recent experiences of acceleration and insecurity (> Nostalgia). They, too, are the target of the *Heimat* Ministry's claim of ensuring the *Geborgenheit* of all Germans, East and West, including immigrants from other countries. The latter, known as 'migrants' in academic discourse, are simply called *Fremde* (strangers) or *Ausländer* (foreigners) in vernacular speech. Nowadays, the government wants them to feel at home and *geborgen* in Germany, and even recognizes their right to have more than one homeland. This was not always the case.

Between 1955, when the Federal Republic signed its first recruitment agreement with Italy, and 1973, when the Brandt government halted labour migration in the face of the oil crisis, about fourteen million 'guest workers' arrived in the country. They were supposed to fill an acute labour shortage in West Germany's 'miracle economy'. When the miracle began to falter, the vast majority returned to their home countries.[38] In any case, the intention from the outset was that their stay would be short and that they would not settle long-term. The majority of 'guests' kept to this plan, but two to three million did stay in the end.

---

[37] Siegfried Suckut, *Volkes Stimmen: 'Ehrlich, aber deutlich' – Privatbriefe an die DDR-Regierung* (Munich: dtv, 2015), 356–58; Lutz Niethammer, 'Zeroing in on Change: In Search of a Popular Experience in the Industrial Province in the German Democratic Republic', in *The History of Everyday Life: Reconstructing Historical Experiences and Ways of Life*, ed. Alf Lüdtke, trans. William Templer (Princeton, NJ: Princeton University Press, 1995), 252–311, here 295; Hockerts, 'Soziale Errungenschaften', 799.

[38] Hedwig Richter, 'Die Komplexität von Integration: Arbeitsmigration in die Bundesrepublik Deutschland von den fünfziger bis in die siebziger Jahre', *Zeitgeschichte-online*, 1 November 2015, http://bit.ly/3mw8ItP, accessed 17 December 2021.

Foreign workers had also been a source of labour in the GDR since the 1960s, some coming from neighbouring Poland and Hungary, but most hailing from more distant 'socialist brother states' such as Angola, Cuba, Nicaragua, Mozambique and Vietnam. They were not expected to remain permanently in the country. The regime only granted them a temporary stay of two years at first, later extended to five, and they lived isolated from the rest of the population. Personal contact was discouraged, and family reunifications were not permitted.[39] In 1989, official statistics documented close to 100,000 such 'contract labourers', who were overwhelmingly Vietnamese.

By contrast, the Federal Republic counted 4.8 million 'foreigners', 1.6 million of whom had come from Turkey. Despite the official halting of recruitment, their numbers had increased significantly since the 1970s, mainly due to family members joining them. Initially, no one attended to their 'assimilation'. It was not until the end of 1964 that a federal president even acknowledged their existence in his annual address and wished them a happy new year. In 1966, Chancellor Kurt Georg Kiesinger included their families as well. Three years later, Willy Brandt dubbed them 'neighbours' and called on his fellow citizens to 'respect them and show them – even through the smallest gestures – that the German people has learnt to accept the foreigner as a friend'.[40]

Brandt's admonishing words shifted the tone of the debate. In 1971, Federal President Gustav Heinemann (SPD) took an even stronger stance when he urged citizens to show moral courage and not stand silently by 'while a guest-worker is being treated like an inferior human being'. As early as 1966, the churches had demanded more compassion and respect with their poster campaign 'A guest worker is also your neighbour' (> Empathy). 'Let us accept them into our community' was how President Karl Carstens voiced his appeal in 1979, though he clearly favoured the more recent repatriates from Eastern Europe who 'want to rediscover their old, never-

---

[39] Ulrich van der Heyden et al., eds, *Mosambikanische Vertragsarbeiter in der DDR-Wirtschaft* (Münster: LIT, 2014).

[40] Kiehl, *Alle Jahre wieder*, 209, 233, 267; Karin Hunn, *'Nächstes Jahr kehren wir zurück...'*: *Die Geschichte der türkischen 'Gastarbeiter' in der Bundesrepublik* (Göttingen: Wallstein, 2005), 277–327. See also Ulrich Herbert and Karin Hunn, 'Guest Workers and Policy on Guest Workers in the Federal Republic: From the Beginning of the Recruitment in 1955 until Its Halt in 1973', in *The Miracle Years: A Cultural History of West Germany, 1949–1968*, ed. Hanna Schissler (Princeton, NJ: Princeton University Press, 2001), 187–218; Sarah Thomsen Vierra, *Turkish Germans in the Federal Republic of Germany: Immigration, Space, and Belonging, 1961–1990* (Cambridge: Cambridge University Press, 2018).

forgotten homeland within ours'. In 1984, Chancellor Helmut Kohl was the first to speak to 'our foreign fellow citizens', only to walk it back again the following year to 'guest workers and their families'. And on it went, this semantic toing and froing.

During his presidential term, Richard von Weizsäcker tried to finally untie the knot. Acknowledging feelings of anxiety and apprehension among migrants 'who have been living with us for years', he made this request in 1987: 'We should approach them. We should let them feel that they have become part of our community.' It was not acceptable, he added in 1988, to go on treating them like strangers. Three years later, with the images of neo-Nazis setting fire to residential hostels for contract labourers and refugees in the Saxon city of Hoyerswerda still fresh in his mind, Weizsäcker provocatively reversed the terms: 'He who takes up his proper place in the order of our lives, and that includes our non-German colleague at work, or the owner of the pizzeria, is our trusted familiar.' What was foreign, on the other hand, were 'the actions of hooligans and radical thugs who happen to be our countrymen'.[41]

Xenophobia

The 1992 riots against contract labourers and asylum seekers in Rostock exposed just how little these words impressed those who, in a deliberate echo of Nazi language (> Hate), preferred to keep their towns and villages 'free of foreigners'. They were only the tip of the iceberg. If right-wing aggression appeared at first to be limited to the territories of the former GDR, the attacks in Mölln that same year and in Solingen in 1993 proved that migrants were not safe in the old Federal Republic either. Here, the murderous violence was directed against Turkish families who had been living in the country for a long time. In the aftermath, there were powerful demonstrations of solidarity and relief efforts organized by the local communities. Yet they could hardly strengthen the feeling of belonging among those affected by the extremist mob.[42]

Nor did the series of murders and attacks by the National Socialist Underground that began in 2000 assist in the emotional 'integration' of migrants. Learning that the authorities' search for perpetrators had focused not on right-wing radicals but on the Turkish 'mafia' dealt another heavy blow to the hope that people with a family history of migration could ever make

---

[41] Kiehl, *Alle Jahre wieder*, 280, 319, 324, 343, 382, 388, 396, 403, 428.
[42] Hunn, *Nächstes Jahr*, 556; Ulrich Herbert, *Geschichte der Ausländerpolitik in Deutschland* (Munich: C. H. Beck, 2001), 304 ff.; Klaus J. Bade, *Ausländer, Aussiedler, Asyl in der Bundesrepublik Deutschland* (Hanover: Niedersächsische Landeszentrale für Politische Bildung, 1994), 36 ff.

Germany their true home. Not even a German passport could protect against the wrath of those who saw in everyone and everything foreign a threat to their own identity (> Fear, > Anger).[43]

There are many reasons why this feeling of threat is finding increasingly aggressive expression in verbal and physical attacks on migrants and refugees. Some are based on facts, others spring from the realm of fantasy. When the best-selling author Thilo Sarrazin claimed in 2010 that Germany was 'abolishing itself', losing its distinctive qualities in the face of Muslim immigration, his alarmism found only scant support in the statistical data. In 2018, out of a total of 83.1 million people living in the country, 10.9 million did not have German citizenship. Turkish citizens were the largest group with 1.5 million, Syrians came in third place with 750,000, and Afghanis in ninth place with 260,000. If one adds the 1.5 million German citizens of Turkish origin and Muslim faith, the number of Muslims totalled around 4 million, or 5.5 per cent of the population. The overwhelming majority of foreigners living in Germany came from Catholic or Christian Orthodox countries in the European Union, especially Poland, Romania, Italy, Croatia, Greece and Bulgaria.[44]

Against this backdrop, the fears of 'Islamization' that draw quite a few citizens to the far right appear puzzling. Their feelings of being overwhelmed by foreigners and losing their own sense of homeland, however, also stem from other sources. From a historical perspective, calls for the protection and affirmation of *Heimat* become particularly loud when people feel threatened by what the present and future hold. Economic and technological as well as cultural and political developments can seem highly dangerous and destructive. In combination, they may present an almost overpowering horror scenario. A yearning for *Heimat* and *Geborgenheit* then becomes synonymous with a desire for manageable circumstances, clear affiliations and, if not secure, then at least calculable horizons of expectation.

Belonging and the 'New Germans'

The precise meanings of *Heimat* have shifted over the past century. That it still carries significant meaning for a lot of people today is evident from a 2019 study: 89 per cent of respondents found home and homeland important. Of

---

[43] Jan Plamper, *We Are All Migrants: A History of Multicultural Germany* (Cambridge: Cambridge University Press, 2023), 79, 98 ff.; Joanna Pfaff-Czarnecka, 'From "Identity" to "Belonging" in Social Research: Plurality, Social Boundaries, and the Political of the Self', in *Ethnicity, Citizenship and Belonging: Practices, Theory and Spatial Dimensions*, ed. Sarah Albiez et al. (Frankfurt: Vervuert 2011), 199–217; Kwame Anthony Appiah, *The Lies That Bind: Rethinking Identity* (London: Profile Books, 2018).

[44] Maximilian Nowroth, 'In Deutschland leben so viele Ausländer wie noch nie: Wo kommen sie her?', *Handelsblatt*, 15 April 2019, https://orange.handelsblatt.com/artikel/29581, accessed 17 December 2021.

these, 88 per cent agreed with the statement that '*Heimat* is where I feel *geborgen*, like I belong'. While 80 per cent connected this feeling with family or a romantic partner, 68 per cent thought of friends and acquaintances. Only 59 per cent drew a link to the nation.[45] National identity is therefore no longer necessarily crucial for feelings of home. If the same question had been asked in 1915 or 1940, the survey results would have been different.

Yet they can also be read this way: in spite of it all, three out of five people still associated *Heimat* with 'Germany'. In view of post-war Germans' proverbial reticence about national > pride, this is an astonishingly high figure. But what exactly was meant by 'Germany'? Some understood it as a cultural entity with a distinct language and a unique history that came with certain claims and responsibilities. For others, 'Germany' was a national sanctuary of protection that was supposed to ward off – or at least cushion – global threats. Still others took refuge in the memory of a country that had never actually existed (> Nostalgia). Just who had permission to call this country 'home' and feel as though they 'belonged' there depended on how Germany was imagined and whether one defined belonging and *Geborgenheit* in broad or narrow, inclusive or exclusive, defensive or offensive terms.

Since the late twentieth century, such definitions have once again become the subject of heated debate and controversy. On the one hand, this testifies to popular feelings of insecurity and people's need for orientation. On the other hand, the controversy is a credit to German democracy, even if not all participants adhere to the same standard of civilized, respectful and non-violent communication. A larger and broader conversation is now taking place over what it means to be 'German', what kind of normative ideas and practical commitments it entails, and what is both expected of, and owed to, immigrants (> Solidarity).

One novelty is that the conversation includes migrants who speak up and play an active part in German society. They no longer want Germany to occupy the role of 'bitter homeland' in their lives, nor do they aim to radically turn away from it. Around the year 2000, when asked whether they feel a 'homeland' connection with Germany, between 20 and 30 per cent of people from Turkish backgrounds answered yes. Between 30 and 40 per cent identified with Turkey, and the same number considered both Germany and Turkey to be their *Heimat*. Since around 2011, however, attachment to Turkey has increased rapidly, while the feeling of belonging to Germany or to both countries has decreased. This is particularly noticeable among members of the third generation and has become known as the 'paradox of integration'. Because they have strongly internalized the principles of equality in German

---

[45] *Die Zeit*, 9 May 2019, 69. For similar survey results in 1979 and 2010, see Habbo Knoch, '"Heimat": Konjunkturen eines politischen Konzepts', *Indes* 4 (2018): 19–34, esp. 28, 31.

society, those younger respond to the experience of unequal treatment and discrimination with 'ethnic withdrawal'. Many feel 'warmer' and more welcome in their parents' or grandparents' country of origin, yet even there, their sense of foreignness and 'unbelonging' is no less intense. This makes the question of identity all the more emotionally complicated.[46]

[46] Semiya Şimşek (with Peter Schwarz), *Schmerzliche Heimat: Deutschland und der Mord an meinem Vater* (Berlin: Rowohlt, 2013); Haci-Halil Uslucan, 'Türkeistämmige in Deutschland: Heimatlos oder überall zuhause?', *Aus Politik und Zeitgeschichte* no. 11–12 (2017): 31–37. The surveys were conducted between 1999 and 2015 in North Rhine-Westphalia. See also Alice Bota et al., *Wir neuen Deutschen* (Reinbek: Rowohlt, 2012).

~

Curiosity

Some people question whether curiosity is an emotion at all. Others are unsure whether to categorize it as good or bad. In 'everyday language', the 1991 *Brockhaus* encyclopaedia noted, curiosity signals an 'inappropriate interest in the affairs of other people'. The curious person, it had stated in 1971, is chiefly 'concerned with experiencing sensations minor or major', preferably from 'the private sphere of those around them (their "gossip" or intimate sphere)'. In early Christianity, *curiositas* was considered a vice and condemned as such.[1]

Only slowly did such judgements disappear, replaced eventually by a general consensus that curiosity was something beneficial. According to this view, curious people exhibit a desire for 'innovation' and an inclination towards experimentation. Educators now champion the importance of fostering curiosity in children as it promotes their capacity to learn and their inquisitiveness and creativity, as well as their 'openness and readiness to engage in the socialization process'. Humans – unlike other mammals – are believed to retain curiosity their whole lives.

Is Curiosity an Emotion?

More recent definitions frame curiosity not as an emotion or feeling but rather as a 'need', 'behaviour' or 'urge'. This is in large part due to the influence of US psychologists, in particular the emotions researcher Paul Ekman. He lists surprise, but not curiosity, among the six or seven 'basic emotions'. His reasoning is that humans show clear facial expressions and cues when they are surprised but do not display similarly identifiable gestures when feeling curious.

Ekman's basic emotions resemble the six primary passions French philosopher René Descartes identified in 1649. Alongside love, hatred, joy and

---

[1] *Brockhaus Enzyklopädie*, 17th ed., vol. 13 (Wiesbaden: Brockhaus, 1971), 333; ibid., 19th ed., vol. 15 (Mannheim: Brockhaus, 1991), 474 (also the following citation). The note about the negative connotation of the everyday term remained until 1998; it was not until the twenty-first edition, in 2006, that it was withdrawn.

sadness, he counted wonder, which encompassed both the 'sudden surprise' and the feeling of admiration. Unlike Ekman, however, Descartes included *le désir*, one of the primary passions of the soul, which spanned the lust for fame and honour and the lust for knowledge. For the Enlightenment thinker, *curiosité* was an important future-oriented emotion.

It suited an era in which people were in the process of transcending borders and discovering new continents as well as new ways of living and thinking. It was not only the encounter with the previously unknown that was new. New things were also expected from the future, which was increasingly imagined as an open space of possibility, replacing perceptions of time as circular and repeating. *Neugier*, greed for the new, summarized this new mood perfectly: curiosity reflected openness, a dismissal of fear and an eagerness for novelty and innovation. Furthermore, it actively aided progress in various fields by inspiring people to make discoveries.

The feeling of curiosity thus served as the godmother to modern science. In the sixteenth and seventeenth centuries, natural scientists such as Nicolaus Copernicus, Johannes Kepler and Maria Sibylla Merian renounced the authority of the ancient canon and placed their trust instead in their own observations, which they acquired through experiments using newly available instruments and techniques. Their efforts, which upturned faith-based systems of knowledge, did not always win them friends. Indeed, Kepler's valiant plea for his mother's freedom when she was tried for witchcraft in Württemberg was hardly met with universal approval.[2]

Scientific Curiosity

It was not until the 1800s that science driven by curiosity and the joy of experimentation gained broader acceptance and institutionalization. Germany was at the forefront of the charge. Research played a central role at the Enlightenment-influenced universities of Halle (founded in 1694) and Göttingen (1737), as well as at the new universities based on the Humboldtian model pioneered in Berlin since 1810. According to this model, professors saw themselves not simply as collectors, archivists and transmitters of knowledge but first and foremost as discoverers, and they wanted to make discoveries together with their students. In any case, this was what the educational reformer and university founder Wilhelm von Humboldt was envisaging when he spoke of the community of students and educators and the unity of teaching and research as guiding principles of the modern university.

---

[2] Lorraine Daston and Katharine Park, *Wonders and the Order of Nature, 1150–1750* (New York: Zone Books, 1998), 303–28; Ulinka Rublack, *The Astronomer and the Witch: Johannes Kepler's Fight for His Mother* (Oxford: Oxford University Press, 2015).

Good research required inquisitive researchers dissatisfied with what was already known. It also needed students with a thirst for knowledge who would hunt in laboratories, libraries and archives for new insights. The move towards scientification affected all disciplines, from history and theology to medicine, law and economics. Particularly rapid were the advances in the experimental natural sciences and engineering, which fuelled economic development and the boom in the electrical engineering and chemical industries from the end of the nineteenth century. It was not by chance that the wealthy Swedish entrepreneur and inventor Alfred Nobel bequeathed his esteemed prize primarily to researchers who had conferred 'the greatest benefit to mankind' in the domains of physics, chemistry, physiology and medicine. Among the first prize winners in 1901 were immunologist Emil von Behring and physicist Wilhelm Conrad Röntgen, while in 1902 the chemist Emil Fischer and, in the field of literature, the scholar of ancient history Theodor Mommsen were recognized for their pathbreaking achievements.

German scientists continued to be lauded in the years to come. Individual performance was not the only feat the prize recognized. It also testified to the level of advancement at academic institutions and their power to facilitate vital research. From 1911, the country's globally renowned universities and technical colleges were joined by a number of non-university institutes under the umbrella of the Kaiser Wilhelm Society, where highly specialized and generously funded research was carried out. Several members of the society would go on to win Nobel Prizes: physicists Max von Laue, Albert Einstein and Werner Heisenberg, and chemists Richard Willstätter, Fritz Haber, Adolf Butenandt and Otto Hahn. After the Second World War, it was renamed and expanded as the Max Planck Society.

Einstein once said that he had 'no special talent', he was 'just passionately curious'. When asked what drives her, biologist Christiane Nüsslein-Volhard replied: 'I think a very big curiosity. I'm very curious and I like to understand things and not only science but also other things where I just try to find out why things work or how things work.' The researcher with the 'curious eye', who was born in 1942, was awarded the Nobel Prize for medicine in 1995 and has not lost her curiosity even in old age. In 2018, she told a journalist from the *Neue Zürcher Zeitung* that she 'fires up quite quickly when something sparks my curiosity'.[3]

As the Max Planck Society, which proudly counts Nüsslein-Volhard among its scientific members, declares, 'research is curiosity'. Curiosity prompts men and women to push the boundaries of science and to pose questions only painstaking and time-consuming work can answer. Conceived as such,

---

[3] Albert Einstein's letter to Carl Seelig, from 11 March 1952, cited in Ulrich Weinzierl, *Carl Seelig, Schriftsteller* (Vienna: Löcker, 1982), 135; http://bit.ly/3ETdbNF; http://bit.ly/3Rvt0z2, both accessed 28 March 2022.

curiosity is not a feeling that flashes up and just as quickly fades away. Rather, it has to be permanently nurtured and sustained, step by step, in the research process. Once awakened, it accompanies scientists throughout their lives and is constantly rekindled. At least that is the impression one gets from listening to successful researchers – although success is certainly relative. Not all research will be crowned with a Nobel Prize, nor does every experiment produce the desired result. Disappointments are a matter of course. Curiosity helps researchers to persevere and to regard setbacks as an incentive to unearth better hypotheses and methods. Under the right conditions, curiosity can move mountains and make history.

Encouraging Curiosity

But where does curiosity come from, and what feeds it? Who is curious and who is not? Psychologists believe that children have a natural inclination to be curious. Initially, they learn by imitation. But they soon begin to discover and explore their environment on their own. Many scientists are now focusing their efforts on encouraging this 'urge to experience'. Since the 1990s, academic institutions have been offering workshops for pupils and kindergarten classes, as well as organizing so-called children's universities. Directors of Max Planck Institutes set up 'science hubs' in order to awaken the 'fun in acquiring knowledge' among little ones. They see the pleasure of learning, coupled with curiosity, as the most vital prerequisite for strengthening Germany's position as a leader in education and science.[4]

Historically, these are new impulses. Looking back, Einstein, who was born in 1879 and completed his schooling in Munich before attending a polytechnic in Zurich, considered it truly miraculous that the 'modern methods of instruction have not yet entirely strangled the holy curiosity of inquiry'.[5] Instead of nurturing curiosity, that 'delicate little plant', with stimulation and freedom, educational institutions often followed the 'Nuremberg Funnel' model, in which knowledge was mechanically drummed into the impressionable minds that trundled through the system. Independent thought was discouraged as it was believed to be disruptive and could undermine the authority of teachers. There was little space in the classrooms of 1900 for curiosity. Students who displayed too much of it were seen as insolent and were swiftly and ruthlessly brought into line.

This happened in primary schools as well as in the secondary or grammar schools that, back then, exclusively educated the sons of the upper-middle classes. Teachers ruled with the utmost discipline and believed in the passive

---

[4] http://bit.ly/3wRNAjs, accessed 20 March 2022.
[5] Albert Einstein, 'Autobiographical Notes', in *Albert Einstein: Philosopher-Scientist*, ed. Paul Arthur Schilpp, 3rd ed. (LaSalle: Open Court, 1970), 2–94, quotes 16.

acquisition of knowledge. Memorization was the custom, the breadth of knowledge required was massive, and critical debate or asking questions was frowned upon. Yet there were always pupils who evaded these strictures or utilized them to feed their 'pleasure in looking and seeking'; Einstein was one of them. Some teachers, too, appreciated bright and inquiring boys who showed initiative and demonstrated intellectual engagement.

Inquisitive Boys, Nosy Girls

For such boys, the German language reserved the term *Wissbegierde* – denoting inquisitiveness and thirst for knowledge. In contrast, girls were thought to be simply curious, without any interest in abstract concepts or intellectual ambitions. In bourgeois families, they were to prepare for a life away from the public sphere; all they needed to take from their schooling was that which would help them in the kitchen, nursery and, at most, the family parlour. In the mid-1890s, theologian Siegfried Lommatzsch shared a common viewpoint: 'ladies' were not suited to university, and if they did attend, they would – to the annoyance of respectable teachers – only 'sit in on lectures to satisfy their curiosity'.[6]

For Professor Lommatzsch and his contemporaries, curiosity or *Neugier* was wholly different to *Wissbegierde*. The former was seen negatively while the latter was praised. Boys were allowed to be inquisitive; girls, however, were considered only superficially curious or nosy, and little inclined to serious education or deep ideas. Their 'trifling spirit' meant they preferred uncovering knowledge of a more personal nature, 'looking through keyholes or even eavesdropping through closed doors'. Educators found this highly indelicate and deserving of censure.[7]

Not every girl or young 'lady' was prepared to accept such censure and conform to the stereotype. Ina Seidel, born in 1885, refused to fill 'the wait for marriage solely with social activities, by dabbling in the fine arts and at the piano, with needlework and dusting'. She and her friends 'were in utter inner turmoil and possessed by a hunger for knowledge, we envied those of our acquaintances who had decided to go to secondary school and university – in my circle there were only two such girls'.[8]

Irma Klausner from Berlin was one of these curious young women, completing her medical studies despite the 'greatest mistrust' on the part of her professors and peers; Rahel Goitein from Karlsruhe was another. In her 1899 graduation speech, Goitein explained why she and her female friends

---

[6] Arthur Kirchhoff, ed., *Die Akademische Frau* (Berlin: Steinitz, 1897), 7.

[7] Karoline S. J. Milde, *Der deutschen Jungfrau Wesen und Wirken*, 12th ed. (Leipzig: Amelang, 1899), 465, 471; Franz Ebhardt, *Der gute Ton*, 13th ed. (Leipzig: Klinkhardt, 1896), 29.

[8] Ina Seidel, *Meine Kindheit und Jugend* (Stuttgart: DVA, 1935), 169.

had committed to 'following this path': 'Above all it was the desire to learn, to know.'[9] Yet this simple desire encountered ferocious resistance. Many professors steadfastly refused to allow women to listen in on their lectures. Just like Lommatzsch, they condemned the 'present educational push' as an aberration and a 'defiance of divine and human laws'. Others were more reluctant to prevent individual talented women from 'cultivating one of the most noble human instincts, the thirst for knowledge'. But they assumed that only a few would in fact pursue academic study out of an 'inner drive and inclination'. They were not actually wrong: even when the official prohibition on women studying was lifted in the early twentieth century, the number of female students remained small. In 1914, before the outbreak of the First World War, there were only 4,000 women enrolled in German universities, less than 7 per cent of the total student population.[10]

In addition to outright hostility to female intellectual endeavours, there were subtler ways of keeping gender differences in place and on track. Reading material, for instance, was highly gendered. On their birthday, boys might receive *The New Universe* (first published in 1880 and still in print today), an annual series that provided information about 'the most interesting inventions and discoveries from all fields'. The tome dealt with transport and industry, technology and machines, physics and chemistry – topics from the supposedly male world of progress and innovation. Toys followed the same pattern: for boys, the German toymaker Märklin created model train sets; for girls, miniature kitchens.

People tended to follow these conventions into adulthood. Men visited public libraries to check out instructive non-fiction books, while women borrowed novels and local stories. These nourished their desire to read about all things human, about love, jealousy, betrayal and the individual search for happiness. Non-fiction books generally examined technical and scientific problems and aimed to arouse the reader's curiosity about possible solutions. This gendered division was present at all levels of society, from working-class to upper-class households.[11]

---

[9] Irma Klausner, 'Dornenweg einer Medizinerin', *Vossische Zeitung*, 25 December 1929, 5; Marco Birn, *Bildung und Gleichberechtigung: Die Anfänge des Frauenstudiums an der Universität Heidelberg (1869–1918)* (Heidelberg: Kurpfälzischer Verlag, 2012), 19–20.

[10] Kirchhoff, *Akademische Frau*, quotes 14, 82, 270, 330; Claudia Huerkamp, *Bildungsbürgerinnen: Frauen im Studium und in akademischen Berufen 1900–1945* (Göttingen: Vandenhoeck & Ruprecht, 1996), 75 ff.; Katharina Rowohlt, *The Educated Woman: Minds, Bodies, and Woman's Higher Education in Britain, Germany, and Spain* (New York: Routledge, 2010), esp. 99–104.

[11] Walter Hofmann, *Die Lektüre der Frau* (Leipzig: Quelle & Meyer, 1931), esp. 30–45 (for the years 1922–1926); Gideon Reuveni, *Reading Germany: Literature and Consumer Culture in Germany before 1933*, trans. Ruth Morris (New York: Berghahn, 2006), esp. fig 3.

Knowledge Is Power

The fact that men from the lower classes also cultivated their intellectual curiosities was thanks primarily to the socialist workers' movement. Under the slogan 'knowledge is power', the movement promised its members a better material and social position. Science and technology were tools that could support workers' emancipation, and for that reason it was important to understand and utilize them. The movement therefore actively participated in the numerous initiatives to popularize science. When, in 1888, the scientific society Urania was founded in Berlin, workers and craftsmen were well-represented among those who attended lectures and events meant to 'spread the joy of knowledge about nature'. Other cities followed suit (Figure 8).

In 1903, the Deutsches Museum opened its doors in Munich and quickly became a major attraction. Exhibiting 'masterpieces of natural science and technology', it drew half a million visitors annually by the late 1920s and 1930s. The Deutsches Hygiene-Museum in Dresden, inaugurated in 1912, was similarly bustling with inquisitive citizens. In 1930 it moved into a modern building, still impressive to this day, which featured an anatomical human figure called *Transparent Man* (joined in 1935 by a *Transparent Woman*) at its heart – thereby affirming its purpose as a 'place of instruction' where 'everyone

Figure 8   The Urania society's physics classroom, Berlin, 1894 (Photo by Bildagentur-online/Universal Images Group via Getty Images)

can acquire knowledge through observation that will enable him to lead a rational and healthy life'.[12]

Instruction and curiosity were not perfect bedfellows, though; too much instruction could in fact stifle curiosity. To prevent this, parties, trade unions, companies and municipalities had founded educational associations and academies in the second half of the nineteenth century, specifically targeting those whose formal schooling had left little room for curiosity or inquisitiveness. By the end of the First World War, these academies were incorporated into local adult-education centres, offering a rich selection of courses and talks on all possible areas of knowledge in exchange for a small fee. They intended 'to turn science into an "experience"' and to relate it, in a novel and sincere way, to people's personal lives. This 'popular movement', as the Prussian minister of culture Carl Heinrich Becker called it, was concerned with the 'development of intellectual and evaluative faculties independent of any practical purpose' and free of any 'class-based division'.[13]

Curiosity for All: Against Educational Inequality

The fight for equality in education has been one of the cornerstones of state policy since the Weimar era. It was believed that every child should have the chance to develop their natural curiosity and to receive the necessary scholastic instruction. The 1919 constitution charged the state with providing the best education for children according to their 'abilities and inclination', and with no regard to the 'economic and social status or the religious confessions' of parents. State and local bodies were to supply 'educational grants for children deemed suitable for instruction in intermediate and secondary schools'. Some educators and politicians campaigned for 'comprehensive schools' and the 'socialization of education'.[14]

Until the early twentieth century, only the sons of well-to-do families had attended university. The push to democratize the education system changed this: universities were henceforth supposed to be open to all young adults,

---

[12] Andreas Daum, *Wissenschaftspopularisierung im 19. Jahrhundert* (Munich: Oldenbourg, 1998), esp. 168–91; Wilhelm Füßl and Helmuth Trischler, eds, *Geschichte des Deutschen Museums* (Munich: Prestel, 2003); Karl August Lingner, *Denkschrift zur Errichtung eines National-Hygiene-Museums in Dresden* (Dresden: Dt. Hygienemuseum, 1912), 5.

[13] Ernst Robert Curtius, 'Max Weber über Wissenschaft als Beruf', *Die Arbeitsgemeinschaft: Monatsschrift für das gesamte Volkshochschulwesen* 1 (1920): 197–98; Carl Heinrich Becker, 'Staat und Volkshochschule', ibid., 5–8; Fritz Borinski, *The German Volkshochschule: An Experiment in Democratic Adult Education under the Weimar Republic* [1944/45], ed. Martha Friedenthal-Haase (Bad Heilbrunn: Klinkhardt, 2014).

[14] Weimarer Reichsverfassung, Art. 146; Becker, 'Staat', 6; Bernd Zymek, 'Schulen, Hochschulen, Lehrer', in *Handbuch der deutschen Bildungsgeschichte*, vol. 5, 155–258, here 159–65, 177–78.

regardless of their gender or social background. Still, the number of female students increased only gradually during the 1920s. In an era of financial scarcity, many daughters from middle-class families had to forego studies – to the benefit of their brothers, who, thanks to the income their sisters earned as secretaries or accountants, could obtain an academic education and pursue an appropriate career. Young men from the lower classes also found it difficult to access the temples of learning, despite the new phenomenon of the 'working student' who earned his bread part-time in factories or trades while studying. In fact, lawyers, doctors and secondary-school teachers from working-class households remained very much the minority and only 3 per cent of university students in 1930 were the children of workers. The vast majority continued to come from (upper) middle-class backgrounds. Even if they possessed neither curiosity nor a desire to learn, these students had their cap, their school diploma and the opportunity for further study practically inscribed on their birth certificate.

Democratic forces made up of Social Democrats, Liberals and the Catholic Centre Party were not the only ones who attempted to change such blatant inequality. National Socialists also mobilized against this form of educational stratification. In *Der Hitlerjunge Quex*, a book for young readers published in 1932 and later turned into a film, grammar-school boy Fritz confesses that he crammed for Latin and Greek solely because his mother wanted him to become a lawyer like his father. He himself rejects the classist education system he was raised in, as he explains to fifteen-year-old apprentice carpenter Heini. Fritz urges him to join the Hitler Youth, where there is no such thing as class, but instead an 'organic community of comrades who have the same blood'. Jewish children were of course excluded from this community. In the 'Third Reich' they became barred from both state schooling and from national youth organizations.[15]

Although the regime preached equality between comrades, the reality in classrooms was quite different. While the newly founded secondary schools did shake up social dynamics, accommodating the interest in education and upward mobility among the lower-middle classes, parents once again had to pay school fees, which not all could manage. This also applied to grammar schools that remained exclusive and exclusionary spaces.

Curiosity and Post-War Schooling

Under National Socialism, the curriculum was strictly aligned with political guidelines that influenced even the teaching of mathematics, not to mention

---

[15] Karl Aloys Schenzinger, *Der Hitlerjunge Quex* (Berlin: Zeitgeschichte-Verlag, 1932), 59 ff. By 1945, around half a million copies had been sold.

subjects like biology and German. The freedom to be curious was curtailed by the heavy rain of ideological doctrine, from which children and adolescents could scarcely escape, especially since the Hitler Youth – the most important educational authority besides the school and family – parroted the regime's beliefs.

Dogma, rather than free-roaming curiosity, continued to mark the peda-gogical landscape after the Second World War in East Germany. Admittedly, the GDR pledged the 'democratic renewal of the German school'. Every child and youth was to receive 'without regard to property, faith or descent, the full education appropriate to his or her inclinations and abilities'. In a truly revolutionary move, the regime abolished the tripartite system of primary, intermediate and secondary schools and replaced it with an eight-grade general school, followed in the late 1950s by a ten-grade 'polytechnic second-ary school'. In 1980, 87 per cent of the relevant age cohort had completed all ten years.

There was no place in the classroom for inquisitive questions, however – let alone doubts. The 'laws' of Marxism-Leninism were unalterable, their position sacrosanct and 'scientifically' grounded. They set the curriculum in the humanities and social sciences, while the natural sciences and technology enjoyed more freedom. Pupils tired of political indoctrination and those who simply wanted to keep their heads down often opted for these subjects.

Political allegiance influenced admission to the extended secondary school that prepared pupils for university entrance qualifications. In 1980, only 8.5 per cent were given the chance to pass through this system, having earned it 'through good performance in class, a high level of ability and willingness, and political, moral and character maturity'. In addition, they needed to have 'demonstrated their attachment to the German Democratic Republic through their attitude and social activity'. Selection committees ensured that 'an appropriate proportion of children from working-class – particularly produc-tion workers – and cooperative farmers' families' were admitted and that 'outstanding achievements of parents in the building of socialism' were also recognized. The educational privilege of the upper classes was thus splintered in favour of a structure that took class and political allegiance into account. Curiosity remained an afterthought.[16]

But then curiosity was not all too common in West German grammar schools either. Until the 1960s, these were primarily filled by the sons, and occasionally the daughters, of civil servants and professionals. Inherited priv-ilege and status did not typically yield curiosity, nor did the methods of teachers who placed greater value on maintaining authority than on giving

---

[16] *Handbuch der deutschen Bildungsgeschichte*, vol. 6, book 2 (Munich: C. H. Beck, 1998), 159 ff., quotes and numbers 163, 191, 193–94.

young people the tools to think for themselves. Social and intellectual strictures around education eased only slowly. With the abolition of school fees, the grammar school gradually lost its reputation as a 'status school for the bourgeoisie' and became, as the Education Council pronounced in 1975, 'a school of advancement also for previously educationally disadvantaged classes'. By then, the proportion of male graduates whose fathers had only an elementary school education had increased to 52 per cent; just 14 per cent came from academic families.[17]

Women also benefited from the expansion of an education system that was both economically required and politically promoted. In 1960, only 8.7 per cent of seventeen-year-old girls were enrolled in a West German grammar school, compared to 13.4 per cent of boys the same age. By 1979, the gap had closed to 20.8 and 20 per cent respectively (a rate more than double that of the GDR). By 2018 – when secondary-school graduates numbered over 40 per cent, and in city states like Hamburg and Berlin over 50 per cent of the relevant age cohort – girls had actually started to surpass their male classmates, both in terms of numbers and grade point averages. Those who had, for a long time, been on the losing end of social opportunities – the proverbial working-class Catholic girl from the countryside – were now among the beneficiaries of the nationwide education strategy, even though working-class parents were still more likely to allow their sons to study at university than their daughters.

A similar phenomenon can be seen in migrant families, where girls do better in school on average than boys. Overall, however, these children's educational outcomes continue to lag behind. This is chiefly due to fundamental disparities before they even get to school: in 2013, 30 per cent of fifteen- to twenty-year-olds from first-generation migrant families were born to parents with no or only minimal formal schooling. Among their non-migrant peers, this figure was 5 per cent. Conversely, 40 per cent of pupils without a recent family history of migration had parents with a high level of education, while just 23 per cent of children from migrant families did.[18]

Families continue to mould the educational prospects of children and young people. Whether a child's curiosity is fostered, what exactly they are curious about and whether their inquisitiveness is sustained over the long term gets shaped first and foremost by their social environment. Kindergartens and schools need parents to ensure that the seeds they plant take root; institutional efforts alone cannot overcome every challenge. The targeted support programmes that many schools now offer compensate for some disadvantages, but not all of them.

---

[17] Ibid., vol. 6, book 1, 307 ff., quotes and numbers 311, 324.
[18] *Grund- und Strukturdaten 1981/82*, ed. Bundesminister für Bildung und Wissenschaft (Bonn: s.n., 1981), 37; *Bildung in Deutschland 2016*, www.bildungsbericht.de/, https://bit .ly/3mmWX9y, accessed 20 March 2022.

Creative Learning

Meanwhile, teachers have far more readily embraced the notion of children as diversely talented and creative beings. Since the 1970s, they have designed new pedagogical methods to encourage critical reflection, replacing the old model of cramming and regurgitating knowledge. The principle of explorative learning encourages young people to use their initiative to seek out the unknown, as in the federal president's History Competition. Since 1973, it has sought to promote independent thought among children and teenagers who engage with local history. Over 130,000 girls and boys have taken part so far.[19] Many more have entered the annual youth research competition, which was founded in 1965, exploring issues from STEM fields and presenting their experimental findings to a jury.

The Nuremberg Funnel has fallen out of favour today; indeed, most children will not even know the expression. Autonomy and interactivity are the order of the day in schools and museums too. Take the Futurium in Berlin, which opened in September 2019. Funded by the Ministry of Education and Research, as well as major research organizations, representatives from industry and various trusts, it markets itself as a 'house of futures' in which visitors can 'discover, try out, discuss'. In the first month of its existence, 100,000 people of all ages and social backgrounds took up this invitation. School groups frequently come to participate in workshops and conduct experiments about nature, humans and machines. Rather than fuelling fears about the future, the Futurium aims to stoke visitors' curiosity and inspire hope that creative solutions can be found for tomorrow's problems.

Curiosity for the Wider World

According to its website, many international visitors have also been lured by the Futurium, adding the site to their list of attractions in Germany's capital. In 2019, fourteen million tourists visited the city, nearly half of them from abroad. They often bring with them an interest in art, culture, architecture – and now science too. Cheap airfares have increased the appeal of short city breaks, particularly among single people and couples without children; at least this was the case until the COVID-19 crisis. Berlin vies with London, Paris and Rome for tourist dollars.

These cities were popular travel destinations in the past as well. From the seventeenth century, noble gentlemen from across Europe converged on Paris, hoping to visit the royal court and acquire the gallant manners and fashionable elegance associated with it. Nearby, Italy beckoned with its ancient and Renaissance-era architectural monuments, while Great Britain and the Netherlands boasted economic and technical advancements that fascinated middle-class travellers, triggering a wave of industrial espionage in the 1800s.

[19] https://eustory.org/general-information-germany, accessed 20 March 2022.

BEWILDERED.

Figure 9   Curious visitors survey Paris's Exposition Universelle, 1889 (Digital Vision Vectors/Getty Images)

Back then, people needed more than curiosity about the wider world and the treasures within it to travel. A substantial sense of adventure and an appetite for risk were also required. Trips to Sicily, Greece or Asia Minor were arduous and hazardous; there were robbers as well as death by malaria to worry about. The tourists who flocked to Paris in 1789 and 1790 to witness the tumult of the revolution did not do so without risk either. A hundred years later, people could travel more safely and comfortably to the Exposition Universelle in the French capital, which saw thirty-two million visitors; in 1900 as many as forty-eight million came. The Austrian writer Stefan Zweig reported in 1910 from the Brussels Fair, this 'tremendous booth' displaying the 'wonders of our time'; in the people present he witnessed a 'beautiful excitement' and a 'dark rushing current of curiosity: restlessly they look, admire, marvel' (Figure 9).[20]

---

[20] Stefan Zweig, 'Die gefangenen Dinge: Gedanken über die Brüsseler Weltausstellung', *Neue Freie Presse*, 17 August 1910, 1–2.

Those who could not travel to faraway lands and cities – the vast majority of people – found other ways to satisfy their curiosity. In the 1920s, travel tales were among the most borrowed books. Leafing through them, readers explored foreign places and ways of life and followed the adventures of real travellers. They read about the dangers and hardships that Alexander von Humboldt, the explorer from Berlin, survived in South America or Central Asia, or what Scottish missionary David Livingstone was doing in Africa in the middle of the nineteenth century, or how Robert Scott and Roald Amundsen launched the race to the South Pole in 1911. Grippingly told and richly illustrated, these tales piqued the curiosity and craving for adventure in readers across many generations, regardless of their age, nationality or social background.

In the tangible world, this craving was usually constrained. Around 1900 there was already talk of a 'generally growing urge to travel'; in 1921 the *Frankfurter Zeitung* reported with some disdain about the 'masses on the move': 'All of Germany is on the road.' Yet the reality was different. No working-class family, no matter how 'inquisitive and fond of sightseeing', could afford to travel at that time. A small consolation was provided by socialist nature-lovers who founded proletarian tourist associations in Austria, Switzerland and Germany at the turn of the century. They gave their members a chance to replace the 'grey city' with a visit to 'green nature' every once in a while. When the Nazis came to power in 1933, they put an end to such escapes, banning the associations and seizing their huts and lodges.[21]

National Socialists created their own travel programme instead. Following the maxim that citizens should be given pleasure as well as work, the German Labour Front soon established a sub-organization called Strength through Joy (Kraft durch Freude, KdF). They organized cultural events such as theatre performances, concerts and art exhibitions, and additionally catered to the wanderlust of the German people. By 1939 the organization had planned and sold forty-three million travel packages, mostly short, afford-able excursions and day trips (Figure 10). Those who wanted to travel further afield by ship, perhaps to Italy, Madeira or Norway, had to part with 150 marks, equivalent to a worker's monthly wages. The colourful posters and

[21] Milde, *Jungfrau*, 476–77; Hermann Bausinger, 'Grenzenlos … Ein Blick auf den moder-nen Tourismus', in *Reisekultur: Von der Pilgerfahrt zum modernen Tourismus*, ed. Hermann Bausinger et al. (Munich: C. H. Beck, 1991), 343–53, quote 346; Wulf Erdmann and Jochen Zimmer, eds, *Hundert Jahre Kampf um die freie Natur: Illustrierte Geschichte der Naturfreunde* (Essen: Klartext, 1991).

Figure 10 KdF holidaymakers keep a lookout, ca. 1936 (Photo by ullstein bild/ullstein bild via Getty Images)

postcards advertising such trips nevertheless inspired many Germans to dream and save.[22]

From 1938, people also started collecting saving stamps for the 'KdF car' (the Beetle) made by Volkswagen. This was another tactic through which the regime served people's longing for mobility and free travel in 'open space'. 'In the motor car', Fritz Todt, the inspector general for roads, gushed in 1937, 'even the little man whose disposition and destiny are hardly that of the bold conqueror is in a position to make his own little journeys of discovery.' The push to build a system of *Reichsautobahnen* or 'Führer's roads' was intended to make these journeys a special experience, though from 1939 it was mostly military vehicles that trundled down them. Millions of German men would eventually cross the borders of their country not as travel-hungry tourists but as soldiers enacting a criminal war of aggression.[23]

---

[22] Kristin Semmens, *Seeing Hitler's Germany: Tourism in the Third Reich* (Basingstoke: Palgrave Macmillan, 2005); Shelley Baranowski, *Strength through Joy: Consumerism and Mass Tourism in the Third Reich* (Cambridge: Cambridge University Press, 2004).

[23] Peter Reichel, *Der schöne Schein des Dritten Reiches* (Munich: Hanser, 1991), 243–54, quote (Todt) 284.

Wanderlust

It was not until the 1960s that Germans started to travel again en masse, this time as civilians. The increase in affluence and motorization enabled millions of West Germans to venture south in their very own cars. Italy was a top destination. People in the GDR travelled too; contingents journeyed to the Black Sea or Hungary's Lake Balaton. The jewels in the state's crown were the cruise ships Völkerfreundschaft (Friendship between nations) and the Fritz Heckert, which began ferrying passengers to Varna, Sochi or Cuba and back in 1960. Shore leave was restricted to excursions in socialist 'brother states'. Of course, only people with sparkling political backgrounds could partake in these subsidized travels, which the state used as a way of recognizing 'deserving activists' and 'top workers'. Showcasing the lucky travellers and their trips in media and propaganda materials would, the regime hoped, motivate others to perform better too (> Envy).[24]

Opinions were divided as to whether travel actually 'educated' people by inciting as well as satisfying their curiosity. Snarky caricatures and scornful critiques of vacationers were not hard to find. The general complaint was that most travellers only wanted to lounge on sunny beaches; they had no interest in the country they were visiting or its people. Quality newspapers disparaged the 'dull' hordes of package-holiday tourists but praised the educated, 'cosmopolitan' men and women who planned their own trips. Yet ordinary lovers of the Adriatic may well have brought back more than a tan and perhaps experienced strange and unfamiliar ways of life, from simple pasta dishes to an understanding of the dolce vita. The young people who snaked their way across Europe via Interrail in the summer also returned with profound impressions of foreign cultures and lifestyles, even if they had only limited contact with local populations.[25]

Curiosity Writes History

Curiosity, the pleasure in and for new things, the urge to discover and experience, took and takes many different forms. In modern society, it is an indispensable emotional resource that moves people to actions and innovations. Back in the nineteenth century, it was assumed that there would always be certain men who would give their curiosity free rein, whether as scientists or

---

[24] Andreas Stirn, Traumschiffe des Sozialismus: Die Geschichte der DDR-Urlauberschiffe 1953–1990 (Berlin: Metropol, 2010).

[25] Rainer Schönhammer, 'Youth Tourism as Appropriation of the World: A Psychological Perspective', Phenomenology + Pedagogy 10 (1992): 19–27; Richard Ivan Jobs, Backpack Ambassadors: How Youth Travel Integrated Europe (Chicago, IL: University of Chicago Press, 2017).

explorers. But it soon become clear that a country bound for scientific and industrial success could not be satisfied with individual accomplishments. In Germany, academies, associations, adult-education centres and museums were founded to spread and stimulate curiosity at a broader societal level. The education strategy of the 1960s finally managed to engage large sections of the populace. Nowadays, the unanimous view is that curiosity serves as the engine of progress. Kindergartens, schools and universities have committed to encouraging and guiding young people to be curious. Not all follow this path, or follow it in the same manner and at the same pace. Some find their own way to be curious about the world beyond institutions.

They are free to do so. Without freedom, Albert Einstein wrote in 1946, curiosity cannot flourish or bear fruit. Liberal democracies have understood this and let their citizens, whether small or grown, ask whatever questions they like and question whatever they like. 'Arts and sciences, research and teaching shall be free', the Basic Law proclaims. That has not always been the case. Some regimes put tight ideological bonds on this freedom. Today, though, the right to be curious is no longer threatened by external forces, but by internal ones instead. Scientific organizations are structured so that researchers' inquisitiveness is often channelled towards fields that enjoy the most funding or guarantee the quickest path to acclaim. This inhibits the principle of curiosity as a free-flowing force, a notion that not only Albert Einstein believed in.

The hunger for knowledge, as the Enlightenment emphasized, is fundamentally different from the hunger for power or material wealth. The Israeli chemist and Nobel laureate Ada Yonath said as much in her 2010 message to young scientists: 'It is not about getting rich or being respected, but about nursing, understanding, and enjoying the inner urge.' Yonath, who was born in Jerusalem in 1939, felt this inner urge and decided to pursue it. Asked what qualities it took to be a good scientist, she replied: 'Curiosity, first. Second, curiosity. And third, curiosity!'[26] That her curiosity was encouraged by her parents, teachers and professors, and her research financially and institutionally supported, was unusual for a woman of her generation. Even more exceptional was her winning of the Nobel Prize, which as of 2021 has been awarded to only twenty-four women in the natural science categories, compared with 606 men: just 4 per cent.

Whether this will change in the future is yet to be determined. These days, girls are permitted to be just as inquisitive as boys; local councils and businesses frequently put on events such as the 'Future Days for Curious Girls', while *The Girl's Book of Adventure* (a work published in

---

[26] 'Ich wollte es allen zeigen', *Zeit online*, 18 January 2010, www.zeit.de/wissen/2010-01/ nobelpreis-yonath-interview; http://bit.ly/3HA0BmH, both accessed 20 March 2022.

German as the 'extraordinary handbook for curious girls') sells very well. But girls still direct their curious impulses towards scientific subjects and phenomena far less frequently than boys do. Instead, they tend to show more interest in aesthetic or social modes of understanding the world. Among the winners of the Nobel Prize for Literature, women accordingly constitute a more visible 13 per cent.

~

Disgust

According to psychologist Paul Ekman, disgust is one of six basic emotions shared by people worldwide and articulated using the same facial expressions. If disgust and contempt are counted separately, this number rises to seven. Contempt, the renowned emotions researcher has argued, is different from disgust chiefly in that it is directed at humans and their behaviour and includes a strong moral component. Disgust, on the other hand, is typically said to be a bodily sensation experienced as nausea: repelling and expelling that which causes the nausea is its chief goal.

Contempt, Disgust and Morality

Hygiene and sanitation expert Valerie Curtis has explained that, from an evolutionary perspective, disgust is primarily a reaction to toxin-producing parasites that can harm the host and spread to other individuals in a group. Humans respond defensively to this perceived threat in an attempt to keep the disgusting thing at bay. Psychologist Paul Rozin also locates the roots of disgust in evolutionary biology. He has identified a 'core disgust' that is activated when people come into contact with unsuitable, possibly pathogenic food, triggering nausea. When they feel disgusted by what they consider 'animalistic', though, they simply want to suppress their genetic kinship with animals, he boldly claims. In a similar vein, philosopher Martha Nussbaum believes that people react with disgust as a way of concealing their own vulnerability and frailty, while anthropologist Mary Douglas has emphasized the cultural importance of purity, arguing anything that tarnishes or threatens it is seen as disgusting filth and rejected.[1]

---

[1] Valerie Curtis, *Don't Look, Don't Touch, Don't Eat: The Science behind Revulsion* (Oxford: Oxford University Press, 2013); Paul Rozin et al., 'Disgust', in *Handbook of Emotions*, 4th ed., ed. Lisa Feldman Barrett et al. (New York: Guildford, 2016), 815–34; Martha C. Nussbaum, *Hiding from Humanity* (Princeton, NJ: Princeton University Press, 2004), ch. 2; Mary Douglas, *Purity and Danger: An Analysis of Concepts of Pollution and Taboo* (New York: Routledge, 1966).

In 1929, the philosopher and journalist Aurel Kolnai likewise saw disgust as
a reaction to 'the element of an unclean condition correlated with a substantial
putrefaction'. But from his phenomenological point of view, being disgusted
by dirtiness crucially had a moral dimension as well, similar to contempt.[2] In
1938, the Austrian citizen, who was born in Budapest in 1900 and converted
from Judaism to Catholicism when he was twenty-six, was proved right.
Neither his religious conversion nor his ultra-conservative politics prevented
him from becoming someone who filled his 'Aryan' countrymen in the so-
called Greater German Empire with disgust.

Discourses of Disgust in the 1920s

The language of purity, filth and disgust was not a National Socialist inven-
tion, nor were the Nazis the first to turn it into a political weapon. When
antisemites in the 1800s ranted about the 'corrosive' power of Jewish people,
they evoked notions of decay and stench that engendered instinctive revulsion.[3] Such notions circulated freely and frequently during and after the First
World War. In 1919, the Association for German Citizenry released a 'wake-
up call' to the German people, urging them to emerge from their 'war fever'
and to 'wash the soiled and stained shield of honour of our people gleaming
and clean' (> Honour). The author of the call, Fritz Hiller from Rostock,
knew precisely who did not want the people to 'recover': the 'parasites,
foreign Russian Jews, who suck us dry and bewitch us'. He mentioned by
name the communist 'scoundrel' Eugen Leviné, who, although born in St
Petersburg, had grown up in Germany and gained German citizenship
in 1913.

In a 1920 edition of the association's magazine, Hans Winkler from Munich
wrote an appeal to his fellow Germans: 'Return to honour and dignity!
Eradicate the unclean maggots, the parasites of the nation, these bloodsuckers
and criminals. And turn away from your unclean idolatry, whereby you
indulge in the idol of pleasure. So often one hears these days: enjoy your
youth, enjoy your life – enjoy, enjoy. And what's left then? Disgust, contempt,
despair.' Well-known writers contributed to the monthly journal, among them
Gabriele Reuter, who, like Hiller, called for 'regeneration' and a healthy
'recovery', as well as university professors who railed 'against the continued
rape' of Germany. The list of members of the association's Essen branch

---

[2] Aurel Kolnai, *On Disgust*, ed. Barry Smith and Carolyn Korsmeyer (Chicago, IL: Open
Court, 2004), 29–91, quote 82.
[3] Renate Schäfer, 'Zur Geschichte des Wortes "zersetzen"', *Zeitschrift für deutsche
Wortforschung* 18 (1962): 40–80, esp. 62 ff.; Uffa Jensen, *Zornpolitik* (Berlin: Suhrkamp,
2017), 55–72.

included factory owners, directors of banks, important businessmen and the local library.[4]

Their less well-heeled or educated contemporaries voiced the language of disgust just as loudly. In 1922, Josef Kreuzhuber, a retired Bavarian gendarmerie constable, addressed a tirade to Prime Minister Hugo von Lerchenfeld about the 'bloodsucker species' raging through Germany's heartlands, among whom he counted surreptitious traders and racketeers as well as usurers and price gougers. He also reprimanded fellow citizens 'polluted primarily by France through de-moralization and demoralization'. The idea of 'moral decline' was similarly invoked by the Volkswartbund (a Catholic association dedicated to upholding public morality) in 1921 when it denounced 'the poison in smut and trash books'. Five years later – with the votes of the Catholic Centre Party, the German National People's Party (DNVP) and the German People's Party (DVP) – the Reichstag passed the Law to Protect Youth from Trashy and Filthy Publications. It did not say exactly what kind of publications it meant, but conceptually posited that such texts poisoned adolescents and sullied their 'purity' and 'cleanliness'.[5]

The debate around the law, which the National Socialists replaced in 1935 with a list of books deemed unsuitable for young people, was reopened after the war. In 1949, Rhineland-Palatinate enacted an identical piece of state legislation; in 1953, with the support of the Christian-conservative parties, the Bundestag passed a nationwide law that cloaked the same aim in different terms. 'Filth' (*Schmutz*) as a 'legally relevant term' disappeared, and preventing the 'distribution of youth-endangering publications' took its place.[6]

The Racist Propaganda of Disgust under National Socialism

This shift did not just signal parliament's retreat from the forms of speech of the 1920s. It also marked its desire to distance itself, whether consciously or not, from the propaganda of disgust that the 'Third Reich' had systematically instrumentalized. Nazi propaganda was racially motivated and tinted, and oriented at everyone and everything that supposedly threatened and

---

[4] Fritz Hiller, *An das deutsche Volk! Ein Weckruf* (Essen: Verlag Dt. Staatsbürgertum, 1919); Hans Winkler, 'Was not tut', *Deutsches Staatsbürgertum: Monatsschrift für staatsbürgerliche Bildung und Erziehung* 3, no. 7/9 (1920): 4; Prof. J. Remke, 'Empor!', ibid., no. 10/12 (1920): 3; Gabriele Reuter, 'Neugesundung', ibid., 4.

[5] Bavarian State Archive Munich, II, MA no. 102386: Kreuzhuber, 20 April 1922; Executive of the Volkswartbund, 23 December 1921; Klaus Petersen, 'The Harmful Publications (Young Persons) Act of 1926: Literary Censorship and the Politics of Morality in the Weimar Republic', *German Studies Review* 15, no. 3 (1992): 505–23.

[6] German Bundestag, Drucksache no. 1/1101 (28 June 1950); Dagmar Herzog, *Sex after Fascism: Memory and Morality in Twentieth-Century Germany* (Princeton, NJ: Princeton University Press, 2005), 108–15.

endangered the ethnically pure *Volkskörper* (body politic) from within. Among them were the Sinti and Roma, who were described as 'pus', 'germs', 'vermin' and 'foreign bodies' from whom the German people must be freed. Homosexuality was considered a 'pestilence' and a 'plague' whose 'ruthless extermination' was rightly ordered. Carriers or spreaders of this 'body- and soul-murdering plague', a local Thuringian newspaper reported in 1937, would henceforth be 'purposefully and inexorably removed from the body politic' and 'eliminated'.[7]

The worst rhetorical attacks were saved for the Jewish population. As he wrote in *Mein Kampf* in 1925, Hitler saw 'the Jew' as 'the perennial parasite, a scrounger who like a harmful bacillus proliferates more and more, as soon as a favourable breeding ground attracts him. The effect of his existence is parasitic too: wherever he emerges, sooner or later the community that hosts him dies.'[8] According to Hitler, parasites preyed especially on female 'hosts', infesting them and, as party member Elsa Walter put it in 1930, trickling poison into their blood. She herself had successfully evaded this fate, writing that she was not directly 'disgusted by Jews, but I wouldn't let one kiss me – my race and my natural feeling refuses to accept that'.

Quite obviously, thirty-two-year-old Walter did not need the massive propaganda campaign launched in 1933 to make her negative feelings about Jewish people known. Even before the 'reign of the Swastika', 'Jewish men' were not allowed to come near her, since her > 'pride and sense of honour' as a Christian and 'German woman' forbade it.[9] Apparently, though, not everybody was filled with the same clear 'sense of sovereignty' and purpose when it came to delineating a border between themselves and the Jewish population. In order to stress the imperative of keeping one's distance, the regime spread the message of disgust through speeches and school textbooks, on posters and in films. The syllabus for the SS and the police, for instance, prescribed that ideological education should highlight the 'corrosive decades-long infection' of the body politic by Jewish 'parasites' and underscore the need to 'eradicate the last traces of this plague'. A Nazi party training text used basic biological concepts to justify the grounds for extermination: the infected body, it claimed, must 'vanquish the invading parasites or it will be vanquished by them. Once it has overcome them, it must have an incentive to cleanse its

---

[7] 'Die Zigeuner und die Jagd', *Deutsches Weidwerk* (26 July 1934): 651–53; Alexander Zinn, '*Aus dem Volkskörper entfernt'? Homosexuelle Männer im Nationalsozialismus* (Frankfurt: Campus, 2018), quotes 264, 463; Günter Grau, ed., *Homosexualität in der NS-Zeit* (Frankfurt: Fischer, 1993), 100, 122.

[8] *Hitler, Mein Kampf: Eine kritische Edition*, ed. Christian Hartmann et al., 4th ed., vol. 1 (Berlin: IfZ, 2016), 793 [323].

[9] *Letters to Hitler*, ed. Henrik Eberle, trans. Steven Randall (Cambridge: Polity Press, 2012), quote 40.

environment of them, to prevent an infection in the future.' What that meant for society was made crystal clear:

> Humanitarian principles are not applied at all, just as they are not applied to the disinfection of a body or a contaminated room. A completely new way of thinking must take hold. Only with such thinking can we reach the final decision which must be made in our time in order to secure the great creative race in its existence and in its great duty in the world.[10]

Antisemitic speech already had a biological tint in the 1800s, and not only in Germany. Racist discourse generally liked (and likes) to conjure quasi-scientific insights.[11] National Socialism, however, did not stop here. By dispatching its message through images and texts, it permeated, as the literary and linguistic scholar Victor Klemperer observed firsthand, 'the flesh and blood of the people through single words, idioms and sentence structures which were imposed on them in a million repetitions and taken on board mechanically and unconsciously'. Since language drove feeling, it was the perfect means of manipulation: 'Words can be like tiny doses of arsenic: they are swallowed unnoticed, appear to have no effect, and then after a little time the toxic reaction sets in after all.'[12]

The impact of biological metaphors and arguments was huge. As in the concept of decomposition, they highlighted aspects of organic life seen as unsanitary and disgusting. Proximity meant danger, which is why a strict boundary or *cordon sanitaire* had to be drawn between those who aroused disgust and the still-healthy but gravely threatened body politic. The filthiness of others stood in stark contrast to one's own purity and cleanliness. Young people in particular were constantly reminded of such dichotomies: since the 'clean' boys and girls of the Hitler Youth and the League of German Girls secured the health of the people, they had to stay away from polluted and polluting 'elements'.[13]

The 1940 film *Der Ewige Jude* (*The Eternal Jew*) also trafficked in strongly antagonistic images. Preceded by a travelling exhibition and officially designated as 'politically valuable', the film broadcast documentary footage taken of Polish citizens under German occupation, with the support of the army and

---

[10] Walther Hofer, ed., *Der Nationalsozialismus: Dokumente 1933–1945* (Frankfurt: Fischer, 1957), quotes 281, 279–80.

[11] Alexander Bein, '"Der jüdische Parasit": Bemerkungen zur Semantik der Judenfrage', *Vierteljahrshefte für Zeitgeschichte* 13 (1965): 121–49.

[12] Victor Klemperer, *The Language of the Third Reich: LTI – Lingua Tertii Imperii: A Philologist's Notebook*, trans. Martin Brady (London: Athlone Press, 2000), 15–16. But Klemperer, who narrowly survived the 'Third Reich' in a 'mixed marriage', was also a child of his time and often spoke in organic metaphors himself. Schäfer ('Geschichte', 80) saw the same phenomenon in Thomas Mann's radio speeches during the war.

[13] That German youth was healthy and clean was a standard topos of the magazine *Das Junge Deutschland* (ibid., 35 (1941), 242; 38 (1944), 89).

Figure 11 Invoking disgust: in 1938 more than 350,000 saw the exhibition *The Eternal Jew* in Vienna. For school children, the visit was obligatory (Photo by Imagno/ Getty Images)

the Ministry of Propaganda led by Joseph Goebbels. It claimed to show Jewish people 'as they really looked before they concealed themselves behind the mask of civilized Europeans': as dirty, devious, cruel (Figure 11). The film compared Jewish migration from Eastern to Western Europe to roaming rats wreaking havoc on the country. Although the film was zealously advertised, and groups of Hitler Youth brought to see it, public turnout was not as high as expected. Those who went were mostly the 'politically active sections of the population', not the 'typical film audience', who instead complained that they were sick of antisemitic propaganda and affronted by the 'repulsive nature of the material'. According to police reports, 'visitors have often been observed leaving the cinema in disgust in the middle of a performance. Statements like "We've seen *Jud Süss* and we've had enough of Jewish filth" have been heard.'[14]

Those who were nauseated by 'Jewish filth' had already internalized the message that Jews were dangerous parasites or vermin. As Supreme Party Court judge Walter Buch put it in 1938: 'The Jew is not a human being. He is a rottenness.'[15] National Socialism stirred > fear and disgust for these beings, who it claimed threatened the vulnerable body politic with infection, deviousness, pestilence and degradation. Propaganda thus bred understanding and acceptance for the brutal eradication of the 'vermin', which began in 1939 when the mass murder of European Jews was set in action.

Political 'Pests' and 'Decomposition' in the GDR

No regime politicized disgust quite as strongly or tied it to a racist logic of extermination like National Socialism. And yet Nazis were not completely alone. Casting political opponents as 'parasites' or destructive insects 'harmful to the people' (*Volksschädlinge*) was common practice in the Stalinist Soviet Union. People were defined as such for being class enemies, not race enemies, but the exclusion and persecution worked in a similar way. The GDR likewise operationalized this vocabulary in the 1950s. In 1952, the police carried out a campaign conceived by the Ministry for State Security (Stasi). It was tellingly called *Aktion Ungeziefer* (Operation Vermin) and relocated citizens deemed unreliable from the areas near the border with West Germany to the interior of the country. On 9 June of that year, the interior minister of Thuringia communicated the 'results of the committee's work to remove vermin' to the ruling party. In 1961, a similar campaign took place, albeit under friendlier aliases such as 'Operation Little Flower', 'Cornflower', 'New Life' and 'Fresh Air'.[16]

In 1959, a poster commissioned by the East Berlin Ministry of Transport put the talk of disgusting vermin and disease-bearing pests in visual terms (Figure 12). It urged railway workers to be vigilant about enemies threatening the GDR. These enemies were depicted in the form of rats moving from the left to the right of the frame, from the west to the east. One rat wore a black,

---

[14] Erwin Leiser, *Nazi Cinema* (London: Secker & Warburg, 1974), 85, 158.

[15] Walter Buch, 'Des nationalsozialistischen Menschen Ehre und Ehrenschutz', *Deutsche Justiz* 100 (21 October 1938): 1657–64, quote 1660.

[16] Manfred Wolter, *Aktion Ungeziefer – die Zwangsaussiedlung an der Elbe* (Rostock: Altstadt, 1997); Manfred Wagner, 'Beseitigung des Ungeziefers ...': *Zwangsaussiedlungen in den thüringischen Landkreisen Saalfeld, Schleiz und Lobenstein 1952 und 1961* (Erfurt: Der Landesbeauftragte des Freistaates Thüringen für die Unterlagen des Staatssicherheitsdienstes der ehemaligen DDR, 2001).

Figure 12   The rats are coming from the west, GDR, 1959 (BPK, Bildagentur)

white and red collar with an iron cross, the symbol of militarism, conservatism and German-nationalist sentiments from the days of the empire and the Weimar Republic. Some had bands with swastikas around their stomachs or NATO helmets on their heads, others SS runes or dollar signs drawn on their coats and flags with the logos of Western media attached to their tails.

The GDR judiciary also used the language of pests when it handed people hefty prison sentences for 'parasite activity' (*Schädlingstätigkeit*) under Paragraph 23 of the Penal Code. In 1955, the twenty-three-year-old chairman of a cooperative for agricultural production received four years in prison for the crime. Although he had 'posed as a progressive person', it was claimed that he was secretly carrying out 'parasite and decomposition activities'. For example, he 'constantly listened to RIAS [i.e. Western] broadcasts' and 'lent equipment and machinery to individual reactionary farmers' without compensation. Also deemed a parasite was the head of the Thuringian construction supervision agency in 1959, because he had allegedly delayed applications from agricultural cooperatives, favouring instead private building projects. Furthermore, he followed and disseminated 'inflammatory West German television broadcasts' including daily and weekly newsreels. A search of his house revealed a 'booklet with the latest recordings of the programmes of West German TV' and 'more than sixty-six books, the contents of which were for the most part vile warmongering'.[17]

Were the judges, party functionaries, Stasi employees and ministers aware that their metaphorical talk of 'parasites' and 'decomposition' continued and reinforced the *Lingua Tertii Imperii* and its exclusionary and stigmatizing aims, as Klemperer had examined? Perhaps not. The Ministry for State Security themselves sought to engage in 'decomposing' activities, and apparently saw nothing objectionable about doing so.[18] After all, Communist Party members socialized during the 1920s and 1930s had come of age with Lenin's remarks about the 'Parasitism and Rottenness of Capitalism'. Many had been part of leftist youth organizations and may have fondly recalled their emphasis on strength, purity and cleanliness.[19]

These values resonated strongly in East Germany's state propaganda. In 1950, official reports on a gigantic youth meeting in Berlin, with up to 700,000 participants, praised it as 'clean, colourful, marvellous'. In 1958, Walter Ulbricht, leader of the ruling Socialist Unity Party (SED), issued the *Ten Commandments for the New Socialist Man*, which became part of the party platform from 1963 until 1976. They spoke about the need to grow and protect the people's property (the implication here was from 'parasites'), and they

---

[17] Andrea Herz, ed., *Nicht – im Namen des Volkes: Politisches Strafrecht in der DDR 1949–1961* (Erfurt: Landeszentrale für politische Bildung Thüringen, 2008), 104, 152–53.

[18] In 'political operative work', 'decomposition' meant covert tactics to 'fragment, paralyze, disorganize and isolate hostile-negative forces' (*Das Wörterbuch der Staatssicherheit*, ed. Siegfried Suckut (Berlin: Links, 1996), 422).

[19] Bein, 'Parasit', 127; Walter Flex, *Der Wanderer zwischen beiden Welten* (Munich: C. H. Beck, 1917), 34, 41; Elisabeth Busse-Wilson, *Die Frau und die Jugendbewegung* [1920] (Berlin: LIT, 2012), 80.

demanded, again, cleanliness, as in the ninth commandment: 'You shall live purely and fairly.'[20]

Cleanliness, like dirt, had a hygienic as well as moral dimension. People who wanted to be and stay pure kept their hearts, bodies and minds spick and span and avoided filthy and impure elements. SED members should, of course, show exemplary behaviour in this regard. When, as in an anonymous letter to Prime Minister Willi Stoph in 1972, functionaries were suspected of being 'guilty of serious offences against the party's 10 commandments', the rhetoric of pests and disgust switched direction. Instead of coming from the top down, it now originated from the bottom and was aimed at men 'with party pins', whom the letter writer called lazy, grubby-moraled 'parasites'. This was followed by a demand for the immediate 'cleansing of all administrations, businesses, etc. of parasites'.[21]

Disgust also rang out in other expressions from 'working people' as a way of distancing themselves from behaviour they found contemptible. An East Berliner writing in 1967 was disgusted by the way the party newspaper *Neues Deutschland* had crawled 'up the butts' of the Russians. In 1978 someone expressed their 'disgust and revulsion' at a government that apparently knew only 'murderous violence'. In 1986, parents from Karl-Marx-Stadt wrote to the regional party leader using their real names and address and voicing their utter 'contempt and disgust' at how their son was being treated by the authorities. After the young man had applied to leave the country, he had been arrested and sentenced in a 'political trial'. In prison, he was 'physically and psychologically battered', but nevertheless had to testify that he had not been harmed. Complaining bitterly about such 'concentration camp' methods, the parents sought to actively break the silence.

Strong negative emotions reverberated in many of the letters sent to state officials and SED functionaries in the GDR. In October 1989, a few weeks before the regime's collapse, a party member 'for almost twenty years' sharply criticized the central youth organization, the FDJ: 'You have still not comprehended that it was you who forced our young people to leave out of sheer disgust.' A group of citizens working 'for glasnost and democracy' expressed their 'disgust' at the 'brazen lies' of the '*Bonzenclique*' – a pejorative term for party bigwigs. Denouncing the men and women who had taken refuge in West German embassies in Hungary or Czechoslovakia as 'counterrevolutionaries, rebels, troublemakers' would not stop the people from 'tearing down their walls', the group warned. A short time later, their words would prove true.[22]

---

[20] *Neues Deutschland*, 25 May 1950, 1; *Protokoll der Verhandlungen des V. Parteitages der SED*, vol. 1 (Berlin: Dietz, 1959), 160–61; *Berliner Zeitung*, 31 March 1950.

[21] Siegfried Suckut, *Volkes Stimmen: 'Ehrlich, aber deutlich' – Privatbriefe an die DDR-Regierung* (Munich: dtv, 2015), 171–75, quotes 173, 175.

[22] Ibid., 124, 240, 346–48, 451, 432–34.

Rhetoric of Filth in West Germany

The tone with which citizens addressed 'the higher-ups' was not always friendly in West Germany either. However, feelings such as disgust, revulsion and contempt were not articulated as often, and politics officially refrained from the rhetoric of disgust. State institutions and parties no longer used it to rally against politically or ethnically determined 'enemies' or to call for their exclusion or extermination. Even the rabid fight against communism in the 1950s relied on > fear rather than disgust.

Nevertheless, the civil and political ruckus over 'filth and rubbish' continued, albeit under different names. In 1964, with church and party support, the citizens of Schweinfurt launched the Clean Screen Campaign, a stand against the 'rising tide of dirty movies', collecting more than a million signatures nationwide (the target was Ingmar Bergman's *The Silence*). Their suspicion that such films or books could 'corrupt' the young was reinforced with pseudo-biological images of nauseating rot.[23] Beneath lurked irritation and concern for the convention-breaking younger generation, whose taste in music seemed as rotten as their style of dress. The 'deadbeats in Germany' who made it onto the cover of the weekly *Der Spiegel* in 1966 were seen as 'scruffy' and unkempt. The GDR bluntly blamed American 'pulp culture' for young people's enthusiasm for beat music, which 'has as little to do with music as a tramp has to do with a washed person'.[24]

The old impulse to paint dirt and deviance as two sides of the same coin had reared its head again. Others took inspiration from the animal kingdom when they called left-wing students 'long-haired apes', as reported in 1968.[25] By then, however, this image had widely lost its negative appeal and no longer worked to evoke disgust. After all, the wildlife filmmaker and zoo director Bernhard Grzimek had cute little monkeys sitting on his lap in his popular television programme *A Place for Animals*, which aired for almost thirty-one years beginning in 1956, and viewers loved it.

---

[23] Philipp von Hugo, '"Eine zeitgemäße Erregung": Der Skandal um Ingmar Bergmans Film "Das Schweigen" (1963) und die Aktion "Saubere Leinwand"', *Zeithistorische Forschungen* 3, no. 2 (2006): 210–30, online edition: https://zeithistorische-forschungen .de/2-2006/4535; Martin Loiperdinger, 'Film Censorship in Germany: Continuity and Change through Five Political Systems', in *Silencing Cinema: Film Censorship around the World*, ed. Daniel Biltereyst and Roel Vande Winkel (New York: Palgrave Macmillan, 2013), 81–96.

[24] *Der Spiegel*, 18 September 1966; Dorothee Wierling, *Geboren im Jahr Eins: Der Jahrgang 1949 in der DDR* (Berlin: Links, 2002), 222.

[25] *Der Spiegel*, 25 February 1968, 23–26, reported on a Berlin anti-APO demonstration on 21 February 1968, with banners carrying the slogan 'Let construction workers work quietly – no money for long-haired apes'.

'Rats and Blowflies'

Other animals proved far more suitable for striking up feelings of revulsion. During the 1972 election campaign, supporters of the conservative CDU stuck bits of paper emblazoned with a red rat onto Social Democratic billboards. Two years later, former minister Franz Josef Strauß summoned the 'courageous citizens who chase the red rats back to where they belong – in their holes'. In 1977, his mouthpiece, the right-wing newspaper *Bayernkurier*, announced that the 'red system changers' were 'emerging like rats out of all their holes'. When Strauß spoke of 'rats and blowflies' at a party gathering in Bavaria in 1978, he had a specific target in mind: the members of a liberal-leftist press committee, whom he felt had insulted him. Instead of suing them – after all, the Penal Code did protect the individual rights and > honour of citizens – the usually hot-headed Strauß 'icily' and without hesitation branded them vermin.[26]

The combative politician was perhaps borrowing his provocative choice of words from former Goebbels associate Eberhard Taubert. The two had been well acquainted since the 1950s. Strauß valued Taubert, who had been trained in anti-communism and antisemitism during the 'Third Reich', as an experienced advisor. A member of the Nazi Party and its violent militia since 1931, Taubert, who held a doctorate in law, had rapidly risen through the ranks. At Goebbels's ministry, he ran the Department for Active Propaganda against Jews. In 1934, he founded the Institute for the Study of the Jewish Question, later called the Antisemitic Campaign. Jews were depicted in the Institute's publications as 'foreign bodies' who 'penetrated every pore of the life of our nation and threatened to poison its organism'. Incidentally, it was Taubert who wrote the script for *The Eternal Jew*, with its images of greedy, swarming rats and the commentary: 'Rats represent among animals the insidious, deceitful, destructive element. Not unlike the Jews among people.'[27]

Regardless of whether it was adopted from Taubert or not, Strauß's invective initially met with only limited protest. Some, like the graphic designer Klaus Staeck, countered with irony: he transformed the red rat on the

---

[26] Gert Heidenreich, *Die ungeliebten Dichter* (Frankfurt: Eichborn, 1981), 7; *Die Zeit*, 29 February 1980.

[27] *Die Juden in Deutschland*, ed. Institut zum Studium der Judenfrage, 4th ed. (Munich: Eher Nachf., 1936), quotes 7, 17; Klaus Körner, 'Erst in Goebbels', dann in Adenauers Diensten', *Die Zeit*, 24 August 1990, www.zeit.de/1990/35/erst-in-goebbels-dann-in-adenauers-diensten, accessed 4 January 2022. In the 1950s, Taubert was 'indispensable' to anti-communist propaganda in the Federal Republic and presided as second chairman over the People's Association for Peace and Freedom, which was subsidized by the Ministry of Intra-German Relations and the United States (*Der Spiegel*, 17 August 1955, 11–13).

1972 stickers into a greeting to the right-wing politician: 'I am a rat.' Many took offence not so much at the animal comparison as at the assertion that they belonged to a 'communist front organization'. The mood changed, though, in 1980, when Strauß ran for chancellor and party secretary Edmund Stoiber explicitly backed his leader's former comments. The CDU mayor of Stuttgart, Manfred Rommel, warned that such words might encourage people to 'go beserk' and want to obliterate the 'vermin'. The *Frankfurter Allgemeine Zeitung* interpreted Stoiber's intervention as an 'aggravation' that 'evokes the worst memories'. Those who used 'disgusting images of negative animals' in lieu of sober arguments were seen to cross the line that separated a democratic state from a National Socialist one. Even the conservative newspaper *Die Welt* was not willing to tolerate this 'pitchfork language' that evidently did not number among the 'highlights of German rhetoric'.[28]

The 'affair of the German word', as *Der Spiegel* called it, thus ended with a stinging rebuke. The defamatory language of disgust was finally discredited as a form of political debate – or so it seemed, until it resurfaced at the beginning of the twenty-first century. In 2005, the high-circulation members' magazine of the industrial trade union IG Metall printed an article about dubious financial investors in German companies; the magazine's cover depicted a grinning mosquito in a tie, a collar and a top hat in the colours of the US flag, under the title 'The Suckers'. The drawing evoked images of bloodsucking insects best resisted with a well-aimed blow, and reminded many of Nazi caricatures of 'Jewish finance capital'. When, at around the same time, Social Democrat Franz Müntefering used the locust metaphor to describe private equity companies, he was also sharply criticized. After all, a plague of locusts needs to be driven out or exterminated. When applied to human beings, such associations awakened uncomfortable memories and no longer spoke to people's political sensibilities.

Yet those sensibilities are not set in stone. They can shift in the future, as they did in the past. This is what contemporary right-wing populist parties have in mind when they, once again, help themselves to this inhumane vocabulary. Calling asylum seekers 'parasites who feed on the lifeblood of the German people' and dismissing homosexuals as a 'degenerate species', as representatives of the new AfD party did in 2016, attempts to resurrect and normalize an older discourse that apparently attracts a considerable number of citizens and voters.[29] Homophobic speech, by the way, is neither limited to right-wing extremists, the majority of whom are men, nor to Muslim migrants who, in this regard, form a paradoxical alliance with those wishing them out of the country. The negative reaction to homosexuality far transcends these two

---

[28] Gert Heidenreich, 'Ratten und Fliegen', *Die Zeit*, 31 August 1979; Heidenreich, *Dichter*, quotes 7, 10, 21, 30; *Der Spiegel*, 24 February 1980, 29–33.
[29] http://bit.ly/3wVEqTf; http://bit.ly/3X9W3t8, both accessed 4 January 2022.

groups: in 2016, four out of ten respondents reportedly found it 'disgusting' when gay people kissed in public (> Love).[30]

Proximity and Distance

Disgust, as Aurel Kolnai pointed out back in 1929, is about proximity. We have an aversion to the thing that rots and ferments right before our eyes and under our nose. From a distance, such processes affect us less and are easier to bear. They might even be a source of pleasure. You can see this regularly on so-called *Ekelfernsehen* ('disgusting television').[31] The term has been around since 2004, when it was coined to describe a reality show on the private German network RTL. The show, based on the British series *I'm a Celebrity ... Get Me Out of Here!*, was set in an Australian jungle camp where stars of varying levels of fame spent several days in each other's company while being filmed around the clock. The highlights of their time together were then shown on screen. They included trials of courage in which participants had to bathe in stinking liquids or vats of cockroaches and eat all kinds of animals not typically found on European menus. Fantastically high viewing figures proved that the showrunners' gamble had paid off: viewers feasted on the disgust felt by the celebrities and could enjoy it all the more intensely the further away they were from the scene. The show set a precedent, entering its fourteenth season in 2020 and inspiring many broadcasters to follow suit.

It is not difficult to see that such scenarios are inspired by classic motifs of disgust: decaying things, maggots, bugs, spiders, faeces, slime. Civilized urbanites usually know how to stay away from them. Occasions for feeling disgust have gradually disappeared from our everyday lives. Compared to the early twentieth century, public space has become far cleaner. Streets are swept, dead animals do not litter pathways, rarely do rats crawl out of the sewers. Slaughterhouses and wastewater treatment stations have moved to the outskirts of the city, and liquid excrement is no longer transported from place to place. Damp homes and cellars full of mould and vermin are largely a thing of the past. Personal hygiene has also improved significantly; daily showers are standard and washing machines spin 24/7. As a result, disgust is less and less part of real life; at most, people see and feel it through the media. It is triggered now and then when a food scandal arises (as in the rotten meat debacle of 2006), and it resonates in the artificially constructed reality of the aforementioned jungle camp. The fact that viewers are given licence to experience

---

[30] www.tagesschau.de/inland/homosexualitaet-toleranz-101.html; http://bit.ly/41Te6rc, both accessed 4 January 2022.

[31] Sarah J. Ablett, *Dramatic Disgust: Aesthetic Theory and Practice from Sophocles to Sarah Kane* (Bielefeld: transcript, 2020), 79–80.

something there that has almost disappeared from their own world increases the enjoyment factor.

Less alien or exotic, however, is the narrative of contamination. People and objects that have come into contact with disgusting and unclean things are themselves deemed unclean and disgusting. Fears of transmission exist still today and affect women in particular. In many places, menstruating women are kept away from certain activities – not for their own protection, but to prevent them from contaminating other substances. In 2003, female students attending a college for social work and education in Thuringia asked the weekly *Die Zeit* for scientific clarification on the matter: 'For years, we have been haunted by the advice of our mothers and grandmothers, which is: don't whip cream when you are menstruating, don't preserve fruit or vegetables, don't take part in slaughters.' Scientifically, there is no proven connection, but the superstition, and the misogyny within it, persists.[32]

Evoking feelings of disgust to stigmatize, defame and discriminate against social groups is therefore not yet a thing of the past. It continues to have a strong hold in India, where ideas of untouchability are deeply embedded in the social imaginary and have visible material effects. And yet, Dalits are seen as a natural and necessary part of Indian society, unlike the Jewish people in Nazi Germany and occupied Europe, whose right to exist was flatly denied. As disgusting 'parasites', they were not only separated from the rest of the population but cleared for extermination. The politics of disgust thus has many faces and consequences. What unites them all is that they negate the basic principles of human dignity and equality. Such principles were inscribed in West Germany's Basic Law of 1949, after being trampled over during the Nazi period. Laws, though, need people to defend them and their spirit against those who, from time to time, resuscitate notions of disgust and impurity for exclusionary purposes.

---

[32] Rozin, 'Disgust', 818; www.zeit.de/2003/35/Stimmts_Menstruation, accessed 4 January 2022.

~

Empathy

Today, the word empathy is everywhere. A hundred years ago, Germans spoke of *Einfühlung*; two hundred years ago, of *Mitgefühl* or fellow-feeling. The latter is how Ludwig Kosegarten translated the concept of sympathy in Adam Smith's 1759 treatise *Theory of Moral Sentiments*. The *Brockhaus* encyclopaedia did not feature an entry for *Empathie* until 1968, defining it as the 'ability to put oneself in another's position'.[1] Meanwhile, the term has become as popular with managers as it is with politicians and educators, psychologists and physicians. It is taken up by opponents and proponents of animal testing alike. Munich's Porsche Club uses the promise of it to recruit new members, who can 'interact with each other with great empathy in a sophisticated environment'. In 2016, Audi presented the concept of the empathetic vehicle with the slogan 'My car cares for me', and other automobile companies followed suit.[2]

Compassion and Sympathy

How can the astonishing career of this emotion word be explained? What makes empathy so attractive that Porsche drivers, among many others, want to adorn themselves with it? And is there a deed behind the word, an emotion that drives action?

The first striking thing is that *Empathie* has relegated classic *Mitleid* to the margins. Held in high esteem by all major religions, *Mitleid* – translated as compassion or pity – was traditionally considered a prerequisite for mercy and charity. From the late eighteenth century onwards, it began to appear in a secular form. Compassionate, sympathetic people, Gotthold Ephraim Lessing noted in 1756, were 'better and more virtuous' than others. The philosopher Arthur Schopenhauer identified compassion as the foundation of human kindness and the basis of morality. It embraces, he wrote in 1840, 'the weak, the guilty, indeed all humanity'. But this was exactly where some saw a problem. In their view, *Mitleid* was not something innocent; instead, it reflected societal and power hierarchies.

---

[1] *Brockhaus Enzyklopädie*, 17th ed., vol. 5 (Wiesbaden: Brockhaus, 1968), 496.
[2] http://bit.ly/3lesaKN (marked in bold on the website); Christiane Köllner, 'Wenn das Auto zum Gesundheitsmanager wird', http://bit.ly/3wZYi7S, both accessed 3 January 2022.

Compassion and pity went along with moralistic evaluations of good or bad people and behaviour, and they fortified social differences. The person demonstrating pity was said to occupy a position of strength and look down on those in need of pity.[3]

This was not deemed appropriate for democratic societies made up of equal citizens. Empathy seems the more relevant term: morally unsuspicious and socially open, it is thought to describe a relationship on equal footing. In actual fact, however, power imbalances do play a role, especially in situations involving the suffering of strangers and requests for active support.

Adam Smith, in his time, had not overlooked this. He was well aware that sympathy knew various shades and gradations, and that their structural components differed. As he saw it, 'fellow-feeling' was not limited to fellow-suffering, but included fellow-joy, fellow-grief, fellow-outrage. And he believed, on the basis of his observations, that people were generally capable of feeling the emotions of others. Whether they really did so was another matter. Yet this was precisely what counted in the modern society Smith anticipated during the second half of the eighteenth century. It could not be based on 'self-love' alone, on the selfish interest of individuals seeking to maximize their resources and profits. It also needed 'the Pleasure of mutual Sympathy'. Sympathy – close in nature to what is called empathy today – was the bond meant to hold society together beyond economic divisions of labour and social stratification.[4]

Requirements and Preconditions

However, this did not happen automatically, nor did it lead without exception to pro-social behaviour. Whether sympathy/empathy was galvanized depended upon conditions such as social and physical proximity or distance. Smith had himself noted that proximity facilitated 'fellow-feeling' and distance impeded it. Empathizing with a family member or friend was easier than with a stranger. The greater the remove, the more difficult it became to regard the stranger as a neighbour and to show them, in line with religious teachings, love, understanding and practical aid. Yet, as the history of the nineteenth and twentieth centuries indicated, the opposite also applied: people were full of sympathy for those suffering far away but averted their eyes from those struggling in the tenements next door.

---

[3] Ute Frevert, *Emotions in History: Lost and Found* (Budapest: Central European University Press, 2011), 149–60; on the distinction between empathy and compassion, see David DeSteno et al., 'Gratitude and Compassion', in *Handbook of Emotions*, 4th ed., ed. Lisa Feldman Barrett et al. (New York: Guildford, 2016), 835–46, esp. 839; Jamil Zaki and Kevin Ochsner, 'Empathy', in ibid., 871–84.

[4] Adam Smith, *The Theory of Moral Sentiments*, 2nd ed. (London: Millar, 1761), 10–15; Adam Smith, *Theorie der sittlichen Gefühle*, trans. Ludwig Kosegarten (Leipzig: Gräffsche Buchhandlung, 1791), 14–19.

Often they kept their distance for social or moral reasons. While one could empathize unconditionally with 'innocent' children and feel their pain like one's own, this did not apply to people who had caused suffering to others and were consequently held accountable. At public executions, which during Smith's time were common practice in Europe, spectators usually showed no sympathy because the criminal being brought to the gallows did not deserve it.[5]

That moralistic judgements can block the human capacity to empathize has been verified by neuroscientific experiments. When a player who has behaved unfairly receives a pain stimulus, other players react without empathy: their neural pain networks remain mute and passive. In contrast, a pain stimulus for someone who has played fairly activates the pain receptors of others: they empathize with the sufferer although they themselves do not experience the pain. As researchers found out, the absence of empathy in the first case is correlated with activation of the brain area responsible for processing rewards. This means no more and no less than that research subjects experienced schadenfreude and satisfaction when the unfair player was punished. Lab studies investigating the relation between empathy and group affiliation have shown similar results. When pain was inflicted on a member of one's own group (in this case a football club), the others not only empathized with the sufferer, but were willing to undergo the pain themselves in order to help. Conversely, when members of the opposing club were mistreated, the familiar reward signal blinked in the brains of the observers.[6]

Is Empathy Female?

The researchers also discovered something else: women reacted differently from men. Even when it was unfair players who were punished, women empathized with them, instead of feeling gratification and schadenfreude. That throws up fundamental questions: are women better people? Are they more sensitive in general, or are there situations in which they also suppress empathy and lust for revenge? Cultural history features numerous women who were just as vengeful as men: Kriemhild, the daughter of a Burgundian king from the Middle High German *Nibelungenlied*, who took gruesome revenge on the murderers of her husband Siegfried at Etzel's court; Medea, the figure

---

[5] Ute Frevert, 'Empathy in the Theater of Horror, or Civilizing the Human Heart', in *Empathy and Its Limits*, ed. Aleida Assmann and Ines Detmers (Basingstoke: Palgrave Macmillan, 2016), 79–99.

[6] Tania Singer et al., 'Empathic Neural Responses Are Modulated by the Perceived Fairness of Others', *Nature* 439 (2006): 466–69; Grit Hein et al., 'Neural Responses to Ingroup and Outgroup Members' Suffering Predict Individual Differences in Costly Helping', *Neuron* 68, no. 1 (2010): 149–60.

from Greek mythology, who killed her own children and her rival in order to wound her unfaithful husband, Jason.

According to the gender ideology of the nineteenth and early twentieth centuries, these women were extreme deviations from the norm. The female mind was generally considered soft and mellow. Women, as the popular philosopher Friedrich Wilhelm Foerster stated in 1909, possessed the 'finer forces of the soul' and were designed for sympathy and compassion. With them, the 'protection of the weak' was in the best of hands and served as the 'greatest means of education' for a culture that would overcome selfishness and exercise 'care for the lives of others'.[7] Women were therefore 'particularly at home' in nursing and social work, as a pedagogical handbook concluded in 1905. The women's movement likewise wanted to reserve these professions for women, because feminine sympathy was believed to be a resource for resolving social problems and bringing peace to disruptive conflicts.[8]

In this respect, little has changed to this day. Women are still thought to have a particular talent for engaging empathetically with other people and behaving caringly towards them. Several feminists claim this to be a special societal virtue: the capacity for empathetic care, in the view of psychologist Carol Gilligan, gives women an advantage when it comes to social cooperation and predestines them to be trailblazers of an ethics that modern societies desperately need. As mothers, but also as teachers, doctors, nurses and lawyers, women practice this ethics of care and compassion to the betterment of their fellow humans. Men, in contrast, orient themselves more towards being arbiters of justice – as neuroscientific experiments into pain and reward perceptions confirm (> Solidarity, > Envy).

Whether such dispositions are inherent in female and male 'nature', as has been asserted for over two hundred years, is questionable. Contemporaries seem not to have trusted this claim, investing significant time and effort in an education that instilled in girls and boys the emotions, attitudes and behaviour they supposedly possessed innately. Female empathy, sympathy and compassion were cultivated in families as they were in schools and in later careers. Girls and young women found role models in their mothers, aunts and teachers, but also in literature for children and young adults.

Moral Disgust and Cultural Superiority

The prescription of roles was not, however, limited to approving of compassion, sympathy and empathy as feminine virtues and paying heed to them in

---

[7] Friedrich Wilhelm Foerster, *Lebensführung* [1909] (Berlin: Reimer, 1917), 226, 261.

[8] *Encyklopädisches Handbuch der Pädagogik*, 2nd ed., vol. 3 (Langensalza: Beyer, 1905), 107; ibid., vol. 5 (1906), 42; Christoph Sachße, *Mütterlichkeit als Beruf: Sozialarbeit, Sozialreform und Frauenbewegung 1871–1919* (Frankfurt: Suhrkamp, 1986), 116, 138–48; Iris Schröder, *Arbeiten für eine bessere Welt: Frauenbewegung und Sozialreform 1890–1914* (Frankfurt: Campus, 2001).

familial or professional life. It also defined who deserved sympathy and who did not; what was considered just and unjust, fair and unfair. 'Innocence' tipped the scales here. A person who was in a desperate situation through no fault of their own was allowed to receive sympathy, while those who only had themselves to blame for their sorry state could not expect it – even if religiously minded people liked to prove their bigger hearts. The incarnations of innocence were infants, small children and, above all, animals. In Germany, the first associations against animal cruelty were formed long before initiatives that sought to protect children from exploitation and abuse.

Adults, in contrast, could hope only for conditional sympathy. When the young doctor Rudolf Virchow visited typhoid-hit Upper Silesia on behalf of the Prussian government in 1848, he found appalling poverty and desperation, but also 'uncleanliness and indolence', laziness and alcoholism. To him, this culture of 'moral and physical sunkenness' made 'such a repulsive impression' that he felt himself 'more moved to disgust than pity'. A 'feeling of unspeakable disgust' regarding the 'moral squalidness and crudeness' of female factory workers was also reported in 1893 by economist Minna Wettstein-Adelt, who had spent several months in a Chemnitz weaving mill.[9]

The moral > disgust that middle-class women and men experienced when faced with the living conditions and behaviours of the lower classes evidently hindered or blocked empathy. It exemplified a sense of cultural superiority that did not merely reflect the social rift between the high and the low but reinforced and widened it. The more that the former believed to observe crudeness, brutality and savagery at the bottom rung of society, the less likely they were to practise the sensitive sympathy that they self-confidently valued in themselves.

The pattern repeated itself in interactions with non-Europeans. Everywhere the Europeans trod as colonizers, they purported to be shocked by the violence and ruthlessness they found. But instead of bringing the 'European culture' of compassion to the colonized, they quickly adapted to what they termed local conventions. Under the pretext that the natives were used to violence and would not understand any other language, they constructed a colonial regime that was rarely surpassed for savagery. Empathy, when it occurred at all, apparently did so only in Europe and among Europeans.

Yet there, too, empathy was in no way neutral or anti-hierarchical. Rather, it suited the self-image of civilized, educated, considerate citizens, who positioned themselves as proud bearers of culture. Empathy developed into a social status symbol: middle-class women showcased their good manners by compassionately attending to the 'protection of the weak' (Foerster),

---

[9] Ute Frevert, *Krankheit als politisches Problem* (Göttingen: Vandenhoeck & Ruprecht, 1984), quote 141–42; Schröder, *Arbeiten*, quote 44.

organizing charity bazaars, collecting donations for the 'shamefaced poor' or making house visits to the ill and the elderly. To prove one's sympathetic heart denoted one's elevated social position as well as a personal sense of duty and virtue. And it went hand in hand with the mission of demonstrating this virtue as a shining example to others, encouraging gratitude and emulation.

Sympathy in National Socialism

The question of who should enjoy the offerings of compassionate virtue and charity was always disputed, and 'innocence' remained an important rationale for their allocation. New boundaries were drawn by nationalist and racist movements, which had been gaining momentum since the late nineteenth century. As of 1939, sympathy was said to presuppose 'the awareness of a certain likeness between ourselves and the alien being'. The more alien or foreign that being was thought to be, the more drastically the capacity for empathy shrank. A regime like National Socialism, which denied other nations and races similarity or equal status, reserved sympathy exclusively for *Gemeinschaftsgenossen*: those living in one's own national and racial community.[10]

Those who did not belong to or who had been painfully excluded from this community could not be sympathized with; people chose to dismiss their suffering and looked away. 'Personal sympathy', according to a local newspaper in 1937, must be silenced – and completely so – when it came to the excision of homosexual 'criminals from the healthy *Volksgemeinschaft* [people's community]'. Four years later, Hans Frank, governor-general of occupied Poland, issued the guideline: 'Basically our sympathy lies with the German people alone and with no other in the world.'[11]

Not everyone adhered to this. As the Hessian farmer Heinrich List set on record in 1942, he had 'felt sorry' for the son of a Jewish business partner and decided to hide him on his farm. List was denounced and murdered in Dachau concentration camp. He was not the only one. Mass observations conducted by the Nazi party's police and security organization frequently documented 'compassionate considerations' and general sentiments of pity. Here, social proximity often played a role. Even those who fundamentally approved of the regime's antisemitic actions and viewed Jews as 'alien beings' showed some reluctance to apply this judgement to their own neighbours or acquaintances. When police reserves who participated in mass shootings in Poland in 1942 talked to Jewish victims and discovered that they were Germans from

---

[10] *Meyers Lexikon*, 8th ed., vol. 7 (Leipzig: Bibliografisches Institut, 1939), 1455.

[11] Alexander Zinn, '*Aus dem Volkskörper entfernt*'? *Homosexuelle Männer im Nationalsozialismus* (Frankfurt: Campus, 2018), quote 463; Helmut Krausnick et al., eds, *Anatomy of the SS State* (New York: Walker & Co, 1965), 94.

Kassel, Hamburg or Bremen, the men resolved to stop participating in the executions and asked for another assignment.[12]

However, proximity and acquaintance were by no means always sufficient for empathy to be felt or practised. Emotions like greed, > envy and resentment could effectively cancel it out. Men and women who wanted to enrich themselves with the 'Aryanized' assets of emigrated or deported Jews did not care about the fate of those who had to leave their belongings behind.

The darkest chapter of German history confers one more lesson about 'fellow-feeling': the men who tortured prisoners in the cellars of the Berlin Gestapo headquarters, and at many other places in Germany and the occupied countries, were hardly callous monsters – on the contrary. Even if some among them were psychopaths, who generally show little disposition to empathy, most had a sense of what their victims felt. That was how they knew exactly which methods of torture elicited the highest pain response. They also used their empathetic ability to uncover the victims' mental sensitivities and traumas, in order to exert calculated pressure.[13]

Instrumentalization and Manipulation

Evidently, empathy does not automatically generate pro-social behaviour. It can also be used to accomplish less beneficial and morally dubious goals. The myriad of current offers to coach and optimize empathy demonstrates that this strategic employment is once again in high demand. Barely a management consultant or leadership coach skips empathy, and corresponding 'academies' pop up like mushrooms. Nurses or doctors are not usually among the clients because, for medical professionals, empathy can be a burden that keeps them from doing their jobs properly. Instead, in the crosshairs of empathy-promoters are business executives, who are encouraged to have an empathetic relationship with – and show empathetic conduct towards – their employees. Empathy, coaches promise, enables one to more easily recognize and handle the positive and negative emotions of colleagues; empathy is thus a key requirement for communicative success and a productive work atmosphere.

Here, empathy is just a prettier word for emotional intelligence. Emotional intelligence entered business culture in the mid-1990s after the American science journalist Daniel Goleman publicized it in his bestselling book. An emotionally intelligent person could decipher and navigate their own feelings as well as those of their peers, and thus maintain the upper hand in every

---

[12] http://bit.ly/3jB7AUw, accessed 13 April 2022; Christopher R. Browning, *Ordinary Men: Reserve Police Battalion 101 and the Final Solution in Poland* (New York: HarperCollins, 1992), 67–68.

[13] Zaki and Ochsner, 'Empathy', 874–75, 879.

situation. Masters of emotional intelligence were, in this respect, masters of emotional literacy and manipulation.

Manipulation, however, does not sound good. That emotions should – or could – be purposefully deployed also seems an unappealing notion because it contradicts the common understanding of emotions as subjective, autonomous and intangible. Every suspicion of manipulation and instrumentalization immediately elicits unease, defensiveness and opposition. This is especially the case for empathy. The idea that strategic calculation could be hiding behind this feel-good term is unwelcome, and therefore often suppressed.

Such calculations are multifaceted. The ability to empathize with others does not necessarily have to be used for selling life-insurance policies or exerting pressure in a police interrogation. Some people may satisfy voyeuristic cravings or enjoy the pleasant feeling, when faced with the suffering of others, of being free of that suffering and able to enjoy life.[14] Others who act on their sympathy may feel like the 'best person' by Lessing's standards and have their positive self-image validated.

The New Sensibility and *Willkommenskultur*

Readiness to alleviate the suffering of fellow human beings significantly increased and spread during the second half of the twentieth century. The heightened awareness of universal human rights after their severe violation under the Nazi regime was a factor here. The 'bourgeois coldness' of distanced spectatorship, without which Auschwitz, in the words of philosopher Theodor W. Adorno, 'would not have been possible', gave way, under the impression left by the images and reports from the concentration and extermination camps, to a sensual-somatic or 'bodily' realization that suffering should not occur and that 'things ought to be different'. This is what Herbert Marcuse, who like Adorno emigrated to the USA in 1934, later called 'the new sensibility' of a new generation that he sought to nurture as an influential mentor of the student movement.[15]

Another factor that spurred the growth of empathy was the post-war experience of large numbers of German citizens. Between 1946 and 1960, ten million families in the West received care packages from American

---

[14] As early as 1798, Immanuel Kant saw the 'principle of contrast' at work when people's 'enjoyment increases through comparison with others' pain, while their own pain is diminished through comparison with similar or even greater suffering of others' (*Anthropology from a Pragmatic Point of View*, ed. and trans. Robert B. Louden (Cambridge: Cambridge University Press, 2009), 135).

[15] Theodor W. Adorno, *Negative Dialectics*, trans. Dennis Redmond (Frankfurt: Suhrkamp, 1970), 393–97, 415; Herbert Marcuse, 'The New Sensibility', in Herbert Marcuse, *An Essay on Liberation* (Boston: Beacon Press, 1969), 23–48.

Figure 13   Enduring empathy: Berlin mayor Ernst Reuter hands over the millionth care package in 1952 (Photo by ullstein bild/ullstein bild via Getty Images)

charitable organizations (Figure 13). Being dependent on the compassion and support of others had a lasting effect. In 1960, West Germans sent thirteen million Christmas parcels to the GDR, an act praised as an expression of human solidarity and readiness to help. Five years later, fifty million packets containing 'gifts of love' were sent to East German friends, relatives and churches. In the early 1980s, many citizens donated money, medication and clothes for people in crisis-ridden Poland. As well as church congregations and social welfare associations, countless individuals got involved, collecting and bringing urgently needed everyday items.[16] Then, in 2015, the

---

[16] Reinhard Kiehl, ed., *Alle Jahre wieder* (Düsseldorf: My favourite book, 2001), 142; Christian Härtel and Petra Kabus, eds, *Das Westpaket* (Berlin: Links, 2000), 127; Volker Ilgen, *CARE-Paket & Co* (Darmstadt: WBG, 2008), 56 ff., 94 ff.; 'Polen-Hilfe: "Eine echte Volksbewegung"', *Der Spiegel*, 7 June 1982, www.spiegel.de/spiegel/print/d-14339926.html, accessed 4 January 2022; Barbara Cöllen et al., eds, *Polenhilfe* (Dresden: Neisse, 2011). On the inter-German exchange of '*Westpakete*' and '*Ostpakete*' and their communicative misunderstandings, see Konstanze Soch, *Eine große Freude? Der innerdeutsche Paketverkehr im Kalten Krieg (1949–1989)* (Frankfurt: Campus, 2018). On the exemplary humanitarian endeavour for post-war Germany, see Godehard Weyerer, 'CARE Packages: Gifts from Overseas to a Defeated and Debilitated Nation', in *The*

Willkommenskultur – which received a great deal of international attention – was put into action by millions of Germans who, not infrequently in remembrance of their own refugee history, welcomed men, women and children who had fled war-torn Syria and other crisis regions, and helped them get a foothold in the country. In this case, empathy actually made history and put pressure on those in power to act.[17]

That open borders would also create problems was clear to all involved. 'We want to help. Our heart is large. But our facilities are finite': this is how Federal President Joachim Gauck, who emphatically praised the compassion of his compatriots, drew attention to the limits of 'welcome culture'. These limits were not only material. Mental and emotional forces, too, could become damaged and dry up if overtaxed. The Italian writer and Auschwitz survivor Primo Levi had observed this from his own very different experience. People were always selective in their sympathy; to suffer with every person suffering would overburden them. 'In the best of cases', what remained was 'only the sporadic pity addressed to the single individual, the *Mitmensch*, the co-man: the human being of flesh and blood standing before us, within the reach of our providentially myopic senses.'[18]

Whether this person was standing there in physical or mediated form is largely irrelevant. The anti-slavery movement of the late eighteenth and nineteenth centuries had bridged the social and spatial distance between its supporters and the slaves crammed onto trading ships and labouring on plantations with striking narratives and pictures. The appeal to common humanity ('Am I not a man and a brother/a woman and a sister?') established an existential closeness to people whom one did not know personally as they lived on different continents and under different circumstances. What was important was that people heard or saw a story about them, depicted in words or images. Since visual media occupied an increasingly prominent place in the twentieth century, a picture spoke 'a thousand words', as a worker for Caritas International stated during the 2012 UN call for donations for the famine-threatened Sahel region. Three years later, the photo of three-year-old Alan Kurdi, who drowned in the Mediterranean Sea during his Syrian family's flight, went all around the world (Figure 14). Described by many as the symbol

---

United States and Germany in the Era of the Cold War, 1945–1990, ed. Detlef Junker et al., vol. 1 (Cambridge: Cambridge University Press, 2004), 522–27.

[17] Jan Plamper, *We Are All Migrants: A History of Multicultural Germany* (Cambridge: Cambridge University Press, 2023), ch. 8 ('Welcome Culture').

[18] 'Unsere Möglichkeiten sind endlich', *Zeit online*, 27 September 2015, http://bit.ly/3jwP9QU, accessed 4 January 2022; Primo Levi, *The Drowned and the Saved*, trans. Raymond Rosenthal (New York: Simon & Schuster, 2017), 45.

Figure 14 Graffiti by artists Justus Becker and Oguz Sen at Frankfurt harbour: Alan Kurdi drowned in the Mediterranean while fleeing from Syria in 2015 (Daniel Roland/ AFP via Getty Images)

of the refugee tragedy, it attained iconic status and unleashed a wave of compassion and willingness to help.[19]

But not every picture, and not every story detailing famines, natural disasters or civil war, provokes the same empathy among those who see the image and hear or read the account. When the media reported on devastating floods in Pakistan in 2010, donations fell far short of the expected amount – probably because at this time a negative image of Pakistan as a Muslim country with terrorist structures was circulating, inhibiting compassion.[20] Political and cultural framings are crucial when it comes to activating the ability to feel and practise empathy.

Nonetheless, empathy's material balance sheet is net positive. The trend in donations is upward. Since the beginning of the twenty-first century, income from private donations in Germany has grown by almost 5 per cent each year; according to estimates, it reached 5.4 billion euros in 2020. In fact, it was even higher, as not all contributions go to NGOs and welfare institutions or

[19] Rebecca Adler-Nissen et al., 'Images, Emotions, and International Politics: The Death of Alan Kurdi', *Review of International Studies* 46, no. 1 (2020): 75–95.
[20] Deniz Yücel, 'Kein Herz für Mullah Omar', *taz*, 18 August 2010 (https://taz.de/Spenden-fuer-Pakistan/!5137170/, accessed 4 January 2022).

are tax-deductible. That donations can be taken off taxable income is intended to encourage citizens to open their hearts and their purses. Many do not need this incentive and donate without receipts, while others want their empathy to be officially affirmed and appreciated.

Increasingly larger sums are collected by transnational humanitarian bodies and flow abroad. From the 1950s onwards, the practice of empathy and compassion has become thoroughly globalized. Since 1958, the Catholic relief organization Misereor has been financing projects in Africa, Asia and Latin America with the aid of donation campaigns for Lent. Protestant churches in Berlin started the campaign 'Bread for the World' a year later, and in one fell swoop raised millions in East and West Germany (> Solidarity). The more examples of and opportunities for empathetic behaviour there were, the more people were inspired to be empathetic. In today's world, anyone who refuses empathy in the face of targeted media campaigns and a broad offering of humanitarian actions and organizations must thoroughly justify their decision – to themselves and to others.

~

Envy

Those who grew up reading *Grimms' Fairy Tales* know envy inside and out. It is found at every turn in the stories collected and put to paper by brothers Wilhelm and Jacob Grimm at the beginning of the 1800s: in the form of the queen who turned 'yellow and green with envy' when she learnt of Snow White's beauty; in the wicked stepmother who wants to marry off her ugly daughter and murders her happily married, beautiful stepdaughter out of envy ('Brother and Sister'); and in the tale of Pechmarie, whose enviousness of her successful stepsister blooms 'in her heart'.

The message is clear: envy is evil, and envy is feminine. It was personified by the archetype of the witch – in the Brothers Grimm's stories one and the same as the beastly stepmother. In the early modern period, witches were thought to be envious beings who poisoned animals, ruined crops and conjured all manner of misfortune on and in people's bodies. Counter-spells offered protection against their harmful incantations – sometimes. The best thing to do was to take the witch out altogether by turning her evil handiwork back on her and ultimately killing her.

Christianity considers envy one of the seven deadly sins; the legal system waged its own battle against it. The term *Neidbau* or 'spite house' was used to describe and criminalize construction projects that deliberately harmed neighbours by depriving them of views or by being erected directly on the property line. The sole purpose of such constructions was to cause trouble.[1] This distinguished envy (an emotion closely related in this instance to schadenfreude) from greed. Envious people begrudged the luck, success, health and wealth of others, aware that they would never enjoy such blessings themselves. As philosopher Max Scheler observed in 1912, envy springs from a feeling of powerlessness. Being 'merely displeased that another person owns a good' does not in itself constitute envy, because one might still acquire this good for oneself 'by means of work, barter, crime, or violence'. Only when this fails 'and the feeling of impotence' sets in does envy present itself.

---

[1] Hans-Peter Haferkamp, '§§ 226–231', in *Historisch-kritischer Kommentar zum BGB*, ed. Mathias Schmoeckel et al., vol. 1 (Tübingen: Mohr Siebeck, 2003), 1035–58, esp. 1038 ff.

In order for envy to materialize, however, something that Scheler called the 'causal delusion' is required: the mistaken idea that those who possess the desired item or quality are the '*cause* of our privation'. This perception then flares up into feelings and acts of hate against the person who possesses the coveted thing – as demonstrated by the characters in the Grimms' fairy tales (> Hate). Scheler coined the term '*resentment* envy' to describe such feelings, which he saw as predominantly oriented towards the 'innate characteristics of groups of individuals'. This included the envy of 'beauty, racial excellence, hereditary character traits', whereas envy of 'power, property, honor, and other values' was secondary.[2]

Penis Envy and Misogyny

Scheler's text was published in a psychiatric journal, for good reason. Alongside philosophy, the author had also studied psychology and was well acquainted with Sigmund Freud's work on pyschoanalysis. Already in 1908, Freud had written about the 'penis envy' allegedly felt by little girls who, as soon as they gazed upon the male body, could identify precisely what they themselves were lacking and desired to have. Upon noticing that their own small, hidden genitals differed from those of their brothers or male playmates, girls 'are overcome by envy for the penis – an envy culminating in the wish, which is so important in its consequences, to be boys themselves'.[3]

Psychoanalyst Karen Horney did not entirely repudiate Freud's observation, but in 1926 she relativized the 'consequences'. Even if girls discover something their brothers have that they themselves do not, this realization does not inevitably cause a lifelong feeling of deficiency and inferiority, Horney argued. In fact, it could work the other way round: maybe women often had difficulties achieving a stable sense of self because society refused them the possibility of doing so. Behind this was a form of envy that Horney had noticed in many of her male patients; they were jealous 'of pregnancy, childbirth, and motherhood'.

Both the penis envy that was, according to Freud, experienced by women and the womb envy felt by men and identified by Horney confirmed Scheler's definition of envy. They pertained to the natural characteristics of individuals or groups that those without them could never attain, even if they fervently wished to. Yet only in men did the feeling of envy give rise to a spiteful attitude. For Horney, this attitude represented the 'impulse to depreciation' of the opposite sex, a drive that characterized an entire culture dominated by

---

[2] Max Scheler, *Ressentiment*, trans. Lewis B. Coser and William W. Holdheim, new ed. (Milwaukee, WI: Marquette University Press, 1994), 31, 34, 35, 39.

[3] Sigmund Freud, *Three Essays on the Theory of Sexuality*, trans. James Strachey (New York: Avon Books, 1972), 93.

men and masculine norms. Evidently, she summarized, men felt 'a greater necessity to depreciate women than conversely'.[4]

Cultural historians had a word for this: misogyny, or the hatred of women. Its causes, expressions and effects were outlined by literary scholar Kate Millett in her pathbreaking 1969 study *Sexual Politics*, which became a second-wave feminist manifesto.[5] According to its critics, it preached and incited misandry. However, the empirical basis for this claim, unlike evidence of the devaluation, degradation and violent humiliation of women, was lacking. Were women as aggressive towards men as men are towards women, the world would look quite different.

Antisemitism: The Begrudging Jew

But is Scheler's finding that envy and hatred are two sides of the same coin really true in all cases? Could one not feel envy without hatred, and hatred without envy? Did women not direct their supposed penis envy first and foremost at themselves, when they felt deficient, imperfect, inferior and had to endure being devalued by men?

Around 1900, the motive of hatred was still largely absent from lexical definitions of envy; envy was simply 'one's own feeling of displeasure, caused by the perception of the pleasure of another' and arose 'from the unsatisfied desire for a good in the possession of others'. Envy, resentment and schadenfreude were considered distinct. He who feels resentment, it was said, 'begrudges his neighbour his good', while the one who feels *schadenfroh* 'rejoices in the misfortune of his neighbour'. The envious person, in contrast, feels 'sadness over a neighbour's good, insofar as this is seen as an impairment of his own happiness'. Fretting over such a situation might under certain circumstances be 'praiseworthy', as long as it yields 'justified competition' and inspires greater 'virtue and perfection'. However, if envy stems from selfishness or grudging resentment, it becomes a sin.[6]

Whether related to hatred or not, clearly envy was not a feeling to be proud of. Envious people did not attract sympathy, in fact, quite the opposite: envy was seen as toxic, caustic, consuming, corrosive – both for the person who felt it and for those around them. Hardly anyone would readily admit to feeling it;

---

[4] Karen Horney, 'The Flight from Womanhood: The Masculinity-Complex in Women as Viewed by Men and by Women', in Karen Horney, *Feminine Psychology*, ed. Harold Kelman (New York: Norton & Co., 1967), 54–70, quotes 60–62.

[5] Kate Millett, *Sexual Politics* (Urbana: University of Illinois Press, 2000). See also Kate Manne, *Down Girl: The Logic of Misogyny* (London: Penguin Books, 2019).

[6] *Brockhaus' Konversations-Lexikon*, 14th ed., vol. 12 (Leipzig: Brockhaus, 1894), 230; *Meyers Großes Konversations-Lexikon*, 6th ed., vol. 14 (Leipzig: Bibliografisches Institut, 1908), 500; *Lexikon der Pädagogik*, ed. Ernst M. Roloff, vol. 3 (Freiburg: Herder, 1914), 876.

indeed, to quote a German psychologist, 'it is always only others' who are envious.[7]

This strange and allegedly foreign feeling was the subject of oft-told stories, like the one of Freudian penis envy or the ubiquitous tales of jealous Jews. Back in the Middle Ages, Jewish people were associated with the colour yellow and, in order to distinguish them from Christians, forced to wear a yellow marking on their clothing. Yellow represented heresy, hypocrisy and envy; to be 'yellow with envy' is an idiomatic German expression still used to this day. It recalls the ancient theory of the four humours, which posited that an excess of yellow bile causes feelings such as jealousy and resentment. Jews, it was claimed, were full of yellow bile. They coveted Christians' honour and privileges and did everything in their power to harm them. Above all, they envied their blood because it reputedly worked miracles in the Jewish body: Christian blood was like a medicine, it made births easier and circumcision wounds heal faster, it neutralized body odour and increased one's sexual stamina. Jews would even kill for this precious elixir – at least this was what the numerous reports of ritualistic murders alleged. As late as 1900, violent antisemitic riots broke out in the small Pomeranian town of Konitz when the corpse of a nineteen-year-old was discovered and a local Jewish family accused of blood libel.[8]

Painting Jewish people as resentful and envious made it easier to excuse their violent treatment as a legitimate form of self-defence. Moreover, doing so was a way to deflect one's own feelings of envy. The fact that Jews in particular attracted such feelings was due to their striking economic and educational success. In 1910, the hundred richest Prussians included twenty-nine men of Jewish faith, most of whom lived in Berlin. The city's Jewish population, 5 per cent of its inhabitants, paid nearly a third of its income taxes. Jews were over-represented in the fields of banking, business, medicine and law. Of course, there were also many poor Jews, predominantly immigrants from Russian-occupied Poland and Galicia. 45 per cent of Hessian and 30 per cent of Bavarian Jews lived in rural communities and were not particularly blessed with wealth.[9] Regardless, the antisemitic image of the wealthy, rapacious Jew jealously guarding his treasures had significant appeal. That he had not acquired these treasures through honest labour but had stolen them from his

---

[7] Rolf Haubl, *Neidisch sind immer nur die anderen: Über die Unfähigkeit, zufrieden zu sein* (Munich: C. H. Beck, 2001); Helmut Schoeck, *The Envy: A Theory of Social Behaviour*, trans. Michael Glenny and Betty Ross (New York: Harcourt, Brace & World, 1969), 24–25.

[8] *Meyers Lexikon*, 8th ed., vol. 9 (Leipzig: Bibliografsches Institut, 1942), 76; Helmut Walser Smith, *The Butcher's Tale: Murder and Anti-Semitism in a German Town* (New York: Norton & Co., 2002), 29, passim.

[9] Monika Richarz, ed., *Jüdisches Leben in Deutschland: Selbstzeugnisse zur Sozialgeschichte im Kaiserreich* (Stuttgart: DVA, 1979), 21–22, 35. See also the reworked English edition, *Jewish Life in Germany: Memoirs from Three Centuries*, trans. Stella P. Rosenfeld and Sidney Rosenfeld (Bloomington: Indiana University Press, 1991).

Christian compatriots through lies and deceit seemed to be a foregone conclusion. It was therefore only right and proper to take them from him again.

In the numerous pogroms and violent attacks on Germany's Jewish community in the nineteenth and early twentieth centuries, a targeted redistribution of material goods did not take place. Mostly, Jewish houses and belongings were set on fire or wantonly destroyed. There was looting, but it was not the rule. The troublemakers were satisfied with causing damage and savouring the misfortune of those they had harmed. This fitted with the classic definition of 'resentment envy' coupled with schadenfreude.

Envy under National Socialism

Another form of envy came to the fore during National Socialism. The Nazi regime, which turned antisemitism into a state dogma, was not satisfied with spreading age-old stereotypes of the envious and begrudging Jew through speeches, texts, images, film and radio. It also aggressively fomented the German people's supposedly justifiable resentment of anyone it considered no longer part of the national community. The Jewish population watched these developments carefully. As the Bavarian civil servant Siegfried Lichtenstaedter put it in 1933, antisemitism was motivated by a combination of social envy, a competitive mindset and the desire to get ahead. The fact that Jews were 'apparently "happier" to a disproportionate degree' aroused 'envy and resentment in the minds and hearts of non-Jews'.[10] These 'hostile feelings' could arise easily and were stoked just as fast.

By no means did this always require encouragement from above. In March 1933, the Hamburg cosmetics producer Queisser & Co sensed an opportunity to beat out their main competitor, Beiersdorf, with a campaign born of envy. It urged pharmacists and drugstore owners to recommend 'national' products 'rather than Jewish specimens'. The company's advertisements urged customers not to use Nivea, the 'Jewish skin cream', any longer: 'Lovana Cream is at least as good, cheaper and purely German!' The pressure on Beiersdorf became so great that its Jewish CEOs resigned so as not to damage the company.

The dressmakers' guilds in their turn battled Jewish companies that had established thriving mail-order businesses selling inexpensive fabrics customers could tailor themselves. In doing so, the guilds complained, the 'avarious Jew' was undercutting 'honest German handicraft'. Brutal actions were directed at Jewish-owned shops and department stores even before the official boycott of 1 April 1933. Right in time for the day of the boycott, the

---

[10] Ne'man [Siegfried Lichtenstaedter], *Jüdische Politik* (Leipzig: Engel, 1933), 21–22, 56; Götz Aly, ed., *Siegfried Lichtenstaedter (1865–1942): Prophet der Vernichtung* (Frankfurt: Fischer, 2019), 186 ff.

management of Karstadt AG decided to dismiss all of its Jewish employees. As 'members of the Jewish race' they had, it was alleged, built a position of power 'on the ruins of the world war and with the help of war mutineers'. Such power 'will have to be completely destroyed and eliminated if the German people and German culture are not to be ruined'.[11]

'Aryan' Germans were thus trying to rid themselves of rivals whose success they envied. Yet they did not stop at inflicting damage on their competitors and relishing the pleasure of seeing this happen. They also immediately helped themselves to the jobs and businesses of those they had forced out. They got rich off their possessions, their apartments, their clothing, their crockery, their furniture, even their linens. When Jewish citizens left Germany and had to sell their houses and businesses for much less than they were worth, gentiles profited hugely. The beneficiaries were party members or employees who wanted to start their own ventures, or mid-sized companies that bought out the competition for cheap. From 1941, which is when the deportations to concentration camps began, the personal effects of Jewish families were put up for auction. Often, the local Nazi elite secured the most valuable items before the rest were sold off to profit the state treasury. In Hamburg, at least 100,000 people benefited from this transfer 'at knock-down prices'; working-class housewives 'were suddenly wearing fur coats, trading in coffee and jewellery, had old furniture and carpets from the port, from Holland or from France'. Everything came from the estates of deported Jews.[12]

Of course, the annexation of other people's property was not always and in all places motivated by envy. The origin of auctioned-off items – from whom and under which circumstances they were taken – interested very few. The more anonymous the redistribution, the less likely it was to cause offence. The active participation of neighbours or colleagues was more frequently the exception than the rule, at least according to Jewish emigrants who left the country following the pogrom of 9 November 1938.[13]

But there were other stories too. Residents of Baisingen, a rural Swabian community, participated without hesitation in the auction of what had only shortly before belonged to their Jewish fellow citizens. Some actually made

[11] Frank Bajohr, 'Aryanisation' in Hamburg: The Economic Exclusion of Jews and the Confiscation of Their Property in Nazi Germany (New York: Berghahn, 2002), 23–24, 27, 35.

[12] Ibid., 279–80; Gertrud Seydelmann, Gefährdete Balance: Ein Leben in Hamburg 1936–1945 (Hamburg: Junius, 1996), 105.

[13] Uta Gerhardt and Thomas Karlauf, eds, The Night of Broken Glass: Eyewitness Accounts of Kristallnacht, trans. Robet Simmons and Nick Somers (Cambridge: Polity Press, 2012); Michael Wildt, Hitler's 'Volksgemeinschaft' and the Dynamics of Racial Exclusion: Violence against Jews in Provincial Germany, 1919–1939, trans. Bernard Heise (New York: Berghahn, 2014), 227–53.

their wishlists known before the deportations began.[14] The number of those who took objects 'on loan' and kept them for the day when their Jewish owners would hopefully return was rather limited.

Thus it was not only top party functionaries who enriched themselves with what the regime took from Jewish people in their own country and throughout occupied Europe, but also large swathes of 'normal' Germans.[15] Antisemitic propaganda that painted Jews as power- and money-hungry representatives of global capital bent on tyrannizing and holding Germany down suppressed any moral scruples. Jews, it was said again and again, envied the strength and unity of the German people and would do everything in their power to destroy the nation from the inside out. This called for radical resistance, the consequences of which the Jews would have brought on themselves.

At the same time, the Nazi regime strove to avoid any suggestion that Germans acted out of personal envy, since this would not have looked good on the world stage. As a result, spontaneous pogroms, looting and the destruction of Jewish property were officially frowned upon. When they did occur, they were sold as an expression of the 'legitimate > anger of the people' and as a reaction to alleged Jewish attacks. For its part, the state provided sober justifications as to why it had imposed an exorbitant 'Flight Tax' on Jews willing and able to emigrate before 1941, as well as severe deductions on any remaining bank balances and bonds.[16] Things were done strictly according to law and order, and official procedures were claimed to be free of rancour or harassment.

Renouncing and Resisting Envy

Admittedly, confessing one's own envy or accusing fellow citizens of such feelings would have put Germans in a morally and socially inferior position to those they envied. After all, even in the 'Third Reich', envy was not one of the virtues of which a good National Socialist should or would boast. *Meyers Lexikon* had not even listed the term in 1940, while it only ever appeared as a negative trait possessed by others in Hitler's *Mein Kampf*. Similarly, as early as 1914, German war propaganda had accused its enemies of 'envy, anger, frustration' in the face of 'German superiority, intellectual

---

[14] Franziska Becker, *Gewalt und Gedächtnis: Erinnerungen an die nationalsozialistische Verfolgung einer jüdischen Landgemeinde* (Göttingen: Schmerse, 1994), 77 ff.

[15] Götz Aly, *Why the Germans? Why the Jews? Envy, Race, Hatred, and the Prehistory of the Holocaust*, trans. Jefferson Chase (New York: Metropolitan Books, 2014); Götz Aly, *Europe against the Jews, 1880–1945*, trans. Jefferson Chase (New York: Picador, 2021).

[16] Martin Dean, *Robbing the Jews: The Confiscation of Jewish Property in the Holocaust 1933–1945* (Cambridge: Cambridge University Press, 2008), esp. 54–171.

Figure 15   Envy campaign? Income comparisons are used to promote the
expropriation of the princes, 1926 (Photo by ullstein bild/ullstein bild via Getty Images)

and moral'. Envy was something felt by the weak and inferior, not by those
who were strong.[17]

For this reason, envy was nowhere to be found in the vocabulary of
socialism either. The nineteenth-century social democratic workers' movement kept just as quiet about envy as their communist offspring in the early
twentieth century. It was not envy of the bourgeoisie and the capitalist class
that motivated the struggles for higher wages, better working conditions and
political emancipation. Rather, people talked about values such as justice,
equality and human dignity as the antithesis of oppression and exploitation.

That did not stop the movement's opponents from denouncing social
democrats as 'envious and hateful' in order to denigrate their demands.[18]
Those who advocated the uncompensated expropriation of the German dynastic houses in 1926 were likewise accused of 'envy, resentment and covetous-
ness' (Figure 15). In the words of a right-wing member of parliament, these

---

[17] Alan Kramer, *Dynamic of Destruction: Culture and Mass Killing in the First World War*
(Oxford: Oxford University Press, 2007), quote 181
[18] *Quellensammlung zur Geschichte der deutschen Sozialpolitik 1867 bis 1914*, sec. 2, vol. 1
(Darmstadt: WBG, 2003), 100 (from a speech by Adolf Stoecker, member of the
Reichstag, 2 December 1881).

were 'the most serious character defects from which the German people suffer'. They were now shamelessly preyed upon by the left to 'stir up the people and spur them to action'. Communists and socialists, agreed the Nazi representative Wilhelm Frick, 'traded on the base instincts of the *Volk*, on envy and resentment'.[19]

The 'Third Reich', which Frick served as interior minister from 1933, generally considered envy between Germans taboo. Those who belonged to the racially grounded people's community were supposed to feel like one equal among many. Hitler boasted that he had eliminated 'envy among the German people' by creating 'the Volkswagen for the lower and ordinary worker'.[20]

After 1945, the envyless *Volksgemeinschaft* was reimagined as a 'community of fate' (> Solidarity), which might in fact have had several reasons for feeling envy. During the war, many had been severely hit by material and immaterial losses, others less, some not at all. While countless city dwellers lost their belongings in bombings, smaller towns and villages remained largely unscathed. Millions who were expelled from the territories in the east and southeast settled in new homelands whose residents seemed to have escaped the war without a scratch. This could lead to envy. Conversely, refugees were envied for receiving payments through the burden-sharing programme and using the money to build modest houses on the outskirts of villages and towns. Resentment, coupled with mistrust, also greeted the returnees who had removed themselves from the National Socialist 'community of shared blood and shared fate' or had forcefully been removed from it. While they had allegedly spent the war years conveniently and safely abroad, they were now demanding compensation. This classified them once again as unloved outsiders who did not belong.

In general, though, envy was not openly discussed or considered socially acceptable in the post-war period. The Federal Republic's 'levelled middle-class society' that sociologist Helmut Schelsky identified in the early 1950s had little use for it. Even if this society never really existed, it spoke to the widespread ideal of an equalizing 'striving for the middle'.[21] The middle, however, were not envious and did not compare themselves to the top or to the bottom. They were comfortable in themselves. Or at least they pretended to be.

---

[19] *Verhandlungen des Reichstags. III. Wahlperiode. Stenographische Berichte* (Berlin: Reichsdruckerei, 1926), vol. 389: 172nd session (6 March 1926), 6023; vol. 390: 190th session (28 April 1926), 6906, 6921.

[20] Heinrich Hoffmann, *Hitler wie ich ihn sah: Aufzeichnungen seines Leibfotografen* (Munich: Herbig, 1974), 214.

[21] Paul Nolte, *Die Ordnung der deutschen Gesellschaft: Selbstentwurf und Selbstbeschreibung im 20. Jahrhundert* (Munich: C. H. Beck, 2000), 318–51.

Whenever politicians ignored those equalizing aspirations, disgruntlement grew. An act that in 1950 set parliamentary allowances for Bundestag members caused 'the nation's soul' to boil, as a citizen observed on his daily train commute. In a letter to the president, he wondered whether 'we can actually afford this expense', adding that his criticism had nothing to do with envy. Although he had seen 'better days' before the war, he was 'satisfied' with his current lot: 'My family is healthy and I have my work.'[22]

Nor was envy an issue among the younger generation. After 1945, those born in the second half of the 1920s – later known as the 'Hitler Youth' or 'Flak helper' generation – rolled up their sleeves to repair and reconstruct the country. They did not immediately harbour any particular sympathy for the new democratic system that had been established in the Federal Republic under the direction of Western allies. Its leading representatives were older and had already had a taste of democracy in the Weimar Republic. Meanwhile, the young, who had grown up in the National Socialist era, kept politics somewhat at arm's length. Schelsky described them as a 'sceptical generation' and attested to their 'mental disenchantment'. Their 'competency at life' coexisted with a marked tendency to reject anything collective, without 'making a counterprogramme of it'. This generation prioritized security above all else and valued prosperity and 'keeping to themselves'. Further removed from ideology and more 'steerable' than their elders, they posed no threat to democracy and were an asset to the economic recovery.[23]

Some benefited more than others from the recovery, without a doubt. Nevertheless, everyone felt they got something out of it and that they were rewarded for their efforts. The elevator effect of economic growth described by sociologist Ulrich Beck reached every part of the population, bestowing on them a collective increase in income, education, mobility and opportunities for consumption.[24] Strong trade unions ensured that blue- and white-collar workers did not lose out in the economic reconstruction. In this land of prosperity, full of optimism for the future, there was little room for envy.

Sources of Envy in the Classless Society

More purposefully and ideologically than the West German state, the GDR sought to tackle envy at the root. There, class difference as a potential cause for envy was a thing of the past. Instead, citizens were promised an equally

---

[22] Theodor Heuss, *Hochverehrter Herr Bundespräsident! Der Briefwechsel mit der Bevölkerung 1949–1959*, ed. Wolfram Werner (Berlin: De Gruyter, 2010), 138–39.

[23] Helmut Schelsky, *Die skeptische Generation: Eine Soziologie der deutschen Jugend* [1957] (Düsseldorf: Diederichs, 1963), 381–82.

[24] Ulrich Beck, *Risk Society: Towards a New Modernity*, trans. Mark Ritter (London: Sage, 1992), 91–92.

satisfactory existence absent major disparities in income or assets. 'Real socialism' knew neither exploiter nor exploited, only a community of workers who
all did their bit to make it a successful model.

At least that was the theory. In practice, there are official records of envy
going back to at least the 1960s. In September 1969, a female resident of
Leipzig complained to SED official (and wife of strongman Walter Ulbricht)
Lotte Ulbricht about how low the minimum pension for women was under the
new provisions: 'With this they have degraded, defamed, declassified and
disparaged us old workers' wives and working women.' That which had been
withheld from them was given instead to 'layabouts, our "national idlers"'.
Among those were state-subsidized 'bums' in the administration, 'as long as
they wear a party pin', as well as 'parasitic GDR citizens', who enjoyed better
pension schemes as officially recognized political persecutees of National
Socialism.[25]

In 1980, a few women born between 1919 and 1925 contacted the head of
state, Erich Honecker, directly. As before, they did not reveal their names 'so
that we do not have to face further hardships in our old age'. They detailed
these privations further in the letter: instead of lowering the retirement age,
they said, 'older women, who, in the difficult years after the war had to bear
every burden alone' and had their 'strength and health' worn away in the
process, were being denied adequate medical care.

> I was personally told: at your age, I am sorry, a treatment spot and health
> cure is not available, we need it for the younger age groups, meaning our
> younger women, who can already make use of every benefit [Housework
> Day, childcare, paid baby year] and also heartily enjoy all the advantages.
> In return, we 'older ones' may spit into our hands again and do the work
> for the 'younger ones'.[26]

The GDR's 'mama policy', which had been gathering steam since the 1970s,
stoked generational envy: older women felt as though they were being set back
and all the work they had done forgotten. The East Berliner who wrote to
Honecker in 1988 with his name, address and a 'socialist greeting' also
criticized these 'shamefully low minimum pensions'. But he had more on his
mind. He was particularly disturbed by the fact that 'the gap between rich and
poor in our republic is getting wider and wider' and national income is

---

[25] Siegfried Suckut, *Volkes Stimmen: 'Ehrlich, aber deutlich' – Privatbriefe an die DDR-
Regierung* (Munich: dtv, 2015), 138–42 (the date of the anonymous letter is erroneously
given as 1968), 223 (letter of a woman from Plauen, 12 September 1977). In 1972 an 'old
Communist' wrote to Walter Ulbricht: 'There have never been so many differences in any
government as there are now. If a woman gets 1000 marks pension because her husband
was locked up for five minutes and another gets 160 marks that can't be fair' (quote 177).
[26] Ibid., 276–77.

'unfairly distributed': 'The real winners in our state are the craftsmen and tradesmen, the racketeers and speculators, the big earners and those for whom Western money flows abundantly through relatives in the Federal Republic. The simple workers and employees as well as the pensioners belong, unfortunately also under socialism, to the losing class.' Completely unacceptable, he continued, was 'the division of society' between those who had, since 1974, been able to buy things in GDR intershops with West German currency and the others, who were 'more than angry' about this.[27]

A single mother whose communist father had survived the Buchenwald concentration camp described her feelings as she leafed through a GDR catalogue advertising products that West Germans could order and have delivered to friends and relatives in the East. Apparently, she and her family were 'third-rate people, because we do not have any Western money'. This form of 'discrimination' was especially hard to bear because one could not do anything about it – one either had relatives in West Germany or one did not. Children and teenagers had a keen sense of this as well. 'The only true cause of material jealousy', recalled journalist Jana Hensel, overcame these 'children of a classless society' when they 'couldn't help but envy classmates who came to school sporting brightly colored T-shirts, Levi's, and Adidas sneakers with Velcro instead of shoelaces' – all things from the capitalist West that were as coveted as they were hard to acquire (Figure 16).[28]

The GDR represented a social order whose egalitarian promises came back to haunt them. The envy produced by the social inequality the state knowingly accepted for financial reasons gnawed at the moral roots of the system. In addition, the regime caused feelings of envy by incessantly deploying overblown comparisons for propangandistic purposes. For one, it constantly compared itself with its sister state in the West to make itself look like the better Germany. According to its self-understanding, East Germany had not only eliminated fascism at its root but also abolished human exploitation at the hands of other humans. It thus emerged as the moral victor in the battle of the systems. In 1979, Walter Ulbricht proclaimed that the GDR would actually

---

[27] Ibid., 390–94.
[28] Ibid., 340 (November 1985), 223–24; Jana Hensel, *After the Wall: Confessions from an East German Childhood and the Life That Came Next* (New York: Public Affairs, 2004), 110. See also Jonathan R. Zatlin, *The Currency of Socialism: Money and Political Culture in East Germany* (Cambridge: Cambridge University Press, 2007), 243–85; David F. Crew, 'Consuming Germany in the Cold War: Consumption and National Identity in East and West Germany, 1949–1989: An Introduction', in *Consuming Germany in the Cold War*, ed. David F. Crew (Oxford: Berg, 2003), 1–19, here 4–6; David Childs, *The Fall of the GDR: Germany's Road to Unity* (Harlow: Longman, 2001), 28–30; Milena Veenis, 'Consumption in East Germany: The Seduction and Betrayal of Things', *Journal of Material Culture* 4, no. 1 (1999): 79–112.

Figure 16   After the fall of the Wall, Berliners from East and West marvel together at objects of desire, November 1989 (Photo by Colin Campbell/Getty Images)

overtake the Federal Republic economically. But the world-class industrial performance it promised failed to materialize, the net income of private households dropped far below Western levels and the production of consumer goods failed to meet demand. From the perspective of most GDR citizens, then, the East clearly fell short in material terms. Disappointment with the state's leadership and envy of the successful Westerners were soon to follow.

Furthermore, competition and the resulting comparisons were firmly embedded in the GDR's blueprint. Not fundamentally dissimilar to capitalist market economies, socialism as a planned economy emphasized performance and encouraged it through financial and symbolic incentives. Awards and bonuses were used to reward high-performing workers and publicly highlight their deservedness (> Honour). This could trigger envy. In 1971 a party member took aim at what he saw as the unfair practice of bestowing awards in factories: 'One gets a bonus, the other does not. Here, too, there is a lot of sinning. It is often always the same people. When a colleague who had recently been given "activist" status received an award, other colleagues were so jealous that he was spanked in the street (in the dark of night).' The fact that in December 1989, operators at the Jena thermal power plant demanded the abolition of 'privileges and advantages for individual workers and employees' as well as 'all bonuses except year-end and loyalty bonuses' spoke for itself.[29]

The strategy of spotlighting and decorating the top performers in schools and youth organizations also sparked envy. Olympiads and sporting events known as Spartakiades were a regular fixture in the lives of young East Germans, as was the battle for the cherished 'Sputnik pin'. The search for the best athletes began especially early and was organized with military precision. The state spent a great deal of money on exceptional performances that made the medal tables of international competitions and demonstrated 'the superiority of our order over the capitalist system in West Germany'.[30] The idea that this might not be well received among the wider populace or that it might contradict the general culture of egalitarianism could be countered with appeals to the socialist spirit of collectivism: every individual achievement was ultimately the work of the collective, the team, the people (and their government). Yet the placards hanging on the walls of factories and schools bore only the names of 'our best'. They were the ones for whom the monetary bonuses and trips abroad beckoned, with high-performing children enjoying a vacation at summer camp or a place in the delegation to national or even international youth meetings.[31] Those who stayed at home might well have been envious of such distinctions.

In Praise of Competition

From a pedagogical point of view, this kind of envy could actually be extremely productive. Realizing that your performance was comparatively poor and that you might be disadvantaged as a result could be an incentive to make more of an effort. As early as 1903, the sociologist and philosopher Georg Simmel had argued as much, writing that societies needed both 'association and competition, favour and disfavour'. Competition increased the level of performance and engagement and placed men, women and children into a fruitful dynamic. This gave rise to a 'tremendous synthesizing power' that ultimately reabsorbed the dissociative, divisive aspects of envy and morally neutralized the feeling.

Simmel was by no means oblivious to the 'tragedy' of modern societies taking competition to extremes and wasting 'endless energy' on it. Yet he considered the positive effects and 'unifying interactions' to be greater and

---

[29] Suckut, *Volkes Stimmen*, 170; Jan Wenzel, ed., *Das Jahr 1990 freilegen* (Leipzig: Spector Books, 2020), 29 (29 December 1989).

[30] Günter Buchstab, 'Sport und Politik im geteilten Deutschland', *Historisch-Politische Mitteilungen* 8, no. 1 (2001): 113–30, quote (from 1958) 122.

[31] Dorothee Wierling, *Geboren im Jahr Eins: Der Jahrgang 1949 in der DDR* (Berlin: Links, 2002), 145, 147, 149–50.

more important. As a struggle for recognition and 'acclaim', competition presupposed the formal equality of competitors. Only when people had a similar chance of aquiring a coveted good or status did they enter into competition with one another. The fact that many people found a certain item desirable also reflected a moment of equality; if their interests and tastes were vastly different, there would be less competition and less envy.[32]

Competition was a crucial pillar in the foundational architecture of the Federal Republic. The market economy was based on competition. The state, for its part, was there to cushion and contain the socio-political effects of the 'free market'. It also guaranteed its citizens equality before the law and enabled them to have roughly equal life chances through access to education, mobility and healthcare. How the individual used their opportunities was up to them. The meritocratic idea of achievement did whatever work was left to fuel competition and justify differences in income; those who achieved more or marketed their skills better need not feel ashamed of their prosperity. In principle, everybody could do just as well, and if they did not, they had no grounds to envy the success of others.

In 1912, Max Scheler found that envy occurred when people did not obtain the item for which they were striving, despite every effort, and accordingly reacted with a 'feeling of impotence'. Impotence, however, had no place in the self-conception of a performance-focused society. The more the state invested in 'human capital', and the more money it spent on education, health and social security, the greater the expectation that the recipients of this investment would make adequate attempts to utilize it. Those who did not only had themselves to blame for the consequences. In such cases, envy seemed not only completely out of place but brazen, even impudent.

Fairness and Feelings of Envy

This interpretation has become more pronounced as calls to effectively combat social inequality have increased. Since the 1990s, social democratic tax plans have been disparaged as 'envy campaigns'. Proponents of liberal economics counter the vocal criticism of high managerial salaries with the accusation that it originates 'from a place of envy'. Those who demand higher income taxes for the rich or transparency when it comes to payments of subsidies in the European Union are unleashing an 'envy debate', they claim. The term 'Neid-Debatte' first appeared in 2002 and has enjoyed growing popularity ever since, if the archives of the Frankfurter Allgemeine Zeitung are anything to go

---

[32] Georg Simmel, 'Sociology of Competition' [1903, trans. Helmut J. Helle], *Canadian Journal of Sociology* 33, no. 4 (2008): 957–78; Georg Simmel, *Sociology: Inquiries into the Construction of Social Forms*, trans. Anthony J. Blasi et al., vol. 1 (Leiden: Brill, 2009), 254–56.

by. 'Neid' ('envy') has also had a stellar career; in the past decade the term appeared in articles more than five times as often as in the 1960s.[33]

Just because journalists are writing more about envy and 'envy debates' does not necessarily mean that envy is in fact more present today than it was half a century ago. Robust and meaningful data to evaluate such a claim are lacking. Even figures on income and wealth distribution are not exactly helpful in this regard. By no means can we assume that envy concomitantly increased when the gap between rich and poor widened in the 1990s. After all, such feelings do not surface as an automatic reaction to inequality, as the historical record shows. Precisely because envy is typically frowned upon, it requires a rationale, a justification and an eloquent defence.

In this context, a representative survey from 2008 proves interesting. Psychologists first asked their interview partners about their feelings of envy. As could be expected, interviewees rarely described themselves as envious, though they did attest to the envy felt by others. They also dismissed accompanying negative feelings such as > anger, > grief or rage; one in three even claimed that they would admire those who had something they wanted as well. Almost 39 per cent explained that it did not bother them at all. Whether that was true is doubtful; respondents may have been giving the answer they felt was most socially acceptable.

The next question was about the call for a 'wealth tax' and whether people considered it to be an expression of 'social envy' or rather of 'social equity'. The vast majority of respondents saw it more as an impulse towards the latter. Those with a university degree, however, more often saw social envy at work, while people with less formal education placed a stronger emphasis on social equity.

But what did equity mean? In order to find out, the authors of the study had their subjects vote on four options: equal distribution of goods, needs-based equity, performance-based equity and individual desires ('everyone should get what they want'). Across all social classes, the largest group (nearly 45 per cent) voted for performance equity, with a sizeable 37 per cent preferring needs-based equity. Equal distribution of goods and desire-based economics came a distant third and fourth (13.5 and 4.3 per cent respectively).[34]

---

[33] In light of the ever-denser rates of reporting on anything and everything, an increase in frequency in itself does not prove much. However, if we compare 'envy' with the far more prominent term 'politics', it becomes clear that the increase is indeed considerable, twice as high as for 'politics'.

[34] Rolf Haubl and Elmar Brähler, 'Neid und Neidbewältigung in Deutschland: Ergebnisse einer repräsentativen Fragebogenuntersuchung', in 'Denk ich an Deutschland ...': Sozialpsychologische Reflexionen, ed. Ulrich Bahrke (Frankfurt: Brandes & Apsel, 2010), 199–213.

This by and large confirmed the findings of previous surveys. Performance as the basis for allocating income is generally considered just. Since the 1980s, seven out of ten West Germans have felt that they are getting their 'fair share' of what the country has to offer. Two-thirds support income inequality as a performance incentive, a number that grew towards the end of the century. Among East Germans polled after 1990, the approval rate is markedly lower: only 40 per cent of respondents in 1994 found income disparities motivating or reasonable. When asked whether they thought social stratifications in Germany were on the whole fair, few answered in the affirmative. As recently as 2000, 60 per cent of East Germans – double the proportion of West Germans – felt that they were not treated at all fairly as far as their standard of living was concerned.[35]

Has this given new impetus to feelings of envy? The 2008 poll speaks of emotional ambivalence. On the one hand, East Germans are far more likely to perceive the 'wealth tax' as a question of social equity than of social envy. This might be due to the more radical rhetoric of equality in the former GDR. More East Germans than West Germans also consider it unfair when they do not have something that others do. On the other hand, expressing admiration for those who possess coveted goods is significantly lower in the East than in the West.[36] This suggests the presence of envy: one envies those who are well off, begrudges them what they have and perhaps even wishes that they might soon lose it all.

This calls to mind a familiar joke: an American walks down the street with his friend. A big Cadillac drives past. The American says to his friend, 'I will drive a car like that one day!' A German walks down the street with his friend. A big BMW drives past. The German says to his friend, 'That guy will soon lose his car and will have to walk as we do.'[37] In the 2008 survey, the American who admires the Cadillac driver and plans to be behind the wheel himself sooner or later corresponded to the West German, while the begrudging and timid German represented the former GDR citizen: he did not dare drive a luxury car, envied the owner's good fortune and wished him the worst.

The joke not only illustrates the difference between envy as deep-seated resentment and what Scheler called 'mere displeasure'. It mirrors the perception of national characteristics. Since the 1800s, people from the USA have been said to possess an irrepressible will to achieve personal success – free from envy – and an equally strong belief in progress and improvement. Continental Europeans, by contrast, are believed to still suffer from a long

---

[35] Bodo Lippl, *Soziale Gerechtigkeit aus der Sicht der deutschen Bevölkerung* (ISJP Arbeitsbericht 95) (Berlin: Humboldt-Universität, 2003), 6, 9–10, 12.

[36] Haubl and Brähler, 'Neid und Neidbewältigung', 210.

[37] Haubl, *Neidisch*, 10.

history of authoritarian control and a fixation on the all-mighty state, despite several revolutions. Instead of a sense of self-confidence and an optimistic spirit, they seem to indulge in envy and resentment.

Behind all stereotypes lurks a kernel of historical truth. This also applies to the caricature that West Germans are confident, self-assured and accomplished, and their frustrated counterparts in the East filled with envy. In fact, the experience of many GDR citizens since 1990 has not done much to convince them that a radically individualized notion of performance is a sound guiding principle. To them, achievement and success have appeared less as something earned through their own efforts than bound to a Western background and unattainable for people without the right upbringing. Fundamentally, the generation born between 1945 and 1955 felt lost and as though they stood no real chance in the rat race of life.

The cliche of the 'envious *Ossis*' (Easterners) beloved in the West overlooks these distinct experiences and ignores the imbalance in life chances that East Germans were faced with from the beginning. But even the supposedly success-spoiled and accordingly arrogant '*Wessi* ' (Westerner) only acquired their self-assurance after a long learning process. If West Germans consider the relevant metrics of performance fair and are able to fend off jealous impulses, this is largely because they have done well by these metrics since the 1950s; East Germans have not had the same opportunities for and experience of success.

Yet they too have found ways of keeping feelings of envy in check. According to a survey conducted in 1996 and 1998, test subjects from the East protected their mental health through 'own-group valorization'. By cultivating a positive East German identity, they could prevent envy of the materially more successful and self-assured West Germans from taking hold and affecting their psychological well-being. In contrast, the self-image of those who had grown up in the West was comparatively bleak, although their > pride in the 'economy and currency' was far stronger. West Germans were also significantly more likely than their East German compatriots to feel constitutional patriotism (> Love) – with men demonstrating more national pride than women.[38]

This brings us back to fairy tales and what they have conveyed about envy as a predominantly feminine trait. Historical and sociological evidence does not support this claim. Recent surveys have only identified gender differences in

---

[38] Manfred Schmitt and Jürgen Maes, 'Stereotypic Ingroup Bias as a Self-defense against Relative Deprivation: Evidence from a Longitudinal Study of the German Unification Process, *European Journal of Social Psychology* 32, no. 3 (2002): 309–26; Manfred Schmitt and Jürgen Maes, 'Perceived Injustice in Unified Germany and Mental Health', *Social Justice Research* 11, no. 1 (1998): 59–78.

the feelings that accompanied envy: women tended to respond with passive sadness, men with aggressive anger, when others possessed something they themselves wished for. This, too, is socially and culturally influenced: men are given permission to direct their negative emotions outwards, while women are supposed to process them quietly and inwardly.[39]

---

[39] Haubl and Brähler, 'Neid und Neidbewältigung', 207.

Fear

What are Germans afraid of? Since 1992, an insurance company has been asking approximately 2,000 people each year – a representative cross-section of the population – how much fear certain topics trigger in them. The list ranges from illness and needing personal care to unemployment, marital crisis, violent crime and war. It is flexible: in 2003, after severe flooding, the fear of natural disasters was added; in 2011, during the European debt crisis, the fear of its costs. In 2015, the fear of being overwhelmed by high numbers of refugees appeared, and in 2018 people were asked whether the policies of US president Donald Trump made the world a more dangerous place. In 2021, 53 per cent of respondents professed that they were afraid of pandemic-related tax increases.[1]

Why the insurance company wants to know all this is unclear, as it does not offer a policy against marital crises, migrants or out-of-control heads of state. At best, politicians could use the surveys as an opportunity to promise citizens more security and implement relevant measures. But even they know the problematic nature of 'desired' answers and their susceptibility to manipulation. The way that questions are worded and the order in which they are posed clearly influences the result. Was Donald Trump really the only politician playing a dangerous game with foreign policy? Certainly not. Moreover, actual and perceived threats often diverge greatly. For instance, the statistical risk of being harmed in a terrorist attack is far lower than the chance of being murdered, robbed or defrauded. Yet only 19 per cent of interviewees said, in 2021, they felt personally threatened by crime, while 32 per cent were afraid of terrorism.

'German Angst' and German Trauma?

The informative value of surveys is thus limited. One can distrust them just as one distrusts the talk of 'German Angst'. Since the 1980s, it has become customary to attest a particular anxiety to Germans. They are supposedly

---

[1] http://bit.ly/3lvzhP7, accessed 3 March 2022.

fearful of everything and everyone: of dying forests and dying in traffic accidents as much as of a third world war. In 1982, a journalist from *Der Spiegel* summarily identified 'German Angst' as 'the nation's consciousness' and warned that it 'blemishes the image of the Federal Republic abroad'. A Western diplomat confided in the *Boston Globe*'s Bonn correspondent that he had 'never seen a country in which the word fear sparked such joy. The Germans love to feel fear.' In 1981, *TIME* magazine ran the title 'West Germany – Moment of Angst'.[2] During the first Iraq war, German media and conservative politicians resurrected the headline in order to discredit pacifist movements. And as recently as 2017, the Free Democratic Party (FDP) ran for election under the slogan 'German Mut statt German Angst' (German courage instead of German Angst).[3]

There is no evidence, though, that Germans are actually particularly fearful or that they allow themselves to be governed by specific or abstract fears any more than other nations. In 2018, the OECD asked 22,000 people worldwide about their personal fears and worries. Germans did not respond more anxiously than the Dutch, Canadians or Israelis, and disclosed far less fear than Greeks, Poles, Portuguese and Mexicans.[4]

But the results of this survey should also be treated with caution. They suggest there is less fear in countries with a high gross national product and a generous social security system than in ones where the economy is struggling and social safety nets are full of holes. Sociological studies construct a similar hypothesis: people with sufficient material resources and a high level of education reportedly feel fear less often than those affected by unemployment, lack of education and scarcity of resources.[5] However, these indicators alone can neither explain nor predict inclinations to fear. As psychoanalysts argue, fears and insecurities are inherited or passed down from generation to generation. Experiences of violence and scarcity can produce trauma that manifests itself not only in the person directly affected but also in their children and their children's children. In particular, the Second World War – with its

[2] Jürgen Leinemann, *Die Angst der Deutschen* (Reinbek: Rowohlt, 1982), 7; 'Germans Fight the Past, Live with Their "Angst"', *Boston Globe*, 8 June 1982, 2; *Time*, no. 34, 24 August 1981. The cover story (8–18) described 'the dark mood of angst' that had descended on West Germany in the past ten months, and which had two sources: the fear of war (in the context of nuclear armament) and the worsening economic situation with rising unemployment and inflation.
[3] See the special issue, 'Angst: Eine deutsche Gefühlslage?', *Museumsmagazin* no. 3 (2018): here 9–10, 13; Frank Biess, *German Angst: Fear and Democracy in the Federal Republic of Germany* (Oxford: Oxford University Press, 2020), 334, 332.
[4] OECD, *Risks That Matter*, www.oecd.org/els/soc/Risks-That-Matter-2018-Main-Findings.pdf, accessed 12 January 2022.
[5] Katja Rackow et al., 'Angst und Ärger: Zur Relevanz emotionaler Dimensionen sozialer Ungleichheit', *Zeitschrift für Soziologie* 41, no. 5 (2012): 392–409.

unparalleled destructive force – is often identified as the cause of deep-seated fears and held responsible for the proverbial 'German Angst'.[6]

Now, the war by no means concerned only Germans. Inhabitants of the many countries that had been trampled by the Wehrmacht after 1938 and swathed in violence and terror had every reason to fear the occupying forces. If they were Jewish, they also reckoned with the fear of denunciation, persecution and deportation. Poland and the Soviet Union suffered far more casualties in total than Germany, and bombs fell not only on Hamburg and Dresden, but on Rotterdam and London too.

This counters the idea of a specifically war-related 'German Angst', as does the fact that between 1933 and 1945 Germans not only experienced different fears but also experienced fear differently. People who politically rejected the Nazi regime or did not conform to its racist and eugenicist tenets lived in constant fear of being beaten up, arrested, taken to concentration camps and murdered. Most citizens, though, did not share this experience. Instead, women feared for their conscripted sons or husbands – unless they felt like the 'nationally proud' woman who wrote to Adolf Hitler in September 1938, 'I have now been married barely a year, and if it should come to a war and I have to be separated from my husband, then I will not despair and will even be proud that my husband may fight under such a glorious Führer and general.'[7]

Fear as Paralysis

Did this woman truly have no fear? Or was she just hiding it behind strong counter-feelings like pride and confidence? Soldiers and military psychologists knew from experience that people could ward off fear using various techniques. Death, wounding and imprisonment were things better blocked out in the wartime everyday. Many had learnt to see fear as their greatest enemy – an enemy that exhausted them and weakened their powers of attack and defence. This view was widespread and could draw on scientific expertise. In 1896, Wilhelm Wundt classified fear as an affect accompanied by physical symptoms of fatigue and limpness.[8] A fatigued or limp body did not perform earth-shattering deeds; it practised avoidant behaviour and shrunk away.

In fact, 'fear' developed etymologically from the Indo-European term for being confined. The German word *Angst* is related to the Latin *angustus*, which is also translated as constriction and distress. Like Wundt, the 1892 *Brockhaus* encyclopaedia associated it with 'mixed bodily sensations' such as 'pressure in the heart area, constriction of the chest and/or the throat, strange

[6] Biess, *German Angst*, ch. 1.
[7] Federal Archive Berlin, NS 51, no. 71: anonymous, 28 September 1938.
[8] Wilhelm Wundt, *Outlines of Psychology*, trans. Charles Hubbard Judd (Leipzig: Engelmann, 1897), 173–82.

sensations in the abdomen, a feeling of general weakness, constriction of numerous arteries'. The 2006 edition specified 'a racing heart, sweating, disturbances of consciousness, thinking or reality, an increase in pulse and breathing rate', as well as feelings of exhaustion, heaviness of the limbs and tightness of the muscles. All in all, it marked a 'usually distressing, always alarming and oppressive emotional state' that occurred in reaction to a 'perceived or actual threat'.[9] It was definitely not something one yearned for, especially not when crucial institutions including family, school and the military made fear taboo and condemned it as leading to cowardice.

Male Heroism and Denial of Fear

Well into the twentieth century and to some extent beyond that, such condemnation primarily affected men who yielded to fear instead of fighting it. The positive counterpart was the hero who overcame internal anxieties and external obstacles and mustered up the courage to place himself unconditionally in the service of an idea or a mission. These heroic figures – almost all of them male – populated the stories and tales that children and adolescents were fed during the nineteenth century. Above all, men who had accomplished great military or political feats were admired, venerated and celebrated as heroes. But those who, as pioneers, discoverers, inventors or scientists, appeared free of fear and baulked at no risk in order to reach their goal – whether this was the South or North Pole, the heart of Africa, the first flight across the Atlantic or the discovery of a pathogen – could also bask in the glow of heroism.

Not everyone had the chance to follow in their footsteps. Still, every German boy was expected to play his part in furthering the greatness and glory of the nation. Personal fears were not allowed to stand in the way. There were various methods to regulate them: one underwent tests of courage that were customary among peers; one joined a student association that practised and rewarded bravery; one moulded oneself after role models as they were portrayed in schoolbooks and children's literature, as well as in films and newsreels. A role model could also be the ordinary Hitler Youth or Labour Service leader or the fellow soldier who kept calm in the greatest danger and by doing so comforted others.

Until the 1960s, boys were educated to be courageous, tough and capable of overcoming fear. 'Boys don't cry', their parents told them; so boys gritted their teeth, stifled the pain and tumbled back into the thick of battle. Fear was something for girls and 'sissies', who were looked down on with a mixture of

---

[9] *Brockhaus' Konversations-Lexikon*, 14th ed., vol. 1 (Leipzig: Brockhaus, 1892), 634; *Brockhaus Enzyklopädie*, 21st ed., vol. 2 (Leipzig: Brockhaus, 2006), 68.

scorn and magnanimity. To be ridiculed as a crybaby was a terrible insult. Conversely, a boy could prove himself a 'man' by offering weak and timid girls his protection. Their fear made his fearlessness shine all the brighter.

Traditional gender roles started to slip in the last decades of the twentieth century, but are far from fully gone. Girls and women no longer let themselves be strictly confined to shy and timorous behaviour (although, given the very real risks of male aggression, they would have every reason to do so). Many arm themselves with pepper spray, take self-defence courses and practise a self-assured, strong demeanour intended to deter attackers. Men, for their part, feel less compelled to deny fear, and instead try out softer role models. This is helped by the fact that the military, until 1945 the authoritative 'school of manhood', has lost its power to genuinely shape male behaviour.

Collective Fears: Inflation versus Unemployment

Fear, however, is not just an emotion that besets individuals at certain moments and is either allowed in or fended off. There are also deep-seated collective fears rooted in social, economic and political experiences. These are transmitted in the cultural memory and shared by broad sections of the population. Since 1945, one of them has been the fear of war and destruction. The fear of wolves is a great deal older. Anyone who grew up with *Grimms' Fairy Tales* as a child imagines wolves as gruesome predators that devour grandmothers and little girls. This explains the panicked commotion that has accompanied the return of the nearly eradicated animals since the turn of the millennium.

While wolves rank as also-rans in the German hierarchy of fears, inflation takes a leading position (Figure 17). Since the early 1920s, when the Reichsbank continually printed banknotes and repeatedly put new trillions of marks into circulation, the spectre has been haunting the country and has entrenched itself in the German imagination. An election poster from 1924 gave this spectre a face and simultaneously promised to banish it. By this time, many middle-class families had lost their savings, or rather what had been left of them after the subscription to war bonds between 1914 and 1918. People who wrote to the president during the 1920s and 1930s complained repeatedly that they were living 'in frugal circumstances' as a result of inflation, which had 'done away with their business and assets', or that they had lost 25,000 Goldmark during the war and never recovered.[10] After the Second World War and the galloping inflation that followed, the currency reform in 1948 was once again to the detriment of middle-class savers. For

---

[10] Federal Archive Berlin, NS 51, no. 51/1: Philipp Seibert, 22 April 1930; R 601, no. 378: Ms. B. Jost, 20 February 1932; ibid., no. 380: Richard Ullrich, 10 March 1932; NS 51, no. 60: Auguste Claussen, 13 December 1934.

Figure 17   The hyperinflation of 1923 was perceived as a deadly threat (Photo by Universal History Archive/Getty Images)

100 Reichsmark they received just 6.50 Deutsche Mark. Owners of material assets and stocks reported far smaller losses.

The aftermath of these dramatic experiences is alive and palpable to this day. In many families, banknotes featuring astronomical figures are passed down from generation to generation and accompanied by corresponding tales of catastrophe. This memory has also left its stamp on politics. When the financial and Euro crises put European governments in a serious predicament in 2008, the German course of austerity and combating inflation was sharply criticized by foreign experts. The American economist and Nobel Prize winner Paul Krugman accused Germans of 'this weirdly lopsided historical memory where everyone remembers 1923, everybody remembers Weimar. And nobody remembers Chancellor Brüning' – whose austerity measures had brought mass unemployment. Mario Draghi, as president of the European

Central Bank, even spoke, in 2014, of the 'perverse angst' of the Germans, who were at odds with his policy of cheap money, not least because of its feared inflationary effects.[11]

Whether perverse, excessive, misguided or not: the fear of inflation has become a driver of German economic and fiscal policy. However, contrary to Krugman's claim, the fear of unemployment has by no means disappeared from collective memory. Although in 2021, only 5.7 per cent of the total labour force were out of work, 24 per cent expressed significant fear of becoming unemployed. Any sign of a looming economic downturn sees the fear-gauge shoot swiftly upwards. The same effect is produced by the debate over digitalization and artificial intelligence, which is conducted with increasing intensity. Many people tend to regard these technological developments – just as they previously regarded the popularization of computers and automation – as 'job-killers' that fill them with fear.

The Business of Fear

Politicians are faced with a dilemma. Which fears do they prioritize? Should they, as Anglo-Saxon economists demand, make more money liquid, boost consumption and the economy and keep unemployment low, even at the risk of causing inflation? What would be the best strategy to deal with fears altogether? Address them as given and actively deflect them with fact-bound information campaigns? Or neutralize them by offering a completely different narrative of things past, present and future?

In fact, fear management became a central political task during the twentieth century, as speeches delivered by leading state officials show. Especially at Christmas and on New Year's Eve, chancellors and presidents have turned to citizens directly – since 1923 over the radio and since 1961 on television too. What they said has subsequently been printed or quoted in the newspaper and so enjoyed a broad audience. Both dates, 25 and 31 December, are ideal for a lingering glance back at the past and then forwards into the future, inviting introspection and contemplation but also messages of hope and confidence. The speeches thus offer pertinent insights into the general sentiment of the nation and reflect, in the words of the first federal president, Theodor Heuss, 'the feelings and wishes that move us all'.[12]

Among these feelings, fear was clearly prominent in the early post-war period. 'The log of German need and hardships' was, Heuss stated on New

---

[11] Martin Hesse and Thomas Schulz, 'Right Now, We Need Expansion' (interview with Paul Krugman), *Der Spiegel*, 23 May 2012, http://bit.ly/3jINVSY; 'Draghi Defends Euro Rescues Policies', *Der Spiegel*, 2 January 2014, http://bit.ly/3IhTpgT, both accessed 12 January 2022.

[12] Reinhard Kiehl, ed., *Alle Jahre wieder* (Düsseldorf: My favourite book, 2001), 39.

Year's Eve 1949, 'immeasurable' and resembled 'a chain of grey misery'. There were worries about the men being held as prisoners of war, about economic reconstruction, about refugees and expellees who had to find and make a new home, and about the high unemployment figures.[13]

But the president and his successors not only articulated the concerns brought to them in countless letters from the general public. They also chose to engage in a politics of emotion, urged patience, sought to allay fears, and kindled > hope for improvement. They explained and justified governmental decisions, solicited approval and gave the impression that they were keeping the ship of state – despite occasional lurching – on a stable course.

At times, though, they themselves operated as merchants of fear.[14] This term commonly refers to manufacturers of weapons, tasers and security technology, whose sales have rapidly increased in recent years. But it has also been used for politicians who magnify threats and in the same breath promise to quell them. Hitler's election campaigns in 1930 and 1932 aggressively played on fears of unemployment and communism. The Christian Democratic Union (CDU), founded in 1946, also enflamed fears of being overpowered by 'Bolsheviks' and contrasted this scenario with the security of being in the transatlantic alliance. When, at Christmas 1950, Chancellor Konrad Adenauer addressed the 'German people', he spoke of his concern 'that peace is under a very serious threat' and located its origin in the 'unchristian' Soviet Union.[15]

The fear of communism occupied a central place in the early years of the Federal Republic. On a CDU election poster from 1949 one saw, in true Nazi propaganda style, the red-tinted face of a man with Asian features, whose greedy hand was grasping for Germany. The same theme turned up – slightly modified – in two more CDU placards for the 1953 parliamentary election: one railed against the SPD with the slogan 'Marxism's roads all lead to Moscow', while the other showed a frightened woman with a small child who, menaced by a huge red hand with clawed fingers, begged for protection (Figure 18). In Adenauer's rhetoric, the concept of security was crucial: as late as 1965, when he had already handed over his office to Ludwig Erhard, he styled himself as a man who had, throughout his long political life, worked 'for the peace, freedom and security of our people'. Election posters concisely proclaimed: 'Our security. CDU.'

This formed a common propagandistic pattern: parties and politicians stirred up fears and portrayed themselves as guarantors who would ensure that what was feared did not become reality. Adenauer followed that very

[13] Ibid., 39–40.
[14] Christopher Catherwood and Joe Di Vanna, *The Merchants of Fear: Why They Want Us to Be Afraid* ... (Guilford: Lyons Press, 2008).
[15] Kiehl, *Alle Jahre wieder*, 44–45.

Figure 18   Politics as the business of fear: posters for the 1953 federal election (KAS/ ACDP 10-001: 414 CC-BY-SA 3.0 DE cf. http://bit.ly/3xetS1F)

pattern in the 1950s when he pushed through rearmament and compulsory military service against huge resistance. Citizens took to the streets in their hundreds of thousands to protest against policies that, in their eyes, made a new war more likely.[16] Conversely, in his 1952 Christmas address, the

---

[16] Michael Geyer, 'Cold War Angst: The Case of West-German Opposition to Rearmament and Nuclear Weapons', in *The Miracle Years: A Cultural History of West Germany, 1949–1968*, ed. Hanna Schissler (Princeton, NJ: Princeton University Press, 2001), 376–408.

chancellor warned against letting fear 'paralyze' and only passively confront-
ing the eminent 'threat from the East'. He had no desire to entertain the
pacifistic slogan 'Better red than dead'. Rather, he accused its adherents of
'cowardice' and advocated uniting against the Soviet 'barbarians' in an 'alliance for the protection of peace'.[17] This alliance was NATO, which the Federal
Republic joined in 1955.

Fears of War on Both Sides of the Wall

In the same year, the GDR government became part of the Warsaw Pact,
together with other Eastern Bloc states whose members assured one another of
'friendship, cooperation and mutual assistance' (> Fondness) against the
'imperialistic warmongers' in the West. While they allegedly made every effort
to turn the Cold War into a hot one, the GDR, President Wilhelm Pieck
declared in his 1956 New Year's Eve message, was valiantly pursuing the
'defence of the peace' and would keep the 'aggressive war bloc' at bay.[18] Two
weeks later, the government passed a law establishing the National People's
Army; compulsory military service, however, was not introduced until after
the construction of the Berlin Wall, so as not to further intensify the continued
stream of young men leaving the GDR for good.

Rearmament had triggered fears in the East as well. But unlike in the Federal
Republic, they could not be openly expressed. There was no pacifist movement, no trade union demonstrations, no press reports about local or national
protests. Instead, there were murmurs, officially dismissed as whinging and
complaining. People aired their concerns to family and friends, though some
also shared their views – anonymously or in their own names – with the
authorities. Among the letters intercepted by the Stasi were many whose
writers dismissed the official assertion that West Germany wanted war as
'totally idiotic'. As an East Berliner stated in May 1967,

> We all have a war behind us, I am truly sick of it, and millions of others
> are too. But what are you doing? Our children are again being summoned
> to the cursed army and tormented, for three long years. I had to have my
> bones shattered for Hitler, now my children are meant to shoot against
> West Germany, against their relatives.

Another letter writer criticized how, 'through the educational programmes of
kindergartens, the military training of schoolchildren and the shooting exercises of "civilian" combat groups', people were being 'systematically raised

---

[17] Kiehl, *Alle Jahre wieder*, 63–65.
[18] *Neues Deutschland*, 1 January 1956, 1.

with a militaristic way of thinking'. This, he warned, stoked fears of war and endangered peace instead of ensuring it.[19]

Many 'whingers and complainers' preferred to express their anxieties under a pseudonym, out of 'fear', as they accusingly confessed, of surveillance and reprisals. Against this background, the movement that formed in the early 1980s against rearmament, specifically against the stationing of new Soviet medium-range missiles in the GDR, appeared even more impressive. Under the roof of the Protestant Church, which in 1982 chose 'Fear – Trust – Peace' for an annual theme, young people appropriated the biblical decree 'Swords into ploughshares'. Stitching it to their clothes, they openly distanced themselves from the government and the decision to introduce military education at school. East Berlin reacted immediately and banned the symbol. Anyone who defied this rule could be expelled from school or university, or lose their apprenticeship.[20]

At the same time, the GDR supported the West German peace movement that opposed the stationing of nuclear-equipped American rockets. In his 1981 New Year's Eve address, Erich Honecker characterized the USA's policy as a 'real threat to humanity' and the preamble to a 'nuclear inferno'.[21] Anti-rearmament activists in the Federal Republic, however, were by no means oblivious to the repression experienced by pacifists east of the Elbe. In comparison, they themselves were at least able to give their fears and concerns free expression, whether in local campaigns or at central demonstrations. In 1981, 1982 and 1983 respectively, several hundred thousand people gathered in the West German capital to voice loud and distinct protest against the new nuclear arms race on their doorstep.

What united them was the fear of death by nuclear catastrophe. 'We are afraid, show your fear! Defend yourselves' was printed on pamphlets. 'Fear is in the air' sang the 150,000 participants of the 1981 Protestant Church Congress in Hamburg, which had chosen the motto 'Fear not'. A seventeen-

---

[19] Siegfried Suckut, *Volkes Stimmen: 'Ehrlich, aber deutlich' – Privatbriefe an die DDR-Regierung* (Munich: dtv, 2015), 122, 338, 411.

[20] Anke Silomon, *'Schwerter zu Pflugscharen' und die DDR* (Göttingen: Vandenhoeck & Ruprecht, 1999), esp. 132 ff., 229.

[21] *Neues Deutschland*, 31 December 1981, 1. In 1982, the chairman of the East German CDU, Gerald Götting, defamed the Peace Movement of the Youth Congregations as one of the pacifist 'attempts at division' by church circles, which aimed to 'weaken our ability to defend ourselves' (*Teurer Genosse! Briefe an Erich Honecker*, ed. Monika Deutz-Schroeder and Jochen Staadt (Berlin: Transit, 1994), 138–39). When the West German rock musician Udo Lindenberg proposed a concert in the GDR to Erich Honecker in 1987, Honecker's deputy Egon Krenz rejected the phrase 'Guitars not guns', as it would 'raise many questions for those active in the FDJ, and especially for young soldiers'. 'Nor can one overlook the textual similarity to the slogan "Swords into ploughshares"' (ibid., 97).

year-old participant frankly told Chancellor Helmut Schmidt, 'Your politics are scaring me', as he did not believe world peace could be secured through further armament.[22]

Fear as a Motive for Protest

To many, such fear appeared overstated and misguided. Schmidt, a Social Democrat known for his sober political style, emphasized the 'passionate will to reason' and in 1981 recommended it to those 'gripped with dread or fear'. Three years later, his CDU successor, Helmut Kohl, squared up against 'bleak pessimism': 'Fear has always been a bad advisor. The courage to believe in a better future grows from the strength of reconciling with the world in which we live.' Reconciliation was, though, out of the question for peace activists. From their perspective, there was nothing paralyzing about fear – quite the opposite. As an emotion that was both individual and shared, it was considered an appropriate, downright rational reaction to the threat of nuclear war. Expressing one's personal worries and concern increased the power of resistance and functioned as an emotional bridge that brought the politically heterogeneous movement together.[23]

Those who acknowledged their own fear and understood it as a strength rather than a weakness treated their emotions differently from those who cultivated habits of sober rationality and 'emotional asceticism'. The latter was the disposition sociologist Theodor Geiger had recommended in 1950 and decidedly favoured over the 'sentimental attitude'.[24] Yet what had promised relief and level-headedness after twelve years of perpetual emotionalization in the 'Third Reich' seemed morally untenable and suspect to the younger generation thirty years later. Social activists instead opted for passionate protest and shared a sentence from Gotthold Ephraim Lessing's 1772 play *Emilia Galotti*: 'he whose understanding can, unshaken, support *certain things*, has none to lose'.[25]

---

[22] Jürgen Leinemann, '"Die halten uns alle für Nicht-Menschen"', *Der Spiegel*, 22 June 1981, 24–26.

[23] Schmidt, who raised awareness of a gap in the military deterrent and called for NATO's nuclear 'upgrading', played his own part in arousing fears, but at the same time vouched for people's safety by referencing his conversations with Soviet general secretary Leonid Brezhnev and GDR head of state Erich Honecker. At their respective meetings, the 'shared experience of war' had apparently been discussed, as had the 'conviction that these horrors must never be allowed to repeat themselves'. Kiehl, *Alle Jahre wieder*, 358–59, 380; Horst-Eberhard Richter, *Zur Psychologie des Friedens* (Reinbek: Rowohlt, 1984), 78 ff.; Biess, *German Angst*, 314–30.

[24] Theodor Geiger, 'Die Legende von der Massengesellschaft', *Archiv für Rechts- und Sozialphilosophie* 39 (1950/51): 305–23.

[25] Gotthold Ephraim Lessing, *Emilia Galotti*, trans. Fanny Holcroft (Philadelphia, PA: Bradford & Inskeep, 1810), 15.

Nuclear armament, forest dieback, acid rain, nuclear power stations with their 'residual risk' demonstrated by Chernobyl in 1986 and the unresolved issue of the disposal of radioactive substances all sparked fears whose collective articulation was perceived as liberating and enacted as a political signal. 'Never again', nurse Anja Röhl said of the months following the reactor catastrophe, did she live 'so militantly as in this time'. She started a group for breastfeeding mothers that turned into 'a tremendous grassroots movement': 'There was an enormous amount of drive among us, we worked day and night on pamphlets, booklets, awareness-raising material.' In May 1986 she spoke in West Berlin at a demonstration of midwives under the slogan 'We won't be talked out of our fear!' Fear of radiation here translated into > anger, and thus felt entirely different from a fear that numbed and paralyzed the senses.

Anger took hold of Röhl at the very moment that she realized her three small children were in acute danger. She was angry at those responsible in politics and media who were downplaying the threat, spreading misinformation and promising a false sense of security.[26] Angry fear differed from powerless, helpless, despairing fear in that it mobilized people and motivated them to take action, whether alone or collectively with others who harboured the same emotions.

A similar principle is followed by the youth-led movement Fridays for Future, which has been rallying around the young Swede Greta Thunberg since 2018, and which calls attention to the climate crisis. 'I want you to panic': this is how the then sixteen-year-old shook up the high-profile attendees of the Davos World Economic Forum in January 2019. 'Adults keep saying: "We owe it to the young people to give them hope." But I don't want your hope. I don't want you to be hopeful. I want you to panic. I want you to feel the fear I feel every day, and then I want you to act. I want you to act as you would in a crisis. I want you to act as if our house is on fire. Because it is' (Figure 19).[27]

Greta Thunberg and her followers see fear as a mobilizing factor that can impel people to change their minds, alter their behaviour and halt the advance of climate change. On the opposite side stand lobbyists and those with vested interests who either ridicule this fear or disavow it as a political conspiracy. 'Après nous le déluge' (After us, the flood): in 1867 Karl Marx placed this saying in the mouths of capitalists who disregarded the future. It still applies to this day as the expression of a way of life that could not care less about its negative consequences.

---

[26] Ulrike Röhr, ed., *Frauen aktiv gegen Atomenergie – Wenn aus Wut Visionen werden: 20 Jahre Tschernobyl* (Norderstedt: Books on Demand, 2006), 33–35.

[27] Greta Thunberg, *No One Is Too Small to Make a Difference* (London: Penguin, 2019), 24; Greta Thunberg, 'Our house is on fire', *The Guardian*, 25 January 2021, http://bit.ly/3lttbz0, accessed 12 January 2022.

Figure 19   A Berlin Fridays for Future march, 29 March 2019 (Photo by Sean Gallup/
Getty Images)

Yet this way of life is not free from fear either. It knows the fear of individual
economic losses, of forfeiting the comfort that has become routine, of the
depreciation of personal assets. Juxtaposed with the wider fear scenarios of
Fridays for Future, which address and aim to include all people on the planet,
the fears of asset managers or shareholders appear utterly individualistic,
selfish and illegitimate. They therefore hide behind socially acceptable concerns and are seldom expressed openly. But they use other routes to achieve
their goals.

Fear: A Political Issue

Fear has thereby once again become a contested, controversially debated
political issue. There is a rivalry between objects of fear and subjects of fear,
between strategies of fear management and various merchants of fear. How
fear is judged and appraised is likewise disputed. The belief that fear paralyzes
and signals despair or even cowardice contends with the claim that fear is a
reaction to real dangers and mobilizes resistance. One position considers fear
menacing; the other extols it as a sign of prudence and care. Some think fear
restricts one's sense of opportunity and appetite for risk, and so limits the
future. The counter-argument is that fear opens people's eyes to what is
going wrong in society and abets a new ethics of responsibility and
political reason.

In the early 1980s, the popular canon 'Nach dieser Erde wäre da keine, die eines Menschen Wohnung wär' (After this earth there'd be none other that'd be a human's home) was sung by peace, anti-nuclear and environmental activists. Critics dismissed it as sentimental 'catastrophe verse'. Four decades later, even rational scientists join the chorus 'There is no Planet B'. Sustainability, the new guiding principle of future-oriented politics, ultimately owes its career to the multifaceted and polyvocal experience of and engagement with fear.

The Federal Republic allowed this engagement to take place, and its emotional signatures have changed as a result. Giving fear significant space and recognition meant partly valourizing it, partly containing and channelling it. As the protest against the 1983 national census or debates about data protection and public video surveillance have shown, it was and is considered legitimate to freely express one's fear of a 'deep state' that knows and observes its citizens all too closely, and to call for limits. This was not the case in the 'Third Reich'; back then, the fear of state terror prevented many from openly criticizing the regime. The GDR also used intimidation, threats and severe reprisals to silence dissidents. There, neither the peace nor the environmental movement found a public forum for their fears.

But then, in October 1989, hundreds of thousands in Leipzig and other cities defied state violence and took to the streets demanding freedom and democratic reforms. They not only ushered in the Peaceful Revolution and the end of the GDR; they also demonstrated how fear could be overcome: first individually and sporadically by participating in collective prayers for peace, then later in a veritable mass movement that could no longer be held back.[28]

Today, admitting one's fear is seen as normal and self-evident. Even men do it (now and then); hardly anyone is ashamed of it. People are regularly asked about their fears in opinion polls, talk shows and interviews. In 2019, an exhibition on *Fear – A German emotional state?* opened in the city of Leipzig. It greeted visitors with the question of which fears society will be most concerned with in the future. The options included digitalization, war, terrorism, demographic and climate change, artificial intelligence, political extremism and migration.[29] Economic anxieties were written in rather small letters or hidden behind other categories.

---

[28] Dirk Philipsen, *We Were the People: Voices from East Germany's Revolutionary Autumn of 1989* (Durham, NC: Duke University Press, 1993), 55, 63, 158, 188; Mary Fulbrook, *Anatomy of a Dictatorship: Inside the GDR 1949–1989* (Oxford: Oxford University Press, 1995), 243–65.

[29] Judith Krause, 'Angst', *Museumsmagazin* no. 1 (2020): 40–41.

COVID-19 and Competing Fears

Within a year the catalogue was completely overturned. With the COVID-19 pandemic, the long-forgotten fear of infectious diseases has made a comeback. It is true that there were isolated epidemics in the twentieth century, usually caused by influenza viruses that each killed tens of thousands of people. Except in the case of HIV/AIDS, however, vaccines were readily available, and the risk of infection remained limited. Even when the 1968 flu pandemic hit Germany with 60,000 estimated deaths, the authorities refrained from administering harsh measures of protection and prevention. Instead, they simply extended the Christmas school holidays by one week, to the joy of pupils and teachers, and imposed some restrictions on public transport.[30] Fifty years later, the federal Robert Koch Institute reacted to the arrival of the new COVID-19 virus with similar calm. But it had to rapidly revise its position. On the advice of medical experts, and learning from what other countries did or did not do, the government swiftly and drastically intervened in order to slow down the spread of infection and protect clinically vulnerable population groups. Since then, fear has been omnipresent, though people have dealt with it differently. Some reacted with panic, some with nonchalance. Younger people, whose risk of dying was low, worried less about their own health than that of their parents or grandparents.

Soon, competing fears were developing. The longer the crisis lasted, the greater became the fear of economic bottlenecks, the loss of the workplace and the closure of companies or shops. These fears sometimes bred irrational behaviour. Many citizens hoarded large amounts of toilet paper and flour without being able to explain why exactly they needed them in such quantities. Others were fearful of plummeting share prices and a looming recession. Quite a few subscribed to angst-ridden conspiracy theories featuring various actors, from international Jewry to domestic elites, from business tycoons like Bill Gates to the 'deep state'. A considerable number of Germans, motivated by fear and a lack of > trust, refused to accept the government's offer of free vaccination. Some instead turned against people they perceived as Asian and

---

[30] Malte Thießen, ed., *Infiziertes Europa: Seuchen im langen 20. Jahrhundert* (Berlin: De Gruyter, 2014); Malte Thießen, *Immunisierte Gesellschaft: Impfen in Deutschland im 19. und 20. Jahrhundert* (Göttingen: Vandenhoeck & Ruprecht, 2017); Malte Thießen, *Auf Abstand: Eine Gesellschaftsgeschichte der Coronapandemie* (Frankfurt: Campus, 2021); Malte Thießen, 'Learning for Life: From Compulsory Vaccination to Vaccination Education in 19th and 20th Century Germany', *on_education: Journal for Research and Debate* 3, no. 8 (2020), DOI: org/10.17899/on_ed.2020.8.1; Kim Yi Dionne and Fulya Felicity Turkmen, 'The Politics of Pandemic Othering: Putting COVID-19 in Global and Historical Context', *International Organization* 74, no. 1 (2020): E213–E230, DOI: 10.1017/S0020818320000405.

considered 'dangerous' because the virus emerged in China. Individuals were insulted and threatened, and in some cases even physically attacked.[31]

Everyday racism against foreigners (> Hate) has intensified – and in turn elicits fear in those targeted. Since the early 1990s, violence against men and women who come from other countries, do not have a light skin tone, or follow non-Christian religions has been happening so frequently that it spreads fear and insecurity. The racially motivated murders committed by the National Socialist Underground between 2000 and 2007 further heated the climate of fear, as did the deadly 2020 attack by a right-wing extremist on shisha bars frequented by people from migrant families. Jewish people also encounter increasing hostility and once again experience fear in Germany.

Unlike after 1933, they are not left to suffer this fear alone, but receive civic tokens of > solidarity and > empathy. Moreover, fear is no longer promulgated, as in the 'Third Reich', by the German state and its willing helpers. Rather, it originates from individuals and groups who settle on the radical fringes of society. They are, though, given ammunition by news media who speak of 'asylum seeker floods' and 'gluts', of 'refugee streams' and 'waves' that, like a natural disaster, threaten to overrun the country.[32]

From 2015 onwards, such fear-stoking scenarios have found a political home in the far-right AfD and have brought the party many voters. The fear of 'being overrun with foreigners' (*Überfremdung*) and the concept of the 'Great Replacement' (*Umvolkung*), which is allegedly causing Germans to lose their language and culture, are key here. The new merchants of fear play their part perfectly: they seize on traditional fears of foreignness, strengthen them and give them a direction that suits their backward-looking agenda of ethnic nationalism. The fact that by doing so they also echo and offer legitimacy to those who commit acts of violence is something they willingly accept – consequences be damned.

---

[31] *Tagesspiegel*, 18 April 2020, 3.
[32] *Bild*'s headline from 2 April 1992 read 'The flood rises – when will the boat sink?'; Jan Plamper, *We Are All Migrants: A History of Multicultural Germany* (Cambridge: Cambridge University Press, 2023), 124.

Fondness

On 11 November 2018, a press photographer captured a special moment: the German chancellor and the president of France, both clad in black, standing cheek to cheek and holding hands in a close embrace. The highly symbolic moment unfolded at a site steeped in history: the northern French town of Compiègne, where military officers and politicians signed the armistice between Germany, France and Britain exactly one hundred years before. In 1918, the demeanour of the participants was ice cold. In 2018, Angela Merkel and Emmanuel Macron were smiling, their body language conveying their mutual fondness (Figure 20).

Whether they actually liked each other or found one another's company pleasant was beside the point. What was important was the public signal their comportment sent: friendship, not enmity, had prevailed. Two newly erected stone plaques in both languages emphasized the 'importance of Franco-German reconciliation in the service of Europe and of peace'. French memorials from the 1920s, in contrast, had depicted a German eagle pierced through with a sword and stated that here 'the criminal pride of the German Empire was vanquished by the free peoples it had sought to enslave'. In June 1940 in the same spot, Hitler had dictated the conditions of surrender to the French and had the obnoxious 'Memorial of Triumph', as he called it, covered in the regime's war flag.[1]

Plans for Europe after 1918

There were few steps towards rapprochement between Germany and France following the First World War. The traces of the battles waged over more than four years were omnipresent in vast military cemeteries and in the form of the millions injured in the war with their missing limbs, their scars and their shell shock. In France the land itself was badly maimed; it still shows to this day. Individuals did endeavour to build bridges and break the ice, especially among

---

[1] http://bit.ly/3XrmI4W, accessed 15 February 2022; Joseph Goebbels, *Die Tagebücher*, ed. Elke Fröhlich, part 1, vol. 4 (Munich: Saur, 1987), 213.

Figure 20   Angela Merkel and Emmanuel Macron in Compiègne, November 2018
(Photo by Philippe Wojazer/Pool/AFP via Getty Images)

the young. Propagandistically, however, the war carried on for domestic
political purposes. In Germany, collective outrage over the 'disgrace' of
Versailles, the 'black horror' of the Rhineland occupation and the Ruhr crisis
drowned out tensions between the polarized political camps. French politicians likewise sought to forge a national alliance over the fallen soldiers (>
Humility). War memorials and annual armistice parades ensured that the
memory of the German 'barbarians' remained fresh and roused the divided
nation to close ranks.

Only gradually did the two nations inch nearer. In 1925, Germany, France
and Belgium signed bilateral arbitration conventions in Locarno, Switzerland,
guaranteeing the inviolability of each country's borders. The French foreign
minister Aristide Briand and his German counterpart, Gustav Stresemann,
were awarded the Nobel Peace Prize in 1926 for their efforts. The same year,
Germany joined the League of Nations, which had been founded in 1920, and
German delegations were welcomed at international conferences and conventions once more. The first talks were held between the German and French
agencies that managed millions of war graves. Eventually, the German side was
given a say in how their military cemeteries in France were designed and
maintained and which symbols should be displayed there (> Grief).

Briand and Stresemann were both freemasons, which may have made it
easier for them to find common ground amid the graves and trenches.

Admittedly, the two foreign ministers were acting first and foremost in the interests of their countries, which had until recently been enemies and were still distrustful of one another. And yet they shared the belief that France and Germany would benefit from a lasting European peace and should actively work to bring it about. Both men were sympathetic to the pan-European movement spearheaded by Austrian Count Richard Coudenhove-Kalergi in the early 1920s, with Briand serving as the movement's honorary president. Stresemann likewise supported the idea of European integration. In 1929, Briand stood in front of the League of Nations and introduced the notion of a 'federal bond' between the states of Europe. What he had in mind was not the – at the time unthinkable – surrender or constraint of political sovereignty, but rather a customs and economic union.

During their frequent meetings, which began in 1925, the ministers came to know each other well. As interpreter Paul Schmidt observed, they developed 'an intimate personal feeling'; even when they disagreed, there was an atmosphere of familiarity, friendliness and fondness surrounding their discussions. When Stresemann died unexpectedly in 1929, Briand went immediately to the German embassy and expressed 'very warm human sympathy'. According to Harry Graf Kessler, 'all the Paris morning papers publish the news of Stresemann's death in the most prominent make-up. It is almost as if an outstanding French statesman had died, the grief is so general and sincere. I feel indeed as if there already were one European fatherland. The French feel Stresemann to have been a sort of European Bismarck.'[2]

Politically, though, international relations were stumbling rather than racing towards a United States of Europe. Vastly more successful were the exchange and collaboration in the art and music scenes. In the Golden Twenties, ideas, styles and people circulated between Paris, Berlin, Barcelona and Moscow with tremendous vitality and at breathtaking speed. Dadaism, a movement founded in Zurich in 1916 by German, Romanian and French artists, inspired an international following, as did Surrealism and the New Objectivity movement. At the Bauhaus schools in Weimar and Dessau, women and men from several nations worked together on collaborative projects. Many were best friends and lovers. Modernist architects also maintained close contacts in the scene. After 1933, these connections were helpful to those who had to leave Germany for political or racial reasons.

[2] Paul Schmidt, *Statist auf diplomatischer Bühne 1923–45* (Bonn: Athenäum-Verlag, 1953), 80–92, 119–20, 123–27, 143–44, 163, 182–84, quote 190; *Harry Graf Kessler, Tagebücher 1918–1937*, ed. Wolfgang Pfeiffer-Belli (Frankfurt: Insel-Verlag, 1982), 629, see also *Berlin in Lights: The Diaries of Count Harry Kessler (1918–1937)*, trans. and ed. Charles Kessler (New York: Grove Press, 2000), 368.

Italo-German Brotherhood in Arms

When the National Socialists took power, the visionary plans for Europe were off the table. Germany left the League of Nations in 1933; fascist Italy followed four years later. The two countries intensified their bilateral relations, with the initiative coming from Berlin. Ever since Benito Mussolini's March on Rome in 1922, Hitler had revered, envied and admired the fascist leader, and he tried to meet 'Il Duce' on several occasions. Mussolini's disinterest only abated after Hitler was installed as chancellor and formed his own dictatorship. In early June 1933, Propaganda Minister Goebbels was given a reception in Rome and was charmed: 'we clicked immediately', he wrote, 'and we talk for an hour, about everything', then 'we part as friends'. Although Mussolini was small in stature, for Goebbels he towered 'quite lonely at the top. A Caesar', whose farewell message was well received: 'Tell Hitler that he can rely on me. I'll stand by him through thick and thin.'[3]

Less than a year later, the two caesars met for the first time. Hitler had asked his idol 'with the expression of the greatest admiration' for a face-to-face meeting, even if only a private one. When he landed in Venice in June 1934, Mussolini was waiting for him in full regalia. But rather than offering a fascist salute, Mussolini shook Hitler's hand, without even removing his glove. To keep his distance, the Duce had his guest put up like a tourist in the Grand Hotel, while he himself stayed in a remote aristocratic palace. Nevertheless, Hitler was deeply impressed, not so much by the cultural programme of Verdi and Wagner as by the parade of 70,000 Blackshirts on Piazza San Marco. There, he later raved, Mussolini had forged 'the closest connection', by making several references to 'Hitler ed io' (Hitler and I) in an address to the fascist troops and subsequently calling him 'comrade'. In any case, the chancellor returned to Berlin 'enthusiastic' and 'happy'. 'Men like Mussolini', he confided to an Italian interlocutor, 'are born only once every thousand years, and Germany can be glad that he is Italian and not French.'

As Hitler saw it, Germany was bound to France by an 'implacable mortal enmity'. He had therefore strenuously attacked Stresemann's policy of concili-ation. Italy, on the other hand, he considered a natural ally because its imperial interests did not overlap with Germany's. This was another reason why the German Führer treated his Italian comrade with the greatest deference. Even when the balance of power shifted and Hitler went from being an imitator to a mastermind in his own right, he left no doubt about his genuine fondness for Mussolini.[4]

---

[3] Goebbels, *Tagebücher*, part 1, vol. 2, 1987, 426–27.

[4] Wolfgang Schieder, *Adolf Hitler: Politischer Zauberlehrling Mussolinis* (Berlin: De Gruyter, 2017), quotes 64, 74–77, 36, 41; Christian Goeschel, *Mussolini and Hitler: The Forging of the Fascist Alliance* (New Haven, CT: Yale University Press, 2018), esp. 45–53.

The – largely one-sided – friendship played out on several levels. First, it was of a personal nature; Hitler felt 'a bond between us on the purely human level', as he confessed privately and publicly, and had 'a deep friendship for this extraordinary man'. In 1938 he called Mussolini the 'leader of the great Fascist state, who is a close personal friend of mine'; in 1940, he said he was happy 'that I myself have the honour to be a friend of this man', whose life 'bears evidence of as many similarities to my own as our two revolutions do to each other'. Their relationship thus went beyond the personal or human level to encompass, second, the political movements the two men had brought into being. National Socialism, Hitler emphasized in his governmental declaration in 1934, had 'consistently' cultivated 'the almost traditional friendship to Fascist Italy' and paid 'high esteem' to the 'great leader of that people'. With 'pleasure' the chancellor announced – this was the third level – that the friendship had now 'been further and variously reinforced in the relations between the two States'. Not just states and governments but people and populations harboured friendly feelings for each other. 'For us Germans', Hitler confirmed in 1938, the friendship was 'indissoluble' and 'the land and borders of this friend inviolable'.[5]

That was certainly not true of other borders, and the 'Third Reich' had no other friends. It approached its Axis partner Japan with racist conceit, even though the East Asian ally proved far more reliable and successful in military terms than Italy. The 'brotherhood of arms' that Germany had forged with Italy in 1939 and immortalized on a postage stamp in 1941 ('two nations and one struggle'), did operate with some reservations. Still, the alliance held, and Hitler saved Mussolini's neck in 1943 when the king, with the support of the fascist Grand Council, removed his prime ministership.

European Friendships

By 1938 it was all too clear that Hitler had his own plans for Europe and lacked neither the will nor the power to implement them ruthlessly. His justification was that he wanted to protect Europe from the 'global threat' of Bolshevism. Nazi propaganda gladly adopted the Catholic-Francoist imagery of a 'crusade' that the Christian Occident had to wage against the godless Soviet Union. This idea was welcomed by small fascist parties in Western and Northern Europe, who recruited volunteers for the crusade and developed bold schemes for a League of Germanic Nations or a Pan-Nordic Federation. For its part, the

---

[5] *Hitler's Table Talk 1941–1944*, intro. H. R. Trevor Roper (London: Phoenix Press, 2000), 267; Max Domarus, ed., *Speeches and Proclamations 1932–1945*, vol. 2: *The Years 1935 to 1938* (London: Tauris & Co., 1990), 1066; vol. 3: *The Years 1939 to 1940*, 2057; vol. 1: *The Years 1932 to 1934*, 427. After the annexation of Austria into Nazi Germany in 1938 it shared a – previously disputed – border with Italy at the Brenner Pass.

Foreign Office also promoted a new solution to the 'European question', drawing up guiding principles in 1943 for a European confederation. As a 'community of sovereign states', albeit under the 'supremacy' of the Greater German Empire, it was to position the continent against England and 'Bolshevism'. 'When this war is over', Goebbels declared in 1940, 'we want to be masters of Europe.'[6]

Alternative models came out of the resistance movement. The Munich-based student group White Rose wanted to forge a 'new Europe of the spirit'. Some called for a European commonwealth 'in which neither Germany nor any other power would claim predominance' and 'internal boundaries would play a less and less important part'. Their goal was a novel 'European consciousness' that alone could 'sustain peace'.[7]

This consciousness was most likely to be formed by those who cultivated personal ties with people from other countries. Helmuth James von Moltke, for example, who was executed by the Nazis in January 1945, was a close friend of Lionel Curtis, with whom he stayed in the mid-1930s while studying for his barrister's examinations in London and Oxford. Curtis introduced Moltke to British debates about a new European order. Both were united by the 'European creed' and the question of how, in post-war Europe, 'the picture of man' could 'be reestablished in the breasts of our fellow-citizens'.[8] Adam von Trott zu Solz, who was likewise sentenced to death for resistance activities, had kept in touch with friends that he had made as a student in Oxford in the early 1930s. Acquainted with the USA through an American grandmother, he used his familial connection to publicize the ideas and plans of the German resistance in the Anglosphere.

Friendships that extended across borders were not just the privilege and domain of noble and well-educated elites. International networks also developed in German concentration camps. Some lasted a lifetime, others long enough to adopt joint declarations and appeals. The *Buchenwald Manifesto*, delivered five days after the camp's liberation and signed by a group of Germans, Austrians, Belgians, Dutch and Czechs, outlined a vision

---

[6] Wolfgang Michalka, ed., *Das Dritte Reich*, vol. 2 (Munich: dtv, 1985), 116–57; Ian Dear, ed., *Oxford Companion to World War II* (Oxford: Oxford University Press, 2001), quote (Goebbels) 367.

[7] Sixth White Rose leaflet, www.holocaustresearchproject.org/revolt/wrleaflets.html, accessed 1 February 2022; Carl Goerdeler, 'Peace Plan', in *Documents on the History of European Integration*, vol. 1: *Continental Plans for European Union 1939–1945*, ed. Walter Lipgens (Berlin: De Gruyter, 1985), 430–32, quote 431; Hermann Brill, *Gegen den Strom* [1946] (Erfurt: FES, 1995), 100.

[8] Michael Balfour and Julian Frisby, *Helmuth von Moltke: A Leader against Hitler* (London: Macmillan, 1972), 185.

of a 'European community of states' and a 'new type of German European' in whose spirit a 'new atmosphere of > trust in Germany' would be established.[9]

Post-War Distances

Trust was an unfamiliar word in 1945. The German populace, fed hateful propaganda until the very last, began to encounter occupying Allied forces who, for their part, had every reason to mistrust the Germans and keep them at arm's length. In November 1944, the British Foreign Office published instructions for the 400,000 soldiers who would soon find themselves stepping onto enemy territory. The guidelines were meant to protect them from brutality but also 'sentimentality' and 'softness'. Instead of being 'taken in by surface resemblances between the Germans and ourselves', succumbing to the inhabitants' tales of misery and the female powers of seduction, servicemen should always be aware that they would not be in Germany 'at all if German crimes had not made this war inevitable'. 'Fraternisation' and marriage were strictly forbidden; similar rules applied in the American military.[10]

On the Soviet side there was no need for an official ban. In newspapers and daily orders from the front, soldiers were exhorted to take revenge on the Germans who had devastated their country for nearly four years, torturing and killing millions of people. 'Remember', read the last message from the Main Political Directorate before the Red Army crossed the border into East Prussia, 'your friends are not there, there is the next of kin of the killers and oppressors'. The soldiers did remember, and women in particular were made to feel their > anger and > hate through sexual violence. On 5 June 1945, Soviet Lieutenant General Vasily Sokolovskii told a British journalist, 'But what do you expect? ... In the first flush of victory our fellows no doubt derived a certain satisfaction from making it hot for those Herrenvolk women. However, that stage is over.'[11]

But only once the Red Army soldiers were finally housed in barracks in 1947 did the sexual assaults cease. Simultaneously, the Soviet military administration began to ease relations between the occupying forces and the populace. To do so, it enlisted the help of returning German communist émigrés, who

---

[9] Brill, *Gegen den Strom*, 96–101, quotes 100; Wolfgang Röll, *Sozialdemokraten im Konzentrationslager Buchenwald 1937–1945* (Göttingen: Wallstein, 2000), 245–60.

[10] *Instructions for British Servicemen in Germany 1944*. First published by the Foreign Office, 1943 (Oxford: Bodleian Library, 2007), 5, 6, 8, 52; Hajo Holborn, *American Military Government: Its Organization and Policies* (Washington, DC: Infantry Journal Press, 1947), 136: 'You will strongly discourage fraternization between Allied troops and the German officials and population' (directive, 28 April 1944).

[11] Norman M. Naimark, *The Russians in Germany: A History of the Soviet Zone of Occupation, 1945–1949* (Cambridge, MA: Belknap Press of Harvard University Press, 1995), 69–140, quotes 72, 79.

proved eager to participate in the formation of a socialist state. Historian Jürgen Kuczynski was tasked with breathing life into the 'idea of friendship with the Soviet Union' and countering the 'stream of prejudices'. Together with novelist Anna Seghers, he presided over the Society for the Study of Soviet Culture, founded in 1947, which two years later became the Society for German-Soviet Friendship (DSF). Initially a purely 'intellectual movement', it developed over time into the second-largest organization in the GDR, numbering 6.4 million members in 1989.[12]

The DSF's aim was to educate East Germans about the 'successes of the Soviet Union' and to stoke goodwill towards it. Under the motto 'Friends always', Kuczynski described the USSR as a 'culture of the most advanced thoughts and the most noble feelings'. Even former National Socialists were encouraged to join the 'friendship movement'.

The relationship was facilitated by the political rhetoric of exoneration. When Stalin telegraphed his congratulations upon the GDR's founding in October 1949, he offered to put the hostile past to rest and to restart on friendly terms. After all, he said, the 'German and Soviet peoples', who had 'made the greatest sacrifices' in the last war, possessed 'the greatest potential in Europe for accomplishing great actions of global significance'. If the Germans loyally sided with the Soviet Union, they would secure 'peace in Europe' and could, the subtext was, be absolved of their war guilt. To ensure that this message was not forgotten, 'good artistic and pedagogical duplicates' of the telegram were hung in every DSF clubhouse.[13]

German–Soviet Friendship

Whether and how many people in the GDR actually had any fondness for the Soviet Union is difficult to say. Quite a few took a very critical view of the proclaimed 'love for our friends'. One man from Leipzig, in a letter to the government in 1971 with his signature and return address, felt that things were going too far if Germany had to 'write off the entire eastern territories and, on top of that, constantly make reparations in the form of economic integration or uneconomic exports to the friendly nations'. Another Leipzig resident complained about a new university building designed in the Moscow style: 'We are indeed the 21st Russian province'. When a crane operator publicly reported in 1971 that every member of his work brigade had joined

---

[12] Jürgen Kuczynski, 'Die Durchsetzung der Freundschaftsidee zur Sowjetunion in unserem Volke', *Beiträge zur Geschichte der Arbeiterbewegung* 21 (1979): 678–81. The largest GDR organization was the Free German Trade Union Confederation (FDGB) with 9.6 million members in 1986.

[13] Jan C. Behrends, *Die erfundene Freundschaft: Propaganda für die Sowjetunion in Polen und in der DDR* (Cologne: Böhlau, 2006), quotes 163, 200.

the DSF in order to improve their chances in the nation-wide 'socialist competition', many protested: 'It is incomprehensible to us that Germans humiliate themselves so much and call themselves friends of the Soviet Union. Have you already forgotten how the Russian beasts (surely they cannot be called people) conducted themselves when they moved in in May 1945?'[14]

The letter of protest that spoke on behalf of 'very many honest and upright German men' was airing a political resentment that could be traced directly back to Nazi propaganda about 'Bolshevik hordes'. But then why did the DSF have millions of members, almost three times as many as the SED? Partly because, as in the case of the crane operator's brigade, the call to join was more or less mandatory. Furthermore, membership of the DSF provided an easy and convenient way to express loyalty without having to belong to the party. 'What is German–Soviet friendship?' the popular actor Manfred Krug asked himself in 1977, shortly before departing for the Federal Republic. 'A badge on the jacket, nothing more.' 'The friendship of socialist countries', he explained, 'is merely the friendship of their anxious governments', who did everything to limit and control their citizens' contact with people in other socialist countries. The privilege of taking a longer 'look behind the wall, even in the eastern direction' was granted to only a select few.[15]

Those who were able to travel included students who were either exceptionally gifted or particularly loyal to the party line, as well as cultural representatives and party functionaries. In 1964, the thirty-year-old author Brigitte Reimann, tasked with writing a report about the experience, chaperoned a delegation to Moscow, Kazakhstan and Siberia. She was overwhelmed by the size of the country and the friendliness of its inhabitants. The Komsomols especially, members of the Soviet Union's youth organization, greeted the Germans with 'the kind of warmth by no means everyone has for guests'. Reimann experienced 'a sense of shame, as if I hadn't earned it – and how could we? Only by showing such warm feelings to them in return' (> Shame). She felt admiration and closeness as she was 'accepted, taken to the bosom of this amazing land'. 'A whole load' of the German delegates, particularly those more advanced in age, thoroughly annoyed her however: 'They are stupid and crude and lose any dignity they might possess as soon as they drink. They turn every gathering into a German beer binge, tell dirty jokes and sing silly songs.' Evidently, the young writer, who often clashed with the official party line, took the German–Soviet friendship far more seriously than the conformist functionaries of the Free German Youth (FDJ).[16]

---

[14] Siegfried Suckut, *Volkes Stimmen: 'Ehrlich, aber deutlich' – Privatbriefe an die DDR-Regierung* (Munich: dtv, 2015), 152, 160, 164–65.

[15] Manfred Krug, *Abgehauen* (Düsseldorf: Econ, 1998), 204.

[16] Brigitte Reimann, *It All Tastes of Farewell: Diaries, 1964–1970*, ed. Angela Drescher, trans. Steph Morris (London: Seagull, 2021), 53 ff., quotes 57, 63, 75, 70.

Reimann, who was repeatedly admonished and criticized for her insufficient 'partisanship', found such loud and self-centred behaviour difficult to bear. She also harboured doubts about the FDJ's general comportment. Like Christa Wolf, the author four years her elder, Reimann, born in 1933, was ashamed of her own 'inglorious past – marching, kerchief, strident instructions'. The sight of Young Pioneers gave her déja vu: 'Jesus, yes, our generation is scarred; we can't bear this kind of thing anymore, damn it.' As a way of leaving the Nazi past behind, she clung enthusiastically to the new notion of friendship among nations and peoples. When she attended the SED's party congress in 1963, she was thrilled by a report on cooperation with other socialist states: 'Here was a glimpse of the world of tomorrow, a united, peaceful world.' She felt 'stirred and moved' when the congress greeted the representatives of 'fraternal parties': 'Seventy countries and their delegates came to us, and the world sat watching, the world that will clearly become communist some day.' This was more than > pride in the lauded 'achievements' of the GDR, more than simple > solidarity with socialist 'brothers and sisters'. Reimann's pathos evoked an overflowing, almost oceanic sense of connection and > belonging to a large, globe-spanning political community.[17]

She did not mention, though, how she felt about the 'fraternal kiss' between party and state leaders of socialist countries. This gesture to express fondness, sympathy and attachment was first practised in the 1960s, and Soviet leaders set the benchmark. While they merely exchanged limp handshakes with delegates from Western countries, representatives of 'fraternal states' received a hug and several kisses. Under Nikita Khrushchev, this form of greeting seemed spontaneous and openhearted. By the time Leonid Brezhnev visited East Berlin in 1973, his three cheek kisses for Erich Honecker had become more ceremonial (Figure 21). They were accompanied by the invocation of 'unshakable brotherhood', 'fraternal friendship' and other incantations rendered meaningless through constant repetition.[18]

In 1981, a GDR citizen writing pseudonymously (not wanting 'a political suicide') aired his objections to such gestures. He stressed that his criticism was intended to be constructive and that he did not want to cast doubt on the historical achievements of the Soviet Union: 'Learning from the SU means learning victory. No communist will doubt that.' Nevertheless, he wrote, it was by no means necessary to adopt 'all the national peculiarities of the Soviet people': 'Must we copy the repugnant kissing between men that was common here only

---

[17] Brigitte Reimann, *I Have No Regrets: Diaries, 1955–1963*, trans. Lucy Jones (London: Seagull Books, 2019), 315.

[18] Dmitri Zakharine, 'Tactile Channels: Brotherly Kisses, Handshakes, and Flogging in a Bathhouse', in *Media and Communication in the Soviet Union (1917–1953): General Perspectives*, ed. Kirill Postoutenko et al. (Cham: Palgrave Macmillan 2022), 121–35, here 126–29; Carola Stern, 'Bruderkuß für Walter Ulbricht', *Die Zeit*, 25 January 1963.

Figure 21 Fraternal kiss between Leonid Brezhnev and Erich Honecker, 4 October 1979 (Photo by Régis BOSSU/Sygma via Getty Images)

among homosexuals or possibly still between family members? Isn't it enough for statesmen or officials to offer a firm and friendly handshake?' Seven years later, as the winds of change were blowing through the Soviet Union, physician Peter S. appealed to Erich Honecker. He also asked, 'as a friend and not as a foe', why the GDR had made it a policy to never utter a critical word against the Communist Party of the Soviet Union: 'What kind of friendship is this, in which there is only praise and adulation and no criticism?' For decades, 'brotherhood with the Soviet Union has been presented as one of the decisive historical pillars of socialism in our country'. But, he pressed on, should the slogan heard 'countless times in schools and universities' not be taken seriously at this very moment? Was it not time to learn from the self-criticism of the Soviet press and drop one's own 'uncritical acclamation'? Rather than answering, Honecker forwarded the letter to Erich Mielke, the all-powerful minister for state security.[19]

Rapprochement in the West

International friendship, as an emotional theme and practice, was also heralded in the West, though it suffered a rockier start there. When the war

[19] Suckut, *Volkes Stimmen*, 307; *Teurer Genosse! Briefe an Erich Honecker*, ed. Monika Deutz-Schroeder and Jochen Staadt (Berlin: Transit, 1994), 87–89.

ended, the moral 'abyss' between Germans 'and other peoples' was there for all to see, as Hannah Arendt wrote in 1948.[20] It further deepened with the Nuremberg trials, which were held before the International Military Tribunal and American military courts beginning in November 1945. Hundreds of journalists and radio reporters from all over the world had been accredited, and they made public detailed information about the crimes that leading Nazi representatives, ministers and military officers as well as doctors, lawyers, policemen and industrialists had committed in the countries Germany occupied between 1939 and 1945.

The first West German government was aware of the debt with which it was starting out. The Allies were not willing to grant it blanket relief, as Stalin had offered the GDR. In his New Year's Eve address in 1949, President Heuss therefore stressed the importance of 'talking with the occupying powers'. Only the increase of 'mutual > trust' could strengthen and vitalize democratic development. Four years later, he praised Chancellor Adenauer, who with 'sobriety and imagination' had succeeded in transforming Germany's image among 'statesmen, and also, emotionally, among nations', who had formerly treated the country with 'disdain'. Adenauer himself was more sceptical. As he explained to his cabinet colleagues in 1952: 'We have to be clear about this: the mood abroad towards us, especially of those countries which were directly at war with us (not the Americans), is still far from what we would like it to be. People have by no means forgotten German terror, they have not forgotten the atrocities of National Socialism, which are very much alive outside the country. They are also afraid of German efficiency once more, having seen how the German people, after all these years, have unexpectedly bounced back economically. They fear and fret about the good qualities of the German people.'[21]

Such fear, aversion and mistrust were particularly stark in France. It was no coincidence that, from day one, West German policy placed particular emphasis on 'clearing away the debris of history that lies between the German and French peoples'. The 'proper and perceptive settlement of Franco-German relations', Heuss stressed over and over again, was 'the central challenge' for the development of a 'European consciousness'. His greatest hope lay with the youth on both sides of the Rhine (Figure 22).[22] Indeed, many young people back then were engaged in federalist movements. In 1950, three hundred students from Germany, France and other countries dismantled barriers at the Franco-German border, calling for a European parliament

[20] Hannah Arendt, *Wahrheit gibt es nur zu zweien: Briefe an die Freunde*, ed. Ingeborg Nordmann (Munich: Piper, 2013), 79.

[21] Reinhard Kiehl, ed., *Alle Jahre wieder* (Düsseldorf: My favourite book, 2001), 41, 77; *Die Kabinettsprotokolle der Bundesregierung*, vol. 5: 1952 (Boppard: Boldt, 1989), 276.

[22] Kiehl, *Alle Jahre wieder*, 41, 77.

Figure 22   Torchlight procession for the idea of Europe: young people at the Franco-German border crossing, 12 January 1952 (Photo by ullstein bild/ullstein bild via Getty Images)

and government. They concluded their surprise action by dancing in front of flabbergasted customs officers.[23]

Negotiations at the governmental level were less jubilant. The first step towards an inter-European organization came with the French foreign minister Robert Schuman's 1950 proposal for a European Coal and Steel Community (ECSC). The proposal took up Briand's plan from 1929 and the groundwork laid by Jean Monnet, the man responsible for modernizing the French economy. Under the plan, Germany and France would cede control over their coal and steel production to an authority tasked with setting maximum prices and production quotas, approving mergers and distributing raw materials in the event of a crisis. This created a common coal and steel market, which Italy and the Benelux countries also joined.

In 1952, the High Authority of the ECSC began its work in Luxemburg, with Monnet as its inaugural president. It was the first supranational West

---

[23] Christina Norwig, *Die erste europäische Generation: Europakonstruktionen in der Europäischen Jugendkampagne 1951–1958* (Göttingen: Wallstein, 2016), 71–81; Richard Ivan Jobs, *Backpack Ambassadors: How Youth Travel Integrated Europe* (Chicago, IL: University of Chicago Press, 2017), 41–42.

European institution and marked the beginning of a process of unification that would gather steam in the years to come, despite some domestic opposition and delay tactics. In 1957 the Treaties of Rome established the European Economic Community, which in 1992 in Maastricht, the Netherlands, became the European Union, an entity with a stronger capacity for political action. In 2004, ten Eastern and Central European states joined the EU; Romania and Bulgaria followed in 2007. Since 2002, citizens of the Eurozone have shared a common currency. There is a European parliament in Strasbourg and a European commission in Brussels, just as the border-crossing students in 1950 demanded. Though its members might not dance together, they do exchange hugs and kisses, albeit with less ceremony than in former socialist states.

Franco-German Friendship

The first public kiss between the complicated neighbours occurred in 1963 at the Élysée Palace in Paris, where President Charles de Gaulle and Chancellor Konrad Adenauer were signing an agreement on Franco-German cooperation. Afterwards, de Gaulle extended his arms, pulled Adenauer towards him and kissed him on each cheek. Bavarian radio called this a 'fraternal kiss'.[24] Adenauer was clearly surprised by the gesture, hesitating a little before accepting the hug and pursing his own lips. Such exuberance and closeness before the cameras were unfamiliar to the eighty-seven-year-old German. The pair, who were almost twenty-five years apart in age, had only ever been photographed shaking hands during previous encounters.

Nonetheless, over the course of their numerous meetings, which sometimes took place in their respective homes, the two statesmen did grow closer.[25] In 1962, they attended a Franco-German military parade on the battlefields of the First World War and then, visibly moved, prayed in the restored Reims Cathedral, which had been destroyed by German shells forty-eight years earlier. There was much that united them: both had lived through the First World War and the Second as well, one as a soldier, the other as a civilian; both were devoted Catholics and anti-communists. Yet they held different ideas about the future of Europe and the role of their own countries

---

[24] http://bit.ly/3Xybr2U, accessed 1 February 2022. See also Corine Defrance, 'The Elysée Treaty in the Context of Franco-German Social-Cultural Relations', *German Politics and Society* 31, no. 1 (2013): 70–91.

[25] Ronald Granieri, 'More Than a Geriatric Romance: Adenauer, de Gaulle, and the Atlantic Alliance', in *A History of Franco-German Relations in Europa: From 'Hereditary Enemies' to Partners*, ed. Carine Germond and Henning Türk (New York: Palgrave Macmillan, 2008), 189–98.

in it. This became apparent soon after the signing of the 1963 'Friendship Treaty'.[26]

Nevertheless, it marked an important new beginning. The treaty not only established regular meetings and consultations between governments and authorities, especially around issues of defence and education; it also raised the prospect of forming an organization that would 'facilitate the encounter and exchange of pupils, students, junior craftsmen and workers'. Young people in particular, the Joint Declaration of 1963 stated, had become conscious of the > solidarity between the two peoples, which was why they had 'a decisive role to play in consolidating Franco-German friendship'. In this spirit, the Franco-German Institute, founded in Ludwigsburg in 1948, soon started to arrange homestay visits for German and French adolescents. Similar initiatives took place in Britain and the USA. Spending time in a London household in 1953, student Karl Heinz Bohrer became acquainted with British institutions, lifestyle and that 'untranslatable English quality: kindness'. He was not alone in finding the experience life-changing: 'It moved him to his core.'[27]

Unlike in the 1920s, cross-border efforts like this gained official support and financial backing after the Second World War. In 1962, de Gaulle gave an enthusiastically received speech to young people in Ludwigsburg, inviting them 'to get closer and closer to each other, and to knit tighter bonds' between 'you and us'. Since its founding in 1963, the Franco-German Youth Office has connected some nine million German and French children, adolescents and young adults. In 2017, nearly 200,000 took part in exchange programmes that now include countries in Central, Eastern and South-Eastern Europe.[28]

Meanwhile the German-Polish Youth Office, established in 1991, reaches some 100,000 youngsters each year through its events. As early as 1966, the

---

[26] Konrad Adenauer, *Erinnerungen 1955–1959* (Stuttgart: DVA, 1967), 424 ff.; Charles de Gaulle, *Memoirs of Hope: Renewal and Endeavor*, trans. Terence Kilmartin (New York: Simon & Schuster, 1971), 173–81; Hans-Peter Schwarz, *Konrad Adenauer: German Politician and Statesman in a Period of War, Revolution and Reconstruction*, vol 2: *The Statesman, 1952–1967* (Providence: Berghahn, 1997), 354 ff. See also Ulrich Lappenküper, 'On the Path to "Hereditary Friendship"? Franco-German Relations since the End of the Second World War', in *History of Franco-German Relations*, ed. Germond and Türk, 151–64; Péter Krisztián Zachar, 'From "Grandeur" to "Sécurité" and "a Special Relationship": The Shift in the French-German Relations in a Historical Perspective', *Prague Papers on the History of International Relations* 2 (2018): 112–35.

[27] Karl Heinz Bohrer, *Granatsplitter: Erzählung einer Jugend* (Munich: Hanser, 2012), 279 ff., quote 284.

[28] Ulrich Krotz and Joachim Schild, *Shaping Europe: France, Germany, and Embedded Bilateralism from the Elysée Treaty to Twenty-First Century Politics* (Oxford: Oxford University Press, 2013), esp. 75–112, quote 86; Ansbert Baumann, *Begegnung der Völker? Der Elysée-Vertrag und die Bundesrepublik Deutschland* (Frankfurt: Lang, 2003); Corine Defrance and Ulrich Pfeil, *50 Jahre Deutsch-Französisches Jugendwerk* (Paris: DFJ, 2013); http://bit.ly/3YrNICH, accessed 15 February 2022.

West German government announced its intention 'to step by step improve relations and promote mutual understanding with our Eastern neighbours'. But unlike in the West, these steps rarely went beyond the governmental level until the lifting of the Iron Curtain in 1989/90. Since then, Europe has grown together from the ground up, thanks to festivals, music and dances but also to seminars and trips that enable young people to visit important sites and explore the often-violent past they share. Fondness, friendship and sometimes even love have grown out of such encounters.[29]

Successful Partnerships

This is the principle behind the creation of so-called twin towns or 'sister cities', of which there are nearly 20,000 across Europe. Most are in France and Germany, but British, Polish, Italian, Hungarian, Czech, Dutch and Scandinavian municipalities also participate. The connections date back to the late 1940s, when West German mayors and administrators accepted the invitation of their British counterparts to come and learn about the democratic organization of local government. In 1950, the first Franco-German *jumelage* or twin town relationship was established between Ludwigsburg and Montbéliard, whose mayor had been imprisoned in the Buchenwald concentration camp. More than 2,000 Franco-German twin-town arrangements have been formed since. They have come about in different ways; sometimes mayors met through the Council of European Municipalities and Regions, founded in 1951, and agreed on closer cooperation, sometimes teachers encountered one another on vacation and did the same.

In the East, the path to understanding was far longer. Not before Ostpolitik and the Helsinki Conference on Security and Cooperation in Europe ended the official ice age between the blocs were the municipalities able to act. In 1975, Saarbrucken signed an official convention with Tbilisi; in 1976, Bremen with Gdansk. These agreements regulated the exchange of information between mayors and municipal councils, but they also enabled schools, choirs and sports clubs to make and maintain contact. Those involved in such partnerships saw as their greatest benefit the 'personal encounters between citizens, which are often perceived as very emotional. The experience of hospitality and the goodwill of strangers in another country', a 2018 study concluded, 'remains in many people's memories a very moving one.'[30]

---

[29] Adrian Gmelch, *Jugendwerke in internationalen Versöhnungsprozessen* (Hamburg: Diplomica, 2017); Kiehl, *Alle Jahre wieder*, 232, 239; *40 deutsch-französische Geschichten* (Berlin: Deutsch-Französisches Jugendwerk, 2005), 52 ff., 71 ff., 106 ff., 113 ff.

[30] Baumann, *Begegnung*, 288–89; Lucie Filipová, *Erfüllte Hoffnung: Städtepartnerschaften als Instrument der deutsch-französischen Aussöhnung, 1950–2000* (Göttingen: Vandenhoeck & Ruprecht, 2015), 76–77, 112 ff.; Ulrich Pfeil, 'The "Other" Franco-

The feeling of fondness and sympathy that emerged between individuals, the knowledge of one another and the resulting mutual emotional concern created the foundations for civic trust, which accompanied and complemented the efforts of 'big politics' to build friendship bonds. If there was a crisis at the top, those at the grassroots could compensate and stabilize the situation. Accordingly, the French ambassador did not let himself be ruffled by a difference of opinion between de Gaulle and Adenauer's successor Ludwig Erhard in 1964. Precisely because 'behind the friendship movement of both nations is the powerful initiative of many groups and individuals', he had 'full confidence' in the 'Franco-German future'.[31] This was sustained in 2020 in the face of the biggest crisis of confidence to date. Although Germany abruptly closed its borders to disrupt the routes of transmission of the COVID-19 virus, local citizens held fast to their principles and experience of cooperation, with hospitals in Kassel and Völklingen treating patients from the sister cities of Mulhouse and Forbach.

Fundamentally, however, the work of building trust at the grassroots depended on understanding at the top. If this was absent, as it was for a long time in relations with the East, civic initiatives were doomed. Unlike encounters between ordinary people, 'big politics' was clearly not about personal fondness. Politicians who invested their time and energy in bilateral and European cooperation self-evidently did so as representatives of their respective states. Only when friendliness and rapprochement were in the national interest did they stand a chance of being enacted. Whether a negotiation partner proved likeable or not was not supposed to matter.

Still, everything was easier and ran more smoothly when the personal chemistry proved right. Regular telephone calls and meetings, which sometimes took place in private homes with no onlookers or aides standing by, helped to ensure that fond feelings could be forged and fortified. 'I liked the personal contact with Mikhail [Gorbachev]', President George Bush (the elder) wrote. 'I liked *him*.'[32]

The importance of individuals liking one another for the success of international relations in general and for European integration in particular is

German Relations: The GDR and France from 1949 to 1990', in *History of Franco-German Relations*, ed. Germond and Türk, 249–59; *Städtepartnerschaften – den europäischen Bürgersinn stärken: Eine empirische Studie der Bertelsmann-Stiftung* (Gütersloh: Bertelsmann, 2018), quote 58; Sohaela Amiri and Efe Sevin, eds, *City Diplomacy* (Cham: Palgrave Macmillan, 2020); Steven Brakman et al., 'Town Twinning and German City Growth', *Journal of Regional Studies* 50, no. 8 (2016): 1420–32.

[31] Gesa Bluhm, 'Vertrauensarbeit: Deutsch-französische Beziehungen nach 1945', in *Vertrauen*, ed. Ute Frevert (Göttingen: Vandenhoeck & Ruprecht, 2003), 365–93, quote 391.

[32] George Bush and Brent Scowcroft, *A World Transformed* (New York: Knopf, 1998), 9 (italics in original).

Figure 23   François Mitterrand and Helmut Kohl on a Verdun battlefield, September 1984 (Photo by Marcel Mochet/AFP via Getty Images)

evidenced by the long list of friendships between high-ranking politicians since 1945, from Charles de Gaulle and Konrad Adenauer to Valéry Giscard d'Estaing and Helmut Schmidt, from Helmut Kohl and Boris Yeltsin to Gerhard Schröder and Vladimir Putin. Even Kohl and François Mitterrand, whose biographies and political opinions differed greatly, managed a profound emotional gesture when they held hands over the graves at Verdun in 1984 (Figure 23). The image has endured, as has that of their predecessors kneeling in Reims in 1962.

Only time will tell whether the snapshot from 11 November 2018 of their smiling successors will have a similar longevity. The expressive power of a political image depends on how it is situated in history. Does it represent the end of something or the beginning? Does it conjure memories of the past? Does it inspire hope for the future? Do the men and women depicted in it lend these memories or hopes a particular or particularly compelling emotional resonance?

Just how much public attention politicians and their relationship with each other attract depends on which countries and nations they represent, and the weight of their common history. At times, every glance, every gesture, every word is noted and charged with meaning. In such contexts, personal fondness or aversion takes on great significance, and conclusions can be quickly inferred about the general state of politics. If the chemistry is off, if congeniality is in

short supply, advisors suggest ways to help it along, as was the case with
Schmidt and Mitterrand.[33]

Less scrutinized but no less important for the future of Europe is the
fondness between ordinary people in their private lives. Countless friendships
and romantic relationships emerged and developed during transnational
encounters like those arranged by the European Union's Erasmus programme.
Between 1987 and 2018, it enabled 4.4 million students, including 650,000
Germans, to spend a term or two at a foreign university. For many of them,
studying abroad had unforeseen consequences: 27 per cent, according to a
2014 study, found a partner for life and love. Among their peers who stayed at
home, only 13 per cent formed international relationships. Projections esti-
mate one million 'Erasmus babies' as a result of these encounters.

Even when one's time abroad yields less profound and permanent results,
programme participants testify to its far-reaching and lasting effects. One
German student even went so far as to describe his year in Florence 'as a
personal contribution to the realization of the idea of "Europe". Because
Europe can only grow together if young people make friends across borders
and keep them for a lifetime.'[34] He was right.

---

[33] Hélène Miard-Delacroix, 'Ungebrochene Kontinuität: François Mitterrand und die
deutschen Kanzler Helmut Schmidt und Helmut Kohl 1981–1984', *Vierteljahrshefte für
Zeitgeschichte* 47, no. 4 (1999): 539–58, esp. 546; Michèle Weihnachter, 'Franco-German
Relations in the Giscard-Schmidt Era 1974–81', in *History of Franco-German Relations*,
ed. Germond and Türk, 223–33; Georges Saunier, 'A Special Relationship: Franco-
German Relations at the Time of François Mitterrand and Helmut Kohl', in ibid.,
235–47; Yuri van Hoef, 'Friendship in World Politics: Assessing the Personal
Relationships between Kohl and Mitterrand, and Bush and Gorbachev', *Amity: Journal
of Friendship Studies* 2 (2014): 62–82.

[34] http://bit.ly/3DXES7d, accessed 13 January 2022; Ute Frevert, *Eurovisionen: Ansichten
guter Europäer im 19. und 20. Jahrhundert* (Frankfurt: Fischer, 2003), quote 154.

Grief

'The life and death of Dietrich von Beulwitz, born 9 July 1896, killed in action 19 October 1914 near Halennes': so reads the title of a 1916 handwritten manuscript authored by the young man's mother. With it, Louise von Beulwitz erected a luminous monument to her firstborn. She described his life: growing up in his family's forester's lodge eighty kilometres northeast of Frankfurt an der Oder, and discovering his 'love for the soldier's life' at the tender age of three; his time in the Dresden Cadet Corps, which he joined in 1908, just before his twelfth birthday; and his 'blazing enthusiasm' for the war in the summer of 1914, in which, 'inspired by feverish desire', he yearned to 'play an active part and distinguish himself'.

Yet she also wrote of her own feelings, which were very far from > joy and enthusiasm: 'Over and over again, tears fell from my eyes in wild, gagging fear. All I could think about was that my boy, my boy, had to go to war. My dear father, an old veteran, chastised my faint-heartedness, but my mother understood me well.' She described their last evening together:

> Immediately after Dietz came to the hotel, we went to a nearby church for the last Communion before the march. At that time, all the churches were always open, and every day people in our situation took the sacrament with loved ones who were heading into the field. It is indescribable what went through our souls; the heart so full, and yet everything drowning in tears that one must not show.

On 19 September 1914, her son 'delightedly' joined his regiment, which fought in northern France. Exactly one month later, aged eighteen and already the 'oldest active officer', he fell; only twelve of the initial sixty officers were left by then. It took two weeks for the field post letter to reach Dietrich's parents:

> We open it and all hope is destroyed in one fell swoop. The colonel himself wrote a heart-wrenching report of his heroic deed and heroic death, as did his battalion leader Demmering. But none of that helps! Nor the thought that it is the same or worse for thousands of others. All you know is: your child is dead and will not be coming back, will never write again. Night has fallen.

After the devastating shock, the family went into frenetic activity: 'We had an ardent wish to bring our Dietz home and bury him in native soil.' His grave, which lay at the foot of a French castle wall under a grove of old trees, was 'lovingly cared for' by the regiment and planted with flowers. Nevertheless, his parents wanted to lay their son to rest in the family tomb. The relevant military authorities gave their consent. His father drove to Lille, got an oak coffin and had the 'beloved body' exhumed. The corpse was wrapped in a 'black silk blanket' that Louise von Beulwitz had embroidered with their coat of arms, name, an oak branch and her son's life-motto, John 15:13. Once the coffin was sealed, it was transported to Rudolstadt by train.

On 30 April 1915, the family met for the final burial 'with drum roll and trumpet call and full military honours'. The eulogy to the young man 'cut down in his prime' was given by garrison pastor Krüger. He extolled the 'high German idealism' and 'burning love of fatherland' that had led Dietrich into the 'murderous war'. He lauded his bravery, his heroism, his loyalty. And he consoled the bereaved:

> You, dear parents and relatives, are in pain, you have lost a piece of your own heart with your bright, gifted son, who was your joy and delight. But his death was a sacrifice, a holy sacrifice. He selflessly gave his life for his comrades. There is no act greater than sacrificing oneself for others. This noble pride shimmers through your tears.

It was in this same spirit that his mother ended her chronicle in 1916: 'He gave his God, his fatherland and his family name much > honour and joy.' Louise von Beulwitz bade her children see to it 'that the memory of their brother never fades, but is faithfully cherished by them and their children'.[1]

Grief and Consolation in 1914

What does this manuscript tell us about grief? A good deal, and in varied tones. Two years after the loss of her son, the mother still found it difficult to revisit the events ('within me, everything is still in turmoil'). She described her fears, worries and the tears she shed as they said goodbye in August 1914. Her memory of the death notice was, in contrast, only brief, whereas the posthumous homecoming and burial were again explained in depth. In keeping with the occasion, her language was 'solemn'. Only one sentence alluded to her pain: 'Our hearts almost broke in two.'

That their hearts did not break completely may have been thanks to the pastor's exalting words (included in the memorial). As a deeply religious Protestant woman, the analogies between her son's 'sacrificial death' and the

---

[1] Manuscript courtesy of granddaughter Maria Kublitz-Kramer, Bielefeld. See also Dorothee Wierling, *Eine Familie im Krieg: Leben, Sterben und Schreiben 1914–1918* (Göttingen: Wallstein, 2013); Gunilla Budde, *Feldpost für Elsbeth: Eine Familie im Ersten Weltkrieg* (Göttingen: Wallstein, 2019).

Passion of Christ were obvious to her right away. She also reiterated Krüger's emphasis on selfless comradeship, because that was how she wanted to see her son: 'A love of home and a feeling of comradeship formed the core of his being.'

Yet there was another source of consolation, as suggested by the terms 'true hero', 'heroic death' and 'heroic loyalty'. Coming from a military family background, the author knew what they were about. Her father, Veit Friedrich von Obernitz, was a Prussian lieutenant general (an 'old soldier'), while other men in the family had served in the armies of Württemberg and Saxony. In these circles, heroism meant sacrificing life and limb for the fatherland or the king, in order to increase one's fame. In principle, every fallen soldier counted as a hero. Before his death, Dietrich von Beulwitz had accomplished an additional 'heroic deed' by capturing eight British soldiers in a daring move. All of this was not only an honour to him but also to the nation for which he fought, and to the family from which he came. It helped them make sense of his death and dampened their grief. In his eulogy, the pastor correctly recognized that self-sacrificing heroism aroused > pride, a pride that 'shimmers through your tears'.

The personal grief of the Beulwitz family was thus moderated by supra-individual, politically charged companion emotions: pride in the patriotic act and appreciation of the religiously draped sacrifice the young man had bequeathed to all sons and daughters of the fatherland.

Such feelings and interpretations were not the sole preserve of Louise von Beulwitz. Turning to the army and navy on 7 August 1914, the German kaiser swore all soldiers to heroic death: 'Each of you knows, should it come to pass, how to die like a hero. Remember our great, glorious past! Remember that you are German!' Grief was not envisioned in this scenario. The Catholic bishop of Speyer, Michael von Faulhaber, 'gladly' let his younger clergymen 'travel to the combat zone and to the field hospital, where they can build morale among the troops and offer spiritual guidance to the dying'. Those who remained behind were instructed to also

> sacrifice themselves entirely to the cause of the fatherland. In the spirit of the glorious proclamation of Your Majesty [the Bavarian king], rather than making the hearts of mourners even heavier with frightful motifs, they should fill all men and women, down to those in the smallest village, with trust and confidence in God, a spirit of sacrifice, and the conviction that this is a holy, just cause, to which all private interests must now take second place.

Personal grief over the loss of a loved family member should therefore not be endorsed or amplified. On the contrary, it was to be subdued and contained in service of the higher common purpose.[2]

---

[2] Bavarian State Archive Munich, III, Geheimes Hausarchiv, Cabinet Files Ludwig III, no. 71: Decree of Wilhelm II on 7 August 1914; Michael von Faulhaber to King Ludwig, 6 August 1914.

This was aimed not least at women who, as wives and mothers of soldiers, seemed emotionally unreliable. As the well-known writer Gabriele Reuter saw it, women, out of sheer selfishness, obstructed the 'path to danger, fame and glorious death' of their husbands, sons and brothers, and burdened them with their own fears and hesitations. What the new era demanded instead was for women 'to surrender their most beloved to the bloody battle for precious Germany'. They should do so with 'gleeful ecstasy'.[3]

Käthe Kollwitz: Private Loss and Public Remembrance

Such an emphatic picture of 'ecstatic sacrificing' disturbed the artist Käthe Kollwitz, whose sons Hans and Peter had volunteered for the army in 1914. 'Where', she wondered, 'do all the women who have watched so carefully over the lives of their beloved ones get the heroism to send them to face the cannon?' With mixed feelings, she herself had bowed to the wish of her youngest son, not yet eighteen, to go to war for Germany. As she later confessed, when he fell in Flanders three days after Dietrich von Beulwitz, she felt 'the hardest blow of [her] life'. It was not until ten days after receiving the death notice that she resumed her diary entries, in which self-flagellation alternated with attacks of despair and numbness:

> There are times when I almost do not feel Peter's death anymore. It is an indifferent state of mind. Instead of emotion, all I feel is emptiness. Then comes a dull longing – bit by bit, over several days. Finally it breaks, and I cry, I cry, and then I feel again with my whole body, my whole soul, that *Peter is dead.*

Relief, and even a feeling of rescue, came through work on a memorial to her dead son: 'I want to honour you with the monument', she wrote, addressing him directly. 'All who loved you keep you in their hearts and you continue to touch all who knew you and know about your death. But I want to honour you differently. I want to honour the death of all young volunteers, sculpted and embodied in your form. The sculpture should be cast in iron or bronze and stand for centuries.'[4]

Käthe Kollwitz carried her private grief into public space. Yet she did more than this: by deviating from her original plan to cast her son 'lying outstretched, father at his head, mother at his feet', and instead depicting only a pair of grieving parents bearing her own and her husband's features, she

---

[3] Gabriele Reuter, 'Was fordert der Krieg von den Frauen?', *Der Tag*, 26 August 1914.

[4] Käthe Kollwitz, *Die Tagebücher*, ed. Jutta Bohnke-Kollwitz (Berlin: Siedler, 1989), 158, 192, 177; Käthe Kollwitz, *Briefe an den Sohn 1904 bis 1945*, ed. Jutta Bohnke-Kollwitz (Berlin: Siedler, 1992), 239–40. See Regina Schulte, 'Käthe Kollwitz's Sacrifice', *History Workshop Journal* 41, no. 1 (1996): 193–221.

Figure 24 Käthe Kollwitz's statue *The Grieving Parents* in the Vladslo German war cemetery, Belgium (Arie J. De Regt/Getty Images)

foregrounded the pain of the bereaved (Figure 24). Her later sculpture *Mother with Dead Son*, which she dedicated to Peter, also showed more mother than son. Begun in 1937, the mother had 'become something of a Pietà', albeit one whose expression was 'no longer one of pain but contemplation' – like the maternal grief felt by 'an old, lonely and sombrely contemplative woman', two decades after the loss.[5]

Kollwitz had never intended to upgrade the 'little sculpture' to a monument. But it was her ardent wish that *The Grieving Parents* be publicly installed. In the mid-1920s, she had received support from Edwin Redslob, who in his official function as national art protector was developing a central plan for honouring the fallen. He envisaged a natural grove, 'where a flame should burn day and night', and suggested that Kollwitz's figures could be placed there. 'It would make me happy', she wrote in her diary, 'if this were to happen and I could speak to, for and as it were on behalf of the whole people through my work. But this is all still up in the air, so it is best not to talk to anyone about it.'

Nothing came of it either. Redslob's plan fell through, and the Prussian government opted for a memorial located in Berlin. It was unveiled in 1931 at

[5] Kollwitz, *Tagebücher*, 690, 698.

the Neue Wache, the historic royal guardhouse on Unter den Linden. In the middle of the otherwise empty interior, a black granite stone was positioned, with an oak leaf wreath and two candelabras, dedicated to the 'fallen of the World War'. There would have been room for Kollwitz's mourners, but the artist did not like the idea, fearing 'monopolization by the right-wing'. Her inkling that nationalist circles would seek to commandeer the memorial could not be dismissed; in fact, a bitter struggle for the sovereignty of interpretation was already raging around the unveiling ceremony. Placing the sculptures on the outside was also out of the question, because here 'they have no security and can be smeared or damaged with swastikas'.

By 1933 it was evident that National Socialists appreciated neither the statements nor the style of this independent artist who sympathized with the Communists. Käthe Kollwitz had to leave the Prussian Academy of Arts, and her works, now considered 'repulsive', were no longer shown in public. In 1936, the plaster original of the grieving mother was removed from where it had been placed in the Kronprinzenpalais (opposite the Neue Wache), along with Ernst Barlach's mourning figures.[6] According to the new regime, the fallen should not be lamented but worshipped as heroes. The National Day of Mourning established during the Weimar Republic was consequently rebranded as a day of heroes and celebrated with militaristic pomp.

From Public Grief to Hero Cult

This ended a controversy that had pulsed through the 1920s. Redslob, in whose vocabulary the 'hero' did not feature, envisaged the official commemoration neither as a ceremony for 'backward dwelling on the past' nor as a bequest to the future. Rather than using the event to justify the millionfold death or burden it with significance, he saw it as an occasion for genuine sadness. This drew protest from conservative and *völkisch* groups, above all the German War Graves Commission, founded in 1919. From their point of view, the fallen victims were heroes who had died for Germany and thus demanded allegiance from Germany. From 1925 onwards, the commission held commemorations in the Reichstag building and invited politicians and parliamentarians to participate. Its members gave speeches that were broadcast on the

---

[6] Ibid., 609, 684, 686, 923. On the Neue Wache, see Peter Reichel, *Politik mit der Erinnerung* (Munich: Hanser, 1995), 231–46. On the history of the creation and installation of *The Grieving Parents*, see Hannelore Fischer, ed., *Käthe Kollwitz: Die trauernden Eltern: Ein Mahnmal für den Frieden* (Cologne: Käthe Kollwitz Museum, 1999); Jay Winter, *Sites of Memory, Sites of Mourning: The War in European Cultural History* (Cambridge: Cambridge University Press, 1995), 108–13; Henriëtte Kets de Vries, 'Mother's Arms', in *Käthe Kollwitz and the Women of War: Feminity, Identity, and Art in Germany during World Wars I and II*, ed. Claire C. Whitner (New Haven, CT: Yale University Press, 2016), 11–19.

Figure 25 Post- and pre-war mourning: Heroes' Remembrance Day, Berlin, 1938
(Photo by Heinrich Hoffmann/ullstein bild via Getty Images)

radio and teemed with references to sacrifice and heroism, national resurrection and future German greatness.[7]

National Socialists could seamlessly build upon this. In 1934, when they declared a new national holiday – the Heroes' Remembrance Day – the War Graves Commission welcomed the name change and expressed satisfaction 'that the sacrifice of those who died in war and during the movement for freedom [the Nazi putsch of 1923] is bearing fruit. We do not remember them in sorrowful pain, but look up to them with stirring pride as the guarantors of a new Germany.' At last, the commission's interpretation officially prevailed: the fallen had actively sacrificed themselves, and their sacrifice demanded emulation (Figure 25).[8]

This demand was fulfilled, and faster than many of the living would have liked. From 1939, lives were once again sacrificed, with the number of deaths steadily increasing. Millions of families received letters of condolence from the

---

[7] Alexandra Kaiser, *Von Helden und Opfern: Eine Geschichte des Volkstrauertags* (Frankfurt: Campus, 2010), 27 ff., 61 ff., 76; Alexandra Kaiser, 'The *Volkstrauertag* (People's Day of Mourning) from 1922 to the Present', in *Memorialization in Germany since 1945*, ed. William John Niven and Chloe E. M. Paver (Basingstoke: Palgrave Macmillan, 2010), 15–25.

[8] Kaiser, *Helden*, 182. See also Sabine Behrenbeck, *Der Kult um die toten Helden: Nationalsozialistische Mythen, Riten und Symbole 1923 bis 1945* (Vierow: SH Verlag, 1996).

respective military commander and, if available, a picture of the grave as 'the only weak, yet nevertheless necessary, consolation'. Sons and husbands always fell 'in the struggle for the freedom of Greater Germany', gave their lives 'for the greatness and future of our eternal German people' and died 'for Führer, Volk and Vaterland'. Obituaries were written in a similar way. 'In proud mourning', under the emblem of the Iron Cross with an embedded swastika, bereaved family members announced the death of their loved one and expressed thanks for 'quiet sympathy'. It is difficult to say whether the mantra-like assurance 'that the sacrifices made for Führer, Volk and Reich will not be in vain' really consoled anyone. After all, despite all the sympathy they received, every mother, every father, every war widow and war orphan was left alone with their loss. Sharing that experience with millions did not make it easier.

Right up to the end, though, the words 'fatherland' and 'heroic death' emblazoned the death notices printed in local newspapers. This suggests that giving the personal loss a political meaning was important and could possibly alleviate personal pain. Public ceremonies to honour fallen heroes were well attended. The higher the death toll climbed, the stronger the call for the Führer became. 'We sometimes have a sombre task', wrote Emilie Weinbrenner from Stuttgart's family support office to Hitler's personal aide in September 1943. 'Women come to us in great anguish when they receive the news of their husband's or son's death.' Yet 'many stand behind our Führer now and forever with faithful hearts and ardently wish to hear him speak again'. Hitler, however, played hard to get and left the mobilization of his fellow Germans to the Ministry of Propaganda. In February 1943, shortly after the capitulation of the 6th Army, Press Chief Otto Dietrich had issued the instruction 'not to whimper words of mourning, but to turn the sacrifice of the men of Stalingrad into a heroic epic'. The Völkischer Beobachter immediately headlined: 'They died so that Germany could live.'[9]

How the soldiers themselves dealt with the death of comrades and friends can be glimpsed through their field post letters. They commented pithily on the 'sad news', describing themselves as 'shaken' and 'beaten'. Enduring feelings of grief, though, could scarcely be conceded, for death was too close and omnipresent. 'Soldier's fate': this is how SS corporal Franz Schädle

---

[9] Klemperer, LTI, 121–24 (on obituary notices and their 'degrees of Nazism'); Oliver Schmitt and Sandra Westenberger, 'Der feine Unterschied im Heldentod', in Volkes Stimme: Skepsis und Führervertrauen im Nationalsozialismus, ed. Götz Aly (Frankfurt: Fischer, 2006), 96–115; Federal Archive Berlin, NS 51, no. 39: Emilie Weinbrenner, 8 September 1943; Klaus Latzel, Deutsche Soldaten - nationalsozialistischer Krieg? (Paderborn: Schöningh, 1998), 265; Utz Jeggle, 'In stolzer Trauer: Umgangsformen mit dem Kriegstod während des 2. Weltkriegs', in Tübinger Beiträge zur Volkskultur, ed. Utz Jeggle et al. (Tübingen: Tübinger Vereinigung für Volkskunde, 1986), 242–59.

summarized the death of a comrade in March 1943, only to then happily report on his own 'soldier's luck' on Eastern European battlefields and the excellent mood of his company. Field letters circulating among former class-mates of a Berlin secondary school from October 1941 onwards also said little about grief. When a comrade fell, it was communicated in stereotypical turns of phrase: 'I received the tremendously sad news that our dear Dieter Pfau met a heroic death in battle at Ilmensee. All our hearts, eyes and hands reach out to you. Outwardly, we must bid you farewell, dear Dieter, but on the inside, a fierce dedication blazes on: "Eternally ours!"' Günther Peters learnt of the 'heroic death of his best friend' during his home leave, which left 'very bitter vermouth drops in the sweet wine of his vacation'. When Peters himself 'had to give up his life for the fatherland' in Italy, his comrades mourned 'with his long-suffering parents'.[10]

In this correspondence, 'heroic death' and 'fatherland' were the most common terms used to share the news. Interestingly, nobody spoke of the Führer, and political or ideological references were also missing. The asser-tions of mutual solidarity and affection thus sounded all the more intimate. Not only did these classmates keep in touch with one another, but 'front and home' were equally bound together 'by hook or by crook', as Wally Haase regularly emphasized. From January 1942, in place of her son, Haase collected written and telephone messages from his former schoolfriends and circulated them as a 'bridge'. She never neglected to thank the 'dear comrades' on behalf of the 'home that is so faithfully defended by all of you' and answered their bravery with an iron will to persevere. 'Sometimes we must stifle our deep suffering, grief and immeasurable worry for you', she wrote, 'we must brace ourselves and resist it with all our energy. We wrestle and fight our way through it until we are back up again, and the darkness has cleared.' She herself held true to this when her own son was reported missing near Stalingrad, and greeted the new year of 1945 'with fresh unwavering > hope, with confidence and with a fervent belief in a change for the better for our dear, precious fatherland'.[11]

Private Grief

It is unknown whether Wally Haase saw her son again or learnt anything more about the circumstances of his disappearance. Of 1.7 million missing-person reports registered with the German Red Cross tracing service in 1950, only

---

[10] Latzel, *Soldaten*, 263; Federal Archive Berlin, NS 51, no. 39: Franz Schädle, 6 March 1943; circular letters of the classmates of the Dietrich Eckart School, hectographed manuscript in possession of the author, no. 9 (January 1943), 3; no. 13 (January 1944), 2–3; no. 17 (January 1945), 4.

[11] Ibid., no. 10 (March 1943), 1; no. 13 (January 1944), 1.

400,000 cases could be solved. Thousands of inquiries still arrive every year, with children, grandchildren and great-grandchildren seeking clarity over the death of their father, grandfather or great-grandfather. As psychoanalysts see it, their grieving work cannot be completed as long as the uncertainty, and the hope and longing, persists. Without a burial ritual and gravestone, they say, grief gets stuck, and the loss is not to be accepted, with sometimes traumatic consequences.[12]

Yet there may be other motives behind these search requests. People deal with grief in very different ways. Simultaneously, they are influenced by cultural habits and social expectations that change over time. Although doctors and psychologists have long endeavoured to design general process and phase models, these are constantly in flux, as documented in the internationally renowned *Diagnostic and Statistical Manual of Mental Disorders* published by the American Psychiatric Association since 1952. The third edition in 1980 recommended that mourners only be classified as depressed and treated accordingly if they still suffered from disordered sleep, loss of appetite, difficulty concentrating and feelings of depression a year after the loss. The fourth edition in 1994 reduced the 'normal' grieving phase to two months, the fifth in 2013 to two weeks. Such concurrent pathologization of grief may serve the interests of the pharmaceutical industry, but it also reflects society's impatience to get grief under medical and therapeutic control as quickly as possible and to keep mourners socially and economically functional.

In fact, deep grief traditionally goes hand in hand with a desire to withdraw from society and bury oneself in the pain. In the past, this was taken for granted and respected. The 1957 *Brockhaus* encyclopaedia still confirmed the 'custom of avoiding social events for a long time when a close relative has died'. The duration of the mourning period varied depending on the degree of kinship, but also on 'respective regional or local custom'. In many places, a 'year of mourning' was observed, a tradition dating back to Roman antiquity. Originally, it had concerned widows who were not permitted to remarry until one year after their husband's death, in order to rule out paternity conflicts. Whether they actually mourned was irrelevant.

In any case, the expectations for how people should grieve differed greatly across time and space. In 1909, *Meyers Lexikon* reported on mourning customs for 'primitive and civilized races'; not surprisingly, it gave significantly better grades to the 'civilized' and their 'very mild form' of mourning. In contrast, the 'wailing women' of southern Italy, who filled the house of the

---

[12] http://bit.ly/3Yr4Ice, accessed 22 December 2021; Henning V. Orlowski et al., 'Psychologie der Vermissung am Beispiel der Kinder von vermissten deutschen Soldaten des Zweiten Weltkriegs', *Zeitschrift für Psychosomatische Medizin und Psychotherapie* 59, no. 2 (2013): 189–97.

deceased 'with their shrieking', incurred unveiled disapproval and were counted among the 'primitive races'.

As the twentieth century progressed, 'mild' forms of mourning grew even milder. According to the 1978 edition of *Meyers Lexikon*, 'traditional rules and timelines for wearing mourning attire' were rarely observed in industrialized countries; the convention of wearing black during 'full mourning' and introducing white, or sometimes grey or violet, features in the later phases of 'half-mourning' and 'quarter-mourning' was vanishing from living memory. Only widows might still adhere to such habits, conforming to and upholding gendered norms of mourning behaviour.[13] The more intimate and emotional family ties had become since the nineteenth century and the more that women profiled themselves as their guardians, the greater and more intense their grief at the loss of a loved family member could be. This entailed dressing in black, sometimes even shrouding themselves in a mourning veil. Men, on the other hand, simply pinned a black ribbon or band to their sleeves or hat. Women were likewise permitted to cry uncontrollably, which was considered inappropriate for men. As women had remained closer to religion and the church, they also made good and ample use of its consolation and support.

In the second half of the twentieth century, this closeness was increasingly lost. The decline in religious observance among men that had begun long before now also gathered pace among women. Religious symbols gradually disappeared from funeral notices and gravestones. In place of a cross, they were adorned with roses, sunflowers, trees, ears of wheat, stars and rainbows. At the same time, grief has gained significance as a self-referential emotional practice. Instead of simply announcing the date of a loved one's passing, obituaries increasingly emphasize the feelings of loss felt by relatives and friends without reference to religion.[14]

This was not the case in the years immediately following the Second World War. Once the political and ideological meaning invested in millions of war deaths was removed, religion was the only anchor of solace left. Religious rituals were again used extensively when designing and staging public mourning events. Monuments to the fallen – the word 'heroes' disappeared from the columns and boulders – often stood on church grounds anyway, and

---

[13] *Der Große Brockhaus*, 16th ed., vol. 11 (Wiesbaden: Brockhaus, 1957), 603; *Brockhaus Enzyklopädie*, 17th ed., vol. 18 (Wiesbaden: Brockhaus, 1973), 826; *Meyers Großes Konversations-Lexikon*, 6th ed., vol. 19 (Leipzig: Bibliografisches Institut, 1909), 676–77; *Meyers enzyklopädisches Lexikon*, 9th ed., vol. 23 (Mannheim: Bibliografisches Institut, 1978), 665.

[14] Angelika Linke, 'Trauer, Öffentlichkeit und Intimität: Zum Wandel der Textsorte "Todesanzeige" in der zweiten Hälfte des 20. Jahrhunderts', in *Zur Kulturspezifik von Textsorten*, ed. Ulla Fix et al. (Tübingen: Stauffenburg, 2001), 195–223.

local commemoration of the dead was combined with a church service until well into the 1960s.

Official Grief

To be commemorated first on National Days of Mourning were Germany's 'own' victims, preferably fallen soldiers and, if need be, those who had died in aerial bombings. In 1961, SPD politician Erhard Eppler harshly criticized such hierarchies and explicitly included 'everyone who had fallen victim to this last war and to an inhumane regime'. The ceremony in the Bundestag likewise remembered 'those who under tyranny became victims for their convictions or beliefs', or who had been murdered 'because they belonged to another people or were assigned to a different race'.[15]

The political language of remembrance thus gradually moved away from privileging active sacrifice over passive victimhood, as it had done so often and momentously in the wake of the First World War. Furthermore, grief in the Federal Republic became increasingly inclusive and embraced many different categories of victims. In this respect it hardly differed from official memory as cultivated in the GDR. In 1960, East Berlin's Neue Wache was reinaugurated as a memorial to the victims of 'fascism and militarism'. Almost completely destroyed in the war, the building's interior received a huge national coat of arms, an eternal flame – Redslob's original idea – and two bronze plaques with the remains of an unknown resistance fighter and an unknown soldier. Fallen Wehrmacht soldiers and officers were thereby declared victims of militarism and buried side by side with those who had fought against the regime and had been murdered in the concentration camps.

In 1993, three years after reunification, the Neue Wache was once more redesigned. On the National Day of Mourning, wreaths were laid in front of the centrally placed sculpture *Mother with Dead Son* by Käthe Kollwitz. While the original 'little sculpture' can be admired in the Cologne Kollwitz Museum, the Neue Wache, Germany's central memorial to 'victims of war and tyranny', houses a copy that has been enlarged fourfold.[16] It remains an open question whether the artist – who died in April 1945 – would have been happy about this magnification and recognition. In 1926, she had admittedly warmed to Redslob's proposal of including *The Grieving Parents* in a national memorial for war victims. In 1937, when she made the profoundly personal sculpture in remembrance of her fallen son, she by no means considered a public installation, which would have been politically impossible anyway. At that time, she

---

[15] Erhard Eppler, *Spannungsfelder* (Stuttgart: Seewald, 1968), 71–76; Meinhold Lurz, *Kriegerdenkmäler in Deutschland*, vol. 6 (Heidelberg: Esprint, 1987), 515; Kaiser, *Von Helden und Opfern*, 210 ff.

[16] Reichel, *Politik*, 240 ff.

neither knew that a second Peter Kollwitz, her grandson, would soon die in another war, nor could she have conceived of the organized murder of millions of Jewish people that Germans would commit. If asked whether and how the perpetrator nation could mourn the death of those murdered, she would, in all likelihood, have had no answer.

Kollwitz never saw the end of the war. Nor did she witness the wrestling in both German states over appropriate forms of grief and memory. The GDR honoured the anti-fascist resistance earlier than the Federal Republic but narrowed the focus to communist prisoners in concentration camps or Nazi torture chambers. The Federal Republic understood earlier than the GDR that, in addition to dead soldiers and civilians killed by Allied bombs, war victims included those who had been slaughtered and annihilated on racial grounds. They began to be actively remembered in the 1980s, initially in local contexts. After nearly two decades of intense public debate, a central Memorial to the Murdered Jews of Europe was finally inaugurated in 2005, next to Berlin's major landmark, the Brandenburg Gate. Monuments to other victim groups – Sinti and Roma, homosexuals, disabled people – followed. Interestingly, all refrained from depicting mourning in the figurative manner of the Neue Wache. Instead, they opted for an abstract visual vocabulary that appeared more fitting for expressing unfathomable suffering.

While heated controversies arose over the design of the respective monuments, the National Day of Mourning drew less and less public and private attention.[17] From the late 1960s onwards, resonance and participation noticeably decreased. Even the annual wreath-laying ceremony and the central commemoration – still in the hands of the National Graves Commission – hardly attracted any interest, despite being broadcast on television.[18] Personal grief, as felt by members of the war generation and their children, gave way to political-moral appeals ('Never again war!', 'Never again Auschwitz!'). In January 2020, when President Frank-Walter Steinmeier bowed 'in deep mourning' to the victims of the Holocaust, the gesture primarily acknowledged that Germany was aware of its responsibility and was taking appropriate action to fight antisemitism and genocide.

State Mourning

The Federal Republic is otherwise rather sparing with mourning rituals and political expressions of grief, reserving them, by order of the president and under the auspices of the Ministry of the Interior, to honour former

---

[17] Thomas E. Schmidt et al., *Nationaler Totenkult: Die Neue Wache* (Berlin: Kramer, 1995); Michael Jeismann, ed., *Mahnmal Mitte* (Cologne: DuMont, 1999); Christoph Stölzl, ed., *Die Neue Wache Unter den Linden* (Berlin: Koehler & Amelang, 1995).

[18] Kaiser, *Von Helden und Opfern*, 409.

chancellors, presidents and ministers after their respective deaths. Some of these state funerals draw a lot of attention and participation from the populace, while others go almost unnoticed. The burial services for Konrad Adenauer in 1967, Willy Brandt in 1992, Helmut Schmidt in 2015 and Helmut Kohl in 2017 were major political events with an extraordinary public response, reflecting the importance attributed to the deceased and the sympathy they still enjoyed years or even decades after their tenure as chancellors ended.

In the 1920s, Edwin Redslob was tasked with giving such mourning ceremonies a dignified tone. Under the former empire, only monarchs and their wives had received state funerals, whereas the Weimar Republic granted this honour exclusively to uncrowned heads: foreign ministers Walther Rathenau and Gustav Stresemann, the president Friedrich Ebert, and thirteen workers from the Krupp factory in Essen who had been shot by French soldiers during the Ruhr uprising in 1923. Like Rathenau, who was murdered by right-wing extremists, they were mourned as 'martyrs'.

The funeral rally and burial held for Rathenau in 1922 was intended as a powerful and impressive profession of faith in the democratic republic. Unions called for the suspension of work. Parliamentarians from the far left to the far right gathered in the elaborately decorated Reichstag where the coffin was set out. Hundreds of thousands waited in front of the building. For Harry Graf Kessler, it was Rathenau's old mother sitting in the imperial box who touched him most, as 'her complexion was as pale as wax and the face behind the veil might have been carved from stone'. The ceremony's 'highest pitch of emotion', according to Kessler, was when Siegfried's funeral march from Richard Wagner's *Götterdämmerung* sounded after the speeches: 'The effect was overwhelming. Many around me wept.'[19]

Friedrich Ebert's funeral in 1925 was likewise a demonstration of national togetherness. Letters and telegrams of condolence poured in from local SPD chapters, democratic clubs and republican women's associations, but also from Wilhelm Schwaner who chaired the *völkisch*-conservative Federation of German Educators. He assured Ebert's widow Louise that 'there are middle-class men and women, too, who express their sympathies for the tragedy that has befallen your family'. Because 'after all, we are all Germans, humans and brothers or sisters'. Berlin-based Agnes Radloff found similar words of consolation: 'Those who cursed and blasphemed him [Ebert] yesterday had to

---

[19] Volker Ackermann, 'Staatsbegräbnisse in Deutschland von Wilhelm I. bis Willy Brandt', in *Emotion und Nation: Deutschland und Frankreich im Vergleich*, ed. Étienne François et al. (Göttingen: Vandenhoeck & Ruprecht, 1995), 252–73; *Berlin in Lights: The Diaries of Count Harry Kessler (1918–1937)*, trans. and ed. Charles Kessler (New York: Grove Press, 2000), 186; *Harry Graf Kessler, Tagebücher 1918–1937*, ed. Wolfgang Pfeiffer-Belli (Frankfurt: Insel-Verlag, 1982), 339–41, and on Stresemann's funeral, 630 ff.

watch today how Berlin, Germany and the whole world honoured the dead. Despite all the sadness in my heart about his passing, I was filled with inner joy when, after the funeral was over, I could read in the newspaper how many had honoured him on his last walk.'[20]

Indeed, almost a million people had gathered in front of the Reichstag; many then followed the funeral procession to the railway station, from where Ebert's coffin was transported by train to Heidelberg, his place of birth. Such abundant and direct participation by the populace was peculiar to the Weimar Republic. In contrast, the Nazi regime, which staged seventy-one (!) acts of state commemoration with pomp and circumstance, kept people at a distance. The GDR, for its part, placed great emphasis on demonstrating the alleged unity of state and people. When Stalin died in 1953, the front page of the ruling party's newspaper *Neues Deutschland* proclaimed him 'the best friend of the German people' and described the moment when the news 'reached us: our hearts seemed to stand still for a moment, our breath stopped, tears of sadness and pain welled in our eyes'. Public buildings set their flags at half-mast, and dance and sporting events were prohibited by order of the Interior Ministry.

On the day of Stalin's funeral, the sirens sounded at 10 a.m., and work and traffic were suspended for five minutes. The official state ceremony began in Berlin's opera house, and those present rose from their seats for 'five minutes of pain-filled silence, sobbing, crying'. Standing and 'with tears in their eyes', the mourners listened to condolences being read out. Sermon-like, theatre director Wolfgang Langhoff recited the verses of Johannes R. Becher's 'Dem Ewig-Lebenden' ('To The Eternal One'), which could hardly be surpassed in pathos. Thereafter, the second movement of Beethoven's Third Symphony penetrated 'into the sad hearts' of the carefully selected audience. The subsequent funeral procession, authorized by the SED and the magistrate of Greater Berlin, was joined by hundreds of thousands, while schools across the country organized 'dignified' obsequies.[21]

Their purpose was explicit: the party, the government and 'the German people' formed a community of mourning focused, beyond the pain of loss, on common political goals set and embodied by the deceased. In 1953, these included the 'struggle for the unity of the German capital, in the interest of the German nation', even though Stalin had enjoyed little sympathy in West Berlin and hardly anyone there shed a tear at the news of his death.

In 1960 there was another opportunity 'for the entire German working class and for the whole German people' to unite in grief. East Berlin's government ordered four days of state mourning in honour of the first and last GDR

---

[20] Federal Archive Berlin, R 601, no. 36; no. 37: Wilhelm Schwaner, 18 March 1925; Agnes Radloff, 11 March 1925.
[21] *Neues Deutschland*, 8 and 10 March 1953, 1.

president, Wilhelm Pieck, and asked the population to give this 'beloved deceased' his last escort. This time, work and traffic were paused for just two minutes. But since the official ceremony was broadcast on radio and television, far more people than in 1953 were able to participate, if only remotely.[22]

German–German Grief?

In the West, very few felt addressed by the GDR's inclusive and politically charged appeals to each and every German. It was a different story, however, in February 1960 when 123 miners were killed in a firedamp accident in a Zwickau coal mine. The West German government announced that it 'shared the grief expressed by the whole German people over this serious accident' in the GDR, and the Ministry of the Interior ordered the flag of mourning be hoisted on federal offices. Mine rescue brigades from the Ruhr area offered their support (which was rejected), trade unions sent a telegram of condolence ('The workers of the Federal Republic mourn with you for these victims of work'), and members of parliament rose for a mourning address. Radio stations adapted their programmes as befitting the 'sombre' mood; the West Berlin Senate cancelled planned youth carnival events. According to the federal minister of all-German affairs, the common grief of 72 million Germans in East and West had made the unity of the people immediately perceptible.[23]

The GDR media, on the other hand, downplayed German–German grief and instead emphasized the sympathy of 'the socialist bloc'. As the *Berliner Zeitung* reported, the accident had 'triggered a surge of > solidarity. With rescue gear from the Soviet Union and the Czechoslovak Republic, with the counsel of good friends, we will continue the fight against death in the burning and smouldering shaft with our strongest physical efforts.' The fact that Algerian trade unions showed compassion was more remarkable than the corresponding statements by West German unions. *Neues Deutschland* did, however, mention that the mourners who paid their last respects to the lost comrades included a delegation of Ruhr miners.[24]

When a no less catastrophic mine accident occurred in Lengede in West Germany three years later, the extent to which the community of mourners transcended the border was even more limited. With the construction of the Berlin Wall in 1961, the GDR abandoned national unity as a state goal and

---

[22] *Berliner Zeitung*, 8 and 9 September 1960, 1.

[23] *Bulletin des Presse- und Informationsamtes der Bundesregierung*, 26 February 1960, 1; *Frankfurter Allgemeine Zeitung*, 29 February 1960; Clemens Heitmann, 'Vor 50 Jahren: Tragödie in Zwickau', *Sächsisches Archivblatt*, 1 (2010): 24–27; Ackermann, 'Staatsbegräbnisse', 256–57.

[24] *Berliner Zeitung*, 26 February 1960, 1; *Neues Deutschland*, 28 February 1960, 1.

prioritized separation. Economic and technological competition may also have played a role: unlike in Zwickau, 100 of the 129 trapped Lengede miners were saved using the latest technology. In any case, GDR media focused more on the 'capitalist tragedy' and 'greed for profit on the backs of the miners' than on expressing their sympathy for the victims and their families.[25]

West German media, in contrast, covered the rescue operations in great detail and emotional language and thus reached millions of citizens who followed the news with bated breath. As much as they celebrated the successful rescue of the lucky hundred, they grieved for the twenty-nine who could not be saved. They were also officially mourned by the state of Lower Saxony, where Lengede was located. In 2015, a similar state ceremony was scheduled for a group of pupils and teachers who had lost their lives in a plane crash intentionally caused by the pilot. The tragedy had sparked horror in many people, far beyond immediate relatives and friends, prompting the need to find a public forum for expressing and sharing empathetic grief. The official ceremony thus enabled a society to collectively mourn its members who had lost their lives in an extraordinary catastrophe. Such mourning was simultaneously private and public, silent and audible. It was civic, but not political.

Cultures of Grief

This was different when state and society grieved for the nine immigrant men and one policewoman murdered by the right-wing terror group National Socialist Underground between 2000 and 2007. Numerous local funeral rallies at which citizens expressed their condolences and voiced their political outrage (> Anger) were followed, in 2012, by a state memorial ceremony in Berlin. Here, Chancellor Angela Merkel publicly apologized for the fact that the authorities had spent far too long looking for the culprits in migrant milieus instead of investigating evidence pointing to the neo-Nazi scene. The official ceremony was therefore intensely political in that it sought to symbolically compensate for the blatant failure of state institutions and, at the same time, summon liberal society's rejection of right-wing terror.

Four years later, citizens mourned those who had been killed or injured in an Islamist attack on a popular Berlin Christmas market. Overnight, a sea of candles, flowers and crosses appeared at the scene (Figure 26). The church right next to the site of terror, in which a memorial service took place in the presence of the federal president and the chancellor, was overcrowded. The parliament held another memorial event shortly after. Still, many citizens felt that this was not enough. Some demanded a minute's silence, others an official

---

[25] *Berliner Zeitung*, 5 November 1963, 1 and 8 November 1963, 2; *Neues Deutschland*, 28 October 1963, 1.

Figure 26   A makeshift memorial for the victims of a terrorist attack in Berlin, December 2016 (John MacDougall/AFP via Getty Images)

state ceremony, similar to what the French government had done after the 2015 terrorist attacks in Paris. Relatives of victims complained about the 'inadequate culture around grieving' on the part of the federal government and the state of Berlin.[26] In their view, victims had been hit at random and the attack had been aimed at society as a whole. An official state mourning ceremony would have been the appropriate response.[27]

Such demands and discussions show how much public grief and its reference points have shifted. In the 1920s, terrorist attacks, almost always carried out by right-wing radicals, targeted prominent representatives of the Weimar Republic. Rathenau was neither the first nor the last victim, and many other politicians and journalists stood in the crosshairs of *völkisch* assassins. For the republic, flying the flag and bestowing the highest state honours upon the murdered victims were acts of political self-assertion. The same went for West Germany in the 1970s and 1980s: when the far-left Red Army Faction cold-bloodedly killed men who, from its point of view, represented the 'fascistic' state apparatus, subsequent memorial services were held on the state's behalf.

[26] Maria Fiedler, 'Linke fordern Staatsakt für Anschlagsopfer', *Tagesspiegel*, 11 January 2017, http://bit.ly/3YEW2hY, accessed 21 December 2021.

[27] In 2022, the annual European Remembrance Day for Victims of Terrorism (established in 2005 to commemorate the Madrid bombings of 11 March 2004) was officially introduced in Germany on a national scale.

The far-right and Islamist attacks of the past two decades, by contrast, have targeted society at large instead of major state officials or public figures. Their victims have consequently asked for and experienced a different, civic form of mourning, with the active participation of local citizens. Grief has come from a broad spectrum of the population, and grieving has been a unifying emotional practice. Politicians and government bodies followed suit, and thus reacted to the sentiments and concerns of civil society, rather than prioritizing the interests of the state as such.

To put it simply, a hundred years ago the state expected citizens to mourn its representatives. Today, citizens expect the state to share their grief and help them cope. Ministers and heads of state are no longer the exclusive subjects of public grief when they pass away. Citizens also mourn fellow citizens who have lost their lives for political reasons or due to natural or man-made disasters. In doing so, they relate to new types of threats and at the same time show greater civic cohesion and personal empathy. This was lucidly demonstrated during the recent COVID-19 crisis. With more than 80,000 dead fourteen months after the pandemic's outbreak, an official mourning ceremony took place in April 2021. It not only catered to the emotional needs of the bereaved but also responded to a broad public sentiment of facing the crisis together and grieving with those who had lost their loved ones to the virus.

How people deal with grief has changed noticeably. After the Berlin attack in 2016, many of those affected wanted psychotherapy instead of prayers and church services. As a general trend, fewer and fewer Germans draw consolation from religious interpretations of loss and the support of priests and pastors. Whereas in 2002, 70 per cent of all burials took place in the presence of a chaplain, numbers had dropped to 52 per cent by 2019 and continue to decline. By no means, though, have people done away entirely with respective rituals and ceremonies. Professional funeral orators are a booming business, offering tailor-made speeches and memorial services. Sometimes close friends or family members of the deceased take on this role, making the farewell far more intimate, participatory and personal than church ceremonies could ever hope to be.

The subsequent 'grieving work' also takes place in a different way.[28] As medicine and psychotherapy identify grief as a potentially pathological adjustment or stress disorder, they offer a variety of methods and tools for managing it. Clubs and associations organize grief counselling and funeral consultations.

---

[28] Joshua M. Gold, 'Generating a Vocabulary of Mourning: Supporting Families through the Process of Grief', *The Family Journal: Counseling and Therapy for Couples and Families* 28, no. 3 (2020): 236–40; Ayten Zara, 'Grief Intensity, Coping and Psychological Health among Family Members and Friends Following a Terrorist Attack', *Death Studies* 44, no. 6 (2020): 366–74; Lidia Borghi and Julia Menichetti, 'Strategies to Cope with the COVID-Related Deaths among Family Members', *Frontiers in Psychiatry* 12 (2021), DOI: 10.3389/fpsyt.2021.622850.

Much happens in cooperation and communion with other affected people. In the wake of collective disasters, but also following personal loss, people often seek proximity to those who are living through similar experiences and fates. Rather than trying to control pain and divert grief, as was the practice until a few decades ago, it is now a matter of 'allowing' oneself to feel pain and grief and accepting one's own vulnerability. The 'problem case' today is the person who feels nothing, or too little.

The reasons for feeling grief are plentiful and not confined to untimely deaths. Those who are abandoned by a loved one can suffer from separation grief, as can those whose cat has run away. There is help for everyone, online and offline. Grief has become a lucrative line of business with numerous consolation providers, for which there was no equivalent a century ago. It has taken new forms and has positioned itself firmly and visibly in the public sphere. Louise von Beulwitz, who mourned her fallen son in 1914 and after, would have felt lost in the new culture of grief and grieving. She died in 1969 at the age of 95.

~

Hate

In the mid-1930s, Bertolt Brecht sent an appeal 'To Those Born Later'. Exiled in Denmark, he spoke of the 'dark times', in which he and many other refugees had to live, and asked future generations for their leniency and understanding. After all, the 'dark times' had invariably produced and left behind emotional scars and distortions: 'O, we who wanted to prepare the ground for friendship could not ourselves be friendly.' Rather, he and his comrades were fuelled by anger and hatred for the National Socialists whose 'horrors' had driven them out of the country. 'Yet we realized: hatred, even of meanness, contorts the features.'[1]

Brecht's poem, first printed in 1939 and later set to music and sung, is a moving piece of exile literature. It speaks of despair and > hope, of mourning and accusation. It is an accusation the author also directed at himself. As Brecht knew only too well, hate made you ugly and hateful, it repulsed and repelled people. Furthermore, it aligned those who hated, albeit for different reasons: when you hate your enemy and your enemy hates you, the two of you become alike in your shared passion for mutual annihilation.

With this text, the poet and communist sympathiser warned against viewing hate as a positive emotion or an effective tool in political struggles. In fact, he seemed to regret the hate he felt because it had been forced on him by those who had tried to take his life and the lives of his comrades. At the same time, though, hate helped him to contend with his situation and channel his despair outward. Hate is a strong and 'hot' emotion; it is no coincidence that we speak of 'blazing', 'burning' and 'smouldering' hatred. Heat supplies energy to the body, it prepares it for resistance. Those who hate do the opposite of those who stoically accept their fate and, in Brecht's words, 'shun the strife of the world'. Hatred is pure, unbridled passion, which, according to *Meyers Lexikon* of 1926, expresses itself 'when sufficiently strong in attitude, face and demeanour'.[2]

---

[1] Bertolt Brecht, 'An die Nachgeborenen', in Bertolt Brecht, *Gedichte*, vol. 4 (Berlin: Aufbau Verlag, 1961), 148–51.
[2] *Meyers Lexikon*, 7th ed., vol. 5 (Leipzig: Bibliografisches Institut, 1926), 1172.

It was precisely this hot passion that saved those who felt it from sinking passively into lethargy or self-pity, or from resigning themselves to the 'horrors' of the other side. Hate could stoke outrage and guide political resistance. Then again, hate was not a pleasant feeling, either for the one who experienced it or for those who witnessed it. Hate was draining, it exhausted and consumed both body and psyche. And it contorted the features, marring one's face and character. In German even the word itself, *Hass*, sounds like a cracking whip. People tried to avoid those consumed with hate because sooner or later their biliousness would poison the relationship.

Wartime Hate

In 1954, the *Brockhaus* encyclopaedia described hate as an 'annihilation affect' with immense destructive intensity.[3] Post 1945, 'annihilation' automatically calls to mind the Nazi war machinery, the Eastern campaign of destruction against Poland and the Soviet Union, the 'extermination of unworthy life' and the Holocaust. Hate seems to have been endemic under National Socialism. It was directed against those that the regime regarded as enemies or vermin, whether socialists, communists, Jews or homosexuals. But hate was not born into the world in 1920 with the founding of the Nazi Party. Already in 1814, the young poet Friedrich Rückert had called on German men to hold 'tremendous hatred' for their enemies. Back then, the enemy was in the west and had a name: Napoleon. His armies occupied large parts of Europe but met with increasing resistance. For Ernst Moritz Arndt, the first preacher of hate in modern German history, '*Volkshass*', people's hatred, was the appropriate response to French rule. Ridding themselves of the occupier and protecting the 'highest human things', namely 'law and freedom', would require the Germans to mobilize 'noble hatred' against 'injustice and disgrace'.[4]

Arndt was the first but hardly the last German to incite his countrymen to hate external foes. A century after his and Rückert's incitements, Berlin writer Ernst Lissauer published his infamous 'Hassgesang', or 'Hymn of Hate against England':

> Hate by water and hate by land
> Hate of the head and hate of the hand
> Hate of the hammer and hate of the crown
> Hate of seventy millions, choking down.

It celebrated those who 'will not forego' their hate and 'hate with a lasting hate'. What is interesting about this rhyme, which was recited gladly and

---

[3] *Der Große Brockhaus*, 16th ed., vol. 5 (Wiesbaden: Brockhaus, 1954), 289.
[4] Friedrich Rückert, *Gesammelte Poetische Werke*, vol. 1 (Frankfurt: Sauerländer, 1882), 43–48, quote 45; Ernst Moritz Arndt, *Ueber Volkshaß* (s.l., 1813), quotes 7, 9.

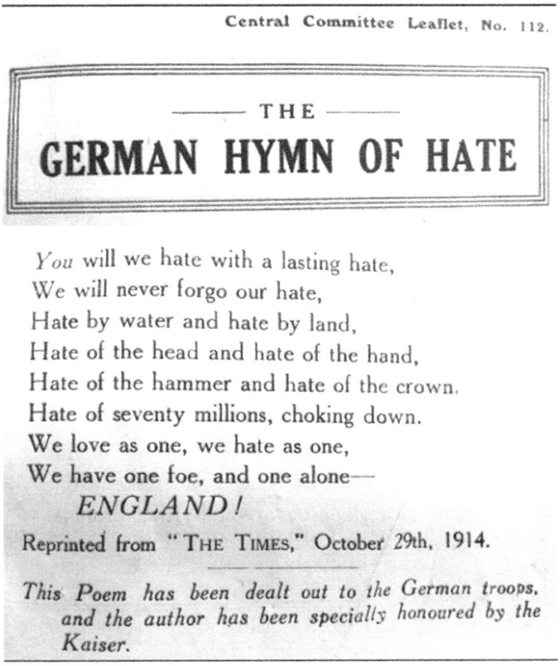

Central Committee Leaflet, No. 112.

——— THE ———

GERMAN HYMN OF HATE

You will we hate with a lasting hate,
We will never forgo our hate,
Hate by water and hate by land,
Hate of the head and hate of the hand,
Hate of the hammer and hate of the crown.
Hate of seventy millions, choking down.
We love as one, we hate as one,
We have one foe, and one alone—
   ENGLAND !

Reprinted from "THE TIMES," October 29th, 1914.

*This Poem has been dealt out to the German troops,
   and the author has been specially honoured by the
   Kaiser.*

Figure 27   Lissauer's 'Hymn of Hate', October 1914

frequently at school celebrations, in concert halls and other venues during the
First World War, is the distinction it makes between nations (Figure 27).
Although Germany was also waging war against Russia and France, according
to Lissauer the Germans did not really care about them; indeed, those countries could and would make peace again one day. England, on the other hand,
pursued Germany with > 'envy' and 'calculating shrewdness' and was the true
enemy worth hating.

What shines through in such sentiments is not only the disappointment
over the decision of the British government to enter the war on the side of
Germany's foes. Particularly in middle-class Anglophile circles, there was a
clear sense of love betrayed and closeness denied. England had been admired
and valued; therefore its 'betrayal' weighed particularly heavy. Answering this
with hate reflected Friedrich Nietzsche's observation: 'We do not hate what we
accord little value, but only what we consider equal or superior.'[5]

---

[5] The 1914 poem was reprinted and newly translated in Richard Millington and Roger
   Smith, '"A Few Bars of the Hymn of Hate": The Reception of Ernst Lissauer's "Haßgesang
   gegen England" in German and English', *Studies in 20th & 21st Century Literature* 41, no.

When Lissauer's song was reprinted in the 1914 Christmas edition of the *Messaggero* newspaper, it sparked intense controversy in Italy, which was still neutral at the time. American expatriates vehemently condemned it, calling hate for an entire people an 'antediluvian sentiment'. But Victor Klemperer, the son of a German rabbi and a lecturer at the University of Naples, spoke 'passionately in defence' of the Jewish author and said 'that with his hate song he spoke to me and to all of us from the soul; he had written our best war poem'.[6]

By no means did all Germans identify with Lissauer, though. One Catholic daily firmly advocated keeping the 'unchristian' 'Hassgesang' away from young people, an opinion the liberal *Berliner Tageblatt* emphatically shared. Even among adults, the *Tageblatt* did not see any need for such 'outpourings', were likewise completely out of place among the 'brave men' in the trenches. The readers of the *Nationalliberale Blätter*, a paragon of patriotism, were told not to give children 'caricatured English or Russian puppets' for Christmas and thereby stoke 'national hate and national revenge'. In the Orthodox Jewish journal *Jeschurun*, Rabbi Joseph Wohlgemuth beseeched his audience to overcome their 'natural' hatred for England through 'moral work', because 'great hatred' encourages 'the brutalization of the self' – an observation that reared its head again with Brecht two decades later. Hate, many agreed, did not suit a civilized nation, and it certainly would not secure or facilitate peace.[7]

From Class to Racial Hatred

Indeed, the peace reached in Versailles in 1919 stood on shaky ground. Internal peace was also in grave danger. A mutinous rumour spreading in right-wing circles, according to which the insurgent home front was to blame for the military defeat, fuelled hatred of the revolution and its alleged masterminds. In 1920, nurse Eleonore Baur was brought to trial in Munich for

---

2 (2017), art. 5, https://doi.org/10.4148/2334-4415.1928; Friedrich Nietzsche, *Beyond Good and Evil*, trans. Judith Norman (Cambridge: Cambridge University Press, 2002), 73. In November 1914, the respected Berlin professor Werner Sombart published an article on *Our Enemies* that repeated Lissauer's message: 'The entire German people, from the lowliest coach driver to the highest official in the Reich' were 'filled with unanimous, burning hate for England.' Apparently, this tirade of hate was so over the top that the editors of the newspaper distanced themselves from it (*Berliner Tageblatt*, 2 November 1914, no. 557, 1–2).

[6] Victor Klemperer, *Curriculum Vitae: Jugend um 1900*, vol. 2 (Berlin: Aufbau-Verlag, 1989), 252, 216.

[7] *Berliner Tageblatt*, 10 August 1915, no. 405; Lissauer's response, ibid., 12 August 1915, no. 409; Joseph Wohlgemuth, *Der Weltkrieg im Lichte des Judentums*, 2nd ed. (Berlin: Jeschurun, 1915), 51–61.

'inciting class hatred'. She was accused of 'harassing the Jews' and publicly blaming them for the misfortunes of recent years. The self-confessed antisemite did not deny this – but was nevertheless acquitted, since she had not directly called for violence.

Baur was a fanatical National Socialist right from the start. Fanaticism, which previously had a negative connotation, gained a favourable reputation in *völkisch* groups after the war. In 1893, *Brockhaus* still understood it as the 'reproving term for very strong convictions that consider any dissenting opinion immoral'. Yet by 1937, *Meyers Lexikon* was praising the fanaticism of the National Socialist who 'unconditionally' committed to 'his leader and his idea'. Here, fanaticism was seen 'in a positive sense, being completely seized and steeped' in personal and ideological loyalty. Unconditional service and full-throated commitment were two qualities Eleonore Baur did not lack – with them she later secured a career for herself in the Dachau concentration camp.[8]

National Socialists also celebrated hate as a constructive force as long as it was their own, legitimate, justified hate. In 1938, *Meyers Lexikon* distinguished between 'the heroic hate of the northern race and cowardly Jewish hate'. Heroic hate, the entry explained, 'involves relentless, but honest, unbowed and courageous rigour, it is controlled by will and insight, it arises predominantly from a sense of duty and responsibility to protect threatened values. In contrast, hate based on cowardice, envy, religious intolerance (Marxist class hatred, religious hatred, etc.) is insidious, base, it rules man.'[9] Not surprisingly, National Socialists claimed heroic, good hate for themselves. Leftists and Jews, by contrast, apparently knew only bad, spineless hate.

'Marxist class hatred' had already been a source of legal concern during the Wilhelmine period. The Penal Code of 1872 threatened to punish anyone who 'publicly incites different classes of the population to acts of violence against each other in a manner that endangers public peace'. In practice, this read as 'incitement to class hatred', meaning the alleged hatred of socialists towards the owners of capital. The 1920 prosecution of Eleonore Baur in Munich proved, however, that other actors and addressees could be included as well. The verdict also demonstrated that the law did not criminalize hate so much as the violence that could follow from it. Since Baur had not specifically called for violence against Jews, her hate could not be legally sanctioned.

Whether Social Democrats actually preached hatred for the capitalist class is open to debate. Their vocabulary certainly contained much talk of struggle and

---

[8] Daniela Andre, 'Eleonore Baur – "Blutschwester Pia" oder "Engel von Dachau"?', in *Rechte Karrieren in München*, ed. Marita Krauss (Munich: Volk Verlag, 2010), 166–85; *Brockhaus' Konversations-Lexikon*, 14th ed., vol. 6 (Leipzig: Brockhaus, 1893), 561; *Meyers Lexikon*, 8th ed., vol. 3 (Leipzig: Bibliografisches Institut, 1937), 1290.

[9] Ibid., vol. 5 (1938), 899.

oppression, exploitation and resistance. Yet hate speech was largely left to the Communists who made glad and ample use of it. In the 1926 campaign to expropriate the princely houses, the KPD urged 'hatred for the crowned thieves' alongside 'class hatred against capitalism and its slave system'.[10] The 'Marxist' narrative that capitalism was to blame for the miserable plight of workers even found some sympathy with Adolf Hitler. What he could not understand, though, was the 'boundless hatred they expressed against their own nation, how they mocked its greatness, polluted its history and dragged the names of the most illustrious men into the gutter'.

As he wrote in *Mein Kampf*, Hitler attributed this attitude to the Jewish influence on 'Marxists' and therefore 'gradually began to hate them'. The book, both a confession and a manifesto, was published in 1925 and conceptualized hatred – of Jews, socialists, parliamentary democracy, the Austrian state and many others – as a personal learning process. Hate was not innate, but developed through experience and critical reflection. 'The longer I stayed in this city [Vienna], the more my hatred grew against the foreign mixture of people who had begun to eat away at this venerable site of German culture.' Later, in the days and nights of Germany's military defeat and the 1918 Revolution, 'hatred grew in me, hatred for those who bore responsibility' for the catastrophe.

Without a doubt, Hitler considered his hate good, heroic even, because it was kindled by the fact that essential values – the German people and its future – were under threat and had to be protected. In contrast, the 'grim hatred' felt by Germany's enemies was deemed vile and treacherous since it was directed at the 'greatest asset' of all, the German army. The Allied decision to severely decimate it with the Treaty of Versailles was, Hitler claimed, the result of the hate felt by those 'who, out of > envy and greed, required and desired the impotence of the Reich and the defencelessness of its citizens'. Of course, he was referring first and foremost to Jews, those 'haters of every true culture' and of the 'white race', which they made every effort to destroy. Knocking non-Jews 'down from their cultural and political heights' was conditional to 'becoming masters themselves'.

The Nazi movement drew its fanatical force and justifications from this reverse logic. It regarded the enmity of its opponents as a 'prerequisite for its own right to exist'. Being hated and slandered was not something Nazis shied away from but something they yearned for and celebrated: 'We were fortunate enough to gain their hatred.' Unlike the hate acted out by Jewish, Marxist or Bolshevik 'rabble-rousers', the defensive hate preached by the National Socialists was not supposed to be envious, nor malevolent or cowardly. On the contrary, as Hitler emphasized time and again, they treasured the

---

[10] *Die Rote Fahne*, 29 May 1926, 1.

'self-evident respect for the hereditary natural otherness of peoples, which overcomes all racial hatred'. What inspired and stirred them was the good, honest and legitimate hatred of all those who were overrunning Germany with their malign forms of offensive hate.

The movement's declared goal was to 'implant in this nation once again the spirit of proud self-assertion, manly defiance and angry hatred'. Already at a party meeting in 1920, Hitler had called, to rapturous applause, for Germans to be inculcated with 'the feeling of hatred against everything foreign'. And so the rhetoric continued, until 1933 and far beyond. In his penultimate radio address, with the Red Army encroaching on Berlin, propaganda minister Joseph Goebbels appealed to Germans to show 'fanatical and fierce resistance' to 'our hateful enemies' and the 'coalition of satanic forces of global ruination', behind which stood the 'international Jewry'. That it was primarily the Hitler Youth who heeded the call to resist the 'powers of hatred' and the 'diabolical rage of destruction' shows how successful this rhetoric of hate had become, especially among children and adolescents who had been bathed in hate speech all their lives and did not know any better.[11]

Young men, too, felt attracted by the Führer's appeal to a legitimate feeling of hate that responded to the hate of others. Violence followed. As a strong bonding experience, it was both enticing and exciting. In the late 1920s and early 1930s, street fighting between Stormtroopers (the party's paramilitary wing), communist Red Front Fighters and the police occurred frequently and with brutal force. No side shied away from such battles, which were often deliberately instigated. Horst Wessel, a young, scrappy Nazi group leader, described the 'invasion of Berlin' in 1928 as follows: 'There is no end to the column. Friend and foe alike stare agog. Bravo, Stormtroopers! Hate and enthusiasm form a guard of honour. A few skirmishes keep things interesting.'[12]

---

[11] *Hitler, Mein Kampf: Eine kritische Edition*, ed. Christian Hartmann et al., 4th ed. (Berlin: IfZ, 2016), vol. 1, 221, 225, 365, 555, 725, 729, 825, 852, 907, 935; vol. 2, 1205, 1581, 1602–3; *Meyers Lexikon*, 8th ed., vol. 9 (Leipzig: Bibliografisches Institut, 1942), 76; *Berliner Morgenpost*, 20 April 1945, 1–2.

[12] Manfred Gailus and Daniel Siemens, eds, *'Hass und Begeisterung bilden Spalier'*: Die politische Autobiographie von Horst Wessel (Berlin: be.bra, 2011), quote 115. See also Dirk Schumann, *Political Violence in the Weimar Republic, 1918–1933: Fight for the Streets and Fear of Civil War* (New York: Berghahn, 2009), chs. 6–8; Molly Loberg, *The Struggle for the Streets of Berlin: Politics, Consumption, and Urban Space, 1914–1945* (Cambridge: Cambridge University Press, 2018), esp. chs. 3 and 4; Sabine Hake, *The Proletarian Dream: Socialism, Culture, and Emotion in Germany, 1863–1933* (Berlin: De Gruyter, 2017), 238–54; Sven Reichardt, 'Fascist Marches in Italy and Germany: *Squadre* and SA before the Seizure of Power', in *The Street as Stage: Protest Marches and Public Rallies since the Nineteenth Century*, ed. Matthias Reiss (Oxford: Oxford University Press, 2007), 169–89.

Hate in the GDR

After 1933, only the Nazis were landing punches. Communists and Social Democrats ended up in concentration camps and torture chambers or went into hiding; exile was granted to a few prominent men and women. It was from exile that Brecht wrote his pensive, self-critical message to the next generation. His own comrades in East Berlin, to whom he returned in 1948, had little appetite for such ambivalences. The GDR drew its own clear distinction between good and bad hate: 'Hatred as a social phenomenon', *Meyers Neues Lexikon* stated in 1973, 'either inhibits or promotes historical development, depending on whether it is an attribute of conservative or progressive social forces. It therefore cannot be subject to any fixed and abstract moral evaluation. It disappears as a social phenomenon with the full maturity of communist society and the complete elimination of capitalism.'[13]

However, as long as capitalism was still ascendant and communist society remained a speck on the horizon, hate found its venerable home in the arsenal of weapons deployed by 'progressive' socialism. The SED leadership regularly exhorted party members and loyal citizens to hate class enemies, imperialists, the saboteurs and traitors in their own ranks, fascists, capitalists and the West in general. Even young children were taught to hate. In 1949, Margot Feist, later Honecker, chairwoman of the Pioneer Organization, demanded that 'our Pioneers should learn to hate all who do not respect humankind, who exploit and oppress it'. 'American imperialism' was chief among them.[14]

In 1962, Minister of Justice Hilde Benjamin wrote an article entitled 'People must learn to love and hate' for the magazine of the Young Pioneers. Telling her young son the truth about his Jewish Communist father murdered in a concentration camp, she argued, had made him understand 'whom and why he had to hate'. Not everybody agreed. In her letter to the *Berliner Zeitung*, Hanna Schober advised pedagogical and political restraint. All parents, she said, try 'to explain to their children what is good and what is ugly [*hässlich*]'. Yet they should not 'burden them with the word hate too early' but instead 'offer positive models for emulation'.[15]

Official politics, however, went the other way. In 1972 the paramilitary Society for Sport and Technology announced that the next university championship would take place under the slogan 'Our love for the GDR, our hate for our enemies'. In 1985, the Stasi declared hate a 'defining component of Chekist sentiments' (Chekists being the umbrella name of the secret services in

---

[13] *Meyers Neues Lexikon*, 2nd GDR ed., vol. 6 (Leipzig: Bibliografisches Institut, 1973), 150.
[14] Leonore Ansorg, *Kinder im Klassenkampf* (Berlin: De Gruyter, 1997), 54. From 1963 to 1989, Margot Feist-Honecker was minister of education.
[15] Marianne Brentzel, *Die Machtfrau: Hilde Benjamin 1902–1989* (Berlin: Links, 1997), 104–5; Hanna Schober, 'Leserbrief', *Berliner Zeitung*, 12 November 1961, 11.

the Eastern Bloc). Hate was more than mere 'disgust and avoidance'. Those who felt hate wished to 'destroy or harm' the enemy. Consequently, the Stasi viewed hate as 'one of the decisive foundations for passionate and irreconcilable struggle against the enemy' as well as 'a lasting and powerful motive for action. It must therefore be consciously mobilized and reinforced as a stimulus for difficult operational tasks.'[16]

Whether all Stasi employees were actually filled with hate when they carried out their clandestine work of 'decomposition' remains an open question. Programmatically, though, hate was an important propaganda tool and educational goal. In 1967, the FDJ magazine stated that collectively performed songs should express 'anger and hate for your friends' murderers'; military recruits were sworn in with the promise to hold 'indelible hatred for the enemies of socialism and peace'.[17]

The state-controlled media, in particular, tried everything to feed and instigate hatred for external and internal opponents. When in 1976 the Lutheran pastor Oskar Brüsewitz died in a public self-immolation to protest the state's church policy, the SED newspaper *Neues Deutschland* wrote that he did not 'have all five senses intact'. The editors received thousands of critical letters in response, all of which disappeared into the archives. Christoph Kunze from Karl-Marx-Stadt explicitly addressed the author of the piece 'regarding your hate hymns. Rarely have I read so much hatred in an article or book. I cannot understand how you can spread such hate. This hate yields absolutely nothing. It would be better if you spread love. There is already enough hate in the world, but love is lacking.' Thirty years later, the paper formally apologized for the article it had printed, reporting that the 'evil slander' had been dictated by the leadership of the ruling party.[18]

At the same time, the GDR criminalized hate and 'rabble-rousing'. The 1968 Penal Code cracked down on 'racial and national hatred' and introduced a special paragraph about 'anti-state agitation'. It prohibited anything 'glorifying fascism or militarism'; a 1979 amendment explicitly mentioned 'race baiting'. That there were good reasons for this addendum, and that the GDR was no stranger to racial and ethnic hatred, became abundantly clear after 1989. Previously, evidence of right-wing extremist groups had been swept

---

[16] *Das Wörterbuch der Staatssicherheit*, ed. Siegfried Suckut (Berlin: Links, 1996), 168; as to the 'work of decomposition', 422–23.

[17] B. H., '"Wir singen, weil wir jung sind. . ."', *Neues Leben*, May 1967, 37; *Vom Sinn des Soldatseins: Ein Ratgeber für den Soldaten*, 34th ed. (Berlin: NVA, 1984), 33.

[18] A. Z., 'Du sollst nicht falsch Zeugnis reden', *Neues Deutschland*, 31 August 1976, 2; Siegfried Suckut, *Volkes Stimmen: 'Ehrlich, aber deutlich' – Privatbriefe an die DDR-Regierung* (Munich: dtv, 2015), 206; 'Warum dieser Hass? Reaktionen auf einen Artikel im ND', *Neues Deutschland*, 12 August 2006, 24; Martin Sabrow, 'Die Wiedergeburt des klassischen Skandals: Öffentliche Empörung in der späten DDR', in *Skandal und Diktatur*, ed. Martin Sabrow (Göttingen: Wallstein, 2004), 231–65, esp. 231–44.

under the carpet. From the 1990s, the signs could no longer be ignored. Their slogans and acts of hate were directed primarily at foreign contract workers and refugees, whom the predominantly young, male neo-Nazis wanted to violently throw out of the country (> Belonging). Xenophobic and antisemitic attitudes remain widespread in the East to this day, much more so than in the West.[19]

Western Hatred

But there were also hate preachers and activists in West Germany. Their actions were likewise punishable under the law, all the more so because across all parties, the official policy – unlike in the GDR – was to unconditionally disavow hate as a political weapon. After 1945, the notion of hate as good, noble or legitimate quickly became a thing of the past. The legislature took this into account when it reformulated the relevant paragraph of the Penal Code in 1960. The new text shared the reference to disturbing the public peace found in the old version, which had been in force since 1872. Added to this was a reference to human dignity and its defence against hatred, violence, insults, slander and malicious contempt. The rewording significantly expanded the scope of criminal offences.

Mounting antisemitic attacks, which culminated in the desecration of the Cologne synagogue on Christmas Eve 1959, formed the backdrop to this revision. Out of concern for their international reputation, but also to avert any 'danger to German democracy', parliament approved the new paragraph – after replacing the term 'incitement' with the 'more sharply defined expression "to incite hatred"'. For the first time, spreading hateful propaganda became a punishable crime.[20]

The paragraph has since undergone further revisions, most recently in 2011. The latest version differs from the 1960 statute in that the 'sections of the population' against which hatred can be incited have been expanded and described in greater detail: the law now protects any 'national, racial, religious

---

[19] According to a representative study conducted in 2018 by sociologists from the University of Leipzig, 47 per cent of East Germans and just under 33 per cent of West Germans were of the opinion that foreigners migrated to the country purely to exploit the welfare state. A similar difference emerged when it came to the question of whether the Federal Republic was 'excessively foreign' (überfremdet): 44.6 per cent of East Germans and 33.3 per cent of West Germans mostly or fully agreed. Regarding the statement 'There is something particular and strange about Jews and they don't really fit in with us', 26 per cent of West Germans agreed, while 39.6 per cent of East Germans did (Süddeutsche Zeitung, 8 November 2018).

[20] Peter Reichel, Vergangenheitsbewältigung in Deutschland (Munich: C. H. Beck, 2001), 146–57, quote 146; 'Entwurf eines Gesetzes gegen Volksverhetzung', in German Bundestag, Drucksache no. 3/918 (5 March 1959), quote 3.

group or a group defined by their ethnic origin' as well as individuals who are attacked due to their 'belonging to one of the aforementioned groups'. The additions enable the courts to penalize hate-fuelled attacks against asylum seekers and migrants.[21]

Such attacks have become commonplace. Antisemitic assaults are also on the rise again, out on the streets as well as in football stadiums.[22] For the most part, attacks are committed by younger, violence-prone men, egged on by far-right ideologues who find an audience in a variety of sect-like groups. They are supported by a party whose appeal and influence have been growing since 2015: the Alternative for Germany. In 2018, AfD leader Alexander Gauland defended hate in the German parliament, claiming: 'Hate is not a crime. Hate has reasons. One day, patience will run out.'[23]

Opinions vary widely as to the reasons and causes behind the feeling of hate, which the Federal Court of Justice defined in 1994 as 'an intensified hostile attitude against certain segments of the population that goes beyond mere rejection or contempt'.[24] The profiles of right-wing extremists often reveal people who have been aggressive since childhood and began committing crimes such as theft or assault at an early age. Joining radical associations gave their destructive behaviour a higher political purpose.[25] Some psychologists connect hate to a perceived slight or threat, which in narcissists provokes outrage and destructive impulses (> Anger, > Fear).[26]

Media experts, meanwhile, point out that such dispositions and perceptions can easily find a space to resonate on the internet, where they are multiplied, amplified and encouraged. The internet also seems to attract people with low levels of > empathy. Those who find it difficult to interact with others are evidently happy to switch to the impersonal, faceless communication of virtual

[21] Law revision, 16 March 2011 (*Bundesgesetzblatt* (2011), part 1, no. 11).

[22] Florian Schubert, *Antisemitismus im Fußball* (Göttingen: Wallstein, 2019), 71–141.

[23] *Die Zeit*, 20 November 2018, 8.

[24] 'BGH-Urteil, 15.3.1994', *Neue Juristische Wochenschrift* 47 (1994): 1421–23, quote 1422.

[25] Klaus Wahl, *Aggression und Gewalt: Ein biologischer, psychologischer und sozialwissenschaftlicher Überblick* (Heidelberg: Spektrum, 2009), 119–20, 159–60. See also Pete Simi et al., 'Narratives of Childhood Adversity and Adolescent Misconduct as Precursors to Violent Extremism: A Life-Course Criminological Approach', *Journal of Research in Crime and Delinquency* 53, no. 4 (2016): 536–63.

[26] Hans-Joachim Maaz, *Die narzisstische Gesellschaft: Ein Psychogramm* (Munich: dtv, 2012), 28–29, 202–3. See also Nicole M. Cain et al., 'Examining the Interpersonal Profiles and Nomological Network Associated with Narcissistic Grandiosity and Narcissistic Vulnerability', *Psychopathology* 54 (2021): 26–38; Emanuela S. Gritti et al., 'Narcissism and Reactions to a Self-Esteem Insult: An Experiment Using Predictions from Self-Report and the Rorschach Task', *Journal of Personality Assessment* 103, no. 5 (2021): 621–33.

spaces, where they can practise invective speech without restraint.[27] In online hate communities, users reinforce the validity of each other's interpretations of reality. A traditional newspaper can only disseminate hate from a central point and administer it to individual readers. New digital media, in contrast, enable and encourage hate to be generated, shared and approvingly commented on collectively and from below. This makes hate attractive and grants it power; hating feels good and foments an emotional community.[28]

Weimar Is Not Berlin

The internet-driven hate-world of the twenty-first century is therefore substantially different from the early twentieth century, even if political-ideological hatred did enjoy a good run back then. Archives house countless hate-filled letters and postcards addressed to the first president of the Weimar Republic, Friedrich Ebert, who served from 1919 to 1925. Many of the anonymous missives contained death threats: 'Usurper! We hate you and will overthrow you as soon as the time is right.'

> You old ass, you drunken dog, you daft saddler's apprentice, you want to govern but you're so drunk on power that you can't even stand up straight, you're too stupid to shit, and you want to swindle decent people. You dirty piece of crap, you and your cronies as well as your old lady will go up against the wall just like the swindler Erzberger. But your corpse, you criminal ass, will still be smeared with shit.

The senders variously identified as monarchists, communists, *völkisch*; everyone considered themselves justified in insulting, slandering and openly hating the Social Democrat at the head of the republic.[29]

Hate speech circulated on the streets, in taverns and in newspapers. In 1921, a sixty-year-old casual labourer from Berlin appealed to Ebert to intervene against the 'rabble-rousers': 'Since the Communists, and even the Social Democrats, to whom I had previously belonged, have recently begun repeatedly cursing and baiting, I must sincerely ask you as a worker: urge the people to keep calm. They are always threatening violence and nothing good comes from it.' In the same year, Hermann Reisner of Hamburg relayed a conversation he had overheard on the train, in which a bailiff had supposedly spouted

---

[27] Martin Melchers et al., 'Low Empathy Is Associated with Problematic Use of the Internet: Empirical Evidence from China and Germany', *Asian Journal of Psychiatry* 17 (2015): 56–60; Teo Keipi et al., *Online Hate and Harmful Content: Cross-national Perspectives* (London: Routledge, 2017), DOI: 10.4324/9781315628370.

[28] Maik Fielitz and Holger Marcks, *Digital Fascism: Challenges for the Open Society in Times of Social Media* (Berkeley, CA: Center for Right-Wing Studies, 2019).

[29] Federal Archive Berlin, R 601, no. 17: anonymous postcard from Berlin, 2 September 1921; anonymous undated, received on 14 September 1921.

scurrilous lies about Ebert and his family. Reisner was non-partisan, he wrote, but his 'political need for purity' let him object to such behaviour, which 'stirs up hatred against the Republic'. He therefore made himself available as a witness and called on the president to prosecute the 'conscienceless slanderer' (> Honour).[30]

Hate speech from the far right and the far left continued to be directed at Ebert's successor, Paul von Hindenburg. In 1927, workers in the Ruhr region were given prison sentences for singing songs about stringing the president up from the nearest lamp post.[31] Such hateful expressions recurred in 1970 when right-wingers protesting against Ostpolitik displayed a banner depicting Chancellor Willy Brandt on the gallows (> Belonging). They were repeated in 2015 at a demonstration in Dresden, when an East German man carried a homemade gallows intended for Angela Merkel and her vice-chancellor Sigmar Gabriel. Although public prosecutors filed criminal charges against the man, proceedings were ultimately discontinued. Only Gabriel's injunction against the online sale of miniature gallows proved successful.[32]

Other politicians (and journalists) have likewise been on the receiving end of obscene hate mail in recent years. Women especially find themselves in the crosshairs of those who, without restraint, spout their misogyny and hatred of Jews and migrants. They usually do so anonymously from the perceived safety of the internet, rarely using their real names. Those who come under attack have defended themselves by reading out the hate messages in public or filing complaints.

Faced with such incidents, many people feel reminded of Weimar. The hate-distorted faces of young and middle-aged men who march against migrants with fists raised paint a clear picture. When right-wingers who deny the health risks caused by the COVID-19 virus and reject protective measures gather with torches at the private homes of prominent politicians and ministers, they adopt a threatening posture that emulates vitriolic practices from the 1920s and early 1930s. Stark hate also exists in the left-wing milieu, among the black-clad radicals who fought 'the system' by burning cars and creating havoc at the G20 summit in Hamburg in 2017. But unlike right-wing extremists, they do not usually direct their hate and violence against individuals, and especially not against those who are structurally marginalized. Moreover, left-wing extremists act in isolation and are neither applauded nor supported by the broader public. In contrast, the far-right movement increasingly extends into mainstream society. In social media, but also in readers' letters to leading broadsheets and in the comments section of their online editions, far-right sentiments find a considerable audience. This is, in no small part, a

---

[30] Ibid., Georg Neumann, 30 August 1921; no. 18: Reisner, 25 March 1921.
[31] Ibid., no. 52: letters from 14 and 18 January 1927.
[32] http://bit.ly/3RUW96S, accessed 5 January 2022.

Figure 28   'Hate is no alternative': Dresden, January 2020

consequence of the sympathy that prominent AfD politicians have expressed for such positions.

The crucial difference between the Weimar Republic and today, however, is in the number and visibility of those who actively defend liberal democracy against vicious assaults and slander. Of course, some citizens did take offence to political hate speech back then. In 1930, a rank-and-file member of the Nazi Party in Westphalia contacted Hitler about

> accusations that many of our speakers often use unparliamentary expressions – such as pig, scoundrels, thugs, etc., which is most offensive in our Protestant Christian circles. The Communists and Social Democrats can allow such language, since it resembles them. I ask you politely but urgently to instruct speakers to refrain from this. Such publicity does not profit us. We must bank on proper, serious Christians, they are the most faithful and finest supporters of our party.

In November 1933, a Bavarian Catholic aired his displeasure that 'those at the top know only hate and terror': 'He who sows hatred cannot reap love.'[33] But such objections remained rare and could neither curb nor prevent the coarsening of speech and the physical violence that emanated from it.

After 1945, a broad consensus was slowly but insistently established: hate was no longer politically or socially acceptable. Distinguishing good from bad hate became a thing of the past, and Bertolt Brecht's warning was eventually heard – not least because the extreme dichotomy of friend or foe has lost its persuasive power and plausibility over seventy years of practising democracy. Certainly, verbal assaults have been and continue to be lobbed both inside and outside parliament's walls, and more than a few politicians and activists pride themselves on their sharp tongues. But it is widely accepted that opposition should not and must not lead to destructive enmity. The lesson has finally been learnt, with exceptions: in democracies, people argue, persistently and vehemently, polemically and pointedly. But they do not hate (Figure 28).

---

[33] Federal Archive Berlin, NS 51, no. 51/1: Carl Scobel, 8 September 1930; Bavarian State Archive Munich, II, Chancellery, no. 5633: anonymous undated (received on 3 November 1933).

~

Honour

Honour is an emotion unfamiliar to many these days. As early as 1974, actress Hanna Schygulla, who played the titular character in Rainer Werner Fassbinder's film adaptation of the novel *Effi Briest* (written by Theodor Fontane in the 1890s), struggled with the concept. Effi's loss of honour due to an extramarital affair and the subsequent pistol duel between her husband and his rival was a situation she found hard to understand.

Hanna Schygulla was not the only one who did not get it. In post-war West Germany, honour was rarely mentioned, let alone felt, though it bravely hung on when children (and sometimes adults) gave their 'word of honour'. Around 1900, however, the term honour had 'a very strong sentimental value', as the criminal law professor Moritz Liepmann put it.[1] In 1943, the year Schygulla was born, German men still 'possessed' honour and felt it 'in their bodies'. Not incidentally, the motto emblazoned on the belt buckles of SS uniforms since 1932 read 'my honour is loyalty'.

Honour and Power

At their 1936 'rally of honour' in Nuremberg, the Nazi party celebrated two major achievements: the reintroduction of compulsory military service and the remilitarization of the Rhineland. Both had, according to Hitler, lifted the 'chain of servitude from Versailles' and restored 'German honour'. The public lauded him for this. In 1935, party member Christian Etzel effusively thanked the Führer for the fact that every young German man may 'again wear the honourable army uniform'. On behalf of all women, Hedwig Elbers joyfully wrote: 'We will never forget that you, my Führer, have given Germany its honour back.'[2]

Honour, military power and sovereignty were intertwined. Not only the Nazis believed that a defenceless state was an honourless one. A country that

---

[1] Moritz Liepmann, *Die Beleidigung* (Berlin: Puttkammer & Mühlbrecht, 1909), 12.
[2] *Reden des Führers am Parteitag der Ehre* (Munich: Eher, 1936), 13–14, 24, 65; Federal Archive Berlin, NS 51, no. 75: Christian Etzel undated (April 1935); Hedwig Elbers, 19 April 1935.

could not defend itself had no power to protect and secure its existence. In the late 1800s, the renowned historian Heinrich von Treitschke explained to his students that 'a state's sense of honour must be highly developed if it is to be true to its own nature. The State is no violet, to bloom unseen; its power should stand proudly, for all the world to see, and it cannot allow even the symbols of it to be questioned.' Whoever impugned its honour 'casts doubt upon the nature of the State'. Therefore, 'if the flag is insulted, the State must claim reparation; should this not be forthcoming, war must follow, however small the occasion may seem; for the State has never any choice but to maintain the respect in which it is held among its fellows'.[3] Insulting its honour was considered a direct attack on the sovereignty of the state and a test of its readiness to stand up for its interests and principles.

This became apparent in 1914, when each party to the war invoked the notion of an honour attacked and to be protected. At least that was how it was communicated to the people who paid the price. On 28 July, the Austrian emperor justified the war against Serbia as being 'in Protection of the Honour of My Monarchy'. Announcing that the country's forces would be mobilized on 29 July, the tsarist ambassador in Vienna explained that Russia had been slighted in its honour as a great power. This obviously left the nation no choice but to respond in kind. The German kaiser refuted the allegation and assured the tsar that 'nobody is threatening the honour or power of Russia'. For his part, Wilhelm II declared on 4 August that he felt obliged to seize arms and stand for 'our might and honour'. Two days later, the British prime minister Herbert Asquith told the House of Commons that Britain was fighting 'in the first place to fulfil a solemn international obligation which, if it had been entered into between private persons in the ordinary concerns of life, would have been regarded as an obligation not only of law but of honour, which no self-respecting man could possibly have repudiated'.[4]

The Culture of Honour

Asquith's remark linked national honour and the individual honour of men, recalling a culture of honour that had been commonplace in nineteenth-century Europe. When journeymen fought over perceived slights it was their honour that was at stake; honour was an indispensable component of

---

[3] Heinrich von Treitschke, *Politics*, trans. Blanche Dugdale and Torben de Bille, vol 2. (London: Constable & Co., 1916), 595.

[4] Imanuel Geiss, ed., *July 1914: The Outbreak of the First World War* (New York: Batsford, 1967), 280, 324; www.dhm.de/lemo/html/dokumente/wilhelm144/, accessed 7 January 2022; Michael Brock, 'Britain Enters the War', in *The Coming of the First World War*, ed. Robert J. W. Evans and Hartmut Pogge von Strandmann (Oxford: Clarendon, 1990), 145–78, quote 177.

mercantile business; there were laws that permitted the immediate dismissal of workers who treated their employer or members of his family dishonourably. The concept of honour was adhered to most stringently and conspicuously by the aristocracy and the upper-middle class, who neatly recorded every violation and demanded vigorous retaliation if their honour was denigrated.

This culture lasted well into the twentieth century. In the summer of 1933, Dr Römer challenged the commissioner in the Ministry of Food and Agriculture, Dr August Hallermann, to a pistol duel. He felt that his honour had been besmirched because Hallermann had brought formal charges against him, leading to disciplinary proceedings. The case was taken to the Halle Court of Honour, which settled disputes among duelling fraternities and military officers. The court deemed the insult serious and decided that a sword fight was necessary. The ministry, however, wanted to prevent the face-off albeit 'without any kind of moral burden arising for Dr Hallermann'. In plain language: Hallermann, as the challenged party, should not give the impression that he would chicken out. One of his superiors therefore asked President von Hindenburg (who knew Römer from the battle of Tannenberg in 1914 and valued his agricultural expertise on his estate) to intervene. But Hindenburg's state secretary Otto Meissner considered it 'no longer possible at this stage to prevent the affair of honour from taking place, although I certainly agree with you that such a handling of official matters does not seem expedient'.[5]

With the outbreak of the war in 1939, Hitler, who had not previously voiced any fundamental opposition to armed duels over honour, ceased to have 'any understanding' for them, whether their reasons were 'official' or private.[6] Nor did the culture of honour hold much political or social sway after the war. The leading groups and circles in which the sentiment had formerly been cultivated lost their influence and prestige. Furthermore, political power no longer centred on honour, reflecting the limitation of sovereignty of both German states. The military heft underpinning state honour was also missing, as neither West nor East Germany had their own armed forces before 1955.

After 1945: Honour on the Wane

Interestingly, though, the government in Bonn linked the country's controversial remilitarization to a retrospective declaration of honour. In 1951, US president Dwight Eisenhower officially declared that German soldiers had fought 'bravely and honorably' for their country during the Second World War. He thus satisfied and appeased the former Wehrmacht officers whom Chancellor Konrad

---

[5] Federal Archive Berlin, R 601, no. 1117: letters from 21 July, 28 September and 20 October 1933. The files say nothing about the outcome of the case.

[6] Ute Frevert, *Men of Honour: A Social and Cultural History of the Duel* (Cambridge: Polity Press, 1995), 225.

Adenauer had asked back to assist the project of a West German 'defence contribution'. Because honour held a firm bastion in the military, Eisenhower's words meant a great deal.[7] They also endorsed the idea that the army had nothing to do with Nazi genocide and mass murders. It took nearly half a century until the first cracks in this image of a clean Wehrmacht began to appear. In the 1990s, exhibitions illustrated just how closely 'normal' soldiers and officers had been involved in the Eastern campaigns of extermination. The phrase 'honourable combat' has since been exposed for what it was: a political cover.

By then, people's reverence for the military had already been waning considerably in West Germany. The Bundeswehr, though conceived as the 'army of parliament' and committed to the ideal of the 'citizen in uniform', was never beloved. Ever more young men who were conscripted into the military from 1956 onwards opted instead for community service. In East Germany, this was not an option. Those who refused to join the armed forces had to serve as non-combat 'construction soldiers' and faced serious disadvantages and reprisals as a result.

The GDR also adhered far more intimately than the Bonn Republic to the concept and sentiment of state honour. In their oath of allegiance, East German soldiers solemnly swore to 'uphold always and everywhere the honour of our Republic and its National People's Army'. Their peers in the West, meanwhile, vowed 'to serve the Federal Republic of Germany loyally and to defend the right and freedom of the German people bravely'. Neither state nor military honour was mentioned here.

The concept that there was a particular honour in being a student or academic also fell out of favour, in both German states. Vociferously defended during the Weimar Republic against any hints of democratic 'egalitarianism', it did live on in the early days of the Federal Republic. Fencing fraternities (which were banned in the GDR) fought tooth and nail to continue their ritualistic sparring. In 1953 the Federal Court of Justice granted their wish, emphasizing the sporting qualities of the *Mensur*. Nevertheless, fraternities rapidly lost their appeal. Neither their elite aura nor their mythologizing of honour and arms seemed appropriate in a society that was fast becoming more civil and democratic.[8]

Women's Honour, Men's Honour

In addition, new ideas about the roles of women and men in society went hand in hand with changing concepts of honour. At the turn of the twentieth

---

[7] Bert-Oliver Manig, *Die Politik der Ehre: Die Rehabilitierung der Berufssoldaten in der frühen Bundesrepublik* (Göttingen: Wallstein, 2004).

[8] Frevert, *Men of Honour*, 229.

century, a man's honour meant 'being able to rely on him, on his word and on his vigour'. A woman's honour, on the other hand, did 'not demand virile behaviour to the outside, but purity in the inner life'.[9] Purity here primarily signified bodily 'shamefacedness' (> Shame). Only married women were allowed to be sexually active. If a woman engaged in sexual relations before or outside her marriage, her 'chastity' and thus her honour were seen as violated.

The possibility that a woman might initiate such encounters was unthinkable, going against her assumed nature and leading as it would to social ostracization. The story of Elisabeth von Bennigsen is a case in point. In 1890, Elisabeth married the landowner Adolf von Bennigsen, with whom she had five children. Initially she resisted the advances of Oswald Falkenhagen, who frequented the Bennigsen house; eventually she 'succumbed' to him. Such wording reinforced the image of the defenceless, passive woman who gave herself to a seducer and thereby ruined her honour in a moment of weakness.

Elisabeth's misstep not only damaged her own honour but her husband's as well. What was done to a woman was done to her husband, who as head of the household assumed responsibility for her. The forty-one-year-old Adolf von Bennigsen accordingly challenged his 'insulter' to a pistol duel, which took place on the morning of 16 January 1902, and ended with the death of the challenger. Duels were forbidden under the law but met with only mild judicial reproval on account of their 'noble' motives and a kaiser who in such cases prioritized mercy over justice. Women who had lost their honour were not as lucky. A 'fallen girl' was guaranteed to feel the heat of public disapproval and private scorn. Following her husband's death, Elisabeth von Bennigsen was cast out by her family and her children were raised by relatives in, as family records show, less than loving circumstances.

Gender imbalance was also reflected in the law that penalized insults. It enabled fathers, husbands and guardians to take legal action if insults were directed at their wives or at 'children under paternal authority'. Furthermore, in line with the concept of 'indirect insult', a man was justified in feeling personally attacked if his wife or children were insulted. He could then pursue legal action to secure 'in his own name his own right', even if the slanderer had no intention of offending him. In the same spirit, the Hague Convention of 1907 defined rape by occupying military forces as an attack on 'the honour and the rights of the family'. Naturally, the family imagined in this definition was headed by a man.

This patriarchal belief was briefly unsettled during the Weimar Republic. In the 1920s, the High Court of Berlin expressed the view 'that an encroachment on the rights of the husband need not at the same time be an affront to his

---

[9] Liepmann, *Beleidigung*, 13; Frevert, *Men of Honour*, 161–62, 185.

honour'. That said, in 1930 the Supreme Court of Justice in Leipzig affirmed the opposite position as one that had 'always been supported by popular wisdom'. Consequently, adultery constituted 'as a rule a disrespect to the injured spouse and an affront to his honour'. Self-evidently, this referred only to male spouses and warranted no further explanation.[10]

The Nazi state adjusted the divergent positions by putting a new spin on the concept of 'family honour'. In accordance with 'healthy popular sentiment', the Supreme Court authoritatively returned the rights of honour to fathers and husbands.[11] This even outlived the end of the 'Third Reich', as a 1947 decision by the Freiburg Higher Regional Court indicated. Although the judges distanced themselves from the 'jurisprudence on family honour developed under the influence of National Socialism', they nevertheless recognized that calling someone's wife a 'whore' was a 'conscious manifestation of contempt for the husband as well'. In 1951 the Magdeburg Regional Court upheld this ruling. However, the Supreme Court of the GDR struck down the argument, denouncing it – incorrectly – as 'purely fascist' and – correctly – as a contradiction of the constitutional principle of equality.[12] Two years later, West Germany followed suit and repealed the law that allowed the husbands and fathers of insulted women and girls to file charges against the person who had insulted them. Such provisions no longer seemed in sync with the Basic Law's article on gender equality.

Sexual Assault

At the same time, the legal practice of classing sexual assault, in whatever form, as an attack on a woman's honour continued. In 1955, the Federal Supreme Court described a doctor's attempt to rape his female patient as a 'violent insult'. In 1967, the Higher Regional Court of Frankfurt explicitly referred to the concept of 'sexual honour' when it declared admissible a charge of sexual violation, battery and slander against a rapist. Similar views persisted in the GDR. In the late 1960s, a district court convicted two railway workers of 'joint coercion to sexual acts' with a sixteen-year-old girl. The regional court overturned the sentence, ordering the lower court to charge the defendants with 'hooliganism' instead. The Supreme Court, however, quashed the verdict,

---

[10] *Juristische Rundschau* 10 (1928): 1065 (court decision OLG Berlin, 19 January 1928); *Entscheidungen des Reichsgerichts in Strafsachen*, vol. 65, 1 (decision II. Criminal Panel, 23 October 1930).

[11] Georg Dahm, 'Der strafrechtliche Ehrenschutz der Familie', *Juristische Wochenschrift* 65 (1936): 2497–503; *Entscheidungen des Reichsgerichts in Strafsachen*, vol. 70, 94–100 (court decision, 13 February 1936, quote 98), 173–76 (court decision, 27 March 1936), 245–51 (court decision, 18 June 1936). Jörg Ernst August Waldow, *Der strafrechtliche Ehrenschutz in der NS-Zeit* (Baden-Baden: Nomos, 2000), esp. 118–50, 186–94.

[12] *Deutsche Rechts-Zeitschrift* 2 (1947): 416; *Neue Justiz* (1952): 123–24.

arguing that the crime was not one of hooliganism but of insult: the defendants 'through indecent harassment had grossly disrespected the personal
dignity of the witness', something a 'socialist society' could not condone.[13]

Significantly, the Supreme Court did not base its decision on honour but on
dignity. It thus conformed to the GDR's new penal code, which came into force
in 1968. Rape was now an offence 'against personal liberty and dignity'. Insults
were classified as attacks on 'personal dignity', while 'lowering the social
reputation of a person or a collective' counted as slander. Meanwhile, the
West German judiciary chose to alternate between dignity and honour without
coming up with sharp definitions or criteria of distinction. A sea change
happened in 1973. What had previously been called 'public decency' was now
renamed 'sexual self-determination'. This transformed what was to be protected
from morally charged and highly gendered notions of sexual 'honour' to the
right of every person to decide their own sexual desires and behaviour.

Legal developments clearly reflected the social, emotional and political
changes that had been taking place in both countries. Equal rights for men
and women, which had already been recognized in the Weimar Constitution
and enshrined both in West Germany's Basic Law of 1949 and in the GDR's
constitution, gained increasing social validity. More and more assertively,
women criticized gender discrimination and made their demands for equality
public, first via traditional organizations and as members of political parties;
later, and more radically, in the West German feminist movement.

They pointed out inequalities in family and criminal law, which often
treated women as if they were men's property instead of human beings with
the same rights to self-determination and bodily integrity. They also could not
stomach the double standard regarding sexual mores: while women were
supposed to adhere to social norms regarding sexual purity (> Disgust) men
enjoyed far greater freedoms. Such hypocrisy had already caught the attention
of the women's movement back in 1900, although they could not do much
about it then. Seventy years later, sensibilities were different, and gender
equality, including when it came to sexual conduct, emerged as a prominent
and widely discussed topic (> Love).

Furthermore, it no longer seemed appropriate to reduce a woman's honour
to her sexuality. Early on, first-wave feminists had protested the fact that
women were perceived only in terms of their 'sexual honour' whereas a man's
honour could be based on many things, be it his profession, public office, his
performance in sports or as a citizen. As soon as women, after the 1918
Revolution, acquired active citizenship, were elected to parliament, held public
office, entered prestigious professions and had careers in sports, they gained

---

[13] *Goltdammer's Archiv für Strafrecht* (1956): 316–17; *Neue Juristische Wochenschrift* no. 44
(1967): 2076; *Neue Justiz* (1970): 303–4.

access to other forms of honour as well. Still, it took them another half-century to cast off the defining power of sexual modesty and purity.

Inclusion and Exclusion

Meanwhile, people's attitudes towards honour had altogether changed. Before 1914, many believed – somewhat grudgingly – that the nobility and the upper-middle classes possessed more honour than other social strata. This became less convincing during the war when the notion of 'national honour' enjoyed enormous popularity. National honour pertained to all citizens, regardless of social, economic and cultural differences. All that mattered was the sense of > belonging to the nation. The promise of inclusion effectively mobilized support for the war. Gertrud Bäumer, a leading figure in the bourgeois women's movement, was not the only one who enthusiastically participated 'in this vast, serious merging of all national forces into a great common will', into a true 'people's community' (*Volksgemeinschaft*).[14]

When the Nazis came to power in 1933, they, too, placed special emphasis on the notion of *Volksgemeinschaft*. It included each and every German, and all had an equal share in the honour of that community. Honour, as stated in 1936, was decidedly 'not bound to ancestry, education or class'.[15] Still, it was by no means strictly and entirely egalitarian. Excluded from the people's community on racial grounds, Jewish Germans had no claim to national honour. The Nuremberg Laws, passed in 1935, ensured 'the protection of German blood and German honour' and forbade Jews 'to hoist the national flag and to display the national colours'. Citizenship was restricted to 'subjects of German or kindred blood' as the sole 'bearers of full political rights'.[16]

By the time compulsory military service was reinstated that same year, Jews were prohibited from the honour of bearing arms and defending the nation, a slight that Königsberg journalist Ludwig Goldstein, among others, regarded as a great humiliation (> Humility). The chemical scientist and entrepreneur Willy Liebermann also felt deeply offended when his student fraternity removed his alumnus status in 1935 because of his Jewish heritage. As someone who had been a member for more than fifty years and 'lived a whole life according to the principles of German honour', he found the exclusion a

---

[14] Gertrud Bäumer, *Lebensweg durch eine Zeitenwende*, 6th ed. (Tübingen: Wunderlich, 1933), 269–70.

[15] Fritz Gürtner, ed., *Das kommende deutsche Strafrecht: Besonderer Teil*, 2nd ed. (Berlin: Vahlen, 1936), 551.

[16] For the Reich Citizenship Law of 15 September 1935, and the First Regulation to the Reich Citizenship Law of 14 November 1935, see https://germanhistorydocs.ghi-dc.org/pdf/eng/English32.pdf, accessed 6 April 2022.

disgrace – not for himself but for the fraternity, which had so shamefully 'kowtowed' to power (> Shame).[17]

Liebermann was equally appalled when an 'Aryan' alumnus who had married a 'Jewish lady' was thrown out. This happened in 1933, two years before marriages and sexual relations between Jews and non-Jews were legally forbidden in order to 'protect the purity of German blood'. Breaking this law meant committing 'race defilement', a crime punishable with imprisonment and public ostracism (> Love). For National Socialism, blood and honour were indivisible. Anyone who betrayed the 'purity' of the German race also endangered the honour of the nation and brought disgrace upon themselves.

From Honour to Dignity

After 1945, both the racist and, initially, classist baggage carried by honour became too much. That it was associated with pre-democratic privileges and anti-democratic exclusions hastened its social and legal demise. The term took a backseat in the reformed penal codes, particularly as lawmakers found it difficult to clearly define the word or draw distinctions between honour, reputation, prestige, recognition or respect. In 1988, the legal literature contained more than sixty different definitions. The Federal Supreme Court did not clarify matters much when, in a 1957 ruling, it distinguished 'inner honour' from a 'good external reputation' and saw the former deriving from 'individual dignity which is inalienably conferred on man from birth'. In 1989, judges no longer found this convincing. Honour, they argued, was only 'one aspect of human dignity' and not the same thing. Equating the two removed the specific contours of honour as a 'legally protected right'.[18]

However, it proved difficult to guess where these contours lay. This is one reason why honour as a legal concept has faded since the 1970s. Some jurists regretted this, holding it responsible for the 'coarsening' of manners, especially in politics. Others pointed out that attacks on a person's honour and right to respect could still be prosecuted, either in accordance with the criminal law sections pertaining to insults, or with the 'common view' in the form of a 'private settlement' before a civil court.[19]

---

[17] Ludwig Goldstein, *Heimatgebunden: Aus dem Leben eines alten Königsbergers*, ed. Monika Boes (Berlin: NORA, 2015), 140; Willy Ritter Liebermann von Wahlendorf, *Erinnerungen eines deutschen Juden 1863–1936* (Munich: Piper, 1988), 42, 262–64.

[18] *JuristenZeitung* 13 (1958): 617; *Entscheidungen des Bundesgerichtshofes in Strafsachen*, vol. 36, 1990, 148.

[19] Rudolf Mackeprang, *Ehrenschutz im Verfassungsstaat* (Berlin: Duncker & Humblot, 1990), 13 ff.; Peter J. Tettinger, *Die Ehre – ein ungeschütztes Verfassungsgut?* (Cologne: Schmidt, 1995), 25 ff.; Georg Nolte, *Beleidigungsschutz in der freiheitlichen Demokratie* (Berlin: Springer, 1992), 5–6, 47–48.

The common view also increasingly tended to replace honour with dignity. The term, closely associated with philosopher Immanuel Kant, featured prominently in the documents drafted by those who actively resisted National Socialism. In 1943, the Kreisau circle, a small group of dissidents centred around Helmuth James and Freya von Moltke, defined the 'inviolable dignity of the human person as the basis of the legal and peace order to be striven for'. A year later, Social Democrats exiled in London imagined 'respect for and protection of the liberty and the dignity of each person' as inalienable principles for a future 'German Republic'. As the experts who drafted the West German Basic Law in August 1948 stipulated in the first of 149 articles: 'The state exists for the sake of man, not man for the sake of the state. Human dignity shall be inviolable. To respect and protect it shall be the duty of all state authority.'[20] With such wording, they clearly distanced themselves from the policy of the 'Third Reich' of putting the state or rather the *Volk* before individual rights.

Moreover, dignity had the advantage of being fundamentally inclusive because it was granted without discrimination to all. This made it a more suitable concept than honour for modern societies that considered themselves egalitarian.

'Honour Killings'

The extent to which dignity successfully replaced and displaced honour in the post-war German emotional economy became glaringly apparent in the 1990s when so-called 'honour killings' were brought to public attention. The term described the deliberate murder of a family member, usually a woman, in retaliation for the alleged disgrace her (sexual) conduct had brought upon herself and her family. Only by getting rid of the shameful woman could the damaged honour of her relatives be restored.

The perpetrators were in most cases men of Turkish or Arab origin. Many came from Kurdish regions, where people adhered to particularly severe regulations and traditions. These impacted young women especially, whose rearing and mores the family closely monitored. Those who transgressed the accepted rules of conduct were held to account. In extreme cases, transgressions might be punished with death at the hands of a brother, father or uncle.[21] The experience of migrating to Germany and other European countries exacerbated the problem since many young women were attracted to the

---

[20] Ignacio Czeguhn, 'Das Verhältnis von Menschenwürde und Menschenrechten in historischer Perspektive', in *Menschenwürde und Demütigung*, ed. Eric Hilgendorf (Baden-Baden: Nomos, 2013), 9–22, quotes 16–19; www.gesetze-im-internet.de/englisch_gg/englisch_gg.html-p0019, accessed 6 April 2022.

[21] Dietrich Oberwittler and Julia Kasselt, 'Honor Killings', in *The Oxford Handbook of Gender, Sex, and Crime*, ed. Rosemary Gartner and Bill McCarthy (Oxford: Oxford University Press, 2014), DOI: 10.1093/oxfordhb/9780199838707.013.0033.

new freedoms on offer. When they rejected the strict dictates imposed by their families, some men reacted aggressively. The more they felt stuck in precarious social and economic circumstances, the greater value they tended to place on preserving their cultural or religious identity and patriarchal authority.

In 2005, the case of Hatun Sürücü hit the headlines. Born in Berlin in 1982 to East Anatolian parents, Sürücü dropped out of high school at her father's request and married a cousin in Istanbul, to whom she fell pregnant in 1999. Shortly thereafter she left her husband and returned to Berlin, where she gave birth to a son and moved into a residential home for underage mothers. She finished her schooling, completed an apprenticeship as an electrician and rented her own apartment. Hatun Sürücü was a practising Muslim but did not wear a headscarf and she dressed in the latest fashions. Her family were deeply critical of these choices and her independent lifestyle. She received repeated death threats, which she reported to the police.

Unfortunately, they were not just threats. On 7 February 2005, Hatun Sürücü was shot on the street by her youngest brother. The murder attracted a great deal of attention. The family expressed no remorse and attempted to cover up the involvement of her other brothers. The German public reacted with horror. Vigils and demonstrations were held, and the local Berlin magistrate erected a plaque to commemorate the murdered woman and all 'other victims of violence against women in this city'.[22]

The idea that this violent act had been done in the name of honour met with general incomprehension. Even though some judges chose to accept such motives as a mitigating factor, with reference to the cultural and religious backgrounds of the perpetrators, mainstream society did not share this view. Using honour as carte blanche to devalue and despise those who thought and lived differently, let alone to kill them, sharply contradicted the now widely accepted principle that every human life is worthy of dignity and respect – even if you disagree with someone's way of living.

Honour, Performance and Service

At present, honour is socially accepted – if at all – mainly in the context of recognizing extraordinary achievements. In German, the podium where athletes receive their medals is called an *Ehrentreppchen* (honour step). In football stadiums, the *Ehrentribüne* or VIP box is reserved for 'honoured guests' from the worlds of politics, sports and entertainment. Pupils who score highly in annual nationwide sports tournaments get an 'honorary certificate' featuring the (printed) signature of the federal president. Academics and non-academics

---

[22] Matthias Deiß and Jo Goll, *Ehrenmord: Ein deutsches Schicksal* (Hamburg: Hoffmann & Campe, 2011).

Figure 29   GDR honorary medal for a 'Meritorious Member of the National People's Army' (Photo by ADN-Bildarchiv/ullstein bild via Getty Images)

can receive an 'honorary doctorate', and since 1980, soldiers might be awarded a 'badge of honour' or, from 2008, an 'honorary cross for bravery'. For as long as it lasted, the GDR created numerous awards to honour citizens for their achievements in the realms of economics, culture and politics and to encourage further service (Figure 29). The Bonn republic also had various medals and decorations relating to merit and honour.[23] Voluntary work is known as an

---

[23]   Christian Bailey, 'Honor Bestowed and Felt? *Verdienstorden* in the Federal Republic after 1945', *Tel Aviver Jahrbuch für deutsche Geschichte* 38 (2010): 61–78; Robin Schnitzler, '*Ehre heißt Planerfüllung!' Zur Geschichte der Instrumentalisierung und Manipulation von*

Ehrenamt (honorary office), a term that gives unpaid labour public recognition.

Honours bestowed by the state have, in the past, been particularly impressive because they signalled the recipient's proximity to power. With the state becoming more democratic, 'rational and disenchanted' state honours have accordingly lost some of their elite status and magic.[24] These days they are mostly seen as an effective way to recognize those who go the extra mile and work for the common good. What this actually means to the recipients depends on how much they identify with the state that honours them. It also depends on numbers. In East Germany, the emotional value of medals decreased the more prevalent they became. Acclaimed 'Heroes of Labour' rarely felt especially heroic, and the 'honoured' woman in Wolfgang Mattheuer's 1973 painting looked anything but happy. The Cross of Honour of the German Mother, which was awarded to millions of particularly fecund women between 1939 and 1945, has fared similarly poorly in the popular imagination – people derogatively named it the 'rabbit medal' (Figure 30).[25]

Other decorations, particularly the rare ones, were very much sought after, however. These included the Pour le Mérite, the Prussian Crown's highest order of merit for officers' bravery, which was first awarded in the eighteenth century. One of the last recipients was twenty-three-year-old Lieutenant Ernst Jünger, who received the honour in September 1918. Four years earlier, the successful business attorney Dr Eduard Bloch had fought for higher civilian honours in Munich. Not without reason could he assume that his Jewish origins stood in his way. Although he already held the honorary title of Privy Councillor of Justice, he did not regard this as a 'special distinction'. Being awarded the Order of Saint Michael had offended more than venerated him as he felt it did not adequately reflect his achievements. Moreover, the fact that it had come without a crown had been noted negatively by the military, which he had joined immediately after the outbreak of the war. He therefore urged the Bavarian chief of cabinet to intervene for 'the upgrade of the minor medal'. He recognized that his request was 'untimely' and 'a great imposition on you. But do not misjudge the importance that this in itself insignificant matter has for me, especially under the current circumstances, and do not scold me for it.' It was not, he explained, out of 'foolish vanity' that he asked such a favour but because he felt set back in comparison to his Christian

Ehre und Geehrten mit Hilfe von Auszeichnungen in der DDR (Berlin: Weißensee-Verlag, 2007).

[24] Georg Dahm, *Völkerrecht*, vol. 3 (Stuttgart: Kohlhammer, 1961), 241.

[25] Irmgard Weyrather, *Muttertag und Mutterkreuz: Der Kult um die 'deutsche Mutter' im Nationalsozialismus* (Frankfurt: Fischer, 1993), ch. 10.

Figure 30   The Cross of Honour of the German Mother was awarded to women with many children, 1940 (Photo by ullstein bild/ullstein bild via Getty Images)

colleagues of the same age and qualifications who had received preferential treatment.[26]

The Jewish lawyer fought so bitterly for official honour and recognition because the state denied him both and treated him as a second-class citizen owing to his religious background. But the incident also proves that medals were worth far more in 1914 than they are today and that they translated directly into social prestige. It would never have occurred to Eduard Bloch to

[26] Bavarian State Archive Munich, III, Geh. Hausarchiv, Cabinet Files Ludwig III. no. 82: letter from Bloch, 5 January and 28 December 1914.

turn down a medal, as Helmut Schmidt or Jan Philipp Reemtsma later did, their refusal safeguarded by the democratic nature of the society they were living in. As proud Hamburgers, they shared the view that the Federal Cross of Merit would contradict the spirit of the Hanseatic constitution.

In 1997, the missionary doctor Margret Marquart returned the Cross of Merit for a different reason: to protest Germany's asylum policies. Such actions refute the assumption that orders are mere baubles. They do express an emotional attachment to the state on the part of those who are or are not honoured, who reject or return them. Before the era of 'rationalization and disenchantment', this attachment was called > love.

~

Hope

'We must be crazy with hope': so begins Wolf Biermann's 'Welcome Song for Marie', a tribute he wrote and recorded to mark the birth of his daughter in 1982. The song contrasts the heart-warming joy Biermann felt at her arrival with apocalyptic images of the environment.

> *All around your cradle*
> *forests of weapons are sown*
> *you're in the battlefield*
> *Marie, and when you're grown*
> *there'll be no air to breathe*
> *and nothing left to eat*
> *the earth's forgetting of us humans*
> *will be total and complete.*

The earth, he continued, *'will become a barren star / just like other barren stars'*. Casting a child into this world would be absolutely foolhardy – were it not for hope (Figure 31).

Hope and the Future

Many people were not as hopeful. Back then, left-wing intellectuals in West Germany liked to talk themselves out of having children by referring to the dire state of the world. The songwriter Biermann, who did his part to bring nine children into existence, clearly thought otherwise. Even in the GDR, where he had been blacklisted from performing or publishing since 1965, the critical communist did not lose hope – despite Stasi 'decomposition measures' that made living and loving difficult for him. After he was stripped of his citizenship in 1976, Biermann returned to his native Hamburg and continued to sing, write poetry and procreate. All around him teemed political, military and ecological threats. When he wrote his song of welcome and hope in 1982, the nuclear arms race was in full swing and a new cold war between the blocs was in the air; the peace activists feared it could turn hot at any moment. Meanwhile, the environmental movement had also gathered momentum, highlighting issues from air and water pollution to acid rain and dying forests.

Figure 31   Hope as Wolf Biermann saw it: LP cover, 1982

In the face of all this, Biermann took Marie's birth as a sign of hope. Admittedly, he acknowledged that he was *verrückt*, crazy. But not because he and the child's mother hoped, despite all evidence to the contrary, that life would go on and could even get better. Rather, it was hope itself that made them 'move out of place' by shifting ('*verrücken*') their perspective and letting them see the future through new eyes. Those who nourished hope refused to accept visions of the apocalypse. Instead, they did everything they could to ensure those visions did not become a reality. Siring children and welcoming them with a beautiful song was one form of resistance, the new social movements of the 1970s and 1980s were another.

Hope is always oriented to the future. Only the dead, as in Dante's *Divine Comedy*, had to abandon all hope as they stepped through the gates of hell. Hopeless people seem dead before their time: lifeless, apathetic, devoid of all joy and vitality. Even in difficult or depressing circumstances, a glimmer of hope generally persists. It is often stronger in the young, for whom much of the future lies ahead, than in the elderly. In 1966, the Austrian writer Jean Améry recalled that in the years immediately following his emigration in 1938, his 'homesickness and longing for the past' were, to a certain extent, 'offset by hope'. Although his past had been torn away from him and his present was not quite 'decipherable', as a man in his mid-twenties he had a future ahead of him, and that future was open. 'But the credit of the person who is aging', he wrote, 'depletes. His horizon presses in on him, his tomorrow and the day-after-tomorrow have no vigor and no certainty.'[1]

Améry, who took his own life in 1978 shortly before his sixty-sixth birthday, somewhat dramatized the experience of ageing, which given his own biography was understandable. In today's world, though, where sprightly seniors remain active and engaged in society well into their eighties, ageing no longer means relinquishing hope or the future. Palliative care doctors and hospice workers speak of people whose time has run out but who nevertheless look forward to the next day, the next visit, the next breakfast – hoping that they will live to see it all. Hope springs eternal and dies last: there is a great deal of wisdom and experience in this saying, which has been passed down in many languages. In Roman antiquity the dictum was *dum spiro spero:* while I breathe, I hope. Since then, the adage has adorned family crests as well as church windows and has functioned as a leitmotif for armies, states and institutions alike.

It retained its practical significance even and especially into the twentieth century. Devastating world wars, mass murder and genocide, displacements and harsh economic slumps took their toll on many people's hopes for the future. Indeed, what kind of future did those locked in Nazi concentration and extermination camps have, and what could they hope for? Yet even there, the hope that they might – against all expectations – escape this hell on earth helped people survive another day.

In Crisis: Conditions in Weimar

Hope was also an important resource for enduring the stark political polarization and severe economic crises of the 1920s and early 1930s. Many citizens gathered 'new courage and hope' from the 1925 election of First World War general Paul von Hindenburg, who succeeded Friedrich Ebert as president. When Hindenburg stood for re-election in 1932, Annie Gerhard, among others, wrote to him explaining that he undoubtedly knew 'what privations and restrictions have been imposed on the low-ranking civil servants.

---

[1] Jean Améry, 'How Much Home Does a Person Need [1966]', in Jean Améry, *At the Mind's Limit,* trans. Sidney Rosenfeld and Stella P. Rosenfeld (Bloomington: Indiana University Press, 1980), 41–61, here 57–58.

Nevertheless, one is willing to hold on if one can at least see a ray of hope. My husband is a railway assistant and his salary is barely enough to live on. But I have not given up hope.' She placed her hopes in Hindenburg, who 'with God's help will now make everything good', 'just as [he] understood throughout the war how to find the right path'.

Luise Sauerteig, a retired teacher from Nuremberg, likewise spoke of a 'ray of hope' as she thanked Hindenburg for running again. Twenty-one-year-old Martha Schneider from Leipzig confided to Hindenburg that she 'stands so often in my room in front of your picture: I draw renewed strength and courage from your determined features'. Mrs Lohmann of Berlin hoped that 'things will get better soon' in her letter to the president. She reported that she had listened 'enthusiastically' to the radio speech Hindenburg had delivered on 10 March 1932 and asked him to amend the 'silly emergency decree': 'For you see, my husband will soon be three years without work and we must often go hungry and freeze because the 13 marks from welfare don't cover anything with a rent of 30 marks.'[2]

In April 1932, almost twenty million voters chose Hindenburg as their beacon of hope – 53 per cent of those who had voted, with a turnout of 83.5 per cent.

The Last Hope: Hitler

Yet for some 13.4 million voters, Hitler was the 'last hope', as one election poster suggested (Figure 32). It depicted an army of unemployed people, predominantly men from various social classes, with blank, desperate faces. Their only hope, according to the poster, lay with Hitler. The illustrator, Hans Herbert Schweitzer, working under the Nordic pseudonym 'Mjölnir', mimicked the style of Käthe Kollwitz, whose expressionistic etchings and lithographs powerfully captured social hardship and hopelessness. Schweitzer dispensed with the combative words and bold colours typical of election posters, choosing sepia rather than red to strikingly juxtapose the bright future the National Socialist movement promised with the oppressive, colourless present.

Sure enough, the rise in unemployment following the global economic crash of 1929 handed the National Socialists more and more votes. In the 1928 Reichstag elections, some 800,000 were cast for the Nazi Party. Over the next two years, this figure jumped to 6.4 million and doubled again by 1932, making the NSDAP almost as strong as the Communists and Social Democrats combined. However, since the KPD saw the 'social-fascist' SPD as

[2] Federal Archive Berlin, R 601, no. 378: Bepler, undated (received on 5 February 1932); Gerhard, 18 February 1932; no. 379: Sauerteig, 10 March 1932; Schneider, 5 March 1932; no. 380: Lohmann, undated (received on 11 March 1932).

Figure 32   The NSDAP election poster from 1932 proclaims 'Our last hope: Hitler' (Photo by Pictures from History/Universal Images Group via Getty Images)

its biggest enemy, a left-wing or even left–liberal coalition against the radical right-wing *völkisch* bloc failed to materialize.

Hitler's supporters and voters placed enormous hopes and expectations on his appointment as chancellor in January 1933. He was not able to deliver on all of these, and certainly not immediately, as the social and economic advancements he had promised were a long way off. While Stormtroopers frequently complained that they were still stagnating 'in the lowest ranks', members of the National Socialist Women's League took aim at these and other 'whingers and doubters'. They firmly clung to the belief 'that our Führer is the right man, the man who can and will secure Germany's future, and that he is connected to all of us in the tightest *Volksgemeinschaft*'. Hedwig Elbers, who wrote to Hitler in 1935 to congratulate him on his forty-sixth birthday, shared this sentiment. 'All of us who think and feel German have just one wish: may our beloved Führer remain with us. Out of the dirt and disgrace like a phoenix from the ashes, "Germany has risen again"! Once more we have a unified, united Germany, led by one hand – and a prudently purposeful one! Small states, impotent parliamentarianism and party strife no longer have a place – to Germany's benefit!'[3]

Hitler fed hopes for twelve long years. With each new promise for the future and each successful political or military action, they swelled until they were endless. Just as Mrs Elbers hoped for an ever larger fatherland and to see 'the country's borders stretch', many Germans dreamt of new Lebensraum in the east, where a lucrative career as a landowner, slaveholder or administrator awaited them. The regime pinned its hopes in turn on the youth, who embodied the glorious future and were well aware that they bore the hopes of the nation. 'I look into the future', sixteen-year-old Hildegard Schade, the daughter of a bricklayer, wrote to Hitler in 1936, 'and I feel so much joy! Germany is being developed and Germany will be great and strong again.' Twenty-two-year-old Lotte Seidel from Kassel introduced herself as a 'German girl' and exclaimed that she could hardly wait to become 'a German woman' and gift her children 'life, this marvellous life in your state'. Meanwhile in 1938, eight-year-old Frank Hendriks noted that he fervently hoped to become 'a German solider' as soon as possible. In this he was not alone.[4]

Miracles

That hope died last even in the 'Third Reich' was primarily thanks to masterful propaganda. Right up until the point of military collapse, Goebbels's apparatus

---

[3] Federal Archive Berlin, NS 51, no. 73: Wilhelm Dörries and Horst Hermann Sagel, 1 January 1935; no. 75: Fanny Caspari, 19 April 1935; Hedwig Elbers, 19 April 1935.

[4] Ibid., no. 63: Hildegard Schade, 29 October 1936; no. 71: Lotte Seidel, 30 September 1938; Franz Hendriks, 19 October 1938.

was churning out notions of ingenious 'miracle weapons' that would turn the tide of the war and secure the 'final victory'. Hitler's rhetoric was full of self-fabricated miracles, raising hopes of further marvels that he alone with his special leadership talents would enable. Likewise, the Ministry of Propaganda played wantonly on the belief in a miracle-filled future.[5] In the popular 1942 movie *The Great Love*, Zarah Leander trilled *I know that someday a miracle will come*. The song was a hit. Its very first line appealed to the power of hope and predicted that 'a thousand fairy tales' would come true, even in times of war and, as one was meant to imagine, not just in terms of love.

Interestingly, the miracle metaphor survived the war's bitter end virtually unscathed. People talked of economic miracles (as they had in the 1930s) and of 'the miracle of Bern' (> Joy) when the German football team unexpectedly won the World Cup in 1954. Those who hoped for a miracle were typically in a poor and difficult situation that, under normal conditions, was unlikely to change. So they desperately needed a miracle, which usually arrived without warning, tempered justice with mercy and brought painful circumstances to an end. In the nineteenth century, composer Richard Wagner located miracles in the realm of the super- and non-human – think *Lohengrin*. In the twentieth century, miracles returned to earth. But even on terra firma, they retained their otherworldly aura and gloss of redemption. Unlike relying on chance, those who hoped for and were granted a miracle could feel uplifted, chosen and blessed.[6]

Future Promises and Disappointed Hopes in the East

Officially, both German states were founded in 1949 not with hopes for a miracle but with ambitious blueprints for the future. Each was eager for National Socialism to become a distant memory and to be known for democracy, although they understood it differently. The GDR expressed its certainty for the future in its national hymn: 'risen from the ruins and facing the future', Germany should become a 'united fatherland'. The third stanza made clear on whose shoulders these hopes rested: the 'German youth', who were described as the 'golden fund of our future' and 'our shiniest and best human material' at a party conference in 1949.

---

[5] *Reden des Führers am Parteitag der Ehre* (Munich: Eher, 1936); Ralf Schabel, *Die Illusion der Wunderwaffen* (Munich: Oldenbourg, 1994). On the Nazi 'miracle weapons', see also Eric Kurlander, *Hitler's Monsters: A Supernatural History of the Third Reich* (New Haven, CT: Yale University Press, 2017), 264–70.

[6] Clemens Risi et al., eds, *Wann geht der nächste Schwan? Aspekte einer Kulturgeschichte des Wunders* (Leipzig: Henschel, 2011); Karlheinz Barck, 'Wunderbar', in *Ästhetische Grundbegriffe*, ed. Karlheinz Barck et al., vol. 6 (Stuttgart: 2005), 730–73.

A 'better future' beckoned this youth, 'a happy future without war and crisis', as the young Pioneer Egon Krenz (who was to become, in 1989, the GDR's last strongman) rejoiced in 1950. As a four-year-old, Krenz had lost his father in the war; the family's house in Kolberg, now Polish, lay in ruins, and they were living near Rostock on a meagre pension. Against this bleak backdrop, the boy placed all his hopes in the 'young German Democratic Republic under the leadership of the workers' president Wilhelm Pieck'.[7]

Others soon abandoned hope and left the country in the hundreds of thousands while the borders were still open. After the Wall was built in 1961, Ernst Bloch, who taught philosophy at the University of Leipzig, similarly decided not to return to the GDR following a trip to West Germany. His major work, The Principle of Hope, written in exile, was published between 1954 and 1959, first in Leipzig and then in Frankfurt am Main. It laid out Bloch's vision of a concrete socialist utopia that would fulfil the unrequited hopes and dreams of the people. The last volume concludes with an emphatic commitment to the 'tomorrow in today':

> The real genesis is not at the beginning but at the end, and it starts to begin only when society and existence become radical, i.e. grasp their roots. But the root of history is the working, creating human being who reshapes and overhauls the given facts. Once he has grasped himself and established what is his, without expropriation and alienation, in real democracy, there arises in the world something which shines into the childhood of all and in which no one has yet been: homeland.[8] (> Belonging)

Thinking of Heimat, homeland, as a place to strive towards rather than a thing of the past suited the political agenda of the GDR just as well as Bloch's eulogy to the working man. Yet what each meant by 'real democracy' differed widely. When Bloch criticized the suppression of the 1956 Hungarian Uprising, the National Prize winner fell into disrepute and was forced into retirement a year later. In 1960s' West Germany, the philosopher found an attentive audience among left-wing liberals, including many influential theologians. The student movement read his work enthusiastically, above all Rudi Dutschke, with whom Bloch formed a fatherly friendship. His articulation of a socialist utopia, which came from the enthusiastic 'warm current' of people's unfulfilled hopes and desires rather than from the sober 'cold current' of Marxist political economy, resonated deeply with the alternative left in the 1970s and 1980s.[9]

---

[7] Leonore Ansorg, Kinder im Klassenkampf (Berlin: De Gruyter, 1997), 55–56; Federal Archive Berlin, DA 4 (Presidential Office GDR, Pieck 1949–1960), no. 1135: Egon Krenz, 16 October 1950.

[8] Ernst Bloch, The Principle of Hope, trans. Neville Plaice et al., vol. 3 (Cambridge, MA: MIT Press, 1995), 1374–76.

[9] Sean A. Forner, German Intellectuals and the Challenge of Democratic Renewal: Culture and Politics after 1945 (Cambridge: Cambridge University Press, 2014); Jack Zipes, Ernst

Back in the walled-in GDR, many had lost hope that, as an anonymous letter to the party newspaper *Neues Deutschland* put it in 1967, 'common sense would one day prevail' and bring an end to the general 'hypocrisy'. In 1978, a worker writing 'on behalf of many colleagues' and sending 'socialist greetings' explained to Chairman Erich Honecker that he himself belonged to the SED and had 'been in favour of our state until now'. However, confronted with severe supply shortages and inequities in the distribution of consumer goods, he found it increasingly difficult to understand the government's policies. 'And', he continued, 'we have little hope that anything will change'. Another 'comrade' reported 'hope and frustration among many people' following the decisions reached at the eleventh party conference in 1986. The first generation of East Germans who helped build the new state had hoped that their efforts would be rewarded with generous social benefits, shorter working hours, longer holidays and bigger pensions, and now found themselves 'profoundly' disappointed. In 1988 a group named Glasnost (referencing Soviet reform policies) emphasized that those who had turned their backs on the GDR and applied for the right of exit – numbers had increased almost fivefold since 1982 – left the country 'out of hopelessness'. 'Understand this, comrades!' they warned. Faced with the wave of departures, others wondered, 'Are we really the stupid remnants'?[10] They continued to 'love our homeland' and wished 'to live here', albeit without the 'corruption, racketeering, embezzlement, bribery' and the 'damned *Schops*' that were perceived as 'moral cesspits'. This referred to the infamous 'Intershops', a government-run chain store that sold coveted goods but accepted only Western currency (> Fondness).[11]

The crowds who had been demonstrating in Leipzig and other cities since September 1989 'for an open country with free people' also wanted to stay and change the GDR for the better. As the numbers of protestors grew, the hope that this could be achieved grew with them, despite excessive police violence, multiple arrests and Stasi 'interventions'. Egon Krenz, who succeeded Honecker on 17 October, was definitely not the one to nourish such hopes. People could not forgive or forget his recent reaction to the bloody suppression of the Chinese democracy movement: 'Something had been done to restore order.'[12]

Bloch: The Pugnacious Philosopher of Hope (Cham: Palgrave Macmillan, 2019); Sven Reichardt, 'Is "Warmth" a Mode of Social Behaviour? Considerations on a Cultural History of the Left-Alternative Milieu from the Late 1960s to the Mid 1980s', *Behemoth* 3, no. 2 (2010): 83–99.

[10] In German, the initials of 'the stupid remnants' (*der dumme Rest*) can be read as DDR (the German acronym for the GDR).

[11] Siegfried Suckut, *Volkes Stimmen: 'Ehrlich, aber deutlich' – Privatbriefe an die DDR-Regierung* (Munich: dtv, 2015), 121, 234–35, 341–42, 411, 340–41.

[12] Bernd Schäfer, 'Die DDR und die "chinesische Lösung"', in *1989 und die Rolle der Gewalt*, ed. Martin Sabrow (Göttingen: Wallstein, 2012), 153–72; David Childs, *The Fall of the*

In the spring of 1990, the great majority of East Germans finally laid their hopes for reform and a new, people-friendly socialism to rest. For decades they had been promised a bright future, one worth endlessly fighting, hating, loving and working overtime for. As this future began to merge with the reality of 'actually existing socialism' in the 1970s, and problems began to pile up not abate, resentment flourished. After the sudden opening of the Berlin Wall and the brief euphoria that followed, many people's patience ran out. Rather than embarking on new experiments, they voted to join the Federal Republic in the first free election in March 1990, hoping for tangible economic benefits and good governance. Politicians from the West had promised them both, raising the bar for their expectations. Disappointment was inevitable and set in quickly. Thirty years after the Wall fell, many voters put their hopes in the AfD, which claimed to be the rightful heir to the Peaceful Revolution and boasted that it alone could fulfil the hopes those in the East had once held (> Nostalgia).[13]

Sources of Hope

Politics is built on hope. This is nothing new, nor is it confined to one side of the political spectrum. The Greens have also campaigned under the banner of hope: they see it in the European project, they have organized a 'cycle tour of hope' and they support the young activists who have been taking to the streets to protest climate change since 2018: 'These young people give us courage and hope.' That women have been prominently involved since the party's founding in 1980 is a matter of principle.

Women, children and young people are considered sources of hope par excellence. Children and youth embody the future, and women enable and secure it by bearing and raising the next generation. Once upon a time, people would say that a woman was *'guter Hoffnung'* ('of good hope') to mean that she was pregnant. This expression has disappeared from common parlance, presumably because most women, thanks to technology and all-round medical care, can now await the birth of their child with confidence and not merely hope. However, the occasion is still associated with individual hopes and wishes, and these accompany the newborn on their journey through life.

GDR: Germany's Road to Unity (Harlow: Longman, 2001), 67. See also Axel Berkofsky, *China-GDR Relations from 1949 to 1989: The (Bad) Company You Keep* (Cham: Springer, 2022), 247–51.

[13] Ilko-Sascha Kowalczuk, *Die Übernahme: Wie Ostdeutschland Teil der Bundesrepublik wurde* (Munich: C. H. Beck, 2019); see also Ilko-Sascha Kowalczuk, 'The Revolution in Germany: The End of the SED Dictatorship, East German Society, and Reunification', in *German Reunification: A Multinational History*, ed. Frédéric Bozo et al. (Abingdon: Routledge, 2017), 15–42.

But hopes are also collectively shared and purposefully kindled to provide pathways for action. This is not only true for the people who, most notably and visibly in 2015, have been leaving Middle Eastern and African countries to lead better, safer lives in Europe. It has been true for Europeans since the 1800s, when the horizon of expectations was detached from the realm of experience and made brighter futures seem humanly possible.[14] When what one wants and expects from life no longer has to be tethered to what one's parents and grandparents lived through, hope becomes an important political resource. Parties, movements, prophets and gurus all bank on people's hopes for redemption, liberation and improvement. The higher these hopes are, the greater the disappointment when the happiness promised fails to appear.

From Ernst Bloch to Fridays for Future

The only hopes resistant to disappointment are those concerning the afterlife, which religious communities and institutions use as currency. Yet their members and adherents are – despite an increase in spiritual diversity – diminishing in number, which demonstrates the decreasing value people place on visions of transcendence. These days, hopes and dreams mostly concern life on this planet and its immediate future. After all, people only live once and claim the right to savour everything that makes their time worth living. Only very few speak of 'concrete utopias' as Ernst Bloch did in the 1940s and 1950s.

Meanwhile, the next generation is beginning to wonder about the 'tomorrow in today' and 'learning hope' for themselves. In many ways, the Fridays for Future movement is reminiscent of what the Marxist philosopher propagated in his time. Bloch wrote that hope is 'in love with success': 'the work of this emotion requires people who throw themselves actively into what is becoming'. Hope, he knew, 'is provocative, is not content just to accept the bad which exists'. Instead, it aims to change the world and shape the future as an 'unclosed space for new development'. The future begins in the here and now: 'The genuine utopian will is definitely not endless striving', nor is it simply focused on the distant future. Rather, it recognizes in the immediate present the 'propensity towards something, tendency towards something, latency of something, and this intended something means fulfilment of the intending'.[15]

Bloch considered hope to be the 'most important expectant emotion', a feeling more attuned to the mood of the late 1940s and 1950s than the fear spread under National Socialism. And he insisted that hope was 'teachable' and learnable through individual reflection and self-analysis as well as

---

[14] Aleida Assmann, *Is the Time out of Joint? On the Rise and Fall of the Modern Time Regime*, trans. Sarah Clift (Ithaca, NY: Cornell University Press, 2020).

[15] Bloch, *Principle of Hope*, vol. 1, 3–18, 75; vol. 3, 1374.

collective effort and activity. Right now, a number of ageing male intellectuals claim that there are no longer grounds for hope in light of global environmental destruction. As a utopian goal, a better future has had its day. Those who speak, think and feel like this have not reckoned with the young, who still have a future before them. Admittedly, some are wondering aloud whether it is still okay to have children and, by doing so, further worsen the CO_2 balance. It is nevertheless unlikely that calls for the end of the human race will find much of an audience. Most probably, the younger generation will also want to bring children into the world and to give them a future. Seldom nine like Wolf Biermann. But then, he was crazy with hope.

~

Humility

When Heinrich Bedford-Strohm, Bavarian bishop and prominent representative of the Protestant Church in Germany, spoke of humility in his 2018 Munich Christmas sermon, the national press took notice. One of the oldest words in the German language, *Demut* appeared to be back in fashion after a long spell where it had been neither seen nor heard.[1] Even politicians tried it out, though it sounded distinctly more assured in the mouths of religious men and women.

Humility had gone unmentioned in politics for a long time. It had made a rare appearance in President Horst Köhler's 2005 Christmas address, as he – referencing the natural catastrophes of the preceding year – stated that nature had 'taught us humility' and 'brought home to us how fragile the world is, and how vulnerable humanity'.[2] Thirteen years later, Bedford-Strohm was likewise concerned with vulnerability and found it personified in Jesus, the Lamb of God, in whom humans recognized their own need for help. At the same time, Bedford-Strohm elucidated, God let them experience his 'inviolability' so that they bow before his power and greatness, grace and mercy, in humility.[3]

Demut stems from the Old High German *dheomodi*: willing to serve. One could be willing to serve in heaven as on earth. Humility was the emotional attitude of the servant who attended his master and accepted without question his lowly place in the world. Humble, however, was also a descriptor applied to the faithful Jew, Christian or Muslim, who recognized the almightiness of God and accepted their own powerlessness and imperfection. The root of the Hebrew word *anavah* contains a reference to bowing or bending down, a gesture signalling one's awareness of another's superiority and showing respect. Immanuel Kant saw in this 'the consciousness and feeling of the

---

[1] *Die Sprache Deutsch*, ed. Heidemarie Anderlik and Katja Kaiser (Dresden: Sandstein-Verlag, 2008), 56: An eighth-century manuscript translated the Latin *abrogans* as the Old High German *dheomodi* (humble), and the Latin *humilis* as *samftmoati* (meek).

[2] *Bulletin der Bundesregierung*, no. 104–1 (24 December 2005): 3.

[3] Heinrich Bedford-Strohm, 'So gehen wir demütig in die Knie vor unserem Gott' (www.evangelisch.de/print/154333, accessed 13 January 2022).

insignificance of one's moral worth', while Nicolai Hartmann defined it as 'the consciousness of falling infinitely short of the mark'. Humility is, Hartmann wrote in 1925, the 'sense of one's own nothingness' relative 'to what is transcendently great'.[4]

The philosophers' attempts to detach humility from its religious context matched the spirit of the modern age. Hartmann's remark that man does not feel humility in the presence of man because doing so would be tantamount to his 'self-degradation' was meant to salvage the emotion for a world that struggled with gestures of submission. The more important and formative values like individual autonomy and self-esteem became, the more humility fell by the wayside. In the educational encyclopaedias of the nineteenth and twentieth centuries it was relegated to the margins, as it was in theological dictionaries and reference works. Whereas the influential Protestant theologian Adolf Harnack had praised it in 1900 as a link between religion and morality, his colleague Paul Tillich, who emigrated to the USA in 1933, distanced himself from a position 'that is not in accordance with human dignity and freedom'. Solely in Catholic theology did humility continue to assert its place.[5]

Humility versus Narcissism

In the same year Tillich bid farewell to humility, it was praised, however, by his fellow émigré and social psychologist Erich Fromm as an 'emotional attitude' upon which reason and objectivity were grounded. In his enduring book *The Art of Loving*, published in 1956, Fromm took up the cudgels for humility: it alone could overcome the selfishness that was running rampant and the related narcissism. Only the person who 'has achieved an attitude of humility' and 'has emerged from the dreams of omniscience and omnipotence which one has as a child' sees people and things '*as they are*' and not as one wishes them to be. This in turn is, for Fromm, the prerequisite for the 'ability to love'.[6]

The Old Testament had placed humility in opposition to arrogance, which was considered a particular form of > pride; the *Brockhaus* encyclopaedia was still emphasizing this juxtaposition in 1901. Fromm, for his part, saw humility

---

[4] Immanuel Kant, *The Metaphysics of Morals*, ed. Lara Denis, trans. Mary Gregor (Cambridge: Cambridge University Press, 2017), 201; Nicolai Hartmann, *Moral Values*, trans. Stanton Coit (Berlin: De Gruyter, 2020), 299, 300. (Originally published in 1923 as the second volume of Hartmann's *Ethik*, first translated into English in 1932.)

[5] Quotes in *Die Religion in Geschichte und Gegenwart*, vol. 1 (Tübingen: Mohr Siebeck, 1909), 2034; ibid., 4th ed., vol. 2 (Tübingen: Mohr Siebeck, 1999), 659.

[6] Erich Fromm, *The Art of Loving* (New York: Harper & Row, 1956), 118–21 (italics in the original). The seventy-third German edition was published in 2018.

in contrast to the new phenomenon of narcissism that received increasing attention in the second half of the twentieth century. It had been known, in fact, as early as 1900, but at that time was described as sexual desire for one's own body and, in the words of psychiatrist Paul Näcke, 'the most severe form of "auto-eroticism"'.[7] Freudian psychoanalysis shared this interpretation, understanding narcissism as the ego-directed libido. Associated with it was low self-esteem, compensated for by the exaggerated perception of one's own importance and the desire for admiration.

Yet as early as 1914, Sigmund Freud had also pinpointed narcissism in incidences where affectionate parents cultivated an emotional relationship with their children characterized by 'overvaluation'.

> They are under a compulsion to ascribe every perfection to the child – which sober observation would find no occasion to do – and to conceal and forget all his shortcomings ... The child shall have a better time than his parents; he shall not be subject to the necessities which they have recognized as paramount in life. Illness, death, renunciation of enjoyment, restrictions on his own will, shall not touch him; the laws of nature and of society shall be abrogated in his favour; he shall once more really be the centre and core of creation – *His Majesty the Baby*, as we once fancied ourselves.[8]

Similar diagnoses can still be read today. Psychologists warn parents against exaggerated praise and overestimation, as these may impart an unrealistic self-perception to children. What in Freud's time pertained to a small group of educated well-to-do families has, since the 1970s, become a parenting style practised by the broader middle classes. Parents started to address their children as friends and fostered a discursive approach to demands, rather than insisting on their own authority.[9] This was part of a macrosocial liberalization, but it was also related to the fact that adults were having fewer and fewer children. A parent who raised just one or two could devote themselves to their offspring more intensively. At the same time, mothers and fathers faced the danger of projecting their 'wishful dreams ... which they never carried out' (Freud) onto their only son and only daughter.

Whether the changed family setup of the late twentieth century can actually explain the oft-observed rise of narcissistic attitudes is difficult to ascertain.

---

[7] Paul Näcke, 'Die sexuellen Perversitäten in der Irrenanstalt', *Wiener klinische Rundschau* 13 (1899): 435–38, 458–60, 478–81, 496–97, quote 496.

[8] Sigmund Freud, 'On Narcissism: An Introduction [1914]', in *The Standard Edition of the Complete Psychological Works of Sigmund Freud*, vol. 14, trans. James Strachey (London: The Hogarth Press, 1974), 67–102, quote 91.

[9] Miriam Gebhardt, *Die Angst vor dem kindlichen Tyrannen: Eine Geschichte der Erziehung im 20. Jahrhundert* (Munich: DVA, 2009), 126–27, 160 ff.

That American authors including Fromm and Christopher Lasch see the
narcissistic age as commencing in the 1950s or 1960s does not negate the
argument, as the change in pedagogical concepts and practices was established
earlier in the USA than in West Germany.[10] Currently, social scientists and
historians are inclined to describe narcissism, a heightened form of selfishness,
as an attendant phenomenon of the neoliberal turn. Since the 1980s, neoli-
beralism has opened up a new view of the 'self' as an entity to be optimized,
and has fuelled high expectations. Each person is supposed to work hard on
themselves in order to improve individual prosperity and market performance
as well as self-confidence and self-esteem. Everyone strives to be special –
particularly beautiful, smart, creative, powerful – and presents themselves as
their own brand.[11] A personal regime like this undoubtedly invites the cultivation of narcissistic behaviours.

That these orientations have their pitfalls and work to the detriment of
society is taken to be self-evident. Under the headline 'Narcissism: The Face of
our Era', *Der Spiegel* reported in 1979 on the 'fight of everyone against
everyone'. *GEO* magazine, which dedicated a cover story to 'excessive self-
love' in 2012, pointed out that it could lead to a gradual 'deformation of
community' (> Solidarity).[12] Even though psychologists and psychiatrists
stress that every healthy person possesses narcissistic qualities without these
significantly harming or devaluing others, there is a widespread unease about
narcissism and its noticeable increase in recent years.[13] Self-centred attitudes,
alongside a strong sense of entitlement, are demonstrably on the rise, more
markedly among men than among women.

---

[10] Christopher Lasch, *The Culture of Narcissism: American Life in an Age of Diminishing
Expectations* (New York: Norton & Co., 1978); Eli Zaretsky, *Secrets of the Soul: A Social
and Cultural History of Psychoanalysis* (New York: Knopf, 2004), 307–31.

[11] As early as 1999, Luc Boltanski and Ève Chiapello noted how the 'new spirit of capitalism'
could activate flexibility, mobility, creativity and individual responsibility to serve specific
aims (*The New Spirit of Capitalism*, London: Verso, 2019). See also Ulrich Bröckling, *The
Entrepreneurial Self: Fabricating a New Type of Subject* (Los Angeles, CA: SAGE, 2016);
Andreas Reckwitz, *The Society of Singularities* (Cambridge: Polity Press, 2020).

[12] 'Narzißmus: Antlitz einer Epoche', *Der Spiegel*, 6 August 1979, 140–42 (review of
Christopher Lasch's book); Hania Luczak, 'Die Liebe zum Ich', *GEO* 9 (2012): 64–80.

[13] Heinz Kohut, *The Analysis of the Self: A Systematic Approach to the Psychoanalytic
Treatment of Narcissistic Personality Disorders* (New York: International Universtities
Press, 1971); Alice Miller, *The Drama of the Gifted Child: The Search for the True Self*
(New York: Basic Books, 1981); Jean M. Twenge and W. Keith Campbell, *The Narcissism
Epidemic: Living in the Age of Entitlement* (New York: Atria Books, 2009); Christopher T.
Barry, *Narcissism and Machiavellianism in Youth: Implications for the Development of
Adaptive and Maladaptive Behavior* (Washington, DC: American Psychological
Asssociation, 2011); Sandy Hotchkiss, *Why Is It Always about You? The Seven Deadly
Sins of Narcissism* (New York: Schuster & Schuster, 2002).

Humility offers itself, as Fromm already proposed, as a counter-strategy. A person who is humble is said to develop modesty and > empathy, and to respect the opinions and needs of others. Out of the existential vulnerability, imperfection and dependence of humanity, the humble person derives an attitude to life that decentres one's own self, instead of making it the sole focus. Or, as the Social Democratic politician and observant Catholic Wolfgang Thierse put it in 2012: 'Humility is the awareness of humanity's worthiness of mercy. The awareness that one commits mistakes and errors and depends on others in order to be forgiven and absolved, and the willingness to do this oneself. A deeper insight into one's own fallibility. And a feeling of gratitude for what works out.'[14]

Friedrich Nietzsche, the freethinking anti-Christian philosopher of the late nineteenth century, had loathed humility as a 'slave morality' and an expression of weakness: 'A worm will twist back on itself when it is stepped on. This is shrewd. It lessens the chance of being stepped on again. In the language of morality: humility.' To contemporaries of the twenty-first century, in contrast, humility appeared in a more positive light; namely as judicious self-limitation that defended against attitudes of omnipotence and deluded belief in unlimited human capabilities. For Sven Giegold, who co-founded the German branch of Attac in 2000 as a 'network for the democratic control of the international finance markets' and had been active in the environmental movement since his school days, humility was neither a religious virtue nor had anything to do with subservience. He experienced it 'most powerfully in nature' and drew from it the decision to actively protect and preserve nature.[15]

Others also discovered humility for themselves. Investment bankers, known for professional ruthlessness, called the industry to 'collective humility' following the financial crisis, and the former Christian Social Union minister Karl-Theodor zu Guttenberg apologized 'with humility' for plagiarizing his doctoral dissertation. Nietzsche's sarcastic aphorism was apt: 'He that humbleth himself wants to be exalted.' As others recognized as well, humility in this instance was calculatedly invoked and followed the adage: 'Now that was embarrassing for me (getting caught).' Genuine humility, on the other hand –

[14] 'Wer demütig ist, spricht nicht darüber', *Spiegel online*, 4 May 2012, http://bit.ly/3RZgkRl, accessed 18 March 2022.

[15] Friedrich Nietzsche, 'Twilight of the Idols', in *The Anti-Christ, Ecce Homo, Twighlight of the Idols and Other Writings*, ed. Aaron Reidley, trans. Judith Norman (Cambridge: Cambridge University Press, 2005), 153–229, quote 160; Mechthild Klein, 'Der Begriff ist tot, es lebe das Gefühl: Die Wiederentdeckung der Demut' (12 January 2008): http://bit .ly/3S1GKSo, accessed 13 January 2022.

Figure 33   Genuine humility: Willy Brandt's genuflection in Warsaw, 1970
(Bettmann/Getty Images)

according to one internet commentator in 2012 – was demonstrated by
Chancellor Willy Brandt as he 'fell to his knees in Warsaw' (Figure 33).[16]

Willy Brandt's Genuflection

That people remembered this event almost half a century after it happened is
remarkable. They may have spelt the chancellor's name wrong ('Willi Brand'),
but what he had done was fixed clearly in their minds. On 7 December 1970,
during his visit to the Polish capital (the first ever by a West German head of
state), Brandt had laid a wreath at the Monument to the Ghetto Heroes. This
honoured the victims of the Holocaust and the Jewish resistance fighters who
had waged a futile battle against their German killers in 1943. For Brandt, the
wreath-laying ceremony was a pressing obligation before the signing of the
Treaty of Warsaw, which was supposed to 'normalize' relations between the
Federal Republic and Poland. After tucking in the wreath ribbons, he did not,

---

[16] http://bit.ly/3lH9rI3, accessed 13 January 2022; Friedrich Nietzsche, *Human, All Too
Human*, trans. R. J. Hollingdale (Cambridge: Cambridge University Press, 1996), 48.

however, stay upright and motionless, as is customary in such situations. Instead, he sank to his knees. Photographers and camera operators captured this moment for eternity, and the image went all around the world.

And it immediately provoked fierce controversy. The Polish prime minister Józef Cyrankiewicz, who had survived two German concentration camps, was moved; his wife wept. The Polish media, though, edited the photo so that it showed Brandt standing, not kneeling. The GDR press also omitted to mention the genuflection. In the Federal Republic, a snap opinion poll reported that 48 per cent found the action excessive, 41 per cent appropriate. Some compared it with Heinrich IV's petition and penitential walk to Canossa in 1076/77, when the German kaiser, apparently on his knees, secured the lifting of the papal ban.

In the Middle Ages, there was nothing unusual about bending the knee before an authority figure, especially an ecclesiastical one. But for politicians of the twentieth century, this penitent gesture no longer seemed befitting. With the dignity of their office, heads of state also carried the honour and dignity of the state they represented. This demanded an upright posture. One showed respect with a slight inclination of the head, ideally without moving one's back. A person who bowed too low gave something away and exposed themselves to the disapproval of the watchful public.

Expressing humility, asking forgiveness, apologizing: in the view of many contemporaries, this did not belong in the political world. In 1958, when the Social Democrat Carlo Schmid signed the visitors' book of the former Gestapo prison in Warsaw 'with deep shame at this site of German disgrace', he was accused back home of violating 'national dignity' (> Shame, > Honour).[17] A similar reproach was brought upon the Protestant Church after it issued, in 1965, a memorandum that acknowledged 'mutual guilt' and recommended the recognition of the Oder-Neiße border as a step towards reconciliation with Poland.[18]

When Brandt, five years later, was reprimanded for kowtowing to Polish interests, his critics ignored the fact that he had knelt before a monument to Jews murdered by Germans. Brandt himself was well aware of this distinction. On the morning of 7 December, as he stopped first at the Tomb of the Unknown Soldier and laid a wreath like all state guests, he had remained upright. But before Nathan Rapoport's sculpture, he 'knew', as he explained that evening to a journalist, 'that it would not be so simple as other wreath

[17] Petra Weber, *Carlo Schmid 1896–1979* (Munich: C. H. Beck, 1996), 599.

[18] Martin Greschat, 'Vom Tübinger Memorandum (1961) zur Ratifizierung der Ostverträge (1972)', in *Versöhnung und Politik*, ed. Friedhelm Boll et al. (Bonn: Dietz, 2009), 29–51, quote 37; Annika Elisabet Frieberg, *Peace at All Costs: Catholic Intelletuals, Journalists, and Media in Postwar Polish-German Reconciliation* (New York: Berghahn, 2019), 128–53.

ceremonies, just bowing one's head. This is a whole different dimension.' In his memoirs two decades later, he found more sober words, 'I had not planned anything, but I had left Wilanów Palace, where I was staying, with a feeling that I must express the exceptional significance of the ghetto memorial. From the bottom of the abyss of German history, under the burden of millions of victims of murder, I did what human beings do when speech fails them.'[19]

Service and Self-Abasement

Although Brandt was not religious, he intuitively fell back on a gesture that has a long religious as well as secular tradition. Since pre-Christian times, people have knelt before their rulers. The church adopted the ritual and demanded it of its members, who thereby testified to their humility and devotion. When European princes abolished the obligatory genuflection of their subjects at the end of the eighteenth century, Catholicism retained it. Up to this very day, the faithful kneel before the pope and pay homage to his high office. Conversely, Christ's representative on earth understands himself to be *Servus servorum Dei*, the servant of the servants of God, when he performs the ritual foot washing each year on Holy Thursday, which he made a duty in cathedrals and abbeys.

This 'serving gesture' is firmly established in the Catholic liturgy. While the group of people on whom it was practised had previously been limited to priests and, in the case of Benedict XVI, lay people close to the church, Pope Francis extended it to anyone from the 'people of God'. In 2016, he attracted a great deal of attention as he washed the feet of refugees. Three years later, he chose twelve foreign prison inmates and emphasized, in his freely delivered sermon, that 'each of us must be servants of others. This is Jesus' rule and the rule of the Gospel: the rule of service, not of dominating, of doing harm, of humiliating others.'[20]

Humble serving, in the view of the pontifex maximus, in no way meant submission or the surrender of one's human dignity. Rather, it arose from a position in which one acknowledged one's own imperfection and so resolved not to be self-righteous towards other people or God. For this, the Lutheran Bible knew the concept of humiliation, without any negative connotations attached. The parable of the Pharisee and the tax collector (Luke 18:9–14) who prayed to God in very different ways – one certain of his self-worth, the other humble and convinced of his sinfulness – ended with the oft-cited sentence: 'For all those who exalt themselves will be humbled, and those who humble themselves will be exalted.' Nietzsche made his own rhyme out of this and

[19] Hermann Schreiber, 'Ein Stück Heimkehr', *Der Spiegel*, 14 December 1970, 29–30; Willy Brandt, *Erinnerungen* (Frankfurt: Ullstein, 1989), 214.

[20] http://bit.ly/3YVOOXd; http://bit.ly/3S1uTnf, both accessed 13 January 2022.

replaced the last *will* with *want* in order to foreground the strategically calculating nature of self-abasement. Pious Catholics will have none of that, because for them humiliation and self-abasement (if they still use the terms at all) belong to a relationship between God and self that lacks any tendency to self-exaltation.

What Nietzsche and pious Catholics do agree on, however, is the categorical rejection of humiliation as a gesture by which the powerful force the powerless into humility. To recognize one's own humility differs greatly from being compelled or coerced to do so by others. In the latter context, humility takes on another meaning: it becomes a degrading submission and debasement, and creates victims who cannot defend themselves.

From Humility to Humiliation

Serving instead of humiliating: with this, Pope Francis touched on a burning issue. Since the turn of the millennium, 'humiliation' has been making increasingly large waves, in politics and beyond. Among those who have frequently and expressively used the term is the Saxon state minister Petra Köpping. In her conversations with former GDR citizens about the post-reunification period, she heard a lot about disadvantages, grievances, personal failures and an absence of recognition. Having grown up in the GDR herself, Köpping summarized those experiences as 'humiliation' and an assault on people's 'dignity'.[21] Especially among the ranks of left-wing parties and the far right, humiliation has become a popular item in the political vocabulary, targeting and resonating with East German voters.

To speak of debasement, degradation and humiliation is to bring out the big guns, using morality to sway listeners. Taking away someone's dignity violates the first and most important article of Germany's Basic Law. The statement that 'human dignity is inviolable' emerged from the painful history of the 'Third Reich'. As disclosed during the Nuremberg trials, the National Socialist regime had trampled human dignity underfoot by humiliating, oppressing and annihilating people on a previously incomprehensible scale. In contrast, liberal democratic societies that value decency and respect – the Israeli philosopher Avishai Margalit calls them 'decent societies' – agree to prohibit any form of humiliation and seek to protect their citizens from it.[22]

---

[21] Anne Hähnig, 'Integriert doch erst mal uns', *Zeit online*, 20 April 2017, www.zeit.de/2017/17/petra-koepping-integration-sachsen-pegida, accessed 18 March 2022. In September 2018, Petra Köpping published her analysis as a book that saw five editions within four months: *Integriert doch erst mal uns! Eine Streitschrift für den Osten* (Integrate us first! A polemic for the East).

[22] Avishai Margalit, *The Decent Society* (Cambridge, MA: Harvard University Press, 1996).

But were the grievances outlined by Köpping really about humiliation? In fact, the men and women who shared their life stories chose less dramatizing words. Reinterpreting disappointment and disregard as humiliation introduced a different political framing and heightened the moral tone. It gave new weight to what people had experienced, and it raised the question of who was responsible. Depending on one's worldview, the culprit was capitalism, arrogant West Germans or Chancellor Angela Merkel who, the allegation went, cared more for refugees and migrants than for her fellow citizens (> Anger). With such imputations it was irrelevant whether the culprits had acted intentionally and deliberately. The subjective feeling of having been humiliated was enough.

Chains of Humiliation

This marks a clear difference with earlier times, when humiliation was considered and employed as a targeted power move. Such was the case after the First World War, when representatives of the Allied powers met with delegates from defeated Germany at the Palace of Versailles to put their signatures to the peace treaty. The 1919 ceremony took place in the famous Hall of Mirrors that had been carefully chosen and prepared by the French prime minister, Georges Clemenceau. Where Germans had, in 1871, proclaimed their empire and celebrated victory over France, they now experienced, in the words of the foreign minister Hermann Müller, the 'worst hour' of their lives. Neither Müller, a Social Democrat with close pre-war connections to French socialists and the British Labour Party, nor his colleague Johannes Bell was permitted to sit at the top table; instead, they were brought in, allowed to sign and immediately escorted out again. Edward House, advisor to the American president Woodrow Wilson, felt reminded of a Roman triumphal procession, where 'the conqueror dragged the conquered at his chariot wheels', on foot with bowed heads. For him the signing lacked any element of 'chivalry' and spoke of the blatant intent to make it 'as humiliating to the enemy as it well could be'.[23]

It was seen and understood as such in Weimar and Berlin. Faced with the charge of being solely to blame for the war, and the peace treaty's harsh terms, the whole country felt humiliated, the old elites as much as the new republicans. The military occupation of the Rhineland, which included the stationing of French units with African soldiers, was perceived as an additional blow. A contemporary pamphlet castigated the 'outrageous humiliation and

---

[23] Margaret MacMillan, *Paris 1919: Six Months That Changed the World* (New York: Random House, 2003), 476–77.

rape of a highly cultivated white race by a still half-barbaric coloured one'. In 1921, middle-class women from Augsburg, among many others, objected to the deployment of 'blacks as tyrants of the white race' and considered it a 'punch into the face': 'The same negro who is treated in France as a second-class human being, and is there kept in check only by the most rigid discipline is allowed to act like a lord and victor in our country; Germany's girls and women have been surrendered, defenceless, to his savage behaviour.'[24]

In 1940 the balance of power reversed: now it was Germany's turn to avenge the humiliation it had suffered. When Wehrmacht troops took Paris on 14 June 1940, Hitler ordered the railway carriage in which the French, British and Germans had signed the armistice on 11 November 1918 in Compiègne be brought back from the museum to its historical site. There, on 22 June, the second ceasefire came into force. Even though, as Minister for Propaganda Joseph Goebbels asserted, the ceremony was not intended as a 'demonstrative humiliation', it did not fail to have an impact on both parties. For Goebbels, 'the ignominy of 1918 is now erased. One feels born again.' The carriage in which Germany had previously been 'humiliated' travelled to Berlin and was displayed in the city centre.[25]

The Politics of Humiliation in the 'Third Reich'

The National Socialist regime was highly familiar with humiliations. As much as it loathed humility as a 'hypocritical degradation of values' and 'hostile temptation', it eagerly used humiliation as an instrument of social and political stigmatization.[26] The measures against the Jewish population had an openly degrading character, regardless of whether they were ordered from above or carried out from below in acts of spontaneous allegiance. The so-called pillory parades, which exposed Jews and their non-Jewish partners from 1933 onwards, were just as focused on humiliation as actions in Vienna after the annexation of Austria on 12 March 1938: Jewish men and women were forced to scrub anti-Nazi graffiti off the pavements, bent double or on their knees, to the amusement of passers-by (Figure 34).[27]

---

[24] Iris Wigger, The 'Black Horror on the Rhine': Intersections of Race, Gender and Class in 1920s Germany (London: Palgrave MacMillan, 2017), ch. 1, quotes 166; Bavarian State Archive Munich, II, MA no. 102383: resolution, 19 February 1921.

[25] Joseph Goebbels, Die Tagebücher, ed. Elke Fröhlich, part 1, vol. 8 (Munich: Saur, 1998), 184–85 (22 June 1940).

[26] Alfred Rosenberg, Der Mythus des 20. Jahrhunderts [1933] (Munich: Hoheneichen, 1935), 185. By 1944, well over a million copies of the book were in circulation.

[27] Ute Frevert, The Politics of Humiliation (Oxford: Oxford University Press, 2020), 54–60; G. E. R. Gedye, Fallen Bastions: The Central European Tragedy (London: Gollantz, 1939), 307–11.

Figure 34   Jews are forced to clean Vienna's streets of political slogans, 1938 (Photo by Universal History Archive/Universal Images Group via Getty Images)

Even in instances where antisemitic policies were not publicly enacted, their effect was intentionally humiliating. In June 1933, the forty-four-year-old Berlin archivist Ludwig Dehio turned to friends and acquaintances with the question of whether they 'still want to view me subjectively as a German comrade of shared blood, although objectively I have ceased to be recognized or treated as such by the German state'. Dehio was referring to a law passed a few months earlier that implemented the dismissal of civil servants who were politically undesirable or of 'non-Aryan descent'. The law applied to him, as his maternal grandfather was from a Jewish family. Although the grandfather had been baptized back in his student days, all that counted in National Socialist ideology was 'blood', not one's religion. Thus the grandson was also considered a Jew and no longer worthy of being a public servant. Dehio felt this to be a 'desecration of his family' at a time when the 'rising of Germany out of dishonour and disgrace', which he had longed for, was finally becoming a reality. 'May you,' he concluded, 'judge how I bear the expulsion from the rising nation! Dispossessed of my Germanness by Germans. With a sincere heart I enclose the wish that you, your relatives, your children and your children's children may remain spared a *humiliation* such as I experienced while composing this letter.'

There was some small comfort for Dehio. Friends forwarded the letter to Hitler's deputy, Franz von Papen, who then turned to President Paul von Hindenburg with a request to recognize the service of the family. Hindenburg's secretary of state subsequently asked Bernhard Rust, the Prussian minister for education, for 'sympathetic examination'. While Rust dismissed approximately 5,000 Jewish officials, he made an exception for Dehio, arguing 'that the civil servant in question was a front-line combatant'. The archivist was transferred to a minor institution where he sat out the Nazi period physically unharmed. How he coped emotionally with the personal humiliation was another matter.[28]

Humiliated was also how Munich lawyer Hans Bloch felt in 1933. As a war volunteer, he had spent three and a half years risking his life for his country and had made it to the rank of lieutenant. Now his admission to a profession that he had been successfully practising since 1924 was put in jeopardy because he was a Jew. This 'disgrace', he wrote in a letter dated 9 August 1933, no longer let him rest; it was only in the memory of the 'years of fighting for Germany', which had 'given direction' to his life, that he found the strength to 'outlast the degradation'. In 1942, after countless further debasements and humiliations, he was murdered in Mauthausen concentration camp.[29]

The Nazi regime humiliated not only Jews, but everyone it considered a political enemy. For this, the president of the Volksgerichtshof ('People's Court'), Roland Freisler, was particularly famous. He did not miss a single opportunity to insult, mock and degrade the defendants he tried for high treason in connection with the attempted assassination of Hitler on 20 July 1944. The officers had to appear before the court in shabby civilian clothing rather than wearing their uniforms. General Field Marshall Erwin von Witzleben's trousers were so big that he had to hold them up. Erich Hoepner, previously a highly decorated colonel general, sat in the dock in a cardigan and without a tie. Freisler addressed them as 'wretches', 'slimy intellectuals', 'swines', 'pansies', sometimes in a cutting tone, often bellowed.[30]

---

[28] Federal Archive Berlin, R 601, no. 1117: correspondence 19 June, 21 June and 12 July 1933. For Ludwig Dehio's work as historian, see Aaron M. Zack, *Hegemonic War and Strategy: Ludwig Dehio, World History, and the American Future* (Lanham, MD: Lexington Books, 2017).

[29] Sinja Strangmann, 'Eduard und Hans Bloch – Zwei Generationen jüdischer Soldaten im Ersten Weltkrieg', in *Krieg! Juden zwischen den Fronten 1914/1918*, ed. Ulrike Heikaus and Julia B. Kohne (Munich: Hentrich & Hentrich, 2014), 254.

[30] Johannes Tuchel, 'Vor dem "Volksgerichtshof": Schauprozesse vor laufender Kamera', in *Das Jahrhundert der Bilder 1900 bis 1949*, ed. Gerhard Paul (Göttingen: Vandenhoeck & Ruprecht, 2009), 648–57; Hannsjoachim W. Koch, *In the Name of the Volk: Political Justice in Hitler's Germany* (London: Tauris, 1997), 196–225.

This was humiliation in its purest form, particularly for military men whose profession had endowed them with a strong sense of > honour and a high -sensitivity to slander.

Sensitization

The contrast with the present is stark. Under National Socialism, humiliation was a deliberate power strategy that state and party systematically used against people who were declared 'inferior' or accused of treason and denied the right to exist. Today, even unintentional slights or structural inequalities have come to be regarded as personal humiliations, and sensitivity has clearly increased. This is related to society's discourse of dignity and how it, since the late 1960s, has been reflected in educational institutions and the judicial system. With families, schools and courts emphasizing the autonomy of the person and strengthening their rights against constraints and violations, children, young people and adults developed a more stable feeling of self-worth. Put-downs that they would previously have overlooked or accepted *nolens volens* they now perceive as intolerable humiliations, and fight back.

Here, the access to digital communication has proven helpful. On social media, the experience of debasement and degradation is easily shared and put on trial. Others react with > empathy and provide support. This is particularly important for members of social groups that suffer from exclusion and stigmatization. To them, the internet offers an effective sounding board for exchanging, disseminating and validating moments of humiliation. At the same time, the significance attributed to those experiences grows, and propels sensitization. The emotion becomes denser, more intense, and, instead of isolating the victim, it enables connection with others.

Power and Powerlessness

However, social media also provides a forum for people out to humiliate others. Since the turn of the millennium, there has been an increase in the number of online platforms where people who are considered too fat, too thin, too pretty, too ugly or who attract malice, mockery and contempt for other reasons are derided. While the state and its institutions have largely withdrawn from the business of humiliation, social groups and cliques have taken their place. Humiliation has become a kind of board game with numerous players. Yet the consequences are hardly trivial; indeed, they are more often than not utterly destructive. And unlike a game, humiliation in real life is always about power and competition for power. People who humiliate others claim power over them and win power in their own group, and this is what keeps the ball rolling.

With humility, on the other hand, powerlessness takes centre stage. Demonstrating and respecting it does not come easy for power-conscious institutions and individuals. Even the pope, who preaches humility and understands himself to be 'servant of the servants', draws narrow boundaries when it is about protecting the power and integrity of his church. One could have expected a humble pope to strongly distance himself from, and remove from office, priests who sexually abused children and adolescents and in doing so inflicted a particularly deceitful humiliation upon them. This did not happen, though, and the official approach to the victims seemed far from humble. For quite some time, German bishops did not think much of humility either. Although, in 2014, after a long chain of accusations and documentation, they appointed an independent research team to investigate the extent of the abuse since 1946, they refused it direct access to files. The wish to shelter one's own 'servants' took priority over humility, acknowledging guilt and apologizing for wrongdoing.

Bishop Franz-Josef Bode, from Osnabrück, showed that this was not the only way. During the Mass for Advent Sunday in 2010, he threw himself before the altar in his cathedral, 'to make plain that the Church has brought guilt upon itself with the incidences of abuse and how they were handled'. Among Catholics, prostration is an established ritual. Before deacons receive ordination, they lie their body flat on the ground to demonstrate that they 'are small before God, and also before the people'. That is seen as the expression of true humility, which has, according to Bode, nothing to do with degradation: 'A person who is created by God is never a degraded being', but 'enlivened through the spirit of the Lord'.[31]

In view of the increasing number of people leaving the church, the bishop's gesture of humility seems futile. In 2018, only 53 per cent of the German population belonged to the two largest Christian denominations; in 1950, it had been a solid 96 per cent in the West and 92 per cent in the East. Between 1990 and 2020, the Catholic Church lost more than six million members and is left with twenty-two million, very few of them practising. In Protestantism, secularization started even earlier and more strongly, and was particularly drastic in the GDR. After reunification, the Protestant Church lost a further nine million members and was down to twenty million in 2020.

Against this background, the Bavarian bishop's plea for humility in his 2018 Christmas sermon sent a remarkable signal. He not only urged believers to emulate Catholics (and Muslims) and go 'humbly on the knees before our God'. He also related humility to courage. Both enabled men and women to

---

[31] 'Wir nehmen uns Menschen nicht demütig genug an', *Spiegel online*, 14 May 2012, https://bit.ly/3Z1h8Hp, accessed 18 March 2022.

stand up for a world without 'hate, selfishness, greed for money, abuse, exploitation of nature', without war and persecution. Such courage and advocacy can, undoubtedly, also come from people who derive their moral bearings from non-religious sources. In all cases, humility helps to counteract morally and socially dysfunctional attitudes like those displayed by the proverbial self-righteous Pharisee.

~~

Joy

Germans, it is often said, can neither be properly joyful, nor do they have a sense of and for (British) humour. Compared to fun-loving Southern Europeans, they are considered grouches and professional pessimists. During the 1930s and 1940s, National Socialism took aim at 'all the doom-merchants and whingers' who sought to belittle and deny the regime's glorious achievements. The GDR was known for its 'complainer culture', while in the Federal Republic Chancellor Helmut Schmidt criticized the 'tendency towards chronic discontentment' in his 1977 New Year's Eve speech. At Christmas two years later, President Karl Carstens voiced the question of 'whether some among us have not lost the capacity to be joyful, to feel joy'. In 1998 Roman Herzog, one of his successors, also decried the 'strange joylessness with which we often make life so difficult for ourselves'.[1]

These comments implied there were many reasons for joy and happiness, and not only at Christmas. West Germans, as Carstens reminded his listeners, enjoyed social security and 'invaluable' individual freedom, unlike East Germans who lacked such liberty. But then, as the GDR regime constantly stressed, the East did not have the > fear of unemployment that had been waxing and waning in the Federal Republic since the 1970s. New Year's speeches addressed to the 'citizens of the German Democratic Republic' thus did not skimp on encouraging words: 'We stride into the new year, cheerful and carefree!' was Walter Ulbricht's message in 1964; 'We celebrate happily, certain of a good future' a year later. In 1969, people were to approach the state's twentieth anniversary 'with confidence, high spirits and a new zest for action'. In 1974, Ulbricht's successor Willi Stoph wished 'all citizens of our

[1] Federal Archive Berlin, R 601, no. 1119: Friedrich Prince Hohenzollern, 24 June 1934; Jochen Staadt, *Eingaben: Die institutionalisierte Meckerkultur in der DDR* (Berlin: Forschungsverbund SED-Staat, 1996); Paul Betts, *Within Walls: Private Life in German Democratic Republic* (Oxford: Oxford University Press, 2010), ch. 6 ('Socialism's Social Contract: Individual Citizens Petitions'); Reinhard Kiehl, ed., *Alle Jahre wieder* (Düsseldorf: My favourite book, 2001), 331, 341, 469.

Figure 35   Exuberant joy: GDR citizens are welcomed by West Berliners, 9 November 1989   (Photo by Thomas Imo/Photothek via Getty Images)

republic good luck and success'; from 1977 onwards, this was done, in the same words, by Erich Honecker.[2]

1989: Jubilation and Other Emotions

By the end of 1989, the tide had turned dramatically. Honecker had resigned as SED general secretary and as chairman of the state council; Egon Krenz lasted just seven weeks. Hans Modrow, the chairman of the council of ministers, delivered an unusually short New Year's message. His words were printed as always in *Neues Deutschland*, which was now no longer the 'organ of the Central Committee of the SED', but simply the 'Socialist Daily Newspaper'. Joy, cheerfulness and happiness were neither addressed nor promised. Instead, Modrow referred to the 'Peaceful Revolution' that was making the citizens' 'dream of freedom, democracy and justice' into reality. Although the GDR was in the midst of a serious crisis, nobody needed to 'feel fear'. After all, a 'better future' was in sight, as long as everyone lent a hand 'to ensure order, an orderly life in city and village'.[3]

Modrow's sober words definitely did not reflect the exhilaration that the opening of the border on 9 November 1989 had triggered in many East Germans (Figure 35). Political rhetoric sounded far more euphoric in the

[2] Printed on the respective front pages of the *Neues Deutschland*.
[3] Ibid., 30/31 December 1989, 1–2.

West, where on New Year's Eve Chancellor Helmut Kohl invoked the 'most touching images' of the fall of the Wall. 'Who would ever forget the joy and happiness on the faces of people who could finally come together again?' President Richard von Weizsäcker likewise placed the 'deep joy' over recent events at the core of his Christmas address. It was particularly important to him that 'virtually the whole world shares in our joy of reunion'. 'Until this point in my lifetime', he recalled,

> the attention paid to us Germans has often been accompanied by other emotions. And even today we would do well not to lose sight of the views and standards of our neighbours. But what we experience these days at Berlin's Brandenburg Gate and all over Germany connects the hearts of the whole world. Journalists from the Soviet Union, the mayor of Jerusalem, Western heads of state and many others wrote to me or called to express their fellow joy. Through their emotions, people move close to one another. (> Empathy)

How long the joy endured is another question. As early as 1990, Weizsäcker found cause for words of warning. A 'fellow citizen' from the East had written to him: 'Our souls are not yet with you.' Upon this, the president urged, 'we should all reflect. What does this mean? Are they supposed to approach us? Why is it not us approaching them? Should they go the whole distance alone? How far, then, have we already gone to meet them?' Meeting halfway, instead of drawing boundaries and devaluing others, seemed necessary to make the reunification – finalized in October 1990 – a success. Time and again, the message was conveyed to old and new citizens alike: there must be no more 'over here' and 'over there'; the 'walls of indifference' should be dismantled; East and West could 'learn a lot from each other', if they only wanted to. At the start of the new millennium, President Johannes Rau took stock: 'This year, we can be joyful about ten years of unity. But we still hold many prejudices and misjudgements about one another. We know too little, we tell each other too little about our different experiences and perspectives.'[4]

The debates that surrounded the thirtieth anniversary of the Peaceful Revolution demonstrated that the situation had not fundamentally improved between 2000 and 2020. For many former GDR citizens, the joy of yore has turned sour – if indeed they ever felt it at all. As the last GDR government pointed out in its New Year's message, millions did take part in the demonstrations of autumn 1989 that finally brought the regime down. Yet millions of others had stayed home, for various reasons. How many SED members – totalling 2.3 million in the mid-1980s – were genuinely happy when the Wall came down? Even party comrades who had previously voiced criticism about

---

[4] Kiehl, *Alle Jahre wieder*, 410–11, 415, 419, 430, 444, 463, 482–83.

the state of affairs reacted less than enthusiastically. Many voters who had joyfully believed in Chancellor Kohl's promise of flourishing regions in the East and, in the first free elections, made the CDU the strongest party there soon thought and felt otherwise. When unemployment figures skyrocketed, joy and optimism gave way to frustration and resentment.

The 'Radiant Faces' of GDR Youth

One of the benefits the new state provided, however, was the freedom to not have to feign joy or express it on command. This had been different in the GDR, whose citizens were expected to profess not only joyful but unreserved enthusiasm for 'real socialism'. Children and young people were raised in this spirit. Schools and youth organizations practised enthusiasm as a civic duty, from honouring the flag or marching in parades to attending the numerous national and international 'friendship' meetings of the FDJ.

In 1950, the Pioneer leader Regina Franke from Jena wrote to 'our president and friend of the youth Wilhelm Pieck'. She was full of 'joy' for the children's 'vigour and enthusiasm, no matter whether it's in sports and working groups, at school or during our great Pioneer mission'. Hilde Seuthe, a fourth-grader from Rostock, referred to Pieck as the 'dad who provides for everyone. We are very happy that you are our president because you have already given us a great deal. We already have more to eat than we did in 1945, now we can bake a cake every Sunday. There are lots more potatoes, bread and vegetables too.' And thirteen-year-old Pioneer Egon Krenz, who would later occupy high offices of party and state, shared joyfully with Pieck that the vote on 15 October 1950 had been celebrated like a 'fair' and 'with chants' such as 'The election's a success, Adenauer will be a mess.'[5]

For the GDR leadership it was key from the start to keep the youth happy and onside because they embodied 'social progress' and the triumph of socialism. In an appeal for 1 May 1946, a public holiday with organized mass demonstrations, a newspaper called upon the young to show their 'confident, radiant faces next to the long-suffering expressions of adult men and women in a united front of workers'. Posters and photographs on front pages showed laughing children and adolescents who looked into the camera 'full of optimism'.[6] *'German youth, best endeavours / of our people united in you / You will be Germany's new life'* was the message in Johannes R. Becher's national anthem. This new life would be blessed with 'joy and peace' and eternal sunshine.

[5] Federal Archive Berlin, DA 4 (Presidential Office GDR, Pieck 1949–1960), no. 1134, 1135.

[6] W. P., 'Der erste Mai im Frieden', *Der Demokrat*, 30 April 1946, 1 (for this and other sources, I thank Juliane Brauer, *Zeitgefühle: Wie die DDR ihre Zukunft besang: Eine Emotionsgeschichte* (Bielefeld: transcript, 2020), 39–139); *Neues Deutschland*, 1 January 1959, 1.

If the sun failed to shine and the youth lacked the due enthusiasm, the regime reacted with something between helplessness and panic. In June 1953, when many citizens took the resentment they felt towards the government's policies to the streets, pupils also participated in the protests. They skived off exams, tore propaganda slogans from the walls, demanded an end to history and Russian lessons, and refused to write essays on Karl Marx. Some defected to the West, others destroyed portraits of the GDR's 'leading comrades'. Teachers and administrators were desperate. In one secondary school in Dresden, they came up with the explanation that 'we attended too much to children's intellect and not enough to their hearts and souls'.[7]

But in fact, the school curriculum had paid close attention to emotions. 'Democratic education' in the early GDR sought not only to generate 'enthusiasm for the struggle for a united Germany' and to 'instil a new work ethic'; its aim was also to awaken 'an optimistic attitude to life'. 'We need joy', the Berlin magistrate declared in 1946, for 'the difficult task of reconstruction'. Leaders of Pioneer organizations were supposed to set an example 'with joy and enthusiasm', and inspire the six- to fourteen-year-olds. Singing together, in particular, 'brightens life, brings joy, banishes sorrow and calls people to fight', stated an FDJ handbook from 1952. In a 1955 teaching directive, the Ministry of National Education advised that singing lessons, by generating 'joy and enthusiasm', greatly 'strengthen the patriotic feelings of pupils' (> Love).[8]

Those appeals did not go unheard. After the war years, there was definitely a willingness – more pronounced in some than in others – to participate in the country's reconstruction. By the summer of 1949, 700,000 children and one million adolescents and young adults had joined the Pioneers and the FDJ, about a third of the respective age groups. Leisure and community activities in particular met with great demand. 'Yes, I felt good', Ellen Fritsch later recalled of her FDJ days in 1948. 'I belonged to them. We sang the songs of the dawning new era with real enthusiasm and fervour.'[9] At the opening ceremony of the 1950 German Youth Meeting in Berlin (Figure 36), 20,000 boys and girls

---

[7] Federal Archive Berlin, DA 4 (Presidential Office GDR, Pieck 1949–1960), no. 948.

[8] F. M. Geidel, ed., *Lieder und Chöre zur Feiergestaltung*, serie 1, 2nd ed. (Berlin: Volk und Wissen, 1950), 63; Magistrat der Stadt Berlin, Abt. Kunst, ed., *Singt alle mit! Lieder für Feier und Gemeinschaft* (Berlin: Das Neue Berlin, 1946), 3; Zentralrat der FDJ, ed., *Handbuch des Pionierleiters* (Berlin: Neues Leben, 1952), 533; for the ministry's directive, see Brauer, *Zeitgefühle*, quote 152. See also Dorothee Wierling, 'Mission to Happiness: The Cohort of 1949 and the Making of East and West Germans', in *The Miracle Years: A Cultural History of West Germany, 1949–1968*, ed. Hanna Schissler (Princeton, NJ: Princeton University Press, 2001), 110–25.

[9] Ellen Fritsch, 'Mein Freund, das Akkordeon', in *'Schade um all die Stimmen...': Erinnerungen an Musik im Alltagsleben*, ed. Dorothea Muthesius (Vienna: Böhlau, 2000), 178–204, here 196.

Figure 36   Young Pioneers at the GDR Youth Rally for Peace, 1950 (Photo by Sovfoto/Universal Images Group via Getty Images)

sang and marched, to the joy of *Neues Deutschland*: 'That is a picture! There the heart laughs.'[10]

But the joy did not last long. On 17 June 1953, cracks had been revealed that could scarcely be papered over with renewed emotional appeals to the heart and soul. Since it was predominantly younger people who fled to the West in their hundreds of thousands before the Wall was built in 1961, the new generation obviously did not always share the 'optimistic attitude to life' under socialism that had been earmarked for them. Slogans seemed increasingly hollow and formulaic. 'Enthusiasm', the writer Günter de Bruyn recalled of the 1970s, 'became sought only from those who wanted to move up' and who therefore continued to wave their flags.[11]

Bearing flags and torches, 100,000 cheering FDJ members paraded past the official gallery in central Berlin on 6 October 1989. They were there to joyfully celebrate the fortieth anniversary of the founding of the republic. A young reporter from the *Berliner Zeitung* dared pose the heretical question of whether torchlight processions were still suited to contemporary times. 'Does the youth of today need thousand-voiced choirs, forests of flags, drum

---

[10] *Neues Deutschland*, 25 May 1950, 1.
[11] Günter de Bruyn, *Vierzig Jahre: Ein Lebensbericht* (Frankfurt: Fischer, 1998), 185–86.

rolls and cheers to express their feelings?' His totally anti-heretical answer was yes. He reported 'storms of enthusiasm' as regional delegations were welcomed, and 'storms of applause' as the first secretary of the FDJ read out the organization's pledge. In this country, the pledge ended, 'we still have much to do. Here we realize our plans and create our happiness. Here we work and learn, study and research, dance and love.' The FDJ members quoted by the journalist spoke of joy and solidarity. Only nineteen-year-old student Gabi Hansch from Gotha disclosed, 'I can't celebrate with such truly high spirits. Because some people are no longer with us, many of them my age, who have left our country. Who, in contrast to me, thought that they had no prospects here. That makes me sad and contemplative.'[12] A short while later, she probably left the FDJ, as almost everybody did. At the start of 1990, only 20,000 of the 2.3 million members remained; by 1994, there were an estimated 300.[13]

Prescribed versus Genuine Enthusiasm

The party leadership knew quite well that the officially ordered and expected enthusiasm was often just an act. Such knowledge came from Stasi informants but also from the many letters that reported on the mood of the general public, either anonymously or signed by name. In 1967, an East Berliner complained vehemently that 'people are being raised to be hypocrites. Nobody dares to share their true opinion anymore unless they are 150 per cent a comrade. In my estimation, at most 5–10 per cent of people really support the GDR. Everybody else is forced to constantly pretend. Including hundreds of thousands of party members.' He himself, as he admitted, did not stay in the country 'out of enthusiasm for Ulbricht's strain of socialism'. Another letter to Walter Ulbricht from 1969 castigated the 'atmosphere of untruthfulness, the permanent hypocrisy': 'Thus you believe you are surrounded by enthusiasm that is, however, not genuine enthusiasm. It is simply smart to clap along, to wave along, to shout along, because it would be unwise not to do so, to attract attention and thereby endanger oneself.' Not even work created 'joy' when people had to 'buy junk and rubbish with our good money', as one 'Anonymous' in 1983 outlined their disappointment over the inadequate provision of consumer goods.[14]

---

[12] Alexander Osang, 'Unter den Linden loderten Tausend Fackeln im Wind', *Berliner Zeitung*, 9 October 1989, 7.

[13] 'Bericht der Unabhängigen Kommission zur Überprüfung des Vermögens der Parteien und Massenorganisationen der DDR über das Vermögen der Freien Deutschen Jugend (FDJ)', in German Bundestag, Drucksache no. 13/5377 (1 August 1996), 12.

[14] Siegfried Suckut, *Volkes Stimmen: 'Ehrlich, aber deutlich' – Privatbriefe an die DDR-Regierung* (Munich: dtv, 2015), 119, 137, 329.

'Genuine' enthusiasm and joy found their place more often in the private sphere, among family and friends and during leisure time. They also sprang up at official sports and music events. The GDR's big international sporting successes, massively promoted by the state leadership for reasons of prestige, aroused > pride in many citizens. This in turn pleased the government. Even if there was some criticism of the 'overblown cult of our medal-winners' during the 1972 Munich Olympics, the regime's investment in sports paid off twice over: it helped joyful integration at home and yielded admiring recognition abroad.[15]

The Miracle of Bern

The regime had been less pleased when, in 1954, the Federal Republic's team unexpectedly won the World Cup final in Bern against the GDR's socialist 'brother state' Hungary. Football fans in Mecklenburg and Saxony, though, who followed the match on the radio cheered loudly and unabatedly and, as the then sixteen-year-old Friedrich Karl Brauns recalled, were 'happy about the three-two by Helmut Rahn'.[16] GDR reporter Wolfgang Hempel, who commentated on the game, did not seem quite so happy. Still, he remained sober and matter-of-fact, in contrast to his West German colleague Herbert Zimmermann, who could barely contain himself: 'Germany lead three to two, with five minutes left of the game. Call me mad, call me crazy. I believe even those less interested in football should have a heart and should rejoice in the enthusiasm of our team and in our own enthusiasm and should now keep their fingers crossed.'[17]

That they did, until the final whistle. Then, as journalists observed, men 'sank together as if released from a spasm' and rushed to the streets 'to pass on the joy that could not be carried alone'. Strangers 'clasped arms, hugged each other and showed without shame the thick teardrops on their cheeks as the national anthem sounded on international soil for a German victory'. The team's journey home turned into a triumphal procession, with tens of thousands welcoming them at Munich's central square.[18]

---

[15] Ibid., 489.

[16] 'Friedrich Karl Brauns im Gespräch mit Astrid Rawohl', 5 July 2014, https://bit.ly/3SggnII, accessed 25 January 2022.

[17] www.das-wunder-von-bern.de/kult_radioreportage.htm, accessed 25 January 2022; Peter Kasza, *1954 – Fußball spielt Geschichte* (Bonn: Bundeszentrale für politische Bildung, 2004), 191–98.

[18] *Frankfurter Allgemeine Zeitung*, 5 July 1954, 6; Nils Havemann, *Samstags um halb 4: Die Geschichte der Fußballbundesliga* (Munich: Siedler, 2013), 28–43. For the impact of the victory on (West) Germans, see Franz-Josef Brüggemeier, 'Das Wunder von Bern: The 1954 Football World Cup, the German Nation and Popular History', in *Popular Historiographies in the 19th and 20th Centuries: Cultural Meanings, Social Practices*, ed. Sylvia Paletschek (Oxford: Berghahn, 2011), 188–200.

As expected, such public storms of enthusiasm held off in the East, but there, too, the Stasi documented several spontaneous jubilant rallies. The party organ *Neues Deutschland*, however, did not forego the opportunity to draw attention to the alleged link between sporting 'triumph' and 'chauvinistic attitudes' in West Germany. Chancellor Adenauer, possessed of 'fascistic impudence', apparently wanted to use the football performance 'for his American propaganda' and to take the victory in Bern as an occasion to 'create the necessary atmosphere for a new military foray'. Not every reader was ready to believe this. A man from Dresden, who had himself played football for many years and closely followed 'international sporting life', asked with irritation what the 'chauvinism that you so emphasize actually has to do with the game'. In reply, the newspaper repeated its claims and warned every 'respectable German sportsperson' against 'indifferently ignoring these ramifications of the World Cup final'.[19]

Expectations of Happiness in the Adenauer Era

Neither the 'fascistically impudent' Konrad Adenauer nor President Heuss made any mention of the 'Miracle of Bern' in their 1954 Christmas and New Year's speeches. In contrast, Chancellor Angela Merkel, who rarely missed an important national team match, liked to reference football in her New Year's addresses. She did so with particular joy in 2006, after the country had hosted the World Cup, with many citizens spending weeks in an exuberant party mood.[20]

The seventy-eight-year-old Adenauer, for his part, was not a football fan. Besides, he found it altogether unnecessary 'to repeatedly pursue variety, distraction, entertainment'. Of the people he had met in his long life, 'those who chased after profit, pleasure, money, power' were not, in his view, the happiest. Heuss, who was eight years younger and a traditionally educated gentleman, also distanced himself from what he saw as a contemporary inclination to 'having fun' and enjoying the organized 'hustle and bustle' of clubs and associations. He instead recommended the reading of a good book as a remedy for 'spiritual loneliness'. Consequently, he stayed well away from regional carnival festivities, not least out of consideration for the economic

---

[19] *Berliner Zeitung*, 6 July 1954, 4; *Neues Deutschland*, 6 July 1954, 6; ibid., 7 July 1954, 6. After the game, many GDR citizens expressed their unhappiness that local media had been biased and political in their reporting and had favoured the Hungarian team (Franz-Josef Brüggemeier, *Weltmeister im Schatten Hitlers: Deutschland und die Fußball-Weltmeisterschaft 1954* (Essen: Klartext, 2014), 229; Kasza, *1954*, 202–3).

[20] *Bulletin der Bundesregierung*, no. 01-1 (1 January 2007). Merkel explicitly praised the 'performance of Jürgen Klinsmann's national football team' – although they only came third in the World Cup.

and emotional 'distress' many people still experienced during the 1950s, and, of course, 'for the Soviet zone'.[21]

West German politicians thereby set a decidedly different tone from the GDR leadership, who went almost overboard with appeals to 'merriment' and 'optimism', and who started to host 'festivals of joy' in the 1960s.[22] National Socialism had likewise attached great importance to festivals and given them plenty of space in its political calendar. In comparison, the events organized by post-war bowling, rifle, carnival and sports associations and disparaged by strict 'Papa Heuss' for their 'pseudo-togetherness' seemed almost primly private, restrained and politically innocent.

Unlike the 'Third Reich' and unlike the GDR, the West German state did not expect its citizens to profess their commitment with ostentatious enthusiasm or gratitude. What it hoped for was an amount of personal contentment proportionate to the general circumstances. In Adenauer's view, this feeling of contentment formed 'the basis of happiness on earth'. The Christian Democrat blamed the fact that it was so rare in the land of the 'economic miracle' on the 'idol of progress' worshipped by many. People who constantly strove for ever more money and pleasure tended, in his opinion, to 'devalue what has been achieved' and would 'never experience joy'.[23]

Here spoke a dyed-in-the-wool conservative who was as critical as he was helpless when confronted with modernity's highly ambiguous faces. Promising and expecting progress was one of them, and economically progress translated into growth. The boom of the 1950s and 1960s raised expectations of the standard of living and made consumer desires accelerate. Improving people's material prospects went hand in hand with increasing their contentment with democracy. Adenauer knew this very well even if he did not particularly like it. But he, along with many others, had learnt the lesson from Weimar, whose young democracy had not survived the massive economic crisis of the late 1920s and early 1930s.

Weimar Progress: Cheers and Rejection

The modern gospel of progress and general improvement had also been sung at the birth of the first German republic. Its constitution boldly professed the aim 'to foster societal progress'. Yet many citizens did not believe in such

[21] Kiehl, *Alle Jahre wieder*, 82, 87; Theodor Heuss, *Hochverehrter Herr Bundespräsident! Der Briefwechsel mit der Bevölkerung 1949–1959*, ed. Wolfram Werner (Berlin: De Gruyter, 2010), 313. In 1954, the German League for Human Rights had requested that Heuss took steps to limit the extravagance, because 'our brothers in the Eastern Zone could perceive the carnival goings-on in the Federal Republic, if they get out of hand, as unbrotherly and lacking in solidarity' (ibid., 312).

[22] Jan Palmowski, *Inventing a Socialist Nation: Heimat and the Politics of Everyday Life in the GDR 1945–1990* (Cambridge: Cambridge University Press, 2009), 77–78, 135, 138.

[23] Kiehl, *Alle Jahre wieder*, 81–82.

progress, or rejected it altogether. Unbridled joy and enthusiasm for the new state were limited. Even those who, like the historian Friedrich Meinecke or the writer Thomas Mann, supported the republic for lack of viable political alternatives and called themselves '*Vernunftrepublikaner*' ('republicans by reason') often remained 'monarchists at heart'.[24]

So by no means everyone welcomed the new state as 'jubilantly' as the citizen Höllmüller did in a telegram he sent to Kurt Eisner in Munich on 11 November 1918. Three days earlier, socialist Eisner had proclaimed the Bavarian Republic and been elected by the workers' and soldiers' council as its first prime minister. On 14 November, the pastor Carl Borromäus Huber from Niedernkirchen also shared his '*enthusiastic* and unlimited respect' as well as his '*exuberant joy*' with the 'most esteemed President'. Miss Link likewise gave a 'cheer' for 'our republic' and expressed her 'joy and gratitude' to Eisner.

Opponents mostly piped up anonymously, as with this clumsily handwritten rallying cry:

> Reflect, my people of Bavaria
> You want to preserve reason
> The convict at the top there
> seduces the blind crowds
> What did your royal family do to you
> that you cast them from the throne
> you believe yourself free, you poor people
> and follow the son of a Jew.[25]

Three months later Eisner was dead, murdered by a student and lieutenant on leave with antisemitic *völkisch*-monarchist beliefs.

If the 1918 Revolution that swept away the monarchy had roused joyful expectations for quite a number of people, they experienced the 1920s with mixed emotions. Only those who possessed enough resources to achieve the modern, culture- and consumption-oriented lifestyle benefited from the Golden Twenties. Many felt at odds with a political system whose personnel changed in rapid succession and whose parties seemed unwilling to enter into dialogue and incapable of compromise. In their eyes, the World War general Paul von Hindenburg, who ran for the presidency in 1925, embodied security, stability and non-partisanship. It is true that the seventy-seven-year-old candidate made no secret of his anti-republican attitudes. Yet people who were weary of the new times or disappointed by them longed for a substitute kaiser

---

[24] Friedrich Meinecke, 'Verfassung und Verwaltung der deutschen Republik [1918/19]', in Friedrich Meinecke, *Politische Schriften und Reden*, ed. Georg Kotowski (Darmstadt: Toeche-Mittler, 1958), 280–98, here 281; Andreas Wirsching and Jürgen Eder, eds, *Vernunftrepublikanismus in der Weimarer Republik* (Stuttgart: Steiner, 2008).

[25] Bavarian State Archive Munich, II, MA no. 102378: Höllmüller, 11 November 1918; C. B. Huber, 14 November 1918; R. Link, 14 November 1918 (italics in the original); anonymous and undated, probably November 1918.

who stood above the parties and symbolized the 'unity of the German people'. In any case, that was how medical student Gerhard Heese from Berlin phrased it in a 1932 letter to Hindenburg.

Auguste Mann, an eighty-seven-year-old veteran's widow from Dresden, listened 'with great enthusiasm and full sympathy' as Hindenburg announced his renewed candidacy over the radio on 10 March 1932. The 'old front-line soldier' Max Jacob from Kaiserslautern, who listened to the speech 'with my family, with a pulsing heart', urged the president 'to finally, with a firm hand and an iron broom, put an end to the political rabble-rousing so that our fatherland again stands united and ceases tearing itself apart'. He voiced the feelings of many. 'Front-line fighter' Wilhelm Meyer from Berlin, who introduced himself as a 'loyal German citizen of Jewish faith' shared the opinion 'that the fatherland comes first, then the party'. And Else Andersch from a Protestant vicarage asked, 'Why the meetings and propaganda! We want to be a united people of brothers, this hatred and discontent is plunging our fatherland into an abyss.' She herself never engaged in politics 'because it only gives cause for dissatisfaction'. More than a few Germans were dissatisfied, as the thirty-two-year-old Wilhelm Bepler from Wetzlar disclosed. He travelled far and wide with his door-to-door sales and encountered lots of people who had 'many a thing to say about state and government'. They complained about the high unemployment as well as slashed wages, pensions and social benefits.[26] Under the 'societal progress' that the constitution announced, they had envisioned something different.

National Socialist Choreographies

Progress was also promised by Adolf Hitler and his National Socialist movement. Prior to 1929 they were largely irrelevant and without influence. But the serious economic crisis brought huge numbers of new supporters; the Nazi Party's share of the vote rose from 2.6 per cent in the 1928 elections to 37.3 per cent in July 1932.[27] For Margarete Rödder from Wiesbaden, who had been following the NSDAP's 'work and flourishing for years with interest, then with wonder and finally with ever-growing admiration', 14 September 1930 was already 'a day of the most triumphant joy', due to the 6.4 million votes (up from 810,000 two years earlier). After Hitler was appointed chancellor on 30 January 1933, widow Lydia Spies sent him handwritten poems she said were inspired by her 'great enthusiasm for you and the *völkisch* movement': '*Heil* and

---

[26] Federal Archive Berlin, R 601, no. 378: W. Bepler, undated (received on 5 February 1932); G. Heese, 15 February 1932; no. 379: A. Mann, 11 March 1932; no. 380: M. Jakob, 10 March 1932; W. Meyer, 11 March 1932; E. Andersch, 11 March 1932.

[27] Jürgen Falter et al., *Wahlen und Abstimmungen in der Weimarer Republik* (Munich: C. H. Beck, 1986), 41, 71, 73.

Figure 37 An excited crowd at Wilhelmplatz, Berlin, the night before Hitler's fiftieth birthday (Photo by Heinz Fremke/ullstein bild via Getty Images)

Sieg! / A million-strong cry jubilantly resounds / The subjugation is over!' In 1935, Anneliese Elkar from Munich, a member of the League of German Girls, congratulated Hitler in a similarly poetic mode: 'And the Germans, they cheer and whoop and sing / Songs of freedom, each louder than the next / *Heil*, the crowd shouts out to the Führer / *Heil* you, O saviour of Germany, you!' (Figure 37). Reading *Mein Kampf*, nineteen-year-old Stormtrooper Georg Eid revealed, gave him 'joy in his heart' and drove away sorrowful thoughts.[28]

Certainly, there were still 'grumblers and doubters' in the 'Third Reich', as Erfurt members of the National Socialist Women's League complained in 1935.

---

[28] Federal Archive Berlin, NS 51, no. 51/1: Marg. Rödder, 20 September 1930; no. 53: Lydia Spies, 15 February 1933; no. 75: Anneliese Elkar, 19 April 1935; Georg Eid, 19 April 1935.

The Hitler Youth also raised the banner 'against detractors and grumblers' and took aim at 'that part of the reaction which comes from the German bourgeoisie', as well as left-wing youth organizations.[29] Not everyone was enthusiastic and joyous about the National Socialist cause, as the Sopade Reports from the exiled SPD in Prague and Paris revealed. Even the SS, which clandestinely observed and charted the 'mood of the population', painted it closer to grey-black than rose-tinted. In 1939 there was little enthusiasm for war to be felt, and anyone looking for cheering men waving their hats like in 1914 looked largely in vain.[30]

Still, the regime consistently managed to mobilize those who conformed to its racial and political ideology. It promised jobs and kept its promise through a policy of accelerated rearmament. When it came to international politics, Hitler gambled on high risk, which paid out and brought him admiration even from circles that had initially taken a distanced approach. Domestically, he declared the end of class-based society and strove to implement, at least symbolically, the national and ethnic *Volksgemeinschaft*. He advertised the Strength through Joy programme for workers to go to concerts or on trips at little cost (> Curiosity), while the Beauty of Labour project sought to make jobs and environments nicer, cleaner and healthier, in order to boost the 'joy in work' and, with it, productivity.[31]

Moreover, Hitler understood how to heighten the cult surrounding his person. To this end, he used sophisticated stage direction and rhetoric that rarely failed to make an impact. At party congresses and other mass events, he immediately captivated those present and sent them into a 'terrific frenzy of enthusiasm', as Minister of Propaganda Joseph Goebbels noted with satisfaction regarding the Berlin 1 May celebrations he had organized in 1933.[32] Even a matter-of-fact Swiss citizen like Denis de Rougemont, who was living in Germany teaching French language classes, sensed 'a special sort of shiver and heartbeat' as he witnessed Hitler in Frankfurt's festival hall on 11 March 1936. Four days previously, the news that German troops had entered the formerly demilitarized Rhineland had triggered nationwide 'euphoria'. Now 40,000 people gathered to see and hear the Führer. Rougemont stood between young girls, militiamen from the National Labour Service, shabbily clothed women and workers. After a four-hour wait, they all raised their right arms 'in a single movement' as Hitler appeared on the

[29] Ibid., NS 51, no. 75: Fanny Caspari et al., 19 April 1935; R 601, no. 1119: Friedrich Prince Hohenzollern, 24 June 1934 (with an enclosed newspaper article about a rally held by the Karlsruhe Hitler Youth).

[30] Ian Kershaw, *The 'Hitler Myth': Image and Reality in the Third Reich* (Oxford: Clarendon Press, 1987), 73–75.

[31] On Beauty of Labour, see Shelley Baranowski, *Strength through Joy: Consumerism and Mass Tourism in the Third Reich* (Cambridge: Cambridge University Press, 2004), 75–117.

[32] Joseph Goebbels, *Die Tagebücher*, ed. Elke Fröhlich, part 1, vol. 2 (Munich: Saur, 1987), 415.

threshold, greeted by 'a deafening thunder of rhythmic *Heils*'. Everybody, Rougemont wrote, 'stands rigidly to attention, motionless and shouting in time, their eyes glued to the illuminated spot, to that face with its ecstatic smile, and tears stream down their faces in the darkness'.[33]

Hitler was betting on this reaction and had deliberately prepared it; he worked with powerful light effects, stepped 'very slowly forwards', welcomed his audience with 'episcopal gestures'. He deliberately drew on the icono-graphy of the Catholic Church and the socialist movement. 'I myself could feel and understand', he had written in 1925, recalling a post-war demonstra-tion 'of Marxism' in Berlin's city centre, 'how easily the man in the street succumbs to the suggestive spell of such a magnificently effective spectacle'. According to Hitler, great rallies produced the 'mass suggestion' that turned the individual man into a 'member of a community' who felt 'all swept up in the tremendous force of the suggestive intoxication and the enthusiasm of three to four thousand others'. This man then left the gathering consolidated, strengthened and emboldened.[34]

Disillusion and a Sense of Proportion

After the lost war, many Germans only reluctantly remembered the euphoria with which they had cheered Hitler and his policies. Young people in particular felt seduced by and disillusioned with their adored Führer. They were the ones the regime had wooed and who had committed themselves to its goals. Confronted with their desires and longings in ruins, many withdrew from politics altogether. But cultivating a 'count me out' attitude was, as President Heuss warned in his 1951 New Year's Eve speech, counterproductive and dangerous. Democracy, as an institution and a way of life, instead needed 'the *"count me in"*'.[35]

Being 'in' and for democracy, however, was by no means synonymous with displaying organized loyalty by featuring, as in the GDR, beaming children, eager adolescents and adults who, out of sheer enthusiasm for real socialism, would work an unpaid extra shift. West of the river Elbe, civil servants were expected to show commitment to the liberal-democratic order, but not demonstrative passion and excitement for the state and its very institutions. Joy was not dictated or stage-managed from above; it remained a private matter. The state merely established the conditions under which its citizens

---

[33] *Travels in the Reich, 1933-1945*, ed. Oliver Lubrich (Chicago, IL: University of Chicago Press, 2004), 84–87 (entries from 9 and 11 March 1936).

[34] *Hitler, Mein Kampf: Eine kritische Edition*, ed. Christian Hartmann et al., 4th ed., vol. 2 (Berlin: IfZ, 2016), 1243 [136], 1211 [121].

[35] Kiehl, *Alle Jahre wieder*, 60. The notion of 'count me out' (*Ohne Mich*) refers to a general attitude of non-participation. More specifically, it designated the post-war pacifist move-ment that resisted rearmament.

could lead a good life, and it demanded neither gratitude nor love in return. Only when the complaining and grumbling of the dissatisfied threatened to take up too much space in public discourse did politicians speak up and warn against losing a sense of proportion.

But what was proportionate? When do people feel happy and content? In 1954, Adenauer believed this related to expectations and aspirations: the more one expected from the future, the more disappointed one would be by what was achieved. Recent empirical research on happiness partly proves him right. It also shows, though, that expectations are complex and go far beyond material aspirations. The willingness to describe oneself as happy in surveys does not increase in line with a higher income and standard of living. In the Federal Republic the real per-capita income, adjusted for price increases, almost doubled between 1970 and 2000 while average life satisfaction remained at approximately the same level. People obviously got used to having a fat wallet and considered it a matter of course, and not a source of joy, to benefit from further growth. Also, comparison with others plays a greater role the more resources are available. If a person's wage does not increase as much as their colleague's, they feel vexed rather than happy. They thus care less about their own gain and more about what they see as a lack of recognition and appreciation.[36]

Happiness and Unhappiness in the Consumer Society

The general horizon of expectations further impacts subjective well-being. In the modern consumer society as it took off in the second half of the twentieth century – in the Federal Republic far more quickly and successfully than in the GDR – citizens' wants and desires soared sky-high. This was fully intentional and had political backing because economic development was essentially dependent upon consumer demand. Rising demand fuelled a booming economy that, through higher wages, offered more opportunities to fulfil needs and maintain the growth trajectory. As in many other capitalist countries, West Germany's so-called economic miracle enabled full employment and rising wages that could pay for consumer goods. Fridges, washing machines, television sets and cars gradually made their way into private homes. Since the mid-1960s the annual holiday, initially and preferably a trip to Italy, has been part of the living standards of ever-broader sections of the population.

But consumption also meant stress, as West Germans swiftly learnt. With cars came traffic jams, with full shop counters jostling crowds at the summer

[36] Bruno Frey et al., *Happiness: A Revolution in Economics* (Cambridge, MA: MIT Press, 2008), here esp. 31–32; Bruno Frey and Alois Stutzer, *Happiness and Economics: How the Economy and Institutions Affect Human Well-Being* (Princeton, NJ: Princeton University Press, 2002).

or winter sales, with washing machines the pressure to keep clothes immaculately clean at all times. Moreover, there was now a constant impulse to compare oneself with others. Each new fashion trend invariably aroused frustration in those who could not afford it, or on whom it looked unflattering and garnered malicious comments from peers. 'Buy yourself happy', as a popular marketing strategy, coupled consumption and well-being but was silent about the risks and side effects. Happiness was – if it existed at all – of ever shorter duration and expired when the colleague, the neighbour or the classmate wore chicer clothes, drove bigger cars or took more exotic foreign holidays (> Envy).

For GDR citizens, these were luxury problems. Particularly in the 1980s, they increasingly complained about high prices, a lack of consumer goods and their poor quality. This undoubtedly dampened the enthusiasm that regular reports of patent economic success were supposed to elicit. One East Berliner, who wrote to Erich Honecker in September 1988 signing his name and address, emphasized that he 'liked living in the GDR'. That was the very reason, he explained, that he monitored economic developments 'with great concern'. The 'discontent among the people' was steadily growing because the living standards in the Federal Republic still proved significantly higher than in the GDR. 'Yet that should actually be the other way round! When will it finally be changed?' He pointed out that West Germans stood in queues neither for everyday items nor for durables, and that they could 'always clothe themselves inexpensively and fashionably for little money. In the GDR this is only possible for those who have the money necessary to buy in "Exquisit" and "Intershops".' The author considered the situation 'intolerable': it provided 'dynamite for an undreamt-of explosion'.[37]

Joy and Disappointment

The explosion materialized, and dissatisfaction with the inadequate supply situation played no small part in it. After reunification, though, the initial enthusiasm over full shelves, new travel opportunities and Western-made cars did not last long. East Germans once again compared themselves with West Germans and felt left behind as their wages were lower and unemployment higher. The fact that inner cities had been spruced up, ruined structures rebuilt, cultural monuments restored, streets and telephone lines extended did not seem to matter. Without a doubt, Czechs, Poles, Slovaks and

---

[37] Suckut, *Volkes Stimmen*, 390–94. Both types of shops were government-owned and operated. They sold rare and high-quality consumer goods at extremely high prices (Exquisit) or in return for Western currencies (Intershop) that officially no East German was allowed to possess.

Hungarians suffered far more from the post-socialist transformation. But, as before 1989, many East Germans preferred to look westwards and were dissatisfied anew.

In the West, excitement ebbed similarly quickly. In 1989/90, people's surprise had been almost greater than their joy. It is true that, year after year, chancellors and presidents had reminded citizens of the wounds caused by the country's post-1945 division. Reversing it remained an indisputable political objective, particularly as the Basic Law called on the 'entire German people' to 'achieve unity and freedom in free self-determination'. Fewer and fewer West Germans, however, believed in this, and many were sincerely indifferent to the walled-in state and its inhabitants. That changed in the historically brief moment when the Wall came down.

Yet euphoria soon gave way, in both parts of the reunified nation, to a widespread feeling of irritation and incomprehension. The political landscape remained split and fractured. In the East, the Party of Democratic Socialism (PDS) initially raked in electoral victories as the SED's successor, and from 2007 onwards Die Linke followed suit. Since 2015, the far-right AfD has gained ground at a pace and scale far exceeding that in the West. Of course, left and right differ fundamentally in their attitudes towards migration and racism. But both are considered reservoirs for the chronically discontent, and come together in their scepticism towards the European Union and affinity with Russia. Neither view finds much favour among West Germans.

And so, three decades after the fall of the Wall, little remains of the collective joy that was felt around the world back then. Such a shift from happiness to disappointment, from exaltation to discontent takes on a particular meaning and importance when placed in the larger context of twentieth-century history. The latter has not offered Germans too many occasions for collective joy. While other countries celebrated the end of both world wars with annual victory parades and fireworks, Germany sank into mourning and contemplation or passed over the days in silence. Even the GDR, which between 1950 and 1967 designated 8 May an official holiday commemorating 'liberation from fascism', failed to get its citizens to feel in a party mood. In the West, it was 1985 before President Richard von Weizsäcker suggested remembering the surrender not as a defeat but as a liberation. Even then, he was asking for historical reflection rather than exuberant cheer. Meanwhile, 8 May has become a 'day of remembrance' in two out of sixteen federal states. Whether it will ever be a day of joy remains in question.

In any case, the Federal Republic has always had difficulty with national festivals and jubilantly choreographed celebrations. As a liberal democracy, it stayed away from overly enthusiastic politics of emotion. Instead, it sought to establish and safeguard the conditions that might make people's contentment and happiness possible. Whether and how citizens use these, however, is considered their own business.

Most show joy primarily in private and value 'small happiness' with family or among friends. In this respect, East Germans do not differ from West Germans, nor Germans from Britons, Italians or Scandinavians. Anyone who watches them at carnivals, in football stadiums or at pop concerts would not think them a miserable, ill-humoured species. Nor is the joy in work a foreign concept. Solely when it comes to politics does the joy-gauge drop, and that has to do with the experience of how often enthusiasm was politically manipulated and instrumentalized throughout the twentieth century.

Some nations have managed to bring together private and public moments of happiness, even if only once a year. When the French or Americans celebrate their national days, they are in high spirits and don their countries' colours for the official programme as well as at the subsequent barbecue or game of boules. Time will tell whether Germans develop a similarly cheerful and relaxed approach to 3 October, the anniversary of reunification and the only national day. At present, it seems a distant prospect.

~

Love

'*I'm falling in love again (can't help it)*', trilled Marlene Dietrich as Lola Lola in Josef von Sternberg's famous 1930 film *The Blue Angel*. Love was Lola's world, '*and nothing else*'. At first glance, she seemed to be validating the expectations placed on women since the 1800s: according to popular encyclopaedias, women were 'representatives of love', their 'whole being' animated by love. This qualified them for the role of loving wife and mother.[1]

Yet the provocative cabaret singer was not in the least interested in fulfilling that role. She basked in the admiration of adoring followers of all ages and enjoyed the attraction she exerted on mortal men: '*Men cluster to me / Like moths around a flame / And if their wings burn / I know I'm not to blame.*' When Lola finally married Professor Rath, a high-school teacher who was besotted with her, she had no intention of playing the part of the faithful, loving and devoted wife. For the archetypal femme fatale, love was episodic, noncommittal, a lark, and thus the opposite of what Rath imagined it to be. The tale, based on Heinrich Mann's successful 1905 novel *Professor Unrat* (Professor Filth), did not end well for him.

Framing the Colourful World of Love

What people in the twentieth century associated with love and how they experienced it is by no means encapsulated in these two figures and figurations alone. Love took many forms: the love of parents, children and siblings, the love between friends, neighbourly love, love of God and for one's homeland (> Belonging) or nation. Even romantic relationships, which increasingly dominate the discourse on love, cover a wide and expansive spectrum. They encompass different types of marriage: the conventional, the 'wild' or de facto marriage, as well as the so-called 'uncle marriage' in which a widowed woman cohabits but does not marry, in order to continue receiving pension benefits. They also include 'free love' and the 'fling', the secret, open or tacitly

---

[1] *Allgemeine deutsche Real-Encyklopädie für die gebildeten Stände*, vol. 3 (Leipzig: Brockhaus, 1824), 877; *Das große Conversations-Lexicon für die gebildeten Stände*, vol. 12 (Hildburghausen: Bibliografisches Institut, 1848), 749–50.

tolerated relationship, lifelong love and serial monogamy, love triangles and polyamorous relationships.

Love exists in various states: it oscillates between hot and burning, tepid and consuming, tender and mild. It alternates, from the deep yearning of infatuation and the frenzy of desire to unconditional devotion and gentle loving care. All of this unfolds between men and women, but also between people of the same gender or diverse genders. Sexuality plays an important role; exactly what that role is differs from relationship to relationship. Moreover, love changes over time and depending on the age of those involved.

That all sounds complex, and it is. What is more, lovers always believe that they are experiencing something utterly individual and unique, something that defies description and classification. That no emotion has had so many words spilled on it as love suggests otherwise, however. Romance novels, love poems and guides fill libraries on every continent and in every language. No opera from the late eighteenth or nineteenth century would have been written if not for the bliss and heartache of love, from Mozart's *Magic Flute* to Wagner's *Tristan and Isolde*. Theatre has drawn from this well too. In the twentieth century, the love story travelled to the small and celluloid screen in the form of comedies, tragedies and melodramas. Without the schmaltz of love, pop songs would probably not exist. Advertisements, typically for jewellery, lingerie and flowers, less frequently for cars and washing machines, proffer ways or wares to help lovers communicate their feelings. The booming market of self-help literature contains its own fair share of tips, recommendations and warnings.

Earlier generations were evidently better versed in the symbolic language of such feelings, or at least they placed greater value on distinguishing between the many different forms and expressions of love. It would not have occurred to them to say 'love you' when bidding farewell to parents, children or friends, as has become general practice in recent years. Instead, they were conversant in the highly varied 'languages of love' taught in novels and advice literature. Among these was the 'language of flowers' meticulously described in popular handbooks on setting the 'right tone' in relationships. What man today is still aware that, instead of dahlias or chrysanthemums, he should give his wife or bride roses, because 'an arrangement of scentless and gaudily coloured flowers will never impart a warm feeling; it can only ever be a sign of cool attention, of worshipful politeness'? The worst mistake a gentleman could make was to send 'a flowerpot, for his gift should be considered merely an acknowledgement of the day itself, and must not give rise to the idea that he intended his person to be remembered for a longer time'.[2]

---

[2] Franz Ebhardt, *Der gute Ton*, 13th ed. (Leipzig: Klinkhardt, 1896), 195.

Around 1900, there were sophisticated rules, prescriptions and explanations not only about flowers and other presents but also for lovers' conduct. Most parents did not mind if betrothed couples saw each other every day, but they did not allow them to be alone. Usually, the mother or a younger sister was present. Unmarried couples, including those who were engaged, were not to appear in public without a chaperone. Tender exchanges in front of others were forbidden as a matter of course: 'The bride must draw the boundary more tightly in this respect than the man may like. If he lacks restraint, she should reject his caresses with friendly demureness.'[3] Sex before marriage was completely taboo – or at least it was supposed to be.

Such stipulations reveal just how much romantic relationships have changed in the last century. Although there are still written and unwritten rules today, they are noticeably more relaxed. Moreover, they do not claim to strike a universal 'right tone' but differ according to social milieu and peer group. Of course, such distinctions existed in 1900 too. Love in working-class or rural circles felt and was experienced differently from that among the urban middle classes, to whom etiquette handbooks were addressed. Nevertheless, the normative hegemony of bourgeois notions and practices of love reigned supreme. This has long since ceased to be the case. The same holds true for the assumption that romantic love only blossoms between men and women.

Advice literature of the late twentieth and early twenty-first century clearly reflects these changes. That such texts, whether books, columns or blogs, continue to circulate at a growing rate and with increasing diversity signals the uncertainty surrounding love – the 'most beautiful feeling in the world', according to *maedchen.de*. Precisely because it is such a wonderful and coveted feeling, people are eager to do it right. To the extent that love has turned into a kind of religion, perhaps even a substitute for religion, it has become rather fragile and precious. In the Romantic tradition, it is regarded as otherworldly and uncontrollable, a gift from the heavens that appears without warning and lands with full force. And yet, women (more often than men) do everything they can to plan and prepare for the moment, aided by fashion, beauty and cosmetic-surgery industries worth billions. Men, meanwhile, invest in muscles and cars; many rely on the erotic appeal of their careers and bank accounts.[4]

Love, then, is not just a feeling. It is also and above all a practice. The conduct of lovers is flanked by an army of professionals, institutions and media, which give love its shape and influence its texture. They develop its

---

[3] Ibid., 141.

[4] www.maedchen.de/love/liebe; Markus Günther, 'Ersatzreligion Liebe', *Frankfurter Allgemeine Zeitung*, 25 September 2014, http://bit.ly/3xRr9M9, both accessed 20 January 2022. The work by sociologist Eva Illouz is instructive, esp. *Consuming the Romantic Utopia: Love and the Cultural Contradictions of Capitalism* (Berkeley: University of California Press, 1997).

modes and customs, they deliver commands and prohibitions. They provide the language – the metaphors, symbols and signs – that brokers love. The supposedly most private and subjective emotion is, then, historically the one most monitored and framed by society. This is precisely what ensures and guarantees change. It also allows politics to enter the picture. Politics sets limits on what forms of love are permissible, and it taps into the power of love and seeks to appropriate it. Love for the state, for the fatherland, for the nation, for the constitution, for the father of the nation, for the Führer or for socialism was an important driver of political action during the twentieth century. This love did not develop on its own, either. Rather, it required careful practice and diligent cultivation.

Regulating Love

'Marriage and the family', the German Basic Law proclaimed, 'shall enjoy the special protection of the state.' The Weimar Constitution had held the same view, deeming marriage 'the basis of family life and the preservation and continuation of the nation'. There was no mention of love in 1919 nor in 1949. Implicitly, however, it was assumed that every marital union was based on love, ideally romantic and exclusive love. Loveless marriages for reasons of finance or convenience did exist, but they were on the wane by the twentieth century. As early as 1900, 'the heart' was permitted to 'speak and to overcome even difficult circumstances'. In 1953, 'almost everyone' dreamt of 'all-conquering and eternal love', according to Walther von Hollander, who was known as the nation's marriage counsellor. By then, the social and economic conditions were in place to enable these dreams to become a reality and to receive official consecration at the registry office or the altar.[5]

At the same time, state and church regulations ensured that certain groups remained barred from official consecration. Well into the 1950s, both branches of Christianity mobilized against mixed-denominational marriages. Wherever possible, local parish priests were supposed to quash love between Catholics and Protestants, which had become commonplace after the post-war Great Migration and its demographic and cultural upheavals. Those who did not share beliefs ought not to share a bed, at least that was the opinion of church leaders – an opinion lovers increasingly disregarded.

The state carried out its own interventions. It determined the age at which people could marry, the obligations that followed and under what

---

[5] Ebhardt, *Der gute Ton*, 131; Walther von Hollander, *Die Krise der Ehe und ihre Überwindung* (Berlin: Dt. Verlag, 1953), 29. On the latter, see also Lu Seegers, 'Walther von Hollander as an Advice Columnist on Marriage and the Family in the Third Reich', in *Private Life and Privacy in Nazi Germany*, ed. Elizabeth Harvey et al. (Cambridge: Cambridge University Press, 2019), 206–29.

circumstances a marriage could be dissolved. It decided who was not allowed to marry and what rights children born out of wedlock had. And it claimed the responsibility to legally buttress social norms around sexuality. Until the early 1970s, 'fundamentally any sexual relationship that lacks the blessing of marriage' was classified as 'fornication'. Under Paragraph 180 of the West German Penal Code, anyone who 'abetted' it by renting apartments or hotel rooms to unmarried couples could face legal action for 'pimping'.[6]

Resistance and Reforms in the Early Twentieth Century

That prohibitions and threats of punishment were necessary in the first place suggests that people repeatedly tried to shake off state and church norms about which kinds of love were permissible and which not. Despite official sanctions, premarital relationships (not to mention extramarital ones) abounded even in the days of the empire. In 1902, physician Willy Hellpach noted that such relations 'reach deep into the middle classes' and that scarcely a single bride went to the altar 'untouched'. Hellpach, who was fond of 'progress' and socialism, saw nothing wrong with this. Why should 'sexual intercourse based on affection be a worse preparation for marriage' than the 'prurient flattering and flirting of our daughters from the top ten thousand or the enforced modesty of middle-class girls with their calamitous ignorance of everything that awaits them later'? After all, he argued, sexuality before marriage was a matter of course in rural and working-class circles, where it was usually accompanied by a promise of marriage.[7]

Doctor Käte Frankenthal, who was born in 1889, did not care for such promises. She never entered into a proper marriage, though nor did she renounce sex, as she confessed in her memoirs. Since her student days she 'voluntarily gave this side of life the place nature has assigned to it'.[8] The author Helene Stöcker, twenty years Frankenthal's senior, likewise defied bourgeois conventions by cohabitating with a man without an official marriage certificate. In 1905, she and others founded the Association for the Protection of Mothers and Sexual Reform, which rallied against the 'lies and hypocrisy' in sexual matters. While women allegedly lost their 'purity' and > honour if they were involved in a premarital relationship, men got off scot-free. If a middle-class woman was expecting a child from a clandestine love affair, her chances for a conventional union were ruined. The father of the

---

[6] Horst Woesner, 'Ohne Ehe alles Unzucht', *Der Spiegel*, 15 April 1968, 67, 69. The author was a senior court judge.

[7] Ernst Gystrow [pseudonym for Willy Hugo Hellpach], *Liebe und Liebesleben im 19. Jahrhundert* (Berlin: Aufklärung, 1902), 21, 24, 34, 38.

[8] 'Käte Frankenthal', in *Before the Holocaust: Three German-Jewish Lives, 1870–1939*, ed. and trans. Thomas Dunlap (Philadelphia, PA: Xlibris, 2011), 29–244, quote 129.

child, on the other hand, was able to shirk his responsibilities without consequence. Until 1970, he was legally considered unrelated to his offspring, and a child born out of wedlock was not entitled to any inheritance.[9]

Helene Stöcker received support in her fight against double standards and for the rights of single mothers from notable feminists including Lily Braun and Hedwig Dohm. Liberal politicians like Friedrich Naumann and professors such as Max Weber and Werner Sombart also joined the association, along with a long list of doctors and eugenicists. Not everyone shared Stöcker's plea to liberate love from the registry office and the church altar. But her campaigns, which continued until 1933, for sexual education, reliable contraception and the right to abortion, and against the criminalization of homosexuals, met with approval far beyond the association.[10]

When it came to love and sexuality, the 1920s in particular were a time of reform and experimentation. Even within bourgeois milieus, formerly strict rules of decency and chastity softened. As reported in 1931, it was 'hardly uncommon' among urban secondary-school pupils of both sexes 'to openly admit to sexual intercourse and to regard it as their right'. Knowledge about contraception was gleaned from relevant handbooks or acquired in municipal or privately run counselling centres. These included, among many others, the Institute for Sexual Science, founded in Berlin in 1919 by physician Magnus Hirschfeld. The institute provided advice and carried out scientific research on homosexuals ('the third sex') and transgender individuals ('sexual intermediates'). Hirschfeld and his colleagues demanded the abolition of Paragraph 175 of the Penal Code, which criminalized homosexual activity, and campaigned for state and social acceptance of same-sex love. Simultaneously, a lively gay, lesbian and transvestite scene was emerging in Berlin's bars, restaurants and nightclubs, where the sex researcher and activist was a welcome and frequent visitor.[11]

Increasingly, marital sexuality also came under the watch of ardent reformers. Marriage and sexual counselling agencies aided couples struggling to find joy in their 'marital duties' and offered extra lessons in eroticism. In 1926, the Dutch gynaecologist Theodoor Hendrik van de Velde released a book about the 'physiology and technique' of the 'ideal marriage'. It was immediately translated into German (among other languages) and by 1932 was already in

[9] Sybille Buske, *Fräulein Mutter und ihr Bastard* (Göttingen: Wallstein, 2004).

[10] Christl Wickert, *Helene Stöcker 1869–1943* (Bonn: Dietz, 1991); Helene Stöcker, *Lebenserinnerungen* (Cologne: Böhlau, 2015). See also Catherine L. Dollard, *The Surplus Woman: Unmarried in Imperial Germany, 1871–1918* (New York: Berghahn, 2009).

[11] *Pädagogisches Lexikon*, ed. Hermann Schwartz, vol. 4 (Bielefeld: Velhagen & Klasing, 1931), 272; Ralf Dose, *Magnus Hirschfeld: The Origins of the Gay Liberation Movement*, trans. Edward H. Willis (New York: Monthly Review Press, 2014); Elena Mancini, *Magnus Hirschfeld and the Quest for Sexual Freedom: A History of the First International Sexual Freedom Movement* (New York: Palgrave Macmillan, 2010).

its forty-second edition. In 1928, the author published two more texts, one on 'the decisive importance' of erotic stimulation, the other on the 'emergence and suppression' of sexual aversion in marriage.

Lectures on these topics were extremely popular, though not with everyone. The Berlin district physician Max Hodann, who talked to pupils in vocational and secondary schools about the 'question of sex', faced a significant backlash for his educational work in the mid-1920s. The Protestant Parents' Association indignantly appealed to Hodann's superiors to immediately put an end to such indecent 'conversations'. The Steel Helmet, a right-wing veterans' organization, called the doctor a 'son of a bitch' and accused him of 'dirty pedagogy' (> Disgust). Both male and female deputies of the liberal-conservative German People's Party (DVP) launched an interpellation in the Prussian parliament, calling on the government to protect 'youth and nation from such damaging influences'. In the Berlin City Assembly, a representative of the far-right German National People's Party (DNVP) accused Hodann of 'raping the youth', degrading the 'honour of women' and destroying the family. Contrary to Hodann's view, 'sexual intercourse' should not be treated 'as a pleasure' but 'as a serious duty to society'.[12]

Writing from Karlsruhe in 1930, thirty-two-year-old National Socialist Elsa Walter similarly aired her displeasure about supposedly rampant immorality: a Social Democratic doctor had given 'a completely shameless lecture on topics whose names I don't even want to write down'. It would 'cause a decent woman to blush', she continued, since 'marriage, love and motherhood' are 'things that one feels and about which one hardly ever speaks, or at least only in such a way as to keep these things sacred for oneself'.[13]

Love under National Socialism

There were no more such talks after 1933. Hodann was removed from his post and went into exile, as did Helene Stöcker, who died impoverished in 1943 in New York. Incessant far-right attacks prompted Hirschfeld to leave the country as early as 1931. His institute was looted and destroyed. Meanwhile, the National Socialists set to work implementing their own ideas about love and sexuality. Homosexuality was criminalized more harshly than ever; instead of jail, the punishment was forced labour and the concentration camp. Abortion was strictly forbidden and the penalties for it intensified, mainly for the 'racially valuable' portion of the populace, whose progeny the state highly

---

[12] Max Hodann, *Bub und Mädel: Gespräche über die Geschlechterfrage*, 5th ed. (Rudolstadt: Greifenverlag, 1926). The first edition was published in 1925, the same year the mentioned campaign took place (132–60).

[13] *Letters to Hitler*, ed. Henrik Eberle, trans. Steven Randall (Cambridge: Polity Press, 2012), 41.

Figure 38   A Jewish man and a non-Jewish woman are pilloried by Nazis for 'racial defilement', July 1933 (History/Universal Images Group via Getty Images)

prized. If a Jewish woman wanted to terminate a pregnancy, this was welcomed. The Nazis also tried to prevent 'racial mixing' and considered marital and extramarital relations between Jews and non-Jews 'race defilement'; both were forbidden (Figure 38). Support was given to healthy 'Aryan' couples for starting a family, and there were monetary incentives to have as many children as possible. Those who did not meet the strict health standards faced other measures, from enforced sterilization and institutionalization to murder through the so-called T4 programme.

Love in the 'Third Reich' was only for 'Aryans' and the 'hereditarily healthy'. The state denied it to everyone else – Jews, Sinti and Roma, homosexuals, disabled people and 'asocials', as well as the millions from occupied territories forced to labour in German factories, mines and quarries during the war. Yet even those whose love was officially condoned were under watch. The regime closed sexual health clinics and made access to contraceptives more difficult, but it could not halt the trend towards the two-child family. Neither abortion bans and Mother's Crosses nor financial benefits and marriage loans would stop couples from limiting the number of children they had.

Still, the birth rate rose because more people were indeed getting married. The grim economic situation in the final phase of the Weimar Republic had made starting a family difficult. Now, National Socialist promises about a bright future raised hopes and expectations. The fact that very few children were born out of wedlock between 1936 and 1939 – representing just 7.7 per cent of all births in comparison to 12.2 per cent between 1926 and 1930 – suggests that couples were more likely and more often willing to marry.[14]

At the same time, the regime tried to dampen societal reservations about unmarried mothers and their children. From 1939, single mothers would no longer be automatically dismissed from the civil service. Women who were expecting a child by an SS man or Wehrmacht soldier but were not married to him could give birth discreetly in *Lebensborn* homes, which were set up in 1935 at the behest of SS leader Heinrich Himmler. Around 12,000 children were born in these homes, every second one out of wedlock.[15]

At first glance, such policies seemed to fulfil the demands Helene Stöcker and her fellow campaigners had made earlier. The motives, though, were wholly different. National Socialism was not interested in enabling women to have self-determined romantic relationships beyond the purview of church, state and society. Its chief concern was increasing the number of 'hereditarily healthy Aryan' children and thus bolstering its claim that it needed to find Lebensraum: living space for its growing population, preferably in Eastern Europe.

The regime used any means to achieve this goal, including amending the divorce laws of 1900. Henceforth, a marriage could be dissolved without fault, as long as the parties had been living apart for three years. The concept of irretrievable breakdown made it easier to divorce, paving the way for new marriages and more children. 'Mixed marriages' between Jews and non-Jews conducted before the 1935 Nuremberg Laws could be ended more swiftly and smoothly thanks to the amendment. By 1939, every fifth divorce proceeded on these grounds.

Love in West Germany

Conservatives and religious people found this hard to accept. In their view, marital love was supposed to last a lifetime and was only severed by death. Whether children came of it was beside the point. The traditional marriage laws that Hitler and Himmler cursed as 'satanic' they held for God-given, and they considered the accelerating divorce rate a sign of the devil's work. After 1945, they did everything in their power to reverse the Nazi-era regulations. Instead of breakdown, the focus was once again put on guilt: if the spouse bringing a divorce claim was largely responsible for destroying the union and

[14] Ute Frevert, *Women in German History: From Bourgeoise Emancipation to Sexual Liberation* (Oxford: Berg, 1997), 230–39.

[15] Amy Carney, *Marriage and Fatherhood in the Nazi SS* (Toronto: University of Toronto Press, 2018); Buske, *Fräulein Mutter*, 166.

the innocent party lodged an objection, family courts generally upheld the marriage. As the Christian Democrat-dominated West German governments of the 1950s and early 1960s saw it, this was meant to help married women. In seven to eight out of ten cases, they bore no 'fault' for the divorce and were allegedly interested in continuing the marriage. That was a gross misunderstanding, however. Women in fact filed for divorce more than twice as often as men, with the obvious intention to dissolve a strained relationship.

Nor did they let legal constraints dissuade them. Divorce rates increased rapidly between the early 1960s and 1977, when Social and Free Democrats re-established the breakdown principle as a valid ground for divorce. By 2003/2004 the number of couples getting divorced reached an all-time high of 214,000; the marriages officiated in the same period totalled only twice this. The reasons are manifold. Women, more likely to be in gainful employment than before, could better afford socially and economically to end a loveless marriage. Furthermore, being divorced was no longer a stigma. The idea that everyone has a right to love and then, when it fades, to find love anew, has become widely accepted in society. A failed marriage is not an argument against trying again (maybe several times). The rate of remarriage among the divorced is accordingly high, and not just for television stars and well-known politicians.

Simultaneously, the expectations placed on love have skyrocketed. People want to experience ultimate happiness with their perfect other half, the kind depicted in Hollywood films, pop songs and glossy magazines. Once they find this person, whether by chance or with the help of commercial matchmaking services, their shared happiness should be given permanence through official approval and legal certification. But there are pitfalls. When marriage is relieved of its social and economic functions and merely represents the ongoing desire for love, its susceptibility to crisis increases. Anyone who hopes for the highest level of trust, the most intimate attention, the exclusive esteem and empathetic consideration of their partner may be easily disappointed – more easily, at any rate, than someone whose emotional demands are set lower and whose primary concern is to know that they and the children are being provided for.

Sexuality has not escaped this whirl of rising expectations either. The more the media reports and represents the sexual conduct of others, the more couples start thinking about their own and looking for improvement. Initially, the task fell to men. Most advice manuals about marriage were aimed at a male readership. Beate Uhse's flourishing mail-order business selling condoms, sexy lingerie and self-help books, which she set up after the Second World War, was no different. By 1957, she had 200,000 loyal customers, all of whom she acquired by sending advertising material to male addressees.

Why did she target specifically men with her wares? Perhaps for practical reasons – very few women had their names in the telephone books from which she copied the addresses. But Uhse's choices also reinforced the notion of feminine modesty, even if she did concede women the right to good sex. It was no contradiction when a catalogue sent out in 1952 set its titular question, 'Is everything in our marriage alright?', under the pretty face of a worried-looking young lady, because it was the husband's job to respond to her worries by buying lingerie, ordering contraceptives or trying out pleasure-enhancing positions and tools. Not surprisingly, then, it was men who sent their thanks as satisfied customers to the perceptive entrepreneur.

Some men, however, felt downright 'insulted' by the unsolicited post that fluttered in from Flensburg. A Catholic law professor from Münster brought a case before the courts in 1949, and dozens more followed, with men declaring that they had been 'attacked in their > honour'. The judges decided one way then the other: in 1955, the Federal Court of Justice invoked the 'concept of decency and morality of the impartial average recipient', who would not see anything offensive about such material. Two years later, the court's Grand Senate ruled that the very title of Uhse's incriminating catalogue was offensive because it 'in a brazen and intrusive manner suggests that the recipient should check whether everything is alright with his sex life'.[16]

Quite obviously, men with conservative and religious backgrounds were particularly unenthused about the intrusion into their love lives. By the 1960s, when the 'sex wave' was sweeping through the media, it was clear that they were fighting a losing battle. The man who rode this wave most spectacularly and successfully was the tabloid journalist Oswalt Kolle. He staged himself as an enlightener who could instruct Germans, men and women alike, about sex. By turning a magazine series (*German man, that's your wife / German woman, that's your husband*) into books and films, he reached a huge audience. The first film, *The Miracle of Love – Sexuality in Marriage* (1968), had six million viewers and was deemed 'important for public health' in the Netherlands (Figure 39). A second instalment on *Sexual Partnership* followed suit and again captivated the public.[17]

Partnership: the term uniquely reflected the guiding principle behind the newly enlightened approach to love. It replaced the outdated concept of 'camaraderie' or companionship predominant in the 1920s. In 1925, an anthology of Hodann's controversial talks on the 'the question of sex' discussed the *Kameradschaft* between 'lads and lasses'. In 1927, a book about *The Companionate Marriage* written by the American authors Ben Lindsey and

---

[16] *JuristenZeitung* 13 (1958): 617–19; Sybille Steinbacher, *Wie der Sex nach Deutschland kam* (Munich: Siedler, 2011), esp. ch. 3; Elizabeth Heineman, *Before Porn Was Legal: The Erotic Empire of Beate Uhse* (Chicago, IL: University of Chicago Press, 2011).

[17] Jürgen Kniep, *'Keine Jugendfreigabe!': Filmzensur in Westdeutschland 1949–1990* (Göttingen: Wallstein, 2010), 229–31; Dagmar Herzog, *Sex after Fascism: Memory and Morality in Twentieth-Century Germany* (Princeton, NJ: Princeton University Press, 2005), 141–83.

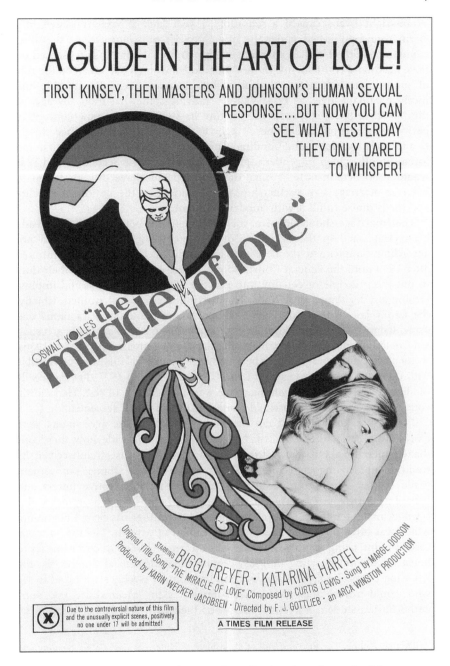

Figure 39 'The Miracle of Love': poster for a film based on the work of German sex educator Oswalt Kolle, 1968 (Photo by Movie Poster Image Art/Getty Images)

Wainwright Evans caused a sensation; a year later it was translated into German and published under the title *Die Kameradschaftsehe*. At the time, companionship offered an alternative to a patriarchal relationship focused on male needs and entitlements. In the older model, women had taken on the role of subordinate helpmates, 'dutiful, willing to make sacrifices, humble and meek in radiant love', as Elsa Walter – rallying somewhat tragically against the liberal zeitgeist she despised – wrote in 1930. But the new concept of parity-based companionship never really took off. Instead, it remained closely tied to male sociability and bonding. Comrades or *Kameraden* were, first and foremost, other men in gender-segregated settings, as the Second World War would soon demonstrate.[18] Since the 1950s, people have thus preferred to describe marriage as a partnership, thereby adopting the notion of equality and the promise to fill it with 'modern' content.[19]

That marriage should involve 'the equal rights of both sexes' had already been established in the Weimar Constitution, though parliament did not accordingly implement the necessary legal-political changes. This continued after 1949 until the Federal Constitutional Court reminded MPs of their duty to put the principle of equality into practice. The task was vast and implied erasing any legislative provisions that discriminated against women. Chiefly, the family law of the 1900 Civil Code contained numerous paragraphs that cemented men's privileges, from the choice of family name to the father's 'casting vote' in the rearing of children. Even after the law was amended in the late 1950s, women were only permitted to be gainfully employed if this was 'compatible with their duties in marriage and family'. It was not until 1977 that the legally binding ideal of the housewife marriage was officially put to rest. Henceforth, couples were to govern 'household management by mutual agreement'.

To be sure, the state did not have a say in how these agreements were reached and what they entailed. Lovers were free to decide how they conducted their love and family lives. Yet this freedom was circumscribed by tradition, upbringing and economic structures, as the new women's movement made crystal clear. From the 1970s, feminism stoked creative unrest and turned its critical gaze on asymmetrical power relations. Such asymmetry also reigned, many feminists believed, in the new trend towards sexual liberation, which was often one-sided and to the detriment of women. The media was a case in point, using scantily or not-at-all clad female bodies as cover images to boost circulation. Starting in 1969, despite their ideological differences, the left-wing political magazine *konkret* and the popular weekly *stern* raced to see who could reveal the most naked female skin. Meanwhile, the anti-authoritarian student movement disclosed their own patriarchal leanings by

---

[18] Thomas Kühne, *The Rise and Fall of Comradeship: Hitler's Soldiers, Male Bonding and Mass Violence in the Twentieth Century* (Cambridge: Cambridge University Press, 2017).
[19] Hollander, *Krise*, 264–65.

subscribing to the motto: 'Whoever sleeps with the same woman twice is part of the establishment.'

Without a doubt, women also enjoyed their newfound sexual freedom, thanks to the contraceptive pill, which became publicly available at the beginning of the 1970s. But they were often the ones who bore the costs and the downsides of this freedom, as the ubiquitous marketing of the female body as a sexual object revealed. As early as 1968, female members of the SDS (a socialist students' association) vented their displeasure by distributing flyers at a general assembly in Hanover calling for 'socialist luminaries to be liberated from their bourgeois cocks'. That women's sexual appetites and experiences might be different from men's was a subject hotly debated in feminist consciousness-raising groups. The widely acclaimed *Hite Report*, released in 1977, provided the empirical proof. Building on findings from the 1950s, its American author painted a new picture of female sexuality, one that diverged considerably from penis-fixated Freudian theories and refused to conceptualize female desire merely as a mirror of male needs.

The issue that male needs set the tone of romantic relationships and might even be enforced with violence was not publicly talked about before the 1970s. Second-wave feminism changed that. It drew attention to the dark sides of love, which women endured far more frequently than men. Just because the state placed marriage under its 'special protection' did not necessarily mean that it protected wives from their husbands' violent assaults and transgressions. As late as 1997, a parliamentary majority eventually supported a collective cross-party motion by female deputies to make rape within marriage a criminal offence.

Love and Marriage – For All?

Twenty years later, a similarly emotional poll took place in the Bundestag. Once again, a conscience vote was allowed, freeing MPs to decide on their own. Almost two-thirds came out in favour of giving same-sex couples a path to the registry office and putting them on an equal footing with heterosexuals. Even among conservative parties, the stand against same-sex marriage crumbled, with one-quarter of CDU and CSU parliamentarians choosing to liberalize marriage laws. The outcome was broadly welcomed; unlike in France, whose parliament made the same move in 2013, there were no passionate protests and demonstrations.

Germany was neither the first nor the last European country to loosen restrictions around marriage. The Netherlands made a start in 2000, Spain followed in 2005, England in 2013 and Ireland in 2015. Denominational differences did not play a decisive role, despite attempts by the Catholic Church to halt the tide. To this day, it limits church weddings to heterosexual couples, while some Protestant churches take a more relaxed view.

In any case, marrying before God is becoming less and less attractive. In 2015, only 22 per cent of couples who appeared in front of a magistrate to have their love certified went on to have a church ceremony; in 1953, 78 per cent did. The move away from the church hastened after German reunification: in 1990, 55 per cent of couples tied the knot in a church; just one year later, the number was down to 46 per cent.

Still, the tendency to formally declare one's love and to place it under state protection through marriage remains strong and has actually grown in recent years. Marriage is important for many same-sex lovers as well, and by no means just because of the legal and financial advantages it brings. Rather, it gives the love of gay and lesbian couples an official recognition they were long denied and which obviously matters a great deal.

Until 1994, same-sex relationships were partly penalized even though both German states had, in the late 1960s, removed the criminalization of sex between adult men (sex between women went unmentioned). However, this did not apply to juveniles under the age of eighteen, and convictions still occurred. In the GDR the relevant paragraph was finally deleted in 1988; a similar motion in 1989 by the Greens in the Bundestag failed due to opposition from the CDU/CSU, Free and Social Democrats alike. Dropping such opposition after reunification was one of the few concessions the West made to the East.

Above all, it was a victory for the gay rights movement. While the GDR forced it to organize furtively under the suspicious watch of the secret police, the movement has been openly flying its colourful flag and asserting its right to love in West Germany since the 1970s.[20] In 1979, 450 people took part in Berlin's Christopher Street Day parade; forty years later there were almost a million. Not all of them were gay or lesbian, but they offered their support for the politics of 'queer' liberation. Initially, support had mainly come from liberals, feminists and the alternative left, while others kept their distance. In 1983, when a rumour arose that a senior general in the Bundeswehr loved men, the defence minister immediately classified him as a security risk and sent him into retirement. Since then, general acceptance of same-sex love has increased considerably; these days even the CDU flies the rainbow flag at Christopher Street Day parades.

What has remained relatively constant throughout these changes are the social signatures and limits of love. The love and marriage market is, to this very day, surprisingly homogeneous and rigid. Rarely does the professor

---

[20] Clayton J. Whisnant, *Male Homosexuality in West Germany: Between Persecution and Freedom, 1945–1969* (Basingstoke: Palgrave Macmillan, 2012); Craig Griffiths, 'Sex, Shame and West German Gay Liberation', *German History* 34, no. 3 (2016): 445–67; Benno Gammerl, *Anders Fühlen: Schwules und lesbisches Leben in der Bundesrepublik: Eine Emotionsgeschichte* (Munich: Hanser, 2021).

match with the mechanic. Women especially seek out 'suitable' partners with the same or ideally even a higher social status and income. Both traditional lonely-hearts advertisements in print media and the newer online dating databases are divided along ethnic, denominational and class lines. Elites seek elites, academics are drawn to fellow academics, Jewish women search for Jewish men, Christian men for Christian women, Muslim men for Muslim women. The number of targeted dating apps and agencies is proliferating just as fast as their diverse user bases. As the options for love grow, the search narrows, and the less likely it is to find an unexpected match.

Love in the GDR

Endogamy also existed in the GDR, but it was less pronounced than in the West, where socio-economic differences were far more visible and starkly felt. Instead, political preferences played a part. In a personal ad, a 'lonely tomcat' from East Berlin sought a 'cute, slim kittycat' who would also preferably share his 'm-l WA' – Marxist-Leninist worldview.[21] The state's youth organization, the FDJ, to which 88 per cent of fourteen- to twenty-five-year-olds belonged in 1989, not only worked to strengthen this position, it also functioned as a matchmaker through youth clubs, holiday trips, summer camps and mass meetings. Youth festivals were a sure-fire way to 'a great love life', it was reported in 1979.[22] Though the regime did not otherwise refrain from all kinds of guidelines, rules and prohibitions, it held an uncommonly long leash when it came to love. From 1972, it gave out the contraceptive pill for free, as well as generous cash grants for the birth of a child. Whether the parents of that child were married or not was irrelevant. The GDR was far more interested in creating children (and workers) than defending 'bourgeois' conventions.

Yet the relevant advice books in general circulation primarily addressed married couples. Marriage was still seen as a preferred part of the 'socialist way of life'.[23] Accordingly, from 1972 onwards, the state offered couples an

---

[21] From the exhibition *Love, Sex and Socialism* at the DDR Museum Berlin, 2018 (Jutta Schütz, '"Schmusekatze" mit marxistischer Weltanschauung gesucht', 23 March 2018, *Welt online*, http://bit.ly/3I4Cfli).

[22] Siegfried Suckut, *Volkes Stimmen: 'Ehrlich, aber deutlich' – Privatbriefe an die DDR-Regierung* (Munich: dtv, 2015), 260.

[23] Till Großmann, 'Moral Economies of Love and Labor in the GDR', in *Moral Economies*, ed. Ute Frevert (Göttingen: Vandenhoeck & Ruprecht, 2019), 213–37; Josie McLellan, *Love in the Time of Communism: Intimacy and Sexuality in the GDR* (Cambridge: Cambridge University Press, 2011), 83–100; Herzog, *Sex after Fascism*, 184–219; for 'sexual > nostalgia', see also Josie McLellan, 'Did Communists Have Better Sex? Sex and the Body in German Unification', in *Remembering the German Democratic Republic: Divided Memory in a United Germany*, ed. David Clarke and Ute Wölfel (Basingstoke: Palgrave Macmillan, 2011), 119–30.

interest-free marriage loan of 5,000 (and later 7,000) marks, which was considered repaid upon the birth of a third child. At the same time, single mothers were also taken care of, in keeping with the stated approach that 'birth out of wedlock is not a stigma', either for the child or for the mother. In 1986, almost every third baby was born outside of marriage (in the Federal Republic, it was every sixth).[24]

When couples did marry, they did so young. This was one reason why the divorce rate reached a formidable 32 per cent in 1980, compared with 21.5 per cent in the West.[25] Extramarital affairs were easier because most women in the GDR were gainfully employed and would meet other men at work. Liaisons between colleagues proved a major issue for marriage therapists and family counselling centres. Generally, love lives seemed to be more eventful in the East than in the West. 'In the East', reported Stefan Wolle, who was born in 1950 in Halle (Saale), 'you had more time for that, more repose, more desire to stray. You're more carefree, everything was taken care of, children were welcome, and jobs secure.'[26]

Citizens' Love

Things were not so carefree when it came to political allegiance and loyalty. From the very start, the GDR regime was intensely concerned with nurturing love for socialism and the Soviet Union among its citizens. Political propaganda and education emphasized, time and again, that the socialist fatherland both demanded and deserved the love of its children. The first generation of East Germans, those born in the late 1940s and early 1950s, were especially raised in this emotional style. Schools taught them 'to love our workers' and peasants' state and its government' as well as the ruling party. For the Young Pioneers (first- to third-graders) and Thälmann Pioneers (fourth- to seventh-graders), the highest commandment was to love 'our socialist fatherland, the

---

[24] http://bit.ly/3lNhHqf. In 2014, the proportion of births out of wedlock was close to 60 per cent in Eastern Germany, compared to less than 30 per cent in Western Germany. 73 per cent of these children grew up with single parents, usually with their mothers: www.iwd .de/artikel/unehelich-na-und-291746/, both accessed 20 January 2022.

[25] https://bit.ly/3SbNqxd, accessed 20 January 2022 (the divorce rate relates the number of marriages contracted in the relevant age group to the number of divorces). See *Lebensstationen in Deutschland 1900–1993*, ed. Rosmarie Beier and Bettina Biedermann (Gießen: Anabas, 1993), esp. 168–73, 221–32, 250–71; Anna Kaminsky, *Frauen in der DDR*, 3rd ed. (Berlin: Links: 2020), 143–78.

[26] Lothar Heinke, 'Liebe, Sex und Sozialismus', *Tagesspiegel*, 27 March 2018, http://bit.ly/ 3xwLBBt, accessed 20 January 2022. Actress Katharina Thalbach, who left the GDR in 1976, made similar comments in 2008: 'We had more sex, and we had more to laugh about – there just weren't as many distractions!' (*Frankfurter Allgemeine Zeitung*, 21 November 2008, 42). See also Konrad Weller, *Das Sexuelle in der deutsch-deutschen Vereinigung* (Leipzig: Forum Verlag, 1991), 10–34.

Figure 40 Republic love in the rain: May demonstration, East Berlin, 1984 (Photo by Reinhard Kaufhold/ullstein bild via Getty Images)

German Democratic Republic' (Figure 40). Love for one's parents came in second or third place. In troops children chanted 'We love our republic' and vowed eternal loyalty to the Communist leader Ernst Thälmann, who had been murdered in the Buchenwald concentration camp in 1944.[27]

For Annette Simon, the 1952-born daughter of writers Christa and Gerhard Wolf, such feelings proved very strong indeed. In 1993, she related her identification with the GDR 'to the deeply felt solidarity with the victims of fascism'. Just like her parents, she had experienced 'a kind of inherited guilt, which I tried to pay off by at least not abandoning the survivors' (> Shame). Only when she was arrested by the police in early October 1989 did 'the last wisp of loyalty leave my body' – to return, one more time, on 3 October 1990, the day that sealed the end of the German Democratic Republic. That evening she felt 'sick to my stomach'.[28]

---

[27] Dorothee Wierling, 'Über die Liebe zum Staat – der Fall der DDR', *Historische Anthropologie* 8, no. 2 (2000): 236–63, here 238–44, 260–62; http://virtuelles-ddrmuseum.de/seiten/ ddralltag3.htm; Leonore Ansorg, *Kinder im Klassenkampf* (Berlin: De Gruyter, 1997), 53–54 (in the original, detailed version); Juliane Brauer, *Zeitgefühle: Wie die DDR ihre Zukunft besang: Eine Emotionsgeschichte* (Bielefeld: transcript, 2020), 141–207.

[28] Annette Simon, *Versuch, mir und anderen die ostdeutsche Moral zu erklären* (Gießen: Psychosozial-Verlag, 1995), 48, 50.

West Germans had a hard time comprehending this. How could a person as actively engaged in the opposition and as hounded for it as Simon feel so emotionally connected to a state that did everything to harm her? More generally, citizens from the 'capitalist' West found it difficult to grasp what love for the state, for a political order, for a fatherland or for the nation might mean. These were concepts that had no place in their own political or emotional world. In 1968, deputy editor-in-chief of *Neues Deutschland*, Günter Schabowski, reported that a visitor from West Germany had asked him 'with raised eyebrows' whether 'it was even possible to love a state'. His response was yes, but only if the state was a socialist one, 'created by the people themselves' and 'in harmony with the laws of social progress'. This was clearly not the case west of the Elbe, as Schabowski explained to the young woman. In the Federal Republic, the state's 'hereditary class disposition' precluded the 'citizen's love'.[29]

Whether this explanation convinced the visitor is not known. For somebody who had grown up in Munich, Hamburg or Frankfurt, civic love was unfamiliar and did not feature in political pedagogy or everyday discourse. Even senior citizens who had been made to swallow stronger doses of patriotism as children and young adults during the 'Third Reich' deliberately kept their distance. When Social Democrat Gustav Heinemann was asked upon his nomination for the presidency in 1969 whether he loved the Federal Republic, he was visibly annoyed and replied curtly, 'No, I don't love states, I love my wife. That's all.'[30] That a soon-to-be head of state said – and could afford to say – this demonstrates just how different West Germany was from the GDR but also from its predecessors.

Love for the King and What Became of It

In 1899, the year Heinemann was born, Social Democrats still had a reputation for being untrustworthy fellows for whom patriotic feelings were totally foreign. At the time, patriotism was synonymous with love for the king, a feeling which proved that one was a good and reliable citizen. In August 1914, new opportunities and ways to demonstrate this attitude emerged. Now, rather than simply throwing hats at festive gatherings to mark the monarch's birthday, men could throw themselves into battle out of love for king and country. During the war, citizens were expressly asked to refrain from such festivities as well as from 'congratulations and blessings' that could disrupt 'telegraphic and postal service communications in the field'. In 1915, Kaiser Wilhelm II decreed that these missives should be dispensed with altogether because he knew from

---

[29] Günter Schabowski, 'Kann man einen Staat lieben', *Neues Deutschland*, 7 October 1968, 9.
[30] Hermann Schreiber, *Gustav Heinemann: Portrait of a President* (Frankfurt: Fischer, 1969), 79.

experience 'the strong bond of love and trust that entwines Me and the German people in powerful concord'.[31]

On 6 August 1914, Bishop Michael von Faulhaber confirmed Wilhelm's experience when he reported on the 'good people's triumphant love of the king'. 'Patriotism and dynastic enthusiasm', he told the Bavarian monarch Ludwig III, had 'awakened moral forces in the soul of the people that one would not have thought possible' considering the fierce partisan struggles during peacetime. In his farewell sermon for local soldiers, Faulhaber hailed the war as 'a pinnacle of love, pure love which is stronger than death. The towering fires of enthusiasm that shine today from all German mountains are not lit by hatred of other peoples and princes, instead they are lit by love for Kaiser and King, for fatherland and homeland'.[32]

When kings and kaiser abdicated at the end of 1918, many people felt the vacuum they left behind. Devotion to the dynasty had been passed down over generations, and the void hurt. Friedrich Ebert, the first Social Democratic president of the Weimar Republic, neither could nor would fill it. He was respected by many, but not loved. Nor was Ebert's successor, World War general Paul von Hindenburg, much suited as an object of love. Nevertheless, some did see in him a potential replacement for the deposed monarch. Whenever he gave radio addresses, on his birthday and on the occasion of his re-election in 1932, he received bundles of letters from people congratulating him with real emotion. Old front-line soldiers assured Hindenburg that 'in our hearts the love for our aged field marshal still burns today'. Young female students saw in him the 'tradition of our grandfathers, whose generation is in many respects closer to ours in soul and spirit than that of our fathers'.[33] More than love, though, the letters spoke of loyalty, > trust and gratitude.

Love for the Führer

If Hindenburg was a fatherly or grandfatherly figure to many of his supporters and voters, Adolf Hitler, forty-two years his junior, filled other roles.

---

[31] Monika Wienfort, 'Kaisergeburtstagsfeiern am 27. Januar 1907', in *Bürgerliche Feste*, ed. Manfred Hettling and Paul Nolte (Göttingen: Vandenhoeck & Ruprecht, 1993), 157–91; see also Bernd Sösemann, 'Hollow-Sounding Jubilees: Forms and Effects of Public Self-Display in Wilhelmine Germany', in *The Kaiser: New Research on Wilhelm II's Role in Imperial Germany*, ed. Annika Mombauer and Wilhelm Deist (Cambridge: Cambridge University Press, 2004), 37–62; *Bayerische Staatszeitung*, 5 January 1915; Bavarian State Archive Munich, III, Geh. Hausarchiv, Cabinet Files Ludwig III, no. 71: decree by Wilhelm II, 13 January 1915.

[32] Ibid., letter from Faulhaber to Ludwig III, 6 and 9 August 1914. The sermon was printed in *Allgemeinen Rundschau: Wochenschrift für Politik und Kultur*, 5 September 1914.

[33] Federal Archive Berlin, R 601, no. 378: Job von Portatius, 9 February 1932; cand. phil. Irmgard von Broesigke, 15 February 1932.

The letters he received reveal an almost irrepressible love for the charismatic Führer. Seventy-four-year-old pastor Heinrich Sayler saw a man who 'glowed' with love for the fatherland, which was why he 'not only honoured him but also loved him'. A Viennese professor referred to his 'genuine devotion for your person', even though devotion was traditionally something felt by women in romantic relationships, not men. Both genders, however, found Hitler an attractive object of love. Women braided him wreaths of edelweiss, his 'favourite flower', and confessed their 'great hunger to be able to speak to our esteemed Führer in person, even for just one brief little moment'. In 1934, Martha Piller from Leipzig could 'barely express in words how much we love our Führer and care for him'. What she found 'most delicious' was 'that this marvellous man belongs to us – to all of us Germans. A marriage, even the greatest, cannot be more wonderful than the gladdening feeling of knowing that the leader of our hearts is married to the whole German people – well, at least to the good ones and those who are of good will.' Hedwig Elbers endorsed the sentiment in 1935: 'Never has the father of a nation been so loved and revered by his people during his service.' In the same breath, she let it be known that Hitler was even more than the father of the nation to her: 'Besides raising my 3 children, my thoughts belong only to you, my Führer, and thus to Germany!' Her husband and father of her children apparently did not warrant further mention.[34]

Hitler also received many letters from children, often in an uninhibited and naïve tone but sometimes clearly written under the instruction of teachers. In 1939, twelve-year-old Elsbeth Stucke from Bad Homburg wrote to congratulate the 'dear Führer' on his birthday, demonstrating through her form of address how personally close to him she felt: 'It's alright to say that to you isn't it, or must one write Excellence and Majesty and so on? No, surely you don't want that. I wouldn't be able to do it either, because I think I love you just as much as my parents.' She was 'terribly fond' of him and concluded the letter with a kiss.

Ten-year-old Lore Bür did not care to go that far. She had listened to Hitler's speeches on the radio, 'some things I do not yet understand but I do know about the Jews and communists'. Her father had explained to her that 'when he saw you for the first time, he could have wept with joy. The most beautiful moments of my life says Daddy.' She was looking forward to growing up and coming 'every year to Nuremberg' for the rallies. In contrast, Mädi Dopple was more focused on the present than the future. She too wrote to Hitler in 1936 to wish him a happy birthday. 'But just think, we have to write

[34] Ibid., NS 51, no. 51/1: Heinrich Sayler, 12 August 1930; Richard Suchenwirth, 28 September 1930; no. 60: Mothers from Danzig, 29 August 1935; Huldi Cronlind, 29 August 1935; no. 73: Martha Piller, 23 December 1934; no. 75: Hedwig Elbers, 19 April 1935.

essays about you all the time and in the long run that will hurt our love for you. Please order our teachers to choose other topics.'[35]

That order never came. Teachers recounted what Hitler said and did and encouraged their students to write to the Führer and express 'their feeling of intense attachment'. 'At school', reported fourth-graders from Breslau in 1936, 'we talk about you every day. Every morning, after the prayers, we recite a motto. Today it was: Being German means being good, being faithful and honest, fighting for truth, freedom and justice!' The letter concluded with the 'most ardent' wish to see Hitler: 'How I envy the little girl who was allowed to wrap her arms around you.' Anneliese Bolz, not yet ten years old, wrote that her class was creating 'a Hitler book. The first part is called Hitler's Childhood and the second is about Hitler in the Great War.' Fifth-graders from Schwerin only had to produce one essay on Hitler, but were extremely taken with a film on the German army, which they had watched one morning:

> Now no one will dare attack us. Here it is much, much better than in Russia, because you have secured unity, work and freedom. We love you very much for that. Unfortunately, we cannot become soldiers, because we are little girls. But we will still help you. Many of us are already members of the Young Girls' League and we are all busily collecting for the Winter Relief. (> Solidarity)

First-graders quoted from their spelling book: '*I shall love you like Father and Mother*, and we want to promise you that today, too.'[36]

Those lines and messages show that textbooks and teachers were doing what the regime instructed them to do: direct the 'child's love' towards the Führer but also to 'state institutions and the National Socialist movement' such as the Hitler Youth. Shaping the 'emotional experience' was key to this education. Love for the Führer was supposed to reflect the love one had for their own people and generate the will to serve him and the people 'in selfless devotion'. That devotion could result in murderous terror and the 'extermination of the Jewish people for the love of our people', for which Heinrich Himmler commended his SS men in 1943, was something the first-graders of 1936 could not imagine and ultimately did not have to experience thanks to their young age.[37]

---

[35] Ibid., no. 71: Elsbeth Stucke, undated (received on 17 April 1939); Lore Bür, undated (received on 23 September 1937); Mädi Dopple, 16 April 1936.

[36] Ibid., no. 76: class IIa of the 6th Leipzig elementary school, 26 March 1936; class IV of school no. 45 Breslau, 18 April 1936; Anneliese Bolz, 16 March 1936; class 5b Schwerin, 28 February 1936; Martha Kirchner, 24 March 1936.

[37] Hermann Kirek, 'Heimatkundeunterricht (1938)', in *Propaganda: Medien und Öffentlichkeit in der NS-Diktatur*, ed. Bernd Sösemann, vol. 2 (Stuttgart: Steiner, 2011), 1277–78. Melita Maschmann, former leader and functionary of the League of German Girls, also stressed that 'what first drew young people to National Socialism was not

Yet they were not spared the experience of learning after the war that the love they had been taught at school and in youth organizations had been attached to the wrong object and was worth nothing. Some clung to it, nevertheless. In 1946, Victor Klemperer, who had barely survived Nazi anti-semitism, met a former student who had joined the party at an early age and spoke to him about 'what it all led to, as the regime's atrocious crimes are now apparent for all to see'. After a long pause, the young man replied 'very quietly: "I accept all that. The others misunderstood him, betrayed him. But I still believe in HIM, I really do."'[38]

Constitutional Patriotism

Younger lads like Günter Schabowski, who was born in 1929 and had been a troop leader in the Hitler Youth, seemingly had less difficulty disposing of their love for the Führer and transferring it to the new state in which they would get ahead. Jürgen Habermas, one of West Germany's leading intellectuals and himself a former *Jungvolkführer*, drew different conclusions. Like Gustav Heinemann, he advocated the radical privatization of love and believed that neither the state nor the so-called fatherland or nation should lay claim to it. What liberal-minded citizens could and should muster instead, he argued, was constitutional patriotism: an identification with the values, institutions and practices laid out in the Basic Law.

This was an emotion in itself, as the inventor of the term, journalist and political scientist Dolf Sternberger, explained in 1970: a 'feeling for the common interest', without which the 'natural divergence of interests in certain situations' would certainly 'lead to collapse'. But it was a moderate and balanced emotion absent burning passion or excessive enthusiasm (> Joy). This was precisely its advantage: in view of the emotional exaltation that National Socialism, but also the GDR, sought to kindle in its populace, a more sober relationship to the state was seen as a good thing.[39]

---

hatred – of "enemy" tendencies or foreigners – but a love of Germany' (Melita Maschmann, *Account Rendered: A Dossier on My Former Self*, trans. Geoffrey Strachan (London: Abelard-Schuman, 1964), 26). For Himmler's Poznań speech, see https://bit.ly/41IuUQH.

[38] Victor Klemperer, *The Language of the Third Reich: LTI – Lingua Tertii Imperii: A Philologist's Notebook*, trans. Martin Brady (London: Athlone Press, 2000), 118. For more on faith in the Führer, see Ian Kershaw, *The 'Hitler Myth': Image and Reality in the Third Reich* (Oxford: Clarendon Press, 1987).

[39] Dolf Sternberger, 'Unvergleichlich lebensvoll, aber stets gefährdet: Ist unsere Verfassung demokratisch genug?', *Frankfurter Allgemeine Zeitung*, 27 January 1970, 11. The term was first popularized by Jürgen Habermas (Jan-Werner Müller, *Constitutional Patriotism* (Princeton, NJ: Princeton University Press, 2007), 6, 15–45).

Such sobriety had emerged already in the 1950s and was observed and practised from above and below. In contrast to the GDR's head of state Wilhelm Pieck, to whom workers collectively expressed their 'total love' and 'love and veneration', Federal President Theodor Heuss received messages of gratitude and > trust. Admittedly, both men were greeted with the expectation of being 'the father of the fatherland' (Heuss) or 'German father' (Pieck). But profoundly loving this father remained a specialty of the East, one robustly supported by mass organizations from the Young Pioneers to the trade unions. In the West, not even the widely respected Bavarian politician and 'father figure' Alfons Goppel, who was showered with 'reverence, esteem, gratitude and affection' by his constituents, was offered love – except from eighty-one-year-old Anny Fichtl who had grown up at a time when loving the king was common: 'We from the countryside', she wrote in 1977, 'really love you.'[40]

Anny Fichtl could not yet have heard about constitutional patriotism, which only started to circulate after 1979, on the thirtieth anniversary of the Basic Law. Even then, it appealed far more to the left-wing and left-liberal milieus of the Federal Republic than to the Bavarian countryside. Whether Anny Fichtl knew of Marlene Dietrich and her 1930 love song is also doubtful. If she had, she probably would not have liked it, because the morals of a femme fatale differed vastly from those prized among her peers. The notion of a woman interested in nothing but love would have seemed just as impudent to her as the type of love for which Lola Lola was hankering. A hundred years ago, love in a Bavarian village followed different laws from love in Berlin and was experienced differently in turn. These laws have since converged; even people in rural areas use online dating services. Instead of church and state, the media now tends to determine what place love occupies in people's emotional economy. Above all, there is broad agreement that love is an entirely private matter and should ideally not be bestowed on the state or a political ideology.

---

[40] Bavarian State Archive Munich, II, Chancellery, no. 12887: Adam Kaiser, 29 September 1975; CSU Ortsverband Neutraubling, 10 October 1975; no. 12153: Leopold Gerblich, 19 May 1977; Th. Sehmer, 23 May 1977; Rudolf Schnell, 24 May 1977; Anny Fichtl, January 1977; Seb. Stocker, 26 January 1977.

Nostalgia

It is often said that nostalgia is an emotion for the old. The less time you have before you, the more likely you are to long for 'the good old days'. This longing frequently goes hand in hand with devaluing the here and now: back then everything seemed sweeter. Children learnt and behaved better, people were friendlier and more polite, food was healthier and daily life less hectic. Even the future, cabaret artist Karl Valentin, who died in 1948, purportedly quipped, used to be better.

Nostalgia, or longing for the past, is more than just an individual emotion triggered by age, however. At times, it has emerged as a collective sentiment, shaping and determining the behaviour of social groups and political activists. The 2016 Brexit movement enticed over half the voters on the British Isles with nostalgic sentiments, tapping into and feeding their dreams of a halcyon past without the European Union. In Germany and France, right-wing nationalists yearn to go back to a time before the existence of 'foreigners' and same-sex marriage. The promise of the future with which they mobilize their supporters is, then, decidedly backward-looking.

When Were the Good Old Days?

Just how far back one needs to go to find this golden past is never clear. Those born in Germany at the turn of the twentieth century grew up in a country marked by food shortages and millions of war casualties; their future prospects were highly uncertain. In 1939, another war broke out in which even more people died, at the front and in bombed-out cities, in concentration and extermination camps, during death marches and on the run. Only after 1945 did the future begin to look brighter for those who had survived such horrific violence. The second half of the twentieth century was a good period for most people, economically, politically and socially, especially in the West.

Yet the murmurs of nostalgia never abated. In 1959 Konrad Adenauer reminisced about the years immediately following the war when Germans were still 'heroic and brave, helpful and charitable', 'full of joy and satisfaction at even the smallest progress'. These 'spiritual forces' had since been 'almost covered up and overgrown' with what the chancellor decried as 'overly strong material thinking'. The lead-up to Christmas in particular, with its 'exaggerated decoration and the splendour of the streets and shop windows' sometimes instilled in him 'fear and concern for the German people' and their capacity for moderation. President Heinrich Lübke sung a similar tune.

In the 1970s people thought back, again with a tinge of regret, to the Adenauer era, when every effort, as Lübke's successor Gustav Heinemann put it in 1973, had been 'directed towards multiplication, towards expansion, towards acceleration'. This had 'created our seductive society of affluence' – which, Heinemann warned, was now reaching its limits (with reference to an acclaimed 1972 study on the *Limits to Growth*).[1] Among environmentalists, meanwhile, men and women did not yearn for the 1950s but for a time much further back, before humans had exploited nature at the expense and to the detriment of future generations.[2]

Clearly each era, social group and person has their own rosy and sunlit past. *Besonnte Vergangenheit* was the title under which Carl Ludwig Schleich, a surgeon and writer born in 1859, released his memoirs in 1920. The Berlin-based publisher Rowohlt landed its first bestseller with the book, which remained in print until 1985. By 1931, it had sold 355,000 copies and boasted a readership of several million. The book shaped the image of the imperial period as a bright time of stability ruined by war and revolution, and kindled nostalgia for this eternally shining and golden epoch of German history.

The First World War was perceived by most contemporaries as a massive rupture. In 1920, Jewish lawyer and royal Bavarian court councillor Luitpold Schülein mourned 'the good old days' before antisemitic provocations had become a part of everyday life. 'The bourgeois age is over', mused Kurt Tucholsky the same year, 'what comes next, nobody knows.' Even Chancellor Adenauer, who was born in 1876, recalled at Christmas 1958 with a touch of melancholy 'those years before 1914, when peace, tranquillity and security still dwelt on this earth and man knew no > fear'.[3]

Yearning for the Kaiser

That may have been the case for many Germans prior to the First World War. But it was hardly true of the Chinese, whose country the Germans, following others, had militarily entered in 1897, or of the Africans living under violently

[1] Reinhard Kiehl, ed., *Alle Jahre wieder* (Düsseldorf: My favourite book, 2001), 123–24, 127, 292–93.

[2] Sven Reichardt, *Authentizität und Gemeinschaft: Linksalternatives Leben in den siebziger und frühen achtziger Jahren* (Berlin: Suhrkamp, 2014), 459–96.

[3] Bavarian State Archive Munich, II, MA no. 102382: Schülein, letter from 10 October 1920; Kurt Tucholsky, *Politische Texte* (Reinbek: Rowohlt, 1971), 104; Kiehl, *Alle Jahre wieder*, 114.

established and maintained German colonial rule. Such downsides of 'peace and security' entered into neither people's views at the time nor their nostalgic recollections. In the days of revolutionary upheaval and unrest following 1918, many yearned to set the clock back and return to an era when the kaiser was still kaiser and had not yet abdicated to make way for the republic.

A robust monarchism persisted, particularly in conservative sectors of German society. In September 1921, a veteran disappointed by the 'high treason and mutiny' told the Social Democratic president, Friedrich Ebert, that 'me and my pals will earnestly help' to 'get a kaiser again'. Forty-one-year-old Minna Raschke, a member of the German National People's Party, was also 'a fanatical supporter of the old regime'. When the former kaiserin, Auguste Viktoria, died in 1921, Raschke – who ran a small cigar shop in Berlin – donned mourning attire and, according to a police report, used every customer interaction as an opportunity to 'vehemently vituperate against the president and other politicians close to him' (> Hate).[4]

The same year, an anonymous letter to the Munich government declared that the 'majority of the Bavarian people' were 'monarchist-minded' and resolutely rejected the republic of 'red bandits'. Few were as magnanimous as the Berlin-based scholar Fritz Castner, who in 1925 wrote to a gravely ill Ebert, 'I am a monarchist to the core, but in spite of that every unbiased person must and will hold you in very high esteem as a human being, even as a role model. A curse on the idiots who wish you dead for political reasons. I cannot and will not believe it.' When First World War general Paul von Hindenburg stood for election following Ebert's death, Luise Sauerteig from Nuremberg welcomed him as someone 'to replace the kaiser of the German people to the best of his ability'. To Margot Oppenheim, however, Hindenburg was merely a placeholder for 'our most revered Kaiser', who would, she hoped in 1932, 'finally return to his homeland' and make 'Germany shine again in the splendour of empire'.[5]

1933/1945: Old Eras or New Ones?

Yet Wilhelm did not come back. National Socialists had never promised to reinstate him or to resurrect the monarchy. On the contrary, they wanted to build a new and better Germany that had nothing in common with the empire or the derided republic. They respected Prussian-German history and ranked Hitler alongside Friedrich II, Bismarck and Hindenburg (Figure 41). But they kept their distance from Wilhelm II and his sons, though they sometimes did

---

[4] Federal Archive Berlin, R 601, no. 17: anonymous, 1 September 1921; no. 20: Police report, 13 January 1922.

[5] Bavarian State Archive Munich, II, MA no. 102386, received on 19 August 1922; Federal Archive Berlin, R 601, no. 36: Fritz Castner, 26 February 1925; no. 379: Luise Sauerteig, 10 March 1932; no. 380: Margot Oppenheim, 10 March 1932.

Was der König – der Fürst – der Feldmarschall – rettete und einigte
eroberte, formte, verteidigte, der Soldat.

Hans von Norden
Nachdruck verboten

Figure 41 Looking back to the future: Hitler's political ancestral gallery (Photo 12/Universal Images Group via Getty Images)

call on their services when it suited them.[6] Germanic 'ancestral heritage' cultivated by leading Nazis such as Heinrich Himmler likewise remained in the shadows; the attempt to instate *Thingspiele*, a genre of open-air theatre, came to nothing. In contrast, the medieval Duke of Saxony, Henry the Fowler, was publicly acclaimed thanks to his invasions and occupations of Slavic territories, an enterprise for which the regime felt a close affinity.

The Nazis saw history as a well-stocked armoury, and they helped themselves to whatever they liked and whatever lent them legitimacy. Still, there was never any question of bringing back the 'good old days'. In what they termed the 'hours of renewal', they propelled themselves, assured of victory, into a 'new era' that would fulfil the boldest visions of German greatness and power.[7] Young people in particular felt committed to this future and they joined in enthusiastically whenever the old workers' song 'We Walk Side by Side' was sung. The tune, with its refrain '*with us the new era dawns*', was printed in the songbooks of the Stormtroopers as well as those of the Hitler Youth and the League of German Girls.

When their 'new era' collapsed in 1945, no one wanted to be seen to mourn its passing. There was no more talk of kaiser or king, either. Nor did the short-

---

[6] Stephan Malinowski, *Nazis and Nobles: The History of a Misalliance* (Oxford: Oxford University Press, 2020).

[7] Christopher Clark, *Time and Power: Visions of History in German Politics, from the Thirty Years' War to the Third Reich* (Princeton, NJ: Princeton University Press, 2019), 171–210.

lived Weimar Republic serve as an object of nostalgia; rather, it was remembered as a period of economic misfortune and political turmoil. The GDR regime laid out a golden socialist future and worked hard to rouse citizens' passionate enthusiasm for it (> Joy). Sparse revolutionary traces were all it borrowed from the 'botched' history of Germany; anything the state considered reactionary was eradicated from the cityscape. In 1950, it had the Berlin royal palace demolished. Only the doorway with the balcony from which KPD founder Karl Liebknecht had proclaimed the German socialist republic in 1918 was preserved; later it was added to the facade of the new government building. Christian Daniel Rauch's equestrian statue of Friedrich II also disappeared in 1950. Its reinstatement to its original location in front of Humboldt University thirty years later reflected an official change in how the ruling party related to Prussian history. Instead of simply considering Prussia a stronghold of reactionary militarism, the regime now saw it as a site of enlightenment, great architecture and science as well. Appreciating those achievements should no longer be the monopoly and prerogative of West Germany.

Being mindful of one's own history and valuing certain traditions does not inevitably make one nostalgic. Most people who join a historical society or are active in their local history group are not motivated by sentimental longing. Hardly anyone who collects knowledge or objects from the past actually wishes that they had lived in those times. Singing old folk songs does not necessarily indicate that someone wants to turn back the clock or that they feel ill at ease in the present. Nor do museums or memorials generally intend to stoke nostalgic sentiments; rather they aim to take visitors on a journey through time that educates, delights, instructs and possibly returns them to the here and now with more insight than they arrived with.

Critique of the Present

Nevertheless, appropriations of the past often go hand in hand with critiques of the present. When left-wing students and activists in Frankfurt began occupying empty late nineteenth-century mansions in 1970, they did not only want to stop rampant property speculation and the construction of further high-rise office blocks. They were also defending a concept of urban living that was under threat from (at the time) modern notions about car-friendly cities. Nor did they act independently of broader social currents and concerns. In 1964, Wolf Jobst Siedler and Elisabeth Niggemeyer had protested the demolition of *Gründerzeit* buildings, the bulldozing of public squares and the felling of old trees in their manifesto *The Murdered City*. A year later, Alexander Mitscherlich railed against 'urban desolation and destruction' in his bestselling book *The Inhospitality of our Cities*. Finally, in 1969, a citizens' initiative was formed in Frankfurt to ensure 'no more old buildings are destroyed without a thought for social aspects and the preservation of the cityscape'. Among its supporters were clergy and trade unionists alike. After the turbulent 'housing war' years, a new law introduced in 1974 enabled threatened residences to be placed under historical protection.[8] Today they fetch top prices on the real-estate market; those who can afford it clamour to live in spacious, renovated *Altbau* apartments, and not only in Frankfurt.

Despite their anti-capitalist furore, the left-wing 'anarchists', as right-wing parties and newspapers called them, were perfectly in step with the times. The Council of Europe had declared 1975 European Architectural Heritage Year, under the motto 'a future for our past'. In the 1950s and 1960s, this past, or what remained of it after the war, was in danger of being swept away by the general tendency towards modernization. It was not just protest-prone students but also conservative-minded contemporaries who railed against such developments. In 1975, the sixty-seven-year-old cofounder and long-time editor of the *Frankfurter Allgemeine Zeitung*, Karl Korn, reported finding consolation in 'how widespread, especially among young people, the inclination, even if fickle, for old buildings is'. This was more than 'fashionable nostalgia', he wrote: rather, 'the feeling of being at home comes from how you live as well as where you live'.[9]

Whether 'fashionable nostalgia' was really so different from the longing to 'feel at home' (> Belonging) is questionable. Since the term first came into use, it has carried with it the painful experience of loss, as the first publication on this topic – a medical dissertation from 1688 – described so well. Its author, a young Swiss doctor, had examined a peculiar clinical condition afflicting soldiers in foreign outposts. His diagnosis was termed 'nostalgia' (from the Greek *nóstos,* meaning return, and *álgos,* pain) and called '*Heimwehe*', homesickness, in German.[10]

Homesickness and Timesickness

Homesickness plagued Swiss mercenaries, but also the apprentice tradesmen who spent several years journeying abroad as part of their training. They parted from mothers and lovers whom they missed dearly, along with their native customs and lands. As folk songs up until the early 1800s captured ('*Must I then, must I then, part from my town*'), journeymen assumed that they would find what they had left unchanged after their years-long absence. The homeland to which they longed to return remained static and frozen in memory.

---

[8] Rudolf Heinrich Appel, *Heißer Boden: Stadtentwicklung und Wohnprobleme* (Frankfurt: Presse- und Informationsamt Frankfurt, 1974), 40–41; Reichardt, *Authentizität*, 498–571.

[9] Karl Korn, 'Heimisch sein', *Frankfurter Allgemeine Zeitung*, 12 August 1975, 15. See also Tobias Becker, 'The Meanings of Nostalgia: Genealogy and Critique', *History and Theory* 57, no. 2 (2018): 234–50.

[10] Ina-Maria Greverus, *Auf der Suche nach Heimat* (Munich: C. H. Beck, 1979), 106–11.

That may have been the case in an era before rapid changes set in. Yet the explosive speed of modern development and the vast upheavals wrought by industrialization left massive imprints on time and place. Even after a short term of absence, one might no longer recognize one's hometown. Cities grew at an astonishing pace, and technological innovations revolutionized daily life. People responded differently to these changes: what one person found fascinating and exciting, gave another reason to > fear. Or they were ambivalent, feeling both drawn to and threatened by these shifts.

That was how Stefan Zweig experienced things in 1910. The Austrian author by no means renounced modernity when he, like many of his peers, recalled with melancholy his love for the pre-1848 Biedermeier era and 'Old Vienna', where life had apparently still been tranquil and unhurried. Thirty years later, however, Zweig looked back at the period around 1910 as a haven of familiarity and > belonging. Although he was also cognizant of what he disliked about the 'world of yesterday', he understandably preferred it to the situation facing him in 1940. Exhausted 'by the long years of wandering without a home' and profoundly depressed by the destruction of his 'spiritual home Europe', he took his own life in Brazilian exile in 1942.[11]

For Zweig, nostalgia or the longing for home was indistinguishable from longing for a certain period in time. His Austrian homeland – which he had had to leave in 1934 because, as a Jew and a pacifist, it no longer provided him with sanctuary – existed only in the past. In the case of émigrés, the rupture was a particularly dramatic and painful experience. In principle, though, it existed in all forms of homesickness.

It is no surprise, then, that the twentieth century, with its dynamics of incessant change, was a heyday of homesickness for things gone by, whether homeland or time period. Indeed, these feelings featured frequently in literature and films. On the other hand, Germans were (and are) not a progress-shy people. They were happy to keep up 'with the times' even if the latter were moving fast and left nothing unturned. That was true of fashion as well as home furnishings, the purchase of technological gadgets, choice of holiday destination or new car. Newlyweds in 1910 would have carefully selected furniture and linen to last them a lifetime. Couples nowadays feel and act differently. Once part of the popular lexicon, the word 'trousseau' or *Aussteuer* has disappeared, as has the dowry insurance that parents took out for their

---

[11] Stefan Zweig, 'Die gefangenen Dinge: Gedanken über die Brüsseler Weltausstellung', *Neue Freie Presse*, 17 August 1910, 1; Stefan Zweig, *The World of Yesterday* (New York: Viking Press, 1943); photograph and translation of Zweig's suicide note: https://blog.nli .org.il/en/djm_zweig/, accessed 18 February 2022. In 1918, the liberal theologian Ernst Troeltsch attributed 'our present-day appreciation of the Biedermeier style and its furniture' to the 'need for reassurance'. (Ernst Troeltsch, *Deutscher Geist und Westeuropa*, ed. Hans Baron (Tübingen: Mohr, 1925), 171).

daughters as late as the 1950s. Anything that no longer appeals or is 'out of fashion' is discarded, while new things not designed to last are bought cheap.

At the same time, the velocity and disposability of modern consumer culture has drawn and continues to draw criticism. Since the 1970s, such criticism and what Karl Korn termed 'fashionable nostalgia' have coalesced; wandering through any of the ever more popular flea markets makes this clear. Anti-capitalism and anti-consumerism, which were widespread among the generation of 1968, bred nostalgia as a 'cultural mood'.[12] It represented the longing for something of lasting value that defied the passage of time, as evidenced by various retro fads. Those who had outgrown their flea-market phase and could afford it might have sought out furniture and silverware from the Biedermeier period so painfully beloved of Zweig. When this market had been exhausted, nostalgic consumers moved on to art nouveau, then to the Bauhaus designs of the 1920s. Later the 1950s were refashioned; currently it is the 1970s that are à la mode. When it comes to clothing, old patterns are trendy again, and vintage shops are popping up on every corner. Strutting down Berlin's Ku'damm in a folksy floral jacket belonging to one's grand-mother is likely to yield approving glances. The eye-catching outfit identifies the wearer as a courageous individualist – who, were they business-minded, might start a new trend and earn money from it.

This is another aspect of the fashionably nostalgic cultural mood: its swift and encompassing commercialization. What was initially intended as a sign of protest and resistance to the dictates of consumption, and would later become a marker of green credentials and sustainability, has also turned out to be a money-maker. In this vein, the billion-dollar conglomerate IKEA, which furnishes almost every home in Germany and beyond, releases limited – and therefore particularly desirable – editions 'full of vintage favourites', providing 'a nice note of nostalgia' with 1950s-inspired designs.[13]

Ostalgie

The wave of *Ostalgie* (a play on the German words for 'east', *Ost*, and nostalgia) that emerged in the late 1990s was likewise keenly marketed. Part ironic, part melancholic, it described a phenomenon that began soon after German reunification. While the GDR had ended not with a bang but a whimper, people soon thought wistfully of the life they had led behind the Wall. They fondly remembered the foodstuffs and laundry products that had vanished from shelves overnight. When it became apparent that 'statement

---

[12] 'Jene Sehnsucht nach den alten Tagen. . .', *Der Spiegel*, 19 January 1973, 86–99; Greverus, *Auf der Suche nach Heimat*, 171–81, Susanne Scharnowski, *Heimat* (Darmstadt: WBG, 2019), 146–64.

[13] http://bit.ly/3XO6naB; http://bit.ly/3XM5vDe, both accessed 10 February 2022.

Figure 42   Traversing today's Berlin in a GDR 'Trabi' (Photo by Sean Gallup/Getty Images)

brands' such as Club Cola and Juwel cigarettes, Rondo coffee and Spreewald gherkins could be peddled to nostalgic buyers, they reappeared on the shelves, beautified but still recognizable. Other products commercialized the much-loved children's television character 'little Sandman' or the iconic East German traffic light men, the *Ampelmännchen*. The Trabant that car owners were only too keen to trade in for a glitzy Western model after the Wall fell gained new, almost cult-like status, giving rise to Trabi fan clubs and Trabi 'safaris' for tourists (Figure 42).[14]

Commercial *Ost*-themed parties have likewise enjoyed great popularity, and both public and private television stations have produced high-rating shows about the East. In 2006, a privately owned GDR museum opened its doors in Berlin; three years later it welcomed its millionth visitor. The museum offers an up-close and interactive insight into politics as well as everyday life, giving people a chance to explore a reconstructed *Plattenbau* apartment and a Stasi control room.[15]

---

[14] Daphne Berdahl, '"(N)ostalgie" for the Present: Memory, Longing, and East German Things', *Ethnos* 64, no. 2 (1999): 192–211; Martin Blum, 'Remaking the East German Past: "Ostalgie", Identity, and Material Culture', *The Journal of Popular Culture* 34, no. 3 (2000): 229–53.

[15] Thomas Ahbe, *Ostalgie: Zu ostdeutschen Erfahrungen und Reaktionen nach dem Umbruch* (Erfurt: Landeszentrale für politische Bildung Thüringen, 2016); see also his 'Competing Master Narratives: Geschichtspolitik and Identity Discourse in Three

It is unclear which feelings exactly are evoked by eating Zetti cornflake clusters or Nudossi spread today. How something tastes or smells is a corporeal experience, stored in the body waiting to be retrieved again. It can be associated with many different emotions – with longing but also with repulsion or > disgust. Just because something is trusted or familiar does not necessarily mean that you value it, miss it or want to have it back.

For that, the political framing is crucial. Recalling the past is bound to feel different according to the circumstances in which you said goodbye to it or were forced to say goodbye to it. Someone who grew up in West Germany may, of course, have pangs of nostalgia thinking about Ahoj Brause (a popular sherbet), Sinalco lemonade or 'Hawaiian' toast. But how this longing for the world of yesteryear expresses itself and how much political and social influence it has depends on how people experienced its disappearance and whether it was replaced by new attractions. As a rule, those who cannot see a place for themselves in the future tend to mourn the past and harbour resentment for the present.

In no small part, changes in the world of work have elicited such resentment and a form of nostalgia steeped in fear of what comes next. The term 'smokestack nostalgia' captures the yearning for the smoking chimneys of heavy industry, which have gradually disappeared from view. Everybody knows that these smokestacks have belched incredible amounts of toxic fumes into the air, but this does not dampen their emotional charge. They are a synecdoche for a lost world that guaranteed jobs – often dirty and dangerous, but passed down through generations – and adequate wages, as well as collegial relationships and housing cooperatives.

This is what links the coal miner in the Ruhr valley, who spent his whole life working in the collieries only to see them close one after the other from 1958 onwards, with the Zwickau woman whose state-owned GDR factory did not outlive privatization in the 1990s. Both have memories of long years of employment, above or below ground. Both probably glorify these years and tend to forget any negative experiences they may have had. And both have responded sometimes with helplessness, sometimes with > anger, to the changes around them.

There are differences, though. In the Ruhr region, where the last mine was sealed in 2018, prudent and long-term crisis management prevented layoffs wherever possible and minimized the social effects of the transition away from coal. This was expensive, but it soothed tempers and gave the authorities time to furnish new perspectives and jobs. There was not the same prudence and

German Societies', in *The GDR Remembered: Representations of the East German State since 1989*, ed. Nick Hodgin and Caroline Pearce (Rochester, NY: Camden House, 2011), 221–49, esp. 232–39; Paul Cooke, *Representing East Germany Since Unification: From Colonization to Nostalgia* (Oxford: Berg, 2005).

patience in the East. Changes and losses hit the population hard and swiftly. As early as 1992 the weekly magazine *Der Spiegel* reported on 'GDR nostalgia in Eisenhüttenstadt', the 'first socialist city in Germany'. Once celebrated as a 'city without a past' but with a bright future, it had been founded in 1950 around a massive steelworks on the Polish border. Only two years after the GDR's collapse, it was clear that its future was over. Most inhabitants would lose their jobs, and there were no new ones on the horizon. Such dim prospects foregrounded citizens' inclination to remember their past lives nostalgically and gloss over darker aspects and disappointments.[16]

In the 2019 elections, the voters of Eisenhüttenstadt handed the AfD candidate a direct mandate for the Brandenburg parliament, with over 30 per cent of the vote. The right-wingers' victory was even greater in the doomed brown-coal region of Lusatia, where the party received almost 36 per cent. Evidently it had understood best how to tap into the popular mood – part nostalgic, part resentful, part anxious about losing out – and how to mobilize people with the narrative of a backward-looking utopia.

This nostalgic gaze back connects the AfD and their supporters to other far-right groups such as 'Identitarians' and *völkisch* settlers who buy farms in depressed regions, invoke nativist customs and cultivate local comradery, borrowing from the blood-and-soil ideology of National Socialism.[17] For them, moving forwards into the future in fact means coming back to an ethnically homogeneous, illiberal, hierarchically ordered national community led by charismatic men, in which gender roles are as narrowly and tradition-ally codified as age and occupational ones. There are people who long for such a future. So far, they remain a small minority.

---

[16] Jan Fleischhauer, 'Ick will meine Ruhe wieder', *Der Spiegel*, 4 May 1992, 117–24.
[17] Andrea Röpke and Andreas Speit, *Völkische Landnahme: Alte Sippen, junge Siedler, rechte Ökos* (Berlin: Links, 2019).

~

Pride

'Germans, we can be proud of our country!' In 1972, this message was printed in bold capital letters on election posters issued by the Social Democratic Party. They showed a confident Chancellor Willy Brandt, who urged voters to return him to office. With the direct address to 'Germans' and the encouragement to be 'proud of our country', he sent a clear national signal. Some comrades flinched; they would have preferred the word 'Germans' to be written in smaller letters. But ultimately, they did not want to leave 'national emotions' to the 'nationalistic bawlers' either. Besides, at campaign events Brandt made sure to put the brakes on any excess of national sentiment by clarifying what was meant by pride: 'Nobody takes away our pride in the results of our hard work.'[1]

That sounded entirely different again, and better suited to the social democratic agenda. The SPD had, throughout its long history, refrained from appeals to national pride. By the end of the nineteenth century, it had taken a clear stance against nationalist ideologies, and it openly proclaimed internationalism as a form of proletarian > solidarity transcending national borders. This had earned party members the reputation of being 'fellows without a fatherland'. At a time when nationalist associations, publications and emotions were soaring, this was not intended as a compliment.

National Pride and Nationalistic Arrogance

Nationalism was more than the joyous commitment to the nation-state that had been created after the Franco-Prussian War. 1871 had marked the fulfilment of a long-held dream, especially for liberals and democrats. Even though the new empire was not as liberal and democratic as they had hoped, national unity outweighed this. People admired Otto von Bismarck as the creator of unity, and bowed down to the military that had made such unity possible on France's battlefields. Even in southern Germany, citizens erected monuments to the Prussian-German chancellor and venerated him as a political hero. They

---

[1] 'Hier stehe ich, der Wähler helfe mir', *Der Spiegel*, 13 November 1972, 38.

felt enormous pride in the new empire, which compared favourably with the toothless German Confederation of former times; consisting of more than forty sovereign states, the latter had never managed to be a major player among European powers. The empire of 1871, in contrast, was constructed so that it could pursue its interests far more confidently. 'For the greater part of the nation', summarized the liberal theologian Ernst Troeltsch in 1918, Bismarck's accomplishment lived up to 'our sacred longing, and today we do not wish to deny the pride with which it filled us.'[2]

Initially, this had little to do with nationalism. To feel strongly about one's own country did not mean cheering it at the expense of others. Patriots who loved their fatherland were not chauvinists who disparaged other fatherlands. The philosopher Aurel Kolnai, in 1931, associated chauvinism not with pride but with arrogant high-mindedness (Hochmut) that 'does not stop at belief in one's "own" superiority or direction (though this be unsubstantiated), but feel what is alien or opposed as somehow "irrelevant"' and 'insignificant'.[3]

Such high-mindedness characterized those who, from the 1880s onwards, had been joining forces in nationalist associations, founding their own newspapers and exerting pressure on the government to embrace more ambitious and aggressive policies. One of the most prominent spokesmen was Heinrich Claß, born in 1868 and politically active into the 1930s. In 1908, he took over the chairmanship of the Pan-German Association, which beat the drum for a German Weltpolitik that involved colonies and accelerated armament. His battle cry was 'Deutschland den Deutschen' (Germany for the Germans), plainly speaking: without Jews or Poles. At the same time, he argued, Germany should expand in size through extensive annexations, as claimed during the First World War.

This domestic and foreign policy agenda contained a violent and antisemitic nationalism that did not vanish after the war was lost but found a new form of sustenance. Many Germans felt insulted and humiliated by the 'dictated peace' of Versailles and reacted with a defiant declaration of national 'honour'. While > honour did not have the same meaning as pride, both involved assertively stating and performing one's own merit and virtue. Anyone who challenged this conviction (as the victorious powers had, from the German perspective, emphatically done in 1919) dealt self-confidence a heavy blow. One either took this blow, ducked away or fended it off with an extra dose of haughty arrogance.

[2] Ernst Troeltsch, Deutscher Geist und Westeuropa, ed. Hans Baron (Tübingen: Mohr, 1925), 209–10.

[3] Aurel Kolnai, 'High-Mindedness', in Aurel Kolnai, Politics, Values, and National Socialism, ed. Graham McAleer, trans. Francis Dunlop (New Brunswick, NJ: Transaction Publishers, 2013), 15–44, quote 19.

Pride, Arrogance, Vanity

The proud and the arrogant, as defined by the 1982 *Brockhaus* encyclopaedia, value 'themselves above all else'. Unlike the vain, they are not focused on garnering applause; instead they ride roughshod over others. The 1909 *Meyers Lexikon*, which separated pride and high-mindedness, had given a more generous verdict: it located high-mindedness in situations where a person overestimated their own importance and allowed themselves 'to be tempted to disregard others'. In contrast, the pride of those who could invoke 'true and actually possessed, even morally valuable' merits such as 'strength of character and scientific or artistic ability' was justified, good and proper; even more so, said the 1957 *Brockhaus*, if society approved of these qualities. A subsequent edition differentiated pride, as 'a form of elevated self-esteem', from arrogance: a proud person was sure of themselves, whereas an arrogant person needed to compare themselves with others.[4]

What becomes clear in all these descriptions, regardless of their different emphases and evaluations, is the moral ambivalence of pride. On the one hand, it was regarded as a positive and vibrant sense of one's own self and achievements. 'A joyful observation of one's own abilities', according to Kolnai, harmed nobody and could 'still be undertaken as > humility, with insight into one's own fragility and imperfection'. On the other hand, the boundary between pride and negatively connoted arrogance and vanity was fluid. In some circumstances, a person equipped with 'healthy' levels of self-confidence might well look down upon others, compare themselves and assign them an accordingly higher or lower value.[5]

The history of national pride is a case in point. When nineteenth-century Germans proudly professed their depth of soul and mind (the untranslatable *Gemüt*), they distanced themselves, in the same breath, from the French, who were denigrated as superficial and lacking *Gemüt*. By contrasting 'German culture' and 'French civilization', First World War propaganda stressed the superiority of one and the inferiority of the other. One's own, of which a person was proud, usually stood in opposition to the foreign, which was, and had to be, considered less valuable.

Yet national pride lacked what the encyclopaedias unanimously emphasized as the source of pride: the feeling of self-esteem derived from individual

---

[4] *Brockhaus' Konversations-Lexikon*, 14th ed., vol. 5 (Leipzig: Brockhaus, 1892), 958; *Meyers Großes Konversations-Lexikon*, 6th ed., vol. 19 (Leipzig: Bibliografisches Institut, 1909), 60; *Der Große Brockhaus*, 16th ed., vol. 11 (Wiesbaden: Brockhaus, 1957), 252; *Brockhaus Enzyklopädie*, 17th ed., vol. 18 (Wiesbaden: Brockhaus, 1973), 161.

[5] Kolnai, 'High-Mindedness', 17. Like Kolnai, in 1925 Nicolai Hartmann saw humility and pride as bound together: pride without humility tips over into arrogance, humility without pride into 'self-degradation' (Nicolai Hartmann, *Moral Values*, trans. Stanton Coit (Berlin: De Gruyter, 2020), 301).

achievements. A person who was proud of their nation invoked a collective to which they attributed particular qualities and merits. Although none of these could be ascribed to their own actions, character or abilities, they were reclaimed because the person had allegedly inherited them as a born member of the nation. Educated citizens liked to cite Goethe's *Faust* here: 'All that you have, bequeathed you by your fathers / Earn it in order to possess it'.[6] These lines were immortalized in countless private poetry books into the 1960s, and even those who could not be spurred to constant 'self-improvement' and high personal performance still conceived of themselves as heirs of national heroic deeds, felt pride and used it to mark political positions.

Noble Pride and Manly Pride

For pride, as the lexical definitions had omitted, was not based solely on one's individual achievements and qualities. One could also be proud of things others had done, just as one could feel ashamed of others (> Shame). In both cases, the precondition was that one must identify with the others in some way: they must be perceived as part of 'one's own'. This applied, in Max Scheler's 1913 view, to children and wives whose parents and husbands had every right to feel proud or ashamed of them. A teacher's pride in his pupil was of a similar kind.[7]

In order to highlight the connection between identification and pride, the philosopher could also have pointed to members of a nation or social class. The nobility, which in the early twentieth century still retained a fair amount of political and economic influence, most notably cultivated a pride pertaining to handed-down accomplishments and positions of power. Anyone born into a noble family automatically inherited the pride in what, from time immemorial, had distinguished their 'lineage'. In Scheler's definition, this strengthened the 'positive feeling of self-value'. One held one's head high and looked around confidently.

It was not only in aristocratic circles that men practised this erect posture. While women continued to curtsy, bows that were too deep and 'slave-like' rapidly became discredited among middle-class gentlemen as well. In 1896, a widely circulated handbook on manners stated that the male body 'must be

---

[6] Johann Wolfgang von Goethe, *Faust: Parts One and Two*, trans. George Madison Priest (Chicago, IL: Benton, 1952), 18.

[7] Max Scheler, 'Shame and Feelings of Modesty', in *Person and Self-Value: Three Essays*, trans. Manfred S. Frings (Dordrecht: Martinus Nijhoff, 1987), 18–19. Scheler left open the question of whether a pupil could be proud of their teacher, a child of their parents or a wife of her husband. Presumably he assumed, as did many of his contemporaries, that influence – and pride in it – only moved in one direction and top-down.

held as straight as possible'; even before high-ranking individuals, 'any curvature of the back' was to be avoided, as 'it creates a ridiculous figure'.[8]

Men held themselves upright and straight not least in the military, where 'manly pride' was carefully cultivated and practised. Under the auspices of general conscription and notwithstanding marked differences in rank, all soldiers possessed, at least theoretically, the same 'manly honour' and displayed the same pride, which remained alive 'in every true man's heart' long after the enlistment period. According to the author of a popular 1917 booklet for adolescents, such feelings brought about 'real miracles' during the First World War, when fighter pilots and submarine crews in particular distinguished themselves with a 'soldier's pride based on heroic deeds'.[9]

Heroes' Pride: 1914 to 1945

Many men who at the beginning of the 1930s turned first to President von Hindenburg and later to Hitler spoke of their pride in having played an active role in the war. In 1935, nine Berliners, all of them volunteers from 1914, wished their Führer a happy birthday. They thanked him for bringing 'prestige and long-missed honour to all of us' and were 'proud of formerly having been privates and trench runners, but even prouder that you, dear comrade of yore, are now the Führer of all'. The letter enclosed photographs that showed the gentlemen in suits and ties, with beer glasses raised.[10]

In this, as in many similar letters, the double face of pride was readily apparent: people were proud of their own achievements, yet also of the deeds of others in whose reflection they could bask, augmenting their own self-esteem. This is how the primary-school teacher and former reserve lieutenant Otto Klünder expressed his feelings to Hindenburg in 1932. As a war combatant, he felt a 'warranted pride' in the 'phenomenal accomplishments of our military leaders' and the 'humble soldier's willingness to sacrifice'. In his civilian profession, it was his 'proudest duty' to pass on this pride to his pupils and 'inculcate in them the respect for the heroic spirit and self-sacrifice of their fallen fathers and brothers, be this through school lessons or hikes in our beautiful homeland', not to forget ceremonies 'at our huge boulder, the memorial stone for the fallen of the parish'.[11]

---

[8] Franz Ebhardt, *Der gute Ton*, 13th ed. (Leipzig: Klinkhardt, 1896), 284–85.

[9] Theodor Lange, 'Mannesstolz vor Königsthronen', in Theodor Lange, *Werde ein Mann*, 10th ed. (Berlin: Spamer, 1917), 219–23. The first edition appeared in 1891 and was aimed at apprentices.

[10] Federal Archive Berlin, NS 51, no. 75: Hermann Engelhardt, 20 April 1935.

[11] Ibid., R 601, no. 380: Otto Klünder, 11 March 1932.

Those who had nothing of which they could personally feel proud found a surrogate in a strictly national ethos. 'It is an elevating feeling', Emma Röttger from Munich wrote to Hitler in 1930, 'to belong to a movement whose leader is a man, upright and proud, who is not swerved by ill will and firmly strives towards his aims.' Two years later, Maria Scherger from Essen, who introduced herself as a 'simple girl', confided in Hindenburg that she had never before been so proud 'to be a German as in this time. Be assured: Germany cannot and will not founder.' Meanwhile, twenty-six-year-old miner Arthur Peuter sounded less certain of the future. He had been unemployed for a year already and consequently felt branded 'a sputum of humanity'. In these circumstances, he stated, it might 'really be called a heroic act to proudly declare one's allegiance to the nation'. This could mean two things: either the job- and party-less Peuter sought, like Maria Scherger, a compensatory pride in the nation that helped him overcome his own depressing situation; or he felt so completely cast out from society that he merely fantasized about such identification as a 'heroic act'.[12]

After 1933, proclamations of pride became more frequent. Two weeks after Hitler had been appointed chancellor, Emmy Spieske from Berlin rejoiced that 'finally, the national emotion is being awakened again among the people'. For her, it was ultimately 'the greatest of all feelings' and stretched 'like a thread through the whole of life'. When Carl Meyer from Arnstadt, who had joined the Nazi Party in 1931, wished the 'esteemed Führer' happy birthday two years later, he added contentedly, 'One can now say again in good conscience that one can be proud of one's Germanness, whereas before 30 January 1933 one could only be ashamed.' In Hedwig Elbers's 1935 letter of congratulation, she thanked Hitler for restoring her pride in her motherhood. Three years later, under the effects of the Sudeten Crisis, a mother-of-five from Gießen promised the 'dear, dear Führer' that in the event of war, she would send her husband and two sons into the field 'to fight for you and Germany'. She felt sure 'that this sacrifice has such a higher purpose today. And I will not become faint-hearted, I will remain joyous and proud that they fell in such a time for this Führer.' A 'nationally proud German woman' from Mannheim joined in exuberantly: 'One can be truly proud to live in this time, in which you, my dear Führer, have raised our beloved Germany to glory and > honour again. One would like to be a man, in order to join your ranks.'[13]

Letters from abroad sent a similar message of admiration and affirmation. 'The youth organizations in particular', Piero Bracci wrote from Livorno, Italy,

---

[12] Ibid., NS 51, no. 51/1: Emma Röttger, 7 April 1930; R 601, no. 380: Maria Scherger, 11 March 1932; Arthur Peuter, undated, probably also 11 March 1932.

[13] Ibid., NS 51, no. 53: Emmy Spieske, 15 February 1933; no. 72: Carl Meyer, 18 April 1933; no. 75: Hedwig Elbers, 19 April 1935; no. 71: L. Hummel, 14 September 1938; anonymous, 28 September 1938.

in 1936, had made a great impression on him: 'I have seen the Hitler Youth marching wonderfully through the streets in their pride; I have seen them carrying the swastika flag with so much pride and with so much beauty that it moved me.'[14] The upright gait, the taut posture, the songs proclaiming love of the fatherland and homeland: all this conveyed an image of proud self-assurance, which rarely failed to make an impact on participants and observers.

Pride was instilled in the younger generation not only through the Hitler Youth. School lessons also aimed to 'awaken in the young person the proud feeling that he belongs to the German people with their superb regions, their heroic disposition, their great past and their high culture'. It was precisely this pride that gave rise to the 'willingness to sacrifice' for *Volk* and Führer.[15] Pride in the 'Third Reich' was thus firmly bound to the national collective. Being part of the heroic people's community imparted the self-esteem that liberal societies saw as based on the individual and their very personal abilities and achievements.

GDR Pride

The GDR was neither liberal nor consistently collectivist. Though it celebrated the 'socialist community', it also allowed individuals their pride, and encouraged it. Personal skills were publicly recognized and commended, whether in competitive sports or in the 1961-founded Mathematic Olympics. Companies, usually state-owned, gave awards not only for joint achievements but also for individual excellence (> Envy).

Pride in one's own work, however, often ran into material constraints, which plagued industrial production from beginning to end. While workers' collectives outwardly expressed pride in having fulfilled or even exceeded the official standards of productivity, they harboured different feelings on the ground. Even trainees noticed 'that there was so much sloppiness everywhere', while their higher-ups were in despair. 'There was always something missing, and building under socialism was almost as impossible as the building of socialism itself': this is how historian Ilko-Sascha Kowalczuk summarizes the experiences of his father-in-law Dieter Arndt, who led a small construction firm close to Magdeburg until 1990. When Arndt was allowed to travel to West Germany for a family visit in the summer of 1989, his first stop was a hardware store. Here, he broke down: 'He cries, is speechless, although he already knew it. Here is everything, standing and lying around in abundance,

---

[14] Ibid., no. 71: Piero Bracci, 13 December 1936.
[15] Hermann Kirek, 'Heimatkundeunterricht (1938)', in *Propaganda: Medien und Öffentlichkeit in der NS-Diktatur*, ed. Bernd Sösemann, vol. 2 (Stuttgart: Steiner, 2011), 1277.

building materials as well as tools, that he is constantly chasing in his day-to-day work. The things he could build, if he didn't have these procurement problems!'[16]

Under such conditions, state-prescribed pride in the 'successes and accomplishments of our socialist republic' did not always come easy.[17] Certainly, citizens were proud of the medals that rained down on top athletes at international competitions. Sigmund Jähn, who in 1978 orbited the earth in a Soviet space capsule ('The first German in space – a citizen of the GDR'), was enthusiastically celebrated by his fellow citizens even before bearing the honorary title 'Hero of the GDR' (> Joy, > Honour; Figure 43).

People were far more ambivalent, though, about the industrial performance shows with which the GDR sought to impress visitors to national and international trade fairs.[18] Many citizens had their doubts about what exactly the 'dynamic increases', which continued to be praised until 1989, pertained to. Other successes the government boasted about seemed immediately evident, though: 'safety and belonging', 'work for all', 'equal educational opportunities for all children' and social security.[19]

A sense of pride also accompanied the 100,000 members of the FDJ who assembled for a torchlight procession on East Berlin's Unter den Linden avenue on the evening of 6 October 1989. Twenty-four-year-old teacher Steffen Matthes experienced the march as 'something very great': 'I felt the need to show that I am proud of this country and its politics. To show that the GDR has every reason to loudly celebrate its fortieth anniversary. Because a lot has been achieved here in a historically short period of time.' Kerstin Thon, the twenty-eight-year-old district secretary of the Wittenberg FDJ, was more concrete and prosaic as she highlighted the organization's accomplishments, from collecting scrap metal to renovating flats.[20]

---

[16] Walter Friedrich and Hartmut Griese, eds, *Jugend und Jugendforschung in der DDR* (Opladen: Leske & Budrich, 1991), 144; Ilko-Sascha Kowalczuk, *Die Übernahme: Wie Ostdeutschland Teil der Bundesrepublik wurde* (Munich: C. H. Beck, 2019), 10.

[17] Siegfried Suckut, *Volkes Stimmen: 'Ehrlich, aber deutlich' – Privatbriefe an die DDR-Regierung* (Munich: dtv, 2015), 166. When the Emnid Institute asked East Germans about GDR nostalgia in 1995, three out of four respondents affirmed the statement: 'I can be proud of my life in the GDR, because I made the best of it and I only went along with the regime as far as was unavoidable.' To be proud of the GDR per se was a foreign concept to most (*Der Spiegel*, 3 July 1995, 40–52).

[18] Martin Wörner, 'Made in Germany – Made in GDR', in *Krauts – Fritz – Piefkes . . . ? Deutschland von außen*, ed. Haus der Geschichte der Bundesrepublik Deutschland (Bonn: Bouvier, 1999), 74–81, esp. 79–81.

[19] Those achievements were celebrated on a poster printed for the GDR's fortieth anniversary in October 1989, under the headline 'This is what we are proud of': www.hdg.de/lemo/bestand/objekt/plakat-darauf-sind-wir-stolz.html, accessed 1 March 2022.

[20] *Berliner Zeitung*, 9 October 1989, 7.

Figure 43   A proud nation honours its hero: GDR cosmonaut Sigmund Jähn,
1978 (Photo by ADN-Bildarchiv/ullstein bild via Getty Images)

However, as long-term studies prove, people like Matthes or Thon were in
the minority. The GDR's Institute for Youth Research in Leipzig, which had
been collecting data on political attitudes since 1966, received increasingly
reserved answers to the question of whether young people were proud 'to be a
citizen of our socialist state'. Until the 1970s, most interviewees were sure that
the GDR's social order served as a role model for the entire world. In the
decade following, fewer and fewer were so convinced. Adolescents and young
adults still felt 'attached' to the state; many valued the secure career prospects,
the anti-fascist ethos and the education system. But in May 1989, only 10 per
cent of apprentices and young workers believed in the 'worldwide victory' of
socialism, and less than 20 per cent identified with the GDR. Among students,

the proportion was slightly higher, with one out of three professing the 'advantages of socialism'.

Self-comparisons with the Federal Republic also proved illuminating. In 1968, when the Leipzig researchers asked ninth- and tenth-graders how they rated 'national pride' and 'attachment to the fatherland' in East and West Germany, the pupils gave the GDR far higher marks. In March 1989, this was reversed.[21]

Pride or Its Absence in the Federal Republic

It may well have been true that national pride in East Germany was on the decline during the 1980s. Whether it was actually on the rise in the Federal Republic, though, is debatable. Under the CDU/CSU-FDP coalition, which had been in office since 1982, some spoke in favour of officially fostering and reviving it. Chancellor Kohl himself took every opportunity to talk citizens into a 'newfound self-confidence'. They had, he stressed in 1986, every reason to be proud: proud 'of our cultural achievements, our solidarity-oriented society, proud of Germany, our homeland, our fatherland'.[22]

But many remained sceptical, their relationship with national identity 'wounded' and 'broken', as Elisabeth Noelle-Neumann from the Allensbach Institute for Public Opinion Research put it in 1987.[23] The criminal legacy of National Socialism and its chauvinist excesses weighed so heavily that national pride was, if not taboo, then still contaminated and thorny. This was one of the reasons why the first federal president, Theodor Heuss, had, in his inaugural speech in 1949, made the case for a 'new national feeling' with 'restraint'. It should be both 'proud' and 'modest' and should distance itself from the 'arrogant hubris that was often enough the case among Germans'.[24]

Yet at the same time, Heuss wanted citizens to nail their political colours to the mast and positively get behind the democratic form of government. This included an unabashed and self-assured handling of national symbols such as the black, red and gold federal flag. These 'German colours' had, since the early nineteenth century, transcended single-state identities and affiliations (Prussian, Bavarian, etc.). Furthermore, they had stood for liberal and democratic principles since the 1848 Revolution. Though controversial, the Weimar

---

[21] Friedrich and Griese, *Jugend*, 131–34, 138–49; Peter Förster, 'Die Entwicklung des politischen Bewußtseins der DDR-Jugend zwischen 1966 und 1989', in *Das Zentralinstitut für Jugendforschung Leipzig 1966–1990*, ed. Walter Friedrich et al. (Berlin: Edition Ost, 1999), 70–165.

[22] Kiehl, *Alle Jahre wieder*, 388.

[23] Elisabeth Noelle-Neumann, 'Nationalgefühl und Glück', in Elisabeth Noelle-Neumann and Renate Köcher, *Die verletzte Nation* (Stuttgart: DVA, 1987), 17–71.

[24] Dolf Sternberger, ed., *Reden der deutschen Bundespräsidenten Heuss/Lübke/Heinemann/Scheel* (Munich: Hanser, 1979), 5–10.

Republic had adopted them for the state flag before the Nazi regime replaced them with the swastika. In both German post-war states, the colours attained a new honour; in 1959 the GDR garnished them with the state emblem of a hammer, compass and wreath of rye.

While the GDR indulged in flags and handed out millions of miniatures – popularly disparaged as 'cheer rags' – for waving at demonstrations, West German citizens held back. In a 1951 survey, only 23 per cent said they felt joy at the sight of the Federal Republic's flag. It was rarely visible anyway. Even on public occasions it was used sparingly, and was most frequently spotted at international sporting events, as West German athletes marched into the stadium or stood on the winners' podium.

How can the lack of joy at the 'German colours' in the early years of the Federal Republic be explained? Some citizens obviously eyed the new state with a considerable amount of scepticism. Others still had the seas of flags brandished during the 'Third Reich' in mind and wished for less national pathos and more political sobriety. Even if the enthusiasm for black-red-gold grew in the following decades, it never reached levels that were customary in other countries. National pride likewise scored far lower between the Rhine and Elbe rivers than in other parts of Europe: asked if they were proud 'to be German', in 1981, only 59 per cent of those interviewed answered in the affirmative.[25]

Three years earlier, Chancellor Helmut Schmidt (SPD) had conceded that one could indeed be 'a little proud' in view of the post-1949 'reconstruction feat'. To nationalistic slogans, however, 'the vast majority of our fellow Germans are unreceptive', a sentiment he approved of. After all, the nation was 'not the ultimate measure of all things'.[26] Here, Schmidt agreed with his predecessor Brandt, who had intended his 1972 campaign slogan similarly: Germans should and could be proud of the successes they had achieved through hard work and effort.

Brandt's clarification invoked the pride in one's profession and work that was firmly anchored in Germans' personal and national value systems. Unlike aristocratic or national pride, this type of pride was based on performance and accomplishments that could be attributed to the individual by virtue of their industriousness, their skills and their knowledge. Since the early twentieth century, the 'Made in Germany' label, originally invented by the British to guard the domestic market against cheap German competition, had become a widely

---

[25] On the survey results of 1951 and 1981: Thomas Petersen, 'Ein Volk kommt zur Ruhe', *Frankfurter Allgemeine Zeitung*, 28 January 2015, 8. See the critical analysis by Jürgen Fleiß et al., 'Nationalstolz zwischen Patriotismus und Nationalismus?', *Berliner Journal für Soziologie* 19, no. 3 (2009): 409–34.

[26] Kiehl, *Alle Jahre wieder*, quote 338.

Figure 44 A 2021 election campaign billboard reads 'To ensure the "Made in Germany" label endures' (Photo by John MacDougall/AFP via Getty Images)

admired seal of quality, signifying 'German workmanship' (Figure 44).[27] Those who manufactured the goods that were exported all over the world used it for self-identification. They felt proud, despite any job-related conflicts, of their work and their employer. As 'Kruppians', for instance, they emotionally related to the company that appreciated and rewarded their services, the results of which met with worldwide demand and acclaim.[28]

After 1945, the rapid economic recovery offered ample grounds for pride, which factory management did their utmost to promote. 'Quality workmanship conquers the global market!' A poster featuring this inscription and a

---

[27] Maiken Umbach, 'Made in Germany', in *Deutsche Erinnerungsorte*, vol. 2, ed. Étienne François and Hagen Schulze (Munich: C. H. Beck, 2001), 405–18; Wörner, 'Made in Germany', 74–78; David Head, *Made in Germany: The Corporate Identity of a Nation* (London: Hodder & Stouton, 1992).

[28] Heinz Reif, '"Ein seltener Kreis von Freunden": Arbeitsprozesse und Arbeitserfahrungen bei Krupp 1840–1914', in *Arbeit und Arbeitserfahrung in der Geschichte*, ed. Klaus Tenfelde (Göttingen: Vandenhoeck & Ruprecht, 1986), 51–91, esp. 68; Klaus Tenfelde, *Bilder von Krupp* (Munich: C. H. Beck, 1994); Alf Lüdtke, '"Deutsche Qualitätsarbeit" (Interview)', in *Arbeit im Nationalsozialismus*, ed. Marc Buggeln and Michael Wildt (Munich: De Gruyter Oldenbourg, 2014), 373–401; Ralf Stremmel, 'Identität, Stolz und Selbstbewusstsein: Erinnerungsort Kruppianer', in *Zeit-Räume Ruhr*, ed. Stefan Berger et al. (Essen: Klartext, 2019), 327–44.

gigantic steamship named Export hung in many factory halls in the 1950s. When the millionth Volkswagen Beetle rolled off the production line in 1955, the Wolfsburg workers and General Director Heinrich Nordhoff looked into the camera with equal pride.[29] In factories that made coveted luxury cars such as Mercedes or BMWs, or that manufactured stainless steel or high-grade chemical products, many employees recognized the value of their contribution and considered themselves proud members of strong companies.

Women were granted this opportunity more rarely as they were less likely than men to work for prestigious firms. Furthermore, they more frequently sought affirmation in the role family policy prescribed and promoted to them: that of mother and housewife. But here, too, there were custom-made opportunities to develop and show pride. A woman could distinguish herself, as advertisements suggested, with a flawlessly neat, spotlessly clean home. Raising her children to be happy and successful was supposed to make her proud, as was her tireless dedication to her husband's physical and emotional well-being. It is only since the 1970s that 'housewife pride' has gradually disappeared from product marketing in favour of a more career-oriented image of women. Still, to this very day, pride remains an emotion that seems less acceptable in women than in men. In psychological tests, proud women prove unpopular with men, while proud men (with chests thrust out and chins raised) score points with women.[30]

In addition to gender-typical preferences, these tests also reflect social hierarchies. Even societies that emphasize equality as a matter of principle distribute prestige and praise unevenly. Certain behaviours and ways of life enjoy wider approval than others; some professions and skills rank higher on the value scale, others lower. This has a direct effect on the self-esteem of those who find themselves classed as inferior. Pride, as the *Brockhaus* pointed out in 1957, generally requires the approving echo of society. If this is lacking, there are consequences, as the nobility learnt during the twentieth century. Courted and privileged as the highest social class in the German Empire, they lost a vast amount of power and standing in the Weimar Republic, and never recovered. Of course, this did not prevent aristocrats from boasting family heritage and connections. But their pride was inward-looking and had little claim to affirmation from the outside world.[31]

---

[29] Knut Hickethier et al., eds, *Das Deutsche Auto: Volkswagenwerbung und Volkskultur* (Gießen: Anabas, 1974), 53, 105, passim.

[30] Jessica L. Tracy und Alec T. Beall, 'Happy Guys Finish Last: The Impact of Emotion Expressions on Sexual Attraction', *Emotion* 11, no. 6 (2011): 1379–87, https://doi.org/10 .1037/a0022902.

[31] Monika Wienfort, *Der Adel in der Moderne* (Göttingen: Vandenhoeck & Ruprecht, 2006), 153–64; Michael Seelig, *Alltagsadel: Der ehemalige ostelbische Adel in der Bundesrepublik Deutschland 1945/49–1975* (Cologne: Böhlau, 2015), 152 ff., 506 ff.

Pride and Prejudice

For other social groups, even inner pride was made difficult or denied altogether. This included people who were criminalized, persecuted and shamed for their sexual orientation. Building a robust self-esteem thus proved extremely tough. Experiencing shaming often led to internalized shame, and many homosexuals sought to hide their desires from themselves as well as from others (> Love). The Gay Pride movement of the 1970s struck like a thunderbolt. In public parades and demonstrations LGBTQ+ people shed their shame and displayed self-confidence. 'Become proud of your homosexuality!' was the message of Rosa von Praunheim's 1971 film *It Is Not the Homosexual Who Is Perverse, But the Society in Which He Lives*. This new-won pride was taken to the streets and increasingly met with approval and respect. More than a million people participated in the 2018 Cologne Pride, now the largest event of its kind in Europe, many heterosexuals among them.[32]

It was no less difficult for migrants to develop and publicly show pride. The 'guest workers' who came to West Germany from the 1950s onwards were rarely received with open arms. At their workplaces, they encountered scepticism and mistrust, if not open rejection, and even trade unions were initially reluctant to build bridges with their new colleagues. Italians, Spaniards and Croatians could at least hope for the support and acceptance of Catholic communities. For the Muslim Turkish workers who joined the West German labour force in the 1960s, there were no such ports of call or networks of > solidarity. When work became scarce but immigration continued, the problem intensified. Against this background, pride could only be built up, if at all, in one's own isolated milieu, often with recourse to concepts of national and family > honour.

But pride might also arise from economic success, as it has increasingly done since the 2000s. Retailers, shopkeepers and restaurant owners with Turkish roots enjoy broad respect and have a clientele not restricted to their compatriots. In Duisburg-Marxloh, locals proudly acknowledge that Turkish-owned bridal shops have made the district famous throughout Germany. The huge selection of decorative clothing attracts crowds of customers willing to pay large sums for shiny outfits.[33] Another source of pride is the sense of

---

[32] Frank Niggemeier, 'Gay Pride: Schwules Selbstbewußtsein aus dem Village', in *West-Wind*, ed. Bernd Polster (Cologne: Dumont, 1995), 179–86; Craig Griffiths, 'Sex, Shame and West German Gay Liberation', *German History* 34, no. 3 (2016): 445–67.

[33] Jochen Oltmer et al., eds, *Das 'Gastarbeiter'-System* (Munich: Oldenbourg, 2012), here particularly the articles by Oliver Trede, 'Misstrauen, Reputation und Integration: Gewerkschaften und "Gastarbeiter" in der Bundesrepublik in den 1950er bis 1970er Jahren' (183–97); Dietrich Thränhardt and Jenni Winterhagen, 'Der Einfluß der katholischen Migrantengemeinden auf die Integration südeuropäischer Einwanderergruppen in Deutschland' (199–215); Anna Caroline Cöster, 'Duisburg-Marxloh' (217–31).

national identity. The fact that, under President Recep Tayyip Erdoğan, Turkey has developed into a potent regional power and is stepping on to the international stage with increasing self-assertiveness has won the government in Ankara the support and approval of many Turkish Germans. A growing majority of the approximately three million people of Turkish descent say in surveys that they feel a stronger sense of belonging to Turkey than to Germany (> Belonging). Waving crescent flags at well-attended Turkish election campaign rallies serve as performative proof of such proud allegiance.[34]

Soft-Voiced Patriotism?

In 2014, 57 per cent of Germans surveyed said they felt joy at the sight of the German flag, a far higher figure than in 1951 (23 per cent).[35] Yet their joy has rarely been so strong that it moved them to hoist the flag or decorate their balconies or front yards with it. The situation that so troubled President Heinrich Lübke back in 1960 – that, unlike in the GDR, 'on national holidays it was practically just official buildings, hardly any private houses, that flew the flag' – has not changed.[36] With one exception, in the summer of 2006: during the football World Cup that the country hosted under the motto 'A time to make friends', there were suddenly black-red-gold flags galore. It was not just Germans who waved them, hung them from windows and fastened them to their cars. Many migrants expressed their support for Germany's eleven in the same way.[37] Although the team was eliminated in the semi-finals, fans were proud of them (Figure 45).

Most observers welcomed the collective > joy as easy-going and harmless; finally, Germany had become a 'normal' nation that accepted itself. Accordingly, Sönke Wortmann titled his documentary film about the 2006 national team *Germany – A Summer's Fairytale*, to contrast with Heinrich Heine's famous epic poem *Germany – A Winter's Tale*. With a mixture of melancholy and sarcasm, the exiled poet had in 1844 criticized the political state of affairs in his homeland, including German chauvinism. As Wortmann saw it, this was precisely what had been absent in 2006. On Berlin's 'fan mile', Germans engaged with their international guests in a genuinely friendly, cheerful and cosmopolitan manner.

But there were also critical voices. It was all too easy, they warned, for 'party patriotism' to morph into xenophobia. Still, most fans rolled up their flags

[34] http://bit.ly/3XQ2emC, accessed 1 March 2022.
[35] Petersen, 'Ein Volk kommt zur Ruhe', 8.
[36] Kiehl, *Alle Jahre wieder*, 141. At that time Lübke, like Heuss in 1949, advocated a 'restrained' use of these 'external symbols of internal solidarity'.
[37] Victoria Schwenzer and Nicole Selmer, 'Fans und Migration', in *Fans: Soziologische Perspektiven*, ed. Jochen Roose et al., 2nd ed. (Wiesbaden: VS Springer, 2017), 343–66.

Figure 45   Berlin 2006: One million people gave the German team a proud heroes'
welcome during their World Cup campaign (Marcus Brandt/AFP via Getty Images)

after the party ended and did not retrieve them from the cupboard until the
next national match. Only far-right extremists make use of them regularly and
with blatant hostility, though they increasingly prefer the Nazi war flag,
without the banned swastika, to the 'German colours'.

The AfD does not go that far. Nevertheless, the party fosters a demonstrative national pride that reaches well beyond what right-wingers debated in the
1980s under the catchphrase of the 'self-confident nation'. Members profess
with 'earnest > love and conviction' that they are 'proud to be a German and
part of this great and magnificent nation'. They promote the idea that one
belongs to that nation through the 'genetic inheritance' of what the 'fore-
fathers' have accomplished. National history, in their view, has 'brought forth
much that is beautiful and worthy of preservation'. Before it, the 'twelve dark
years' pale in comparison; besides, every nation ultimately has 'its light and
dark chapters'.[38]

Most citizens, though, reject such revisionist versions of history. The general
sentiment was both captured and echoed by President Frank-Walter
Steinmeier in 2019 when he, commemorating the centenary of the Weimar

[38] https://bit.ly/3ENey0n; on the 'dark chapters', see also the 2018 'bird shit' speech by AfD
cofounder Alexander Gauland: http://bit.ly/3Si6daa, both accessed 1 March 2022;
Gabriele Kämper, 'Selbstbewusstsein', *WerkstattGeschichte* 37 (2004): 64–79.

Constitution, propagated a 'democratic patriotism'. Like Heuss seventy years earlier, he declared the German flag to be the 'emblem of our democracy', a 'proud ribbon' that tied the democrats of the early nineteenth century to the present and was out of place in the hands of those who 'want to ignite new nationalistic > hate'. Above all, he stressed, the patriotic gaze must not mask or minimize the 'contradictions and aberrations' of German history. Against a background of dictatorship, war and the Holocaust, patriotism could 'only ever be a patriotism of soft voices and mixed emotions'.[39] A pinch of pride, à la Willy Brandt or Helmut Schmidt, would do no harm, if paired with the modesty that Theodor Heuss had advised.

[39] http://bit.ly/3Z2Pfz6, accessed 1 March 2022. On 8 May 2020, the seventy-fifth anniversary of the end of the war, Steinmeier spoke of how, for the aforementioned reasons, 'this country can only be loved with a broken heart' (200508-75-Jahre-Ende-WKII-Englisch.pdf (bundespraesident.de), accessed 11 February 2022).

~

Shame

On 9 October 2019, a twenty-seven-year-old man carried out an attack on the Halle synagogue in which the congregation was celebrating Yom Kippur, the most sacred of Jewish holidays. When the heavy door withstood the assault, the perpetrator shot two people at random. The following day, President Frank-Walter Steinmeier visited the scene and declared 9 October a 'day of shame and disgrace'.[1]

Disgrace and Shame

Technically, Steinmeier should have inverted the terms, because first came disgrace, followed by shame. Disgrace is the opposite of > honour; anyone who disgraces themselves and others loses honour and respect. Like honour, disgrace is not an objective, immutable fact. Rather, it touches upon moral conventions, which differ from each other temporally, spatially and socially. A person who 'through his behaviour violates morality, good custom or the demands of rank, profession, etc.' caused disgrace and reaped 'contempt', according to *Meyers Lexikon* in 1909. A century later, the *Brockhaus* defined disgrace as a 'state of being despised, into which one has fallen primarily through one's own fault', without specifying the fault in detail. Between the two definitions lay a time during which ideas of custom, morality and honour fundamentally changed; who, today, would know what 'honour of estate' (*Standesehre*) means?

And what about shame? In 1909, it was said that contempt and the perception that 'other people's respect for us has genuinely or presumably diminished' could trigger the 'unwelcome emotion' of shame. In 1977, *Meyers* emphasized that shame was 'instilled' by means of education and experience, and linked with the awareness 'of having, through certain behaviour or remarks, fallen short of social expectations or violated important norms or values'. Summarizing this observation, the 1992 *Brockhaus* noted that shame

---

[1] *Süddeutsche Zeitung*, 11 October 2019, 1.

reflects 'failure before an ideal norm' and is 'experienced in the form of an embarrassing awareness of the otherness or inferiority of one's own self'.[2]

It is unlikely that the attacker from Halle was ashamed of or embarrassed by his heinous act. He was so obsessed with his belief that the Jews, once again, were to blame for all that was wrong with the world that he did not even perceive the immoral and despicable nature of what he had done. His 'ideal norm' was not congruent with the norms of the society in which he lived. Instead, it conformed to the worldview of antisemites and right-wing extremists, among whom he felt he belonged. With them, there was no place for shame.

But this was not the point President Steinmeier was trying to make. For him, shame was the predominant feeling of the society in whose midst the perpetrator had committed his attack. Citizens felt shame that they had not been able to protect their Jewish neighbours and, above all, that murderous antisemitism was still at home in Germany, eight decades after the Holocaust. This could not be reconciled with the republic's fundamental values and implied a dismal assessment of the manifold pedagogical and political efforts to drive antisemitism out of the country and its inhabitants.

Collective Shame after 1945

Knowingly or unknowingly, Steinmeier continued the first federal president's attempts to grasp and frame people's emotions. Invited in 1949 by the newly founded Society for Christian-Jewish Cooperation, Theodor Heuss spoke of the 'collective shame' that Germans felt in the face of the murder of millions of Jews. The population as a whole may not bear the guilt directly, he said, as they had neither ordered, carried out nor sanctioned this monstrous crime. But they were ashamed it had been done in their name, and even more ashamed of giving Hitler and his helpers free rein instead of bringing them down.[3]

Such expressions of and appeals to shame were not at all unusual after the end of the war. As early as May 1945, British and American occupying forces confronted Germans with film footage from liberated concentration camps in order to show them what had taken place there and to trigger shame (Figure 46).[4] In June 1945, the German Communist Party (KPD) declared that 'in every German, the shame must burn that the German people bear a

---

[2] *Meyers Großes Konversations-Lexikon*, 6th ed., vol. 17 (Leipzig: Bibliografisches Institut, 1909), 621, 688; ibid., 9th ed., vol. 20 (1977), 820; *Brockhaus-Enzyklopädie*, 19th ed., vol. 19 (Mannheim: Brockhaus, 1992), 281; ibid., 21st ed., vol. 21 (2006), 153.

[3] Thorsten Eitz and Georg Stötzel, *Wörterbuch der 'Vergangenheitsbewältigung'* (Hildesheim: Olms, 2007), 383.

[4] Ulrike Weckel, 'Shamed by Nazi Crimes: The First Step towards Germans' Reeducation or a Catalyst for Their Wish to Forget?', in *Reverberations of Nazi Violence in Germany and Beyond: Disturbing Pasts*, ed. Stephanie Bird et al. (London: Bloomsbury, 2016), 33–46.

Figure 46   May 1945: US troops take Ludwigslust citizens to view a nearby
concentration camp (Courtesy of the National Archives/Newsmakers)

significant share of complicity' in the atrocities of the Nazi regime. For
prominent East German intellectuals such as Anna Seghers, Arnold Zweig,
Johannes R. Becher and Stephan Hermlin, shame was the key emotion that
made repentance, catharsis and a new beginning possible. 'Felt deeply', it could
make 'the whole person red hot, and burn out the dross of the rotten old in us',
Becher wrote in September 1945.[5] Shame was, in his view, the purgatory that
would cleanse Germans of the national disgrace of having committed innumerable crimes against humanity.

Thanks to a sophisticated strategy of administered anti-fascism, the GDR
managed to officially absolve its population of responsibility for those crimes
while simultaneously eliciting their shame. Of course, everyone knew only too

[5] Helmut Peitsch, 'Verordneter Antifaschismus', in *1949/1989: Cultural Perspectives on
Division and Unity in East and West*, ed. Clare Flanagan and Stuart Taberner
(Amsterdam: Rodopi, 2000), 1–26, esp. 2–3; Heidrun Kämper, *Der Schulddiskurs in der
frühen Nachkriegszeit* (Berlin: De Gruyter, 2005), 296–301.

well that there had been few anti-fascists before 1945, and the ruling party left no doubt about this. In retrospect, the 1912-born writer and former Wehrmacht soldier Erwin Strittmatter lucidly described how such politics of humiliation had worked for his generation: 'You showed us the cruelty in the concentration camps and the murder and torture of political opponents that we tolerated with our silence and lack of protest. We understood and were grateful to the teachers you sent to us to make us see and have insights. After that, we did as it suited you.' Strittmatter's colleague Christa Wolf, born in 1929, was similarly ashamed of her childhood and teenage enthusiasm for the 'Third Reich', and so declared herself resolutely on the side of socialism. Identifying with those who had resisted the Nazis was supposed to drown out the shame of one's own complicity. In reality, though, it kept alive the feeling, the passive-powerless undertone of which played into the hands of the SED and reinforced the regime's legitimacy.[6]

Not surprisingly, Strittmatter referred solely to 'political opponents', i.e. communists (and social democrats) as victims of Nazi terror. Not saying a word about the far larger number of people whose life was taken on racist grounds reflected the GDR's hierarchy of values. Correspondingly, Willy Brandt's 1970 Warsaw genuflection, which was addressed to the Jewish victims of the Nazi regime, fell flat in East Berlin; the state-controlled press did not find it worth mentioning.

Yet the gesture was also controversial in the Federal Republic, since it broke through the silence of shame that large sections of the West German population chose to maintain. Even though shame, as Heuss had emphasized time and again, could not be shaken off, few followed his proposal of overcoming 'the shame into which Hitler has forced us Germans' by means of an impressive 'counteraction'. One organization that did was the Action Reconciliation Service for Peace, founded in 1958 by the Protestant Church. They sent young volunteers first to Western European countries and later also to Israel and Eastern Europe, where they helped build synagogues and kindergartens or worked with the elderly and on social projects.[7] The vast majority of

---

[6] Erwin Strittmatter, *Nachrichten aus meinem Leben: Aus den Tagebüchern 1954–1973* (Berlin: Aufbau-Verlag, 2012), 333; Christa Wolf, *A Model Childhood*, trans. Ursule Molinaro and Hedwig Rappolt (New York: Farrar, Straus & Giroux, 1980); Ralph Giordano, 'Der verordnete Antifaschismus', in Ralph Giordano, *Die zweite Schuld oder Von der Last, Deutscher zu sein* (Hamburg: Rasch & Röhring, 1987), 215–28; Christiane Wienand, 'Remembered Change and Changes of Remembrance: East German Narratives of Anti-fascist Conversion', in *Becoming East German: Socialist Structures and Sensibilities after Hitler*, ed. Mary Fulbrook and Andrew I. Port (New York: Berghahn, 2013), 99–118.

[7] Christiane Wienand, 'From Atonement to Peace? *Aktion Sühnezeichen*, German-Israeli Relations and the Role of Youth in Reconciliation Discourse and Practice', in *Reconciliation, Civil Society, and the Politics of Memory: Transnational Initiatives in the 20th and 21st Century*, ed. Birgit Schwelling (Bielefeld: transcript, 2012), 201–35;

Germans, however, practised a remote and suppressive silence that was only occasionally disrupted by trials against individual Nazi perpetrators in the late 1950s and 1960s.[8]

Brandt's genuflection came without words, too, and yet was anything but silent. It embodied > humility before the victims, as well as shame of the crimes that Germans had committed against them. Although the Social Democratic chancellor had spent the years 1933 to 1945 in exile and carried no personal guilt, he publicly acknowledged his responsibility as a German citizen and head of state. For this he found a symbol that was as eloquent as it was ambivalent. People who feel ashamed generally want to make themselves invisible; they fall silent and lower their gaze. But Brandt, kneeling, looked straight ahead at the monument to the Warsaw Ghetto fighters and the victims of the Holocaust. He accepted the shame and translated it into a gesture that, because it was unusual and meaningful, stuck in the memory.

Defence against Shame

Apart from acceptance and silence, there was a third way to handle shame: one could deflect it. Shame is usually considered an unpleasant emotion, so strong and uncomfortable that people prefer to keep it at bay. After 1945, defence mechanisms were readily available. For one thing, people could place the responsibility exclusively on those who had worked in the apparatus of party and state. Heuss's phrasing – Hitler 'forced' the Germans into shame – was in this vein. Even the men who had carried out mass killings invoked superior orders that they had been required to obey, alleging that they would have been shot had they refused. This could not be proven, but the more the claim was repeated, the more entrenched it became. According to this logic, culpability lay solely with Adolf Hitler – who had conveniently escaped it through suicide.

Secondly, people sought to relativize their own actions by referring to the wartime context ('Where wood is chopped, there splinters will fall') or proclaiming that the other side had been no better. Hitler had himself justified the extremely brutal warfare by suggesting that the enemy, especially the 'barbaric'

Christiane Wienand, 'Reverberations of a Disturbing Past: Reconciliation Activities of Young West Germans in the 1960s and 1970s', in *Reverberations of Nazi Violence*, ed. Bird, 215–32; Johannes Becke, 'German Guilt and Hebrew Redemption: *Aktion Sühnezeichen Friedensdienste* and the Legacy of Left-Wing Protestant Philozionism', in *Jews and Protestants: From the Reformation to the Present*, ed. Irene Aue-Ben David et al. (Berlin: De Gruyter, 2020), 241–55; Jonathan Huener, 'Antifascist Pilgrimage and Rehabilitation at Auschwitz: The Political Tourism of "Aktion Sühnezeichen" and "Sozialistische Jugend"', *German Studies Review* 24, no. 3 (2001): 513–32.

[8] Mary Fulbrook, 'Reframing the Past: Justice, Guilt, and Consolidation in East and West Germany after Nazism', *Central European History* 53, no. 2 (2020): 294–313.

Soviet Union, was doing even worse. The mass rapes by the Red Army as well as the nuclear bombing of two Japanese cities by the USA in the summer of 1945 provided new ammunition for this argument.

Most of all, however, people weighed their own suffering against what they had inflicted upon others. In view of the hundreds of thousands killed by bombs and the millions of expellees and refugees, it was easy to perceive and pity oneself as a victim. When Adenauer's government agreed under international pressure in 1952 to deliver goods worth 3 billion Deutsche Mark to Israel and allocate 450 million Deutsche Mark to Jewish organizations, the public was taken aback. Most considered such reparations an 'annoyance' and reacted with the 'tenacious resistance of sluggish and obdurate hearts', as the CDU parliamentarian Franz Böhm put it.[9] Hearts opened, instead, towards their own war victims – widows and orphans, disabled veterans, those bombed or chased out of their homes – whose provision was seen as the clear priority.

In the GDR, views were not so different. Among the victims of the Nazi regime, communist 'anti-fascist resistance fighters' came first and received comparatively high honorary pensions. Sinti and Roma were left, as in the Federal Republic, empty-handed; the same held true for homosexuals. Jewish property for which there were no local heirs fell to the state. Not a single penny flowed to Israel. In April 1990, the last East German parliament – the first decided by free elections – asked forgiveness from 'all Jews around the world', and apologized to the Israeli people for the 'hypocrisy and hostility in the official GDR policy'.[10]

Remembering the Victims

At this time, the list of victim groups who were entitled to compensation had long since been expanded in West Germany. The year 1979 marked a sea change, and the dam with which the 'nation of the perpetrators' had shielded themselves from confrontation with the Jewish victims finally started to burst. Millions sat in front of the television watching the American mini-series

---

[9] Franz Böhm, 'Wie besiegen wir die Trägheit des Herzens?', *Frankfurter Allgemeine Zeitung*, 13 January 1955, 2.

[10] Hans Günter Hockerts, '*Wiedergutmachung* in Germany: Balancing Historical Accounts 1945-2000', in *Restitution and Memory: Material Restoration in Europe*, ed. Dan Diner and Gotthart Wunberg (New York: Berghahn, 2007), 323–81; Constantin Goschler, *Schuld und Schulden: Die Politik der Wiedergutmachung für NS-Verfolgte seit 1945* (Göttingen: Wallstein, 2005); Constantin Goschler, 'Disputed Victims: The West German Discourse on Restitution for the Victims of Nazism', in *Historical Justice in International Perspective: How Societies Are Trying to Right the Wrongs of the Past*, ed. Manfred Berg and Bernd Schäfer (Cambridge: Cambridge University Press, 2009), 93–110; Angelika Timm, 'The Burdened Relationship between the GDR and the State of Israel', *Israel Studies* 2, no. 1 (1997): 22–49, quote 43.

Figure 47   The practice of remembering: *Stolpersteine*, or 'stumbling stones', are installed in Berlin's Friedrichstrasse, where Jewish victims of Nazi genocide lived (John MacDougall/AFP via Getty Images)

Holocaust and following the Weiss family's dire fate from Berlin to the Warsaw ghetto, from the Buchenwald concentration camp to Auschwitz. Quite a few subsequently turned in tears to the producers, giving their shame and grief free expression. Only a small minority persisted with the pointed deflection of shame.[11]

The memorialization drive of the 1980s, then, did what the first federal president had called for in the 1950s: it sought to overcome shame through 'counteraction'. Local citizens worked to preserve the traces of the Jewish men, women and children who had been forced out of Germany or killed after 1933. Many cities established sites of remembrance. Moreover, they invited survivors and their descendants to visit their former homeland and bade them a sincere welcome.

That active remembrance had suddenly become a matter close to the heart was largely due to generational change (Figure 47). Three or four decades after the end of the war, a new generation held sway who had no personal

---

[11] Julius H. Schoeps, 'The Emotional Impact of the Broadcast of *Holocaust* in the Federal Republic (1979)', https://ghdi.ghi-dc.org/sub_document.cfm?document_id=1155, accessed 9 March 2022.

experience or involvement with National Socialism. When Chancellor Helmut Kohl stated in 1985 that 'We as Germans acknowledge our shame, our responsibility before history', he could be sure of broad assent. The 'mercy of late birth' to which he often referred enabled those born after 1945 to look at Nazi history in a more distanced and objective way. The shame against which the older generation had armoured themselves no longer burnt the younger's skin.[12]

This was reflected in political semantics. As early as 1955, President Heuss had associated '1945' not only with the 'destruction of centuries-long state and national history', but also with the 'feeling of being liberated' from deceit, despotism and violence. Yet it was not until thirty years later that Richard von Weizsäcker first made liberation the sole focus, when he spoke on the fortieth anniversary of German capitulation. He thereby sent a radical political message accompanied by a firm statement against any and every form of softening and relativizing National Socialism.

This statement seemed all the more impressive because the 1920-born Weizsäcker belonged to an age cohort who had spent their formative years in the 'Third Reich'. Weizsäcker himself had been a highly decorated Wehrmacht officer; his father, a top diplomat, had been convicted of crimes against humanity in Nuremberg. That he now, as president, self-critically scrutinized his generation was somewhat unexpected. His 1985 verdict was succinct: even if they had not been directly involved in the planning and enactment of genocide, they could not have remained unsuspecting or ignorant. He clearly did not want to exonerate himself and his contemporaries from individual and collective failure.

As he memorialized the war casualties and the victims of Nazi terror, Weizsäcker named the murdered Jews first. He then remembered Soviet and Polish victims, before turning to German soldiers. Sinti and Roma, homosexuals, disabled people and those who had undergone forced sterilization were also mentioned. Expanding the victim groups was not mere lip service. It also meant paying compensation and securing justice, material as well as immaterial, for the men and women who had been deprived of their dignity, health and lives by the Nazi state and its 'willing executioners'.

Responsibility, Liability and External Shame

The notion of shame no longer loomed in Weizsäcker's 1985 speech. Instead, he spoke of responsibility, which he also assigned to 'young people'. They were 'not responsible for what happened over forty years ago. But they are responsible for the historical consequences' – and for ensuring that it was not

---

[12] Eitz and Stötzel, *Wörterbuch*, 388.

forgotten.[13] Such responsibility, though, did not come without shame. In modern understanding, a person feels shame not only for their own actions but also for the actions of people with whom they are in some way connected: friends, relatives or, more generally, fellow members of a community or nation. Shame for others (*Fremdschämen*) entered the *Duden* dictionary in 2009 as a kind of extended self-shame: those who a person is ashamed of have transgressed against that person's 'self-value' or 'ideal norm'.[14] Shame, as a social emotion, follows both the evaluative gaze of others and one's own conscience, including the standards and expectations a person sets for themselves and for those close to them.

This was how President Steinmeier used the word in 2019: as personal and societal shame in the face of an antisemitism that, after 1945, was no longer supposed to have a place in Germany. Fifty years earlier, philosopher Herbert Marcuse had spoken of shame similarly and yet differently. While celebrating the revolts of the student youth movement on both sides of the Atlantic as a departure from a social and psychological system of oppression, he lauded the rebelling students as men and women 'who do not have to be ashamed of themselves anymore'. In his view, they had 'learned not to identify themselves with the false fathers who have built and tolerated and forgotten the Auschwitzs and Vietnams'. As a result, they would be able to prevent the recommencement of such crimes.[15]

Was Marcuse's diagnosis correct? As German post-war history in the East and West amply demonstrates, it is impossible to break away from one's generational ties and bonds. Those who distance themselves from their guilty fathers still assume liability for their deeds and failures. Even if there is nothing that one personally has to feel ashamed of, shame for the shameful acts of elders remains. Marcuse's notion that the young generation possessed enough inner freedom to transform the world into a state of paradise free of shame thus sounded all too optimistic.

Shame as Repression

It did, however, fit a time that had no shortage of liberation utopias. People wanted to liberate and emancipate themselves, not least from shame, which they regarded as a first-rate instrument of social repression. In focus, though,

[13] https://bit.ly/3KCWzxl, accessed 9 February 2022.

[14] The philosopher Max Scheler spoke of 'self-value' in 1913; it was the precondition for shame, which he also assigned to the '*feelings of ourselves*' (italics in original; Max Scheler, 'Shame and Feelings of Modesty', in *Person and Self-Value: Three Essays*, trans. Manfred S. Frings (Dordrecht: Martinus Nijhoff, 1987), 1–86; here 38, 15).

[15] Herbert Marcuse, 'The New Sensibility', in Herbert Marcuse, *An Essay on Liberation* (Boston, MA: Beacon Press, 1969), 24–25.

was less the shame of parents and their politics during Nazism and more the shame used to control the young and train them into conformity. Anyone who violated the shame-reinforcing norms of good conduct experienced shaming. This began in the nursery and continued into church pews and workplaces, practised by priests as well as parents, teachers and superiors. Drumming shame into those who behaved inappropriately ensured social compliance and obedience.

The power of shame and shaming was felt acutely by girls and young women, and they were the first to rebel against it. 'The shame is over', feminists started declaring in the late 1960s. They refused to be ashamed of anything and everything to do with their bodies. And they demanded that women, too, be given the freedom to explore their sexuality in line with their own desires, instead of adjusting to traditional moral standards (> Love).[16]

During the nineteenth century, these standards had become considerably stricter and more rigid. Religious as well as secular authorities strongly believed in the natural shamefacedness of the female sex and made sure that women respected, at all times and in all places, the boundaries drawn by nature and fortified by state and society. An 1874 pedagogical handbook stated that, as 'the female soul and mind' was 'by nature' designed for shamefacedness, 'we make particularly high demands on the female in this respect'. Shame was meant to determine the way women clothed themselves, chose their words and directed their gaze downwards; above all it was to be demonstrated in the 'sexual domain', in the preservation of 'chastity' and 'modesty'. In 1956, a Catholic lexicon extolled feelings of shame and honour as 'essential driving forces of the human soul', whereby the feeling of shame lay closer to 'female reserve'; the feeling of honour, to 'male vigour'. Female shame was therefore connected with passive avoidance and caution, while male > honour proved itself in active engagement.[17]

These stereotypes fed a double standard of morality that granted men far greater freedom than women. From early on, girls were accosted with lessons about indecent glances and worse. Mothers told their daughters to feel ashamed of every speck on their blouse, every tear in their skirt, every loose

---

[16] In 1976, the German translation of the book *The Shame Is Over* by Dutch author Anja Meulenbelt was published by a feminist press; by 1995, it had received sixteen editions. Back in 1913, Scheler had seen the 'sexual shame' of women as stemming 'from tradition' and thereby referenced the formative influence of familial socialization; at the same time, though, he considered it a 'natural' fact (Scheler, 'Shame and Feelings of Modesty', 20, 30).

[17] *Handwörterbuch für den Deutschen Volksschullehrer*, ed. E. Petzold (Dresden: Schulbuchhandlung, 1874), 149–50; *Der Große Herder*, 5th ed., vol. 8 (Freiburg: Herder, 1956), 181.

strand of hair, every pimple on their forehead. Being 'slatternly' was a devastating judgement. If a young woman strayed from the path of bourgeois respectability, she was considered a harlot, whore or 'fallen woman'. There was no direct male equivalent – except when a man was openly homosexual and brought disgrace upon his family.

Rebelling against the gendered shame-diktat, as women did around 1970, was not the end of it. The repressive function of shame and shaming showed up in many social domains and met with increasing discontent. Pupils refused to accept a staple of classroom shaming, standing in the corner, and turned it into an ironic performance. Adolescents and young adults confidently flouted 'decent' dress codes and thumbed their nose at good society's disapproval and > disgust. Intergenerational communication took on a new tone that older people found disrespectful and tactless. What they embraced as valid standards of propriety were deliberately disregarded by younger men and women who, on top of this, resisted any attempt to make them feel ashamed of such transgression.

A Shameless Society?

For some observers, this resulted in a shameless society that prioritized selfish gratification over civilized behaviour. Even if they disparaged shaming as a practice of control, they regretted the decline of social shame, which they saw as a necessary corrective to individual misbehaviour and bad manners. In their view, boundless greed, corruption, tax fraud, elbowing tactics and rampant ruthlessness mirrored the loss of the sense of shame. Similarly, the cultural revolutionaries of the 1960s and 1970s who slated shame as reactionary and repressive were accused of damaging civilization's roots and jeopardizing social cohesion.[18]

From today's perspective, such doom-laden warnings sound shrill and overstated. Certainly, social regulations and conventions have been relaxed, owing to what sociologists call informalization and liberalization. There is no doubt that the authority of teachers and elders has suffered, and their rather timid attempts at shaming often prove futile. At the same time, contemporary youth culture has by no means swept away all rules and established an anarchistic state of *anything goes*. Peer groups define and follow their own concepts of appropriate and accepted behaviour, and their members know. Regardless of all the coolness and nonconformity on display, they abide by unwritten terms and guidelines, the transgression of which is bound to trigger

---

[18] American proponents of this view included, among others, Eric Hoffer, 'Long Live Shame!', *The New York Times*, 18 October 1974, 41 (Hoffer was a popular moral philosopher) and the New York psychoanalyst Henry Lowenfeld, 'Notes on Shamelessness', *The Psychoanalytic Quarterly* 45 (1976): 62–72.

shame sanctions. It was no different in the supposedly shameless generation of 1968. Anyone who eschewed the clothing style, skirted the rituals of flat-sharing and wore a wedding ring instead of enjoying free sexuality sensed the effects of collective disdain. As a result, they either felt ashamed and conformed, or left the group and looked for another.

That it has become possible to question and switch group affiliations is one of the achievements of late-modern liberal societies. They offer their members unprecedented space for individual freedom and decision-making and thus inevitably weaken the power of the collective. With this, shame has not altogether disappeared. But it has lost its central place and mandatory grammar. Neither religion and the church nor secular institutions like schools or professions are in a position to set generally binding rules and impose authoritative standards. Their ability to assign shame has suffered in turn.

Shamers and Their Motives

They are replaced by a large number of social stakeholders who, for their part, want to stipulate which behaviour is morally upstanding and which deserves to be shamed. Since they imagine themselves to be in possession of the correct morality, they feel justified in publicly rebuking others. They, too, trust in shame's power to manufacture conformity to rules. In a liberal, highly indi-vidualized society, however, the enforcement of such rules usually meets with fierce resistance.

Morality-driven political struggles and campaigns are a novelty of recent years. Not coincidentally, at least three new shame-words emerged in German in 2019: *Fleischscham* ('Meat-shame'), *Flugscham* ('Flight-shame') and *Kinderscham* ('Children-shame'). *Fleischscham* befalls those who damage the climate through their meat consumption. *Flugscham* is experienced by travellers who have a guilty conscience when they enlarge their personal carbon footprint through frequent flying, or who have this guilty conscience impressed upon them by the young activists of the Fridays for Future movement.

Environmental issues have been widely discussed since the 1970s; the 1980-founded Green Party has made a pivotal and enduring contribution. Still, the massive consequences of global warming have only lately penetrated general consciousness. At the same time, the field of action has shifted. Whereas the focus used to be on abstract causalities – acid rain, pesticides or CFC-based propellants – criticism is now directed towards the concrete lifestyles and behaviours of each and every individual that cause and exacerbate global warming. To achieve change, climate activists rely on information and know-ledge – and on shame.

Among the factors that irreparably damage and destroy the environment, some even count childbearing. Anti-natalist philosophers, as well as women who go on ecologically motivated 'birth strike', designate abstaining from procreation as the moral order of the day. At a minimum, they demand that the number of children – already low in Europe – be reduced even further. In their view, those who act differently are sinning against the world's climate and should be ashamed. This is what the neologism *Kinderscham* denotes (> Hope).[19]

As these examples show, shame continues to be in vogue despite all efforts to banish it from society and permit everyone a shame-free way of life according to their own liking. Even the social movements and stakeholders that locate themselves on the left or liberal side of the political spectrum use shame and shaming as political weapons and engines for desired change.

Meanwhile, most incidents of shaming that circulate on social media are not explicitly political. But they are enormously effective. It is primarily young girls and women who serve as targets, as the female body still appears superbly suited to invoking and being instilled with shame. The popular model cult has hugely raised the bar for perfection. This is demonstrated by television shows like *Germany's Next Top Model*, which have been enjoying consistently high viewing figures since 2006, or by the latest wave of so-called influencers who thanks to Photoshop always appear slender and symmetrical. People who fail to fit the ideal measurements receive derisive comments; shame follows swiftly after.

People feel shame for other reasons as well. In a society whose self-image revolves around performance and accomplishments and in which self-optimization has, since the late twentieth century, been determining individual happiness, it is easy to feel shame when one's own achievements fall short of expectations. In the GDR it was not so much personally attributable effort but rather the work done collectively that decided a person's fate and assigned them their life chances. When millions of East Germans were put out of work after 1990, they also lost their sense of > belonging. Many reacted with shame, which could translate into > anger and resentment.

In the former West, quite a few families have been living on benefits for several generations without being ashamed. For others who have accepted and internalized society's performance norms, this would be unthinkable. If they ever found themselves in hardship, they would likely belong to the 'shame-faced poor' who hide their unfortunate situation for as long as possible. Even visiting the *Tafel*, a foodbank that since 1993 has been distributing groceries to those in need, would be shame-laden and dishonourable.

Shame has thus by no means disappeared from society. But it wears a different face from that it did a hundred years ago, has other facets and fault lines. In 1913, the philosopher Max Scheler wrote that people were ashamed

---

[19] Meredith Haaf, 'Kinderscham statt Kinderschar', *Süddeutsche Zeitung*, 13 September 2019, 13. On the 'BirthStrike movement' see e.g. http://bit.ly/3SywmC2, accessed 9 February 2022.

not only of their obvious mistakes but also of their virtues; exhibiting such merits apparently aroused even 'deeper and purer shame'.[20] This is far from the case today. Anyone applying for a new job or scholarship is prompted and coached to emphasize their unique selling points. Boasting about personal achievements and skills may not necessarily make someone a popular figure, but it is certainly no cause for shame.

What has also changed is the hierarchy and direction of shaming. Around 1900, it was rarely possible to trigger shame at the top of society from below. A worker could not shame his superior, nor a wife her husband, nor a child an adult. Shaming functioned only from a position of power, and shame was usually felt by the powerless. Over the course of the twentieth century, this has levelled out. In 2012, the employees of an insolvent drugstore chain shouted 'shame on you' at the owners. The 20,000-plus women who suddenly found themselves without work or income were not ashamed. Instead, they shamed those who bore responsibility for the situation and who had fallen short.

[20] Scheler, 'Shame and Feelings of Modesty', 20.

~

Solidarity

On 11 March 2020, as the events of the COVID-19 pandemic were unfolding and the authorities were announcing new measures to contain the extremely contagious virus on an almost hourly basis, Chancellor Angela Merkel addressed German citizens on television. She urged them to protect older people and those with pre-existing conditions in particular because they were most at risk from the virus: 'This is a test for our solidarity, our common sense and care for each other.'[1]

Solidarity and Brotherhood

Linking solidarity with care and common sense accurately illustrates the semantic field in which the term and the associated practice developed historically. In legal matters, solidarity initially meant only that debtors who had made a contractual commitment were jointly liable and vouched for each other ('all for one'). When the socialist workers' movement started using it in the early 1860s, the term fused rationality and emotion, common sense and care. At the time, socialist Johann Philipp Becker summarized solidarity as 'systematic total liability' including 'common property, cooperative production, management and beneficial use'. Solidarity was, he added, a 'brotherhood of deeds' that clearly differentiated itself from any 'brotherhood of words' as privileged by bourgeois circles.[2]

Brotherhood here described not only a narrow range of family ties but above all a caring and fond relationship. The fact that relatives and even brothers could be deadly enemies was well-known from the Old Testament. But the idea that people should act like good brothers to one another also had religious roots. Notably, the Pietist congregations of the eighteenth century

---

[1] 'Angela Merkel Calls for Solidarity', 11 March 2020, www.bundesregierung.de/breg-en/news/merkel-zu-corona-1729906, accessed 17 March 2022; Arjen Boin et al., *Governing the Pandemic: The Politics of Navigating a Mega-Crisis* (Cham: Palgrave Macmillan, 2021), 65.

[2] Wolfgang Schieder, 'Brüderlichkeit', in *Geschichtliche Grundbegriffe*, ed. Otto Brunner et al., vol. 1 (Stuttgart: Klett-Cotta, 1972), 552–81, here 579.

exercized brotherly love as an inclusive Christian practice. As a secular concept, brotherhood first emerged with the Freemasons and in 1786 found its way into Friedrich Schiller's 'Ode to Joy'. The poet's brotherly kiss was meant for the whole world, his embrace for the millions. When Ludwig van Beethoven set the ode to music in his ninth and last symphony, which premiered in 1824, he accentuated the line 'All people shall be brothers'. It suited a period in which many dreamt of a new cosmopolitan order that, as the poet Christoph Martin Wieland put it in 1770, would make 'a brotherhood of men of all the nations of the earth'.[3]

Wieland's hope was shared by some of the French revolutionaries who toppled the old order in 1789 and set about building a society under the maxim *Liberté, égalité, fraternité*. In the military campaigns that followed, the desire to export *fraternité* and let other peoples benefit from it was professed. But since the French armies usually acted as imperial occupying forces rather than as brothers, *fraternité* was not welcomed. Nevertheless, the term migrated into the German language and was translated as *Bruderliebe* (brotherly love) or *Brüderlichkeit* (brotherhood). In 1801, the educator Joachim Heinrich Campe understood it as meaning the 'brotherly ethos and brotherly conduct' of those who were, in one way or another, closely connected.[4]

International, National, Social Levels of Solidarity

The convergence of ethos and conduct, of feeling and practice gave the term a political career in which different meanings mixed. Firstly, there was the cosmopolitan interpretation favoured by the Philhellenic and pro-Polish associations of the early nineteenth century. Their members actively supported the liberation struggles of the Greeks (against the Ottoman Empire) and the Poles (against Russia), and offered refugees shelter and support. The Young Europe movement, which the liberal revolutionary Giuseppe Mazzini launched in 1834 with representatives from Italy, Poland and Germany, likewise committed itself to the 'brotherhood of nations'.

Alongside these international perspectives emerged a national one, which had already been visible and palpable during the French Revolution. In 1789, Campe had, 'not without emotion', noticed in Paris the 'peaceful, friendly and affectionate conduct of the liberated French towards each other'. Such an attitude of brotherhood allegedly encompassed all members of the French nation, overcoming social or religious barriers of any kind. This was the spirit in which those gathered on 14 July 1790 at the Parisian Champ de Mars for the

---

[3] Ibid., 560–65.
[4] Joachim Heinrich Campe, *Wörterbuch zur Erklärung und Verdeutschung der unserer Sprache aufgedrungenen fremden Ausdrücke*, vol. 2 (Braunschweig: Schulbuchhandlung, 1801), 375.

anniversary celebration of the storming of the Bastille swore to remain united
with all French citizens by 'the indissoluble bonds of brotherhood'. In 1832,
the liberal-democratic Hambach Festival saw Germans 'united as brothers'.
The emotionally charged image of brotherhood referred to the creation of a
nation that would transcend social or regional differences and embrace all
citizens as equal.

It obtained a different hue during and after the 1848 revolution. When
numerous workers' associations across Germany joined forces to establish the
General German Brotherhood of Workers, this indeed became a supra-local
and supra-regional movement. It intended, furthermore, to bridge the divides
between the various professions even though civil servants, merchants and
employers were excluded from the brotherhood. Women were also supposed
to stay out, a view young activist Louise Otto criticized in a friendly but firm
manner. In a public missive she reminded the brotherhood of workers that
'you have *sisters*', who were suffering under 'the dominance of capital' as well.
Back in 1801, Campe had pointed to the possibility that brotherhood could be
accompanied by a 'sisterhood' fostering equivalent attitudes and modes of
behaviour among the female sex. But when a lady from a middle-class family
like Otto's stood up for working women and treated them as her 'poor sisters',
she clearly violated the principles of the new workers' organization, which
emphasized collective self-help and autonomy. Consequently, Louise Otto
turned away from the male brotherhood to found, in 1849, a *Women's
Newspaper* under the motto 'Sisters, unite with me' and, in 1865, the first
general women's association.[5]

For Mutuality

Meanwhile, the male association actively set about 'building a strong union
that, grounded in mutuality and brotherhood, is to connect the rights and wills
of individuals into one body, joining work and benefits'. Workers were advised
to organize, above all, in the production cooperatives that had been developing
since the 1850s. Their members were meant to operate and make decisions
collectively, and share the profits – which usually did not last long.
Substantially more successful were the retail and housing cooperatives. They
existed well into the second half of the twentieth century (and are currently
undergoing a revival). Many were called 'Solidarity' and carried their moral-
political agenda in their name.[6]

---

[5] Louise Otto, 'Sendschreiben an alle "Verbrüderten" [1848]', in *"Dem Reich der Freiheit
  werb' ich Bürgerinnen": Die Frauen-Zeitung von Louise Otto*, ed. Ute Gerhard et al.
  (Frankfurt: Syndikat, 1980), 57–58.
[6] Schieder, 'Brüderlichkeit', 575; Christiane Eisenberg, *Frühe Arbeiterbewegung und
  Genossenschaften* (Bonn: Neue Gesellschaft, 1985); Christiane Eisenberg, 'Working Class

So, solidarity actually became, as demanded by Becker, a brotherhood of deeds. At the start, it was still largely used synonymously with *Brüderlichkeit* but gradually supplanted the older term. Following socialist doctrine, it was based upon common interests that arose from a shared class position. And it was expressed in collective undertakings 'for mutuality'. These could be retail cooperatives or cycling leagues, like the one founded in 1896 under the name 'Solidarity'. Since 1912, it has organized bicycle manufacturing and fought for 'Truth, Freedom, Brotherhood'; it still exists today (Figure 48).

Solidarity was particularly necessary when it came to protecting people from risk. Not for nothing did all nineteenth-century workers' associations and trade unions affiliate themselves with relief funds that members paid into in order to receive financial subsidies in the event of illness or unemployment. The contributions, often graded in line with income, financed equal benefits for everyone in need.

Early fire insurance as well as state insurance systems, which have been established and expanded since the 1880s, functioned according to the same principle. In addition, the government made employers liable and required them to cover one third of their workforce's health insurance, while being the sole payer of accident insurance fees and contributing an equal share to occupational pension schemes. This meant spreading the financial impact of workers becoming ill and disabled across multiple shoulders and added another layer of solidarity to the original group-based concept.

It also sent a political message, in that workers and 'capitalists' moved closer together, on a national scale. In contrast, the international perspective of workers' solidarity receded into the background. In 1889, on the centenary of the French Revolution, delegates from twenty states met in London for an international socialist congress. One of their resolutions was to designate 1 May a global day of struggle for the working classes. In 1910, International Women's Day was added; both have continued to the present day in Germany, as in many other countries. Commitments to a solidarity that transcended individual nation-states did not, however, alter the fact that the Socialist International broke apart during the First World War. Partly autonomously, partly under state pressure, parties sided with their respective governments and prioritized national solidarity.

Not only in Germany was this war touted as a shared experience in which the nation would overcome all differences. 'I no longer know parties, I only know Germans': this is how Kaiser Wilhelm II summarized the promise and necessity of national unity and consensus. Yet, before long, conflicts and

and Middle Class Associations: An Anglo-German Comparison, 1820–1870', in *Bourgeois Society in Nineteenth-Century Europe*, ed. Jürgen Kocka and Allan Mitchell (Oxford: Berg, 1993), 151–78; Klaus Novy and Michael Prinz, *Illustrierte Geschichte der Gemeinwirtschaft* (Berlin: Dietz, 1985), 22.

Figure 48 Setting things in motion: postcards by the proletarian cyclist league Solidarity, ca. 1900 (Radfahrerbund)

tensions arose about the war's aims as well as the distribution of scarce resources and the question of whether all sections of the population had contributed equally to the war's costs and sacrifices. Tensions culminated in the revolution of November 1918, which right-wing circles defamed as a 'stab in the back' of the supposedly undaunted and undefeated army. These accusations were a heavy burden for the new, post-revolutionary state to bear.

Solidarity in the Weimar Welfare State

Nonetheless, the republic started strong and with an ambitious social agenda that was fundamentally shaped by the SPD. Solidarity as ethos, emotional attitude and practice, fostered primarily in the social democratic labour force, was now intended to hold for the whole of society. Everyone was entitled to expect it from everyone else by virtue of common citizenship and belonging to the German nation-state. This transformed both the basic concept of solidarity and its vernacular architecture. If class-based solidarity was a wilful commitment that one entered into intentionally and voluntarily, then national solidarity was something people were born into – whether they liked it or not. Moreover, in the trade union and cooperative movements, solidarity functioned on an equal footing: all members were in need of and eligible for it. With state-wide solidarity, however, the stronger were meant to take responsibility for the weaker. Glimpses of such a practice had previously been visible in the 1890s, when the Prussian government introduced a progressive system of income tax. The more wealthy were assessed at a higher tax rate than the poor and contributed correspondingly more to the financing of governmental responsibilities.

In the Weimar Republic, those responsibilities underwent a considerable expansion. The state henceforth took charge not only of the country's internal administration and external security, but also of supporting citizens who could not help themselves. The constitution ruled in no uncertain terms that every German was obliged 'to earn his livelihood through efficient work', but 'insofar as appropriate employment opportunities for him cannot be established, his necessary sustenance will be provided for'. Such provision normally happened through insurance; in 1927, unemployment insurance was added to the branches of social insurance that had existed since the late nineteenth century, with its contributions paid jointly by employees and employers.

The Weimar state added yet another dimension to its welfare policies by pledging all citizens a 'dignified existence'. For this purpose, it constructed a complex, graded communal system of public welfare that assessed individual need and provided support. The system was funded from the tax pool, into which the middle and upper classes paid significantly more in percentage terms than the lower classes. Here, too, solidarity proved itself a 'brotherhood of deeds', this time at a macrosocial level. Simultaneously, though, solidarity shrank to an abstract, emotionally empty principle. Cast in laws and regulations and impersonally executed by a well-ordered bureaucracy, it lost its 'human face'. The feeling of connectedness, of a brotherly and affectionate spirit, that Campe had so admired in the Paris of 1789, drifted away from the modern welfare state – even though it had inspired its creation.

Catholic Solidarity and Nazi Community

It had also spurred Catholic social thought since the beginning of the twentieth century. Known as the founder of solidarism (*Solidarismus*) in Germany, the Jesuit Heinrich Pesch (1854–1926) distanced himself both from liberal notions centring the individual and their 'own gain', and from socialism, which celebrated the collective of equals and the concept of class struggle. Instead, he envisioned a society where every person and social group contributed to 'securing the well-being of the whole and its weaker parts'. Such solidarity, which was directed towards 'public welfare and the general common good', was conceived of as greater and broader than the solidarity of individual associations like trade unions or cooperatives. As a 'social principle of law' it formed, as Pesch's influential student Oswald von Nell-Breuning outlined, one of two crucial 'building blocks' of society (the other was subsidiarity or 'helpful assistance'). In 1931, Nell-Breuning was instrumental in co-writing the papal social encyclical that stressed the equivalence of capital and labour, emphasized the mutual responsibility (i.e. solidarity) of all members of society, and stipulated the social obligations of property.[7]

Eleven years later, *Meyers Lexikon* set the doctrine of solidarism in stark opposition to National Socialism, which was purportedly achieving 'social levelling through a socialism of the national community, based on blood and soil'. Since solidarity was traded as a Marxist-communist catchword, it hardly ever appeared in the vocabulary of the 'Third Reich', which preferred to speak of the racially defined unit of the *Volksgemeinschaft*. Nazi ideology and political practice deliberately restricted solidarity to this 'people's community' and its best interest. What counted was not what the individual wanted but what was good and useful for the *Volk*: 'You are nothing, your *Volk* is everything' was drilled into children from an early age. A great many citizens found the message of community highly attractive.[8]

---

[7] Heinrich Pesch, 'Solidarismus', in *Stimmen aus Maria-Laach: Katholische Blätter* 63 (1902): 38–60, 307–24; Oswald von Nell-Breuning, *Baugesetze der Gesellschaft: Solidarität und Subsidiarität* (Freiburg: Herder, 1990). See also Jonas Hagedorn, *Oswald von Nell-Breuning SJ: Aufbrüche der katholischen Soziallehre in der Weimarer Republik* (Paderborn: Schöningh, 2018).

[8] Michael Wildt, '*Volksgemeinschaft*: A Modern Perspective on National Socialist Society', in *Visions of Community in Nazi Germany: Social Engineering and Private Lives*, ed.

Back in the Weimar period, quite a few had bemoaned the nation's inner turmoil and fragmentation in letters to the president. As early as 1919, Friedrich Ebert received correspondence from Richard Walter in Berlin, who introduced himself as a 'stiff-collar proletarian' and ex-soldier. He urged Ebert to teach the people an important lesson: they should 'not only appear to reach out a brotherly hand over all differences of religion, regional origin and party affiliation, but henceforth feel truly brotherly, so that never again will one be the fiend of the other, but instead the supporter of the other'. Ebert expressed his thanks and suggested that Walter play his part 'through appropriate elucidation in the social circles accessible to you'.

In 1932, the Social Democrat Theodor Kretschmann from Wesermünde told President Paul von Hindenburg why he would vote for him in the upcoming election: 'I do not disavow my political ideology, but in the nation's current distress and danger, I feel first and foremost German. A person who still privileges the party over the unity of the people is not worthy of being a German. Only in consensus and unity do I see the assurance of liberation from the monstrous burdens, and of economic recovery.' A former captain by the name of Breucker, who served as director of a Bonn-based dynamite company, voiced similar sentiments while making no secret of his right-wing conservative stance. 'I have experienced, in many years of cooperation with our labour force whose national thinking has been strengthened by foreign occupation, how bitterly necessary unity between all social classes – for which Your Excellency has always campaigned with the entire strength of your personality – is for our country's rise and advancement.' Another letter writer from Lübeck wished that 'as in 1914, all Germans would come together in one *Volksgemeinschaft* and unanimously strive towards reconstruction'.[9]

National Socialism placed this *Volksgemeinschaft* at the centre of its propaganda and politics, promising an end to class struggle and enforcing the cooperation of all workers of 'mind and fist', together with their employers. And it did not stop at promises. Symbolically and practically, it sought to orchestrate social unity and equality and make them visible for all to see and feel. Elaborate festivals were organized, starting with 1 May 1933, the traditional day of the socialist workers' movement, which was henceforth a paid 'holiday of national work'. Minister of Propaganda Joseph Goebbels staged it as a 'magnificent demonstration of the people's will'. In Berlin, over a million

---

Martina Steber and Bernhard Gotto (Oxford: Oxford University Press, 2014), 43–59; Michael Wildt, 'Volksgemeinschaft: A Controversy', in *Beyond the Racial State: Rethinking Nazi Germany*, ed. Devin O. Pendas et al. (Cambridge: Cambridge University Press, 2017), 317–34.

[9] Federal Archive Berlin, R 601, no. 370: Richard Walter, 12 February 1919; reply, 22 February 1919; no. 378: Theodor Kretschmann, 20 February 1932; Breucker, 2 March 1932; no. 380: Wolf von Waldenburg, 10 March 1932.

men, women and children took part in the 'mass event': 'worker and bourgeois, high and low, employer and subordinate, now the differences are
obliterated, only one German people marches', Goebbels noted euphorically
in his diary. 'Here nobody can exclude himself, here we all belong together,
and it is no longer just a phrase: we have become a single *Volk* of brothers.'[10]

Things were also supposed to be fraternal in the German Labour Front,
which after the destruction of the trade unions claimed to represent the 'real
national and economic community of all Germans' as a united federation of
blue- and white-collar workers and their employers. Instead of waging class
wars and labour struggles, all members were instructed to work together. Even
the military smoothed over social hierarchies. Unlike in the German Empire,
compulsory military service, abolished in 1919 at the instigation of the victorious powers and reintroduced in 1935, no longer stipulated property and
educational privileges. Any man 'with a good military training' could now
become a reserve officer – a privilege restricted to the middle classes before
1918 – as long as they could prove their 'Aryan descent'. Social eligibility
requirements were lowered for professional officers as well.[11]

Equality and unity were also showcased in civil life, especially on Sundays.
Larger cities held public community meals where needy and well-off citizens
shared a meal from the stewpot (Figure 49). Instead of the Sunday roast,
housewives were advised to put an inexpensive dish on the table and donate
the money saved to the Winter Relief agency. Members of the Hitler Youth
and the League of German Girls went from door to door collecting donations.
This figured as the 'socialism of deeds' and initially served to alleviate the acute
hardship experienced by the unemployed and homeless. Later, the donations
filled the coffers of the National Socialist People's Welfare, whose seventeen
million members and hundreds of thousands of volunteers testified to the
solidarity of the *Volksgemeinschaft*.[12]

Yet the community had racial and social limits, which the regime demar-
cated from the very beginning. Excluded from solidarity were not only Jewish
Germans but also men and women 'alien to' or 'incapable of community'. In

[10] Joseph Goebbels, *Die Tagebücher*, ed. Elke Fröhlich, part 1, vol. 2 (Munich: Saur, 1987),
408, 413–15.

[11] Tilla Siegel, *Leistung und Lohn in der nationalsozialistischen 'Ordnung der Arbeit'*
(Opladen: Westdeutscher Verlag, 1989), 62–124; Ute Frevert, *A Nation in Barracks:
Modern Germany, Military Conscription and Civil Society*, trans. Andrew Boreham with
Daniel Brückenhaus (New York: Berg, 2004), 252–55; see also Timothy W. Mason, *Social
Policy in the Third Reich: The Working Class and the 'National Community'*, trans. John
Broadwin (Oxford: Berg, 1993), 88–108.

[12] Norbert Frei, *1945 und wir: Das Dritte Reich im Bewußtsein der Deutschen* (Munich:
C. H. Beck, 2005), 107–28; Norbert Frei, *Nationalist Socialist Rule in Germany: The
Führer State 1933–1945*, trans. Simon B. Steyne (Oxford: Blackwell, 1993), 77–83; Eckard
Hansen, *Wohlfahrtspolitik im NS-Staat* (Augsburg: Maro-Verlag, 1991).

Figure 49   *Eintopfsonntag* (stewpot Sunday): a large pot acts as a reminder of national solidarity (Photo by Imagno/Getty Images)

principle, anyone who was not healthy and performing well was deemed ballast that might endanger the 'existence of the whole people', as the president of the public health department worded it in 1939. Four years earlier, the Berlin exhibition *Miracle of Life* had used diagrams to present the threats the 'inferior' posed to the 'superior'. In mathematics lessons, pupils learnt to calculate a person's worth or, rather, worthlessness: 'According to conservative estimates', one arithmetical problem for pupils aged 11–15 stated in 1936, 'there are 300,000 mental patients, epileptics etc. in institutional care in Germany. What is the total annual cost of this at a rate of 4 Reichsmark? How many marriage loans at 1000 Reichsmark each – waiving later repayment – could be issued annually from this money?' Under the heading

'Here you take weight', a biology textbook for fifth-graders depicted a sturdy young man whose back was bending under the weight of two people with hereditary diseases.[13] The message was clear: one did not need to act in solidarity with people who were 'unworthy of life' – quite the contrary.

Volkssolidarität in the GDR

'Germans of all classes, regions and professions, join hands! United, we march into the new era,' Goebbels had demanded and declared in 1933.[14] When the march came to a standstill in 1945 and the next 'new era' dawned, the entwined hands – the traditional motif of the workers' movement for solidarity – found another application. As a symbol of the historic handshake between Social Democrats and Communists in 1946, they henceforth served as the emblem of the Socialist Unity Party (SED), which from this point on decided GDR politics.[15] Furthermore, they epitomized the various forms of solidarity that 'real socialism' would put into practice.

To start with, there was the Volkssolidarität, launched in Dresden in October 1945 'against winter hardship' and subsequently continued as a charity for the elderly. With the iconic squeeze of the hand, the newly founded parties and unions, as well as church representatives, appealed for 'brotherly help' for those suffering most from the consequences of the war. 'Everybody who still has a home' was prompted to 'give all they can spare for those who are left with nothing'. As a mass organization that profited from citizens' apparently ever-increasing 'willingness to show active solidarity', Volkssolidarität primarily attended to pensioners and veterans, providing them with 'care and belonging' and enabling them to participate in social life through clubs. As one of the few institutions that survived the end of the GDR, it is still active today in East German welfare work.[16]

Solidarity was also writ large among colleagues. In the 'socialist work collectives' there was, despite occasional feelings of > envy, little competition and lots

---

[13] Hans-Walter Schmuhl, *Rassenhygiene, Nationalsozialismus, Euthanasie: Von der Verhütung zur Vernichtung 'lebensunwerten Lebens', 1890–1945*, 2nd ed. (Göttingen: Vandenhoeck & Ruprecht, 1992), quotes 86, 175; Christina Vanja, ed., *Euthanasie in Hadamar* (Kassel: Landeswohlfahrtsverband Hessen, 1991), 20, 205. On the 'politicized pedagogy' and 'racial hygiene' in school education, see Sheila Faith Weiss, *The Nazi Symbiosis: Human Genetics and Politics in the Third Reich* (Chicago, IL: University of Chicago Press, 2010), 219–64.

[14] 'Aufruf zum 1. Mai "An das ganze deutsche Volk!"', *Berliner Morgenpost*, 25 April 1933, 1.

[15] Gottfried Korff, 'History of Symbols as Social History? Ten Preliminary Notes on the Image and Sign Systems of Social Movements in Germany', *International Review of Social History* 38, suppl. 1 (1993): 105–25, here 122–25.

[16] http://bit.ly/3SzUa8C, accessed 17 March 2022; *Neue Zeit*, 23 April 1972, 1.

of 'comradely cooperation and mutual aid'. Particularly after 1989, when many lost their jobs, this was wistfully recalled (> Nostalgia). According to an older skilled worker, who otherwise had nothing good to say about the GDR, 'we who grew up in the time of socialism were actually all colleagues. We were in the brigades, brigade life was encouraged, and it was actually a good relationship. And I would like to say that even retrospectively this still holds true.' In a 1995 survey on 'GDR nostalgia', one working mother stated that 'the team spirit among acquaintances, neighbours and colleagues' had been 'very good'. In fact, 89 per cent of respondents were convinced that solidarity, cooperation and social cohesion had been far 'stronger in the GDR than it is today'.[17]

The regime had also placed great value on international solidarity. As a member of the socialist bloc, it supported 'anti-imperialist' states, movements and individuals such as the African American civil rights activist Angela Davis, who in 1970 was imprisoned in the USA. The SED immediately started a large-scale solidarity campaign with demonstrations, fundraising drives and postcards printed with roses sent to the admired 'freedom fighter' in jail. This went down particularly well with young people. When Davis visited East Berlin in 1972 after her acquittal, 50,000 youngsters welcomed her with chants of 'Peace, Freedom, Solidarity'; official sources had expected 2,000–3,000 to turn up. At the World Festival of Youth and Students, which in 1973 took place in East Berlin under the slogan 'For anti-imperialist solidarity, peace and friendship', Angela Davis was a celebrated guest of honour (Figure 50). Expressly crediting the postcards of solidarity and protest letters with playing an important role in her release, she reinforced her fans' feelings of having done the right thing in the right state.[18]

Not all solidarity campaigns were met with such requited love. In 1971, an SED party member complained that the Vietnam and other 'solidarity dona-tions' trade unionists paid every month out of their own pocket were 'not voluntary but compulsory'. Factual obligation, however, precluded 'personal desire'. If solidarity was not a heartfelt matter but rather a 'voluntary coercion', then it lost its emotional value and became just empty words.

Over and over again, GDR citizens suggested 'devoting so-called solidarity funds to our own reconstruction'. In November 1980, one 'well-intentioned' man from Glauchau feared that, given the dire circumstances in neighbouring Poland, 'us GDR citizens would once more be saddled with a burden': 'Must we, time and again, only take responsibility for others?' In an extensive,

---

[17] Werner Schmidt, 'Metamorphosen des Betriebskollektivs', *Soziale Welt* 46, no. 3 (1995): 305–25, quote 309; 'Stolz aufs eigene Leben', *Der Spiegel*, 3 July 1995, 40–52, here 41, 49.
[18] Sophie Lorenz, 'Heroine of the Other America: The East German Solidarity Movement in Support of Angela Davis, 1970–73', in *The Routledge Handbook of the Global Sixties: Between Protest and Nation-Building*, ed. Chen Jian et al. (New York: Routledge, 2018), 548–63.

Figure 50   International solidarity in East Berlin: Angela Davis at the opening of the World Festival of Youth and Students, 1973 (Photo by ADN-Bildarchiv/ullstein bild via Getty Images)

soberly argued memorandum sent to leading SED functionaries under a pseudonym in 1981, Point 21 stated: 'Who would not be in favour of international solidarity? It is, however, dubious that our GDR donates millions of marks to Vietnam, for example, although wonderful fruit (peaches) is delivered not to the GDR but instead the FRG. Don't we need peaches?' Solidarity was thus perceived as a one-way street and a 'dupery of the masses that nobody believes in anymore'.[19]

Solidarity in the Federal Republic

Back then, the Federal Republic was still far from imposing a national obligation of solidarity on its citizens. It was not until the mid-1990s that this was officially implemented and designated as such, with 'solidarity surcharges'

[19] Siegfried Suckut, *Volkes Stimmen: 'Ehrlich, aber deutlich' – Privatbriefe an die DDR-Regierung* (Munich: dtv, 2015), 167–70, 230–32, 295, 315, 228.

(*Soli*) and 'solidarity pacts' worth billions that were to finance the 'costs of unity' and the modernization of infrastructure in the East. Before this, solidarity had been a rather galvanizing term that enjoyed particular popularity in left-wing circles. Students of the late 1960s appropriated old socialist traditions, established solidarity committees, chanted 'Here's to international solidarity' and demonstrated for Vietnam's freedom, the release of Angela Davis and the liberation movements in Zimbabwe or Mozambique. In 1973, after the military coup against the democratically elected socialist government in Chile, many people took to the streets in solidarity with the Chileans who had fled into exile. Later, they shifted their sympathies to the Sandinista Revolution in Nicaragua. Solidarity thus always had two sides: it expressed an ideological affinity with political groups and actors abroad, and it was a protest against the politics of the Federal Republic, the European colonial powers and the USA.[20]

This duality made the term highly attractive but also overloaded it and hollowed it out. Solidarity was more declaimed than actually felt. Barely anyone went as far as the 'hippy radical' and banker's son Tom Koenigs, who in 1973 gave his inheritance to the Vietcong and Chilean resistance fighters. Almost half a century later, Koenigs, who in the meantime had been a Frankfurt city treasurer for the Green Party as well as the federal government's representative for human rights policy, took on a five-year sponsorship for a Syrian refugee, acting as his legal guarantor. He remained true to his practical commitment to those in need, even if the emphasis on political solidarity had faded considerably in the intervening years. That connected him with many other members of his generation.

In any case, the West German left had never had a monopoly on sentiments and actions of solidarity. The concept had acquired a good name in Christian communities as well. Helping oppressed and endangered people at home and abroad was and is part of the self-image of church congregations, and the institution of 'church sanctuary', revived in the 1980s, would not function without the active support of individual members. For them, solidarity comprised what former generations would have called the spirit and practices of brotherhood and sisterhood respectively. Over time, solidarity had evidently extended its appeal across cultural, class and party lines.

Back in 1968, the CDU had named solidarity 'built upon a person's individual responsibility' as a pillar of Christian-Democratic politics. With the clarifying amendment, they brought on board the principle of subsidiarity, which had been equally important for Catholic social thought as developed by Nell-Breuning and others. In contrast, the SPD committed to solidarity in their

---

[20] Frank Bösch et al., eds, *Internationale Solidarität: Globales Engagement in der Bundesrepublik und der DDR* (Göttingen: Wallstein, 2018).

Godesberg Programme of 1959 as a 'mutual obligation resulting from the common bond', which ranked alongside freedom and justice as 'core values of the socialist spirit'. Although Social Democrats by then distanced themselves from class struggle and Marxist vocabulary, they kept solidarity as a traditional leitmotif and organizational principle. They saw it embodied chiefly in the trade unions, which concentrated the 'solidarity-driven, democratically controlled power' of employees. Yet, at the same time, they extended the concept and linked it, as had been rudimentarily done in the Weimar Republic, to the logic and substance of the welfare state.

Welfare State versus Civic Solidarity

The Basic Law of 1949 had already laid the foundations for a social policy that aimed to balance economically stronger and weaker segments of the population. In 1952, the Equalization of Burdens Act imposed, for reasons of 'social justice', a financial levy on the wealthy, from which expellees and refugees – including those from the GDR – were to be compensated for property losses. The pension reforms of 1957 established a new 'intergenerational contract', as from this time onwards, it was younger people still in the workforce whose contributions paid for the older generation's retirement. This also counted as a form of solidarity, and enabled pensions to substantially rise and benefit from wage growth.

Additionally, the state co-finances people's retirement schemes, as it has since Bismarck's time. Its subsidies have increased significantly in recent decades. In 2017, they amounted to 28 per cent of the federal budget and 66 per cent of the welfare budget. They are funded, as is social security spending, from tax revenue. As a result of the progressive mode of taxation, high earners contribute far more than low earners, and this likewise figures as a statement of solidarity and social justice. According to a representative survey in 2012/13, 73 per cent of the population supported the tax rate rising the more a person earns. State benefits and transfer payments received equally high levels of approval. Fairness and cooperation were expected from recipients in return; in a 2018 survey, 65 per cent agreed that a person who refused reasonable employment ought to be sanctioned for doing so. Among CDU supporters this was as high as 70 per cent, while it was still 52 per cent among SPD voters.[21]

Solidarity is evidently not limitless, but subject to certain conditions. This had also been the case for the early 'communities of solidarity' within the workers' movement. They continually and carefully checked whether those benefiting from the collectively procured support used it responsibly. When the principle of solidarity broadened and became fixed as a legal entitlement,

---

[21] http://bit.ly/3xRQOEr; http://bit.ly/3SuskKE, both accessed 17 March 2022.

social benefits were anonymized and morality taken out. From the perspective of the recipients, that had unmistakable advantages. But it had disadvantages, too: back in 1963, Chancellor Ludwig Erhard lamented the 'unfeelingness' of many citizens and their 'flight from their fellow humans'. Instead of recognizing and experiencing 'the high value of empathy, compassion and fellow joy', people referred 'to the calculated formulas of social legislation'.[22] The more responsibility the state bore for the social security of its citizens, the more civic solidarity was reduced to a financial relationship and forfeited its social and emotional binding force. When people nowadays talk so persistently of > empathy, they partly try to fill such a vacuum.

But even empathy is no panacea, at least not when it is limited to a feeling. Solidarity, as a 'brotherhood of deeds', proves itself in practice; 'ethos' and 'conduct', as per Campe, flow into each other. The fact that there is still plenty of solidarity, despite all gloomy predictions, is less apparent in everyday life than in exceptional emergency situations. When Hamburg and the surrounding area were stricken by severe flooding in 1962, the spontaneous willingness to help knew no borders. After the Oderbruch floods of 1997, the overflowing of the Elbe river in 2002 and the catastrophic flooding of 2021, citizens not only donated considerable sums of money; they also showed up in large numbers to lend a hand. And they practised 'international solidarity' completely non-ideologically as they assisted affected areas in Poland and the Czech Republic. Similarly transnational was the solidarity felt and displayed with the victims of the Islamist attackers who, in 2015, stormed the Paris offices of the satirical magazine *Charlie Hebdo* and shot eleven people. On the same day, many gathered outside the French Embassy in Berlin, bearing signs that declared *Je suis Charlie*.

The 2015 'refugee crisis' demonstrated that national and international solidarity do not always interact so harmoniously. On the one hand, it triggered an impressive wave of solidarity in Germany; innumerable volunteers made the '*Willkommenskultur* ' into a much-marvelled-at reality. On the other hand, it was not long before citizens complained about unearned benefits being lavished on 'the foreigners'. In the East, this argument found an especially strong echo. 'The asylum seekers are pampered. The people are scorned' appeared on a placard that AfD members carried through Magdeburg in 2015. Many East Germans, who despite solidarity pacts and transfer payments from their West German 'brothers and sisters' felt they had not been treated in a 'brotherly' or 'sisterly' manner, reacted with irritation to what they judged an excessively generous demonstration of international solidarity. The sense that they had not got their piece of the pie fuelled, as it had done in GDR times, resentment against those who allegedly did not belong (> Anger, > Belonging).

---

[22] Reinhard Kiehl, ed., *Alle Jahre wieder* (Düsseldorf: My favourite book, 2001), 185.

Who owes or gives which amount of solidarity to whom is a contested and never-ending issue in modern history, and not only in Germany. Solidarity nevertheless constitutes an important anchoring principle of liberal democratic societies that is both claimed and practised by numerous stakeholders. While traditional communities of solidarity (especially the unions) have suffered a loss of organizational power, and social democracy – the concept's midwife, mouthpiece and disseminator – struggles, others have adopted or rediscovered it. Never before has the number of volunteers been greater: 30 to 40 per cent of those older than fourteen donate their time and take care of others, be they ill neighbours, children from socially precarious and migrant families, or senior citizens. At the peak of the 2015 'refugee crisis', every second person had become active. Community organizations and civic foundations are booming, and many offer assistance with homework and refugee sponsorships. Nor was there any shortage of caring behaviour and acts of direct solidarity during the first weeks of the COVID-19 pandemic – only topped, once again, by the outpouring of practical help for the hundreds of thousands of Ukrainian refugees, who, since late February 2022, have left their war-stricken country to seek safety in neighbouring states. Germans have shown their solidarity in many ways: at demonstrations, by waving Ukrainian flags or posting messages like 'Stand with Ukraine' or 'We stay united'. But they have also opened their private homes to refugees, taken them in and offered personal help and comfort (Figure 51).

Figure 51   Berlin, February 2022 (Photo by Odd Andersen/AFP via Getty Images)

Such voluntary acts and initiatives, which embody the caring heart of solidarity, are an important barometer for the emotional temperature of a society. At the same time, they serve as a striking counterweight to the tendencies towards competitive individualization and egotistical attitudes that have been escalating since the 1990s. At least in times of crisis, solidarity remains, and impressively so.

~

Trust

In 1977, Bavaria was on edge. Alfons Goppel, who had been the state premier since 1962 and was so beloved that under his leadership the Christian Social Union (CSU) took nearly two-thirds of the vote in 1974, received stacks of mail from citizens who begged him to stay in office rather than handing over to Franz Josef Strauß any sooner than necessary. While they had 'inner trust' in their 'good father of the country', they obviously did not trust his appointed successor. Unlike Goppel, Strauß was not seen as an 'exemplary figure' but rather as an 'unscrupulous ladder climber and man of violence', one who spoke 'hastily and angrily much of the time' and was 'ambitious and striving' to a fault. Johannes Lorenzer, a priest and long-time CSU member, summed it up: 'Bear in mind', he beseeched Goppel, 'that he is no statesman. He is hard, ruthless and without mercy. He has not handled his fame and talent well. He does not want to take a back seat as a member of the opposition, where he is not allowed to play first fiddle. He always wants to play first fiddle.' A fellow party member agreed, warning that as state premier Strauß would endanger not only the 'reputation of the CSU but also trust in the democratic constitutional bodies'.[1]

Trust came up threefold in these communications: trust in the individual person, in the office and in the system.[2] The correspondents gave Goppel good and Strauß poor marks in every arena. In their view, Strauß lacked the qualities, character traits and record to prove that he could act in the manner required of a good *Landesvater*. He seemed consumed by ambition and a 'desire for power and self-interest' – a man who could not curb his temper and showed no consideration either for the members of his own party or for the opposition. A figure like this inspired deep distrust.

---

[1] Bavarian State Archive Munich, II, Chancellery, no. 12153: T. Aicher, 20 November 1977; Jörg Bornebusch, 27 January 1977; Annemarie Herterich, 11 February 1977; Johannes Lorenzer, 30 January 1977; Barbara Lang, 1 February 1977; Servatius Maeßen, 2 March 1977.

[2] See, on different types of trust, Anthony Giddens, *The Consequences of Modernity* (Cambridge: Polity Press, 1990), 79–123; Annette C. Baier, *Moral Prejudices: Essays on Ethics* (Cambridge, MA: Harvard University Press, 1994), 95–203; Geoffrey Hosking, *Trust: A History* (Oxford: Oxford University Press, 2014).

A year later, Strauß did become the state premier of Bavaria, a role he held for ten years. He never enjoyed the level of popularity Goppel did though, and the CSU lost votes. Many citizens were fed up with the scandals he generated and with the political polarization for which he was famed. And yet, the majority still placed their trust in him. When he died in 1988, his funeral procession was the largest the city of Munich had ever seen (> Grief).

Definitions and Purposes of Trust

Trust plays a central role in political communication, but it is indispensable in other domains as well.[3] In 1957, the *Brockhaus* encyclopaedia described trust as 'one of the cornerstones of collective solidarity: in family, marriage, friendship, in the relationship between doctor and patient'. As a 'human-ethical component', it was equally crucial 'where functional considerations otherwise predominate: in professional and economic life ("crisis of confidence"), in politics as a prerequisite for continuity and stability'. In order to make social interactions succeed, people needed to have an 'attitude of "trusting" the other, i.e. not expecting anything ill from him'. Furthermore, they should be 'inclined to consider him reliable in character, so that one can have faith in his words and especially in his promises'. Such trust was 'never merely an opinion of the other, but a personal relationship entered into with him, and thus an act of chance'. Taking this chance, though, might 'strengthen the will in the other to justify the trust placed in him'.[4]

This interpretation conceived of trust as an attitude, opinion, inclination and relationship, not an emotion. But then how to explain the concept of 'basic trust' that psychoanalyst Erik Erikson traced back to the 'quality of the maternal relationship'? Nearly everyone, he argued in 1950, possesses a primary or basic trust in the world, acquired from and through interactions with their caregiver in the first year of life. It is impossible for this kind of trust to be rooted in 'attitudes' or 'opinions' since infants hold neither. Instead, Erikson used affective terms to describe the 'sense of trust' that builds between mothers (there was no mention of fathers at the time) and their newborns. While the child learns to trust the mother as a reliable and friendly person, her caring affection likewise gives them a 'firm sense of personal trustworthiness'.[5] Trust

---

[3] 'Trust' (*Vertrauen*) and 'confidence' (*Zuversicht*) are at times used interchangeably. In German, *Vertrauen* is far more common than *Zuversicht*, which mainly focuses on attitudes towards the future.

[4] *Der Große Brockhaus*, 16th ed., vol. 12 (Wiesbaden: Brockhaus, 1957), 173; *Brockhaus Enzyklopädie*, 17th ed., vol. 19 (Wiesbaden: Brockhaus, 1974), 574.

[5] Erik H. Erikson, *Childhood and Society* [1950], 2nd ed. (New York: Norton & Co., 1963), 249.

is therefore something that can be learnt and practised, but also unlearnt or lost over the course of one's life, depending on experience.

Experience teaches us that trusting is often risky, whether in interactions with strangers or intimates. Ostensibly, the stranger might seem more deserving of mistrust than the friend. If trust, following Georg Simmel's 1908 definition, takes 'a middle position between knowledge and ignorance of others', then the risk of being let down increases with the unknown element: in this case, the stranger.[6] On the other hand, one can never fully know one's friends or lovers. They too are capable of abusing or misusing trust, and that turns out to be particularly painful.

In recent decades, this pain may have become more common as people place ever-greater expectations on their romantic and platonic relationships. The ideal of close friendship and enduring love as the union of two souls is of course older than the twentieth century. Yet it only began to have a broad impact when the social, economic and media conditions were aligned. Since then, everyone dreams of romance. People of all genders search indefatigably for partners capable of providing the most perfect > love and absolute trust. The exceptional standards placed on relationships (in large part by the media) have put them under considerable stress. The more exclusive and total a relationship is expected to be, the more likely it is to fall short. Deceit, betrayal and breaches of trust weaken its foundations and hasten its breakdown. Some attempt to mitigate the risk by spreading their options for love and friendship across many people and cycling through relationships more quickly, reasoning that the less trust they invest, the less likely they are to feel hurt if anything goes wrong.

Economies of Trust

Sociologists and psychologists like to differentiate between 'thin' and 'thick' trust, and locate the latter primarily in intimate relationships. 'Thin' trust, in turn, exists in brief encounters and remote transactions with lower emotional and material stakes. The intensity and significance of the trust relationship therefore depends on how reliant one is on the person in whom one is placing one's trust and whether one has other options. The technician who fixes your washing machine generally demands and receives less trust than the doctor whose diagnosis and cure might mean the difference between life and death.

Doing business necessitates an extension of trust in advance. This is true for long-distance trades as well as everyday consumer decisions. The customer

---

[6] Georg Simmel, *Sociology: Inquiries into the Construction of Social Forms*, trans. Anthony J. Blasi et al., vol. 1 (Leiden: Brill, 2009), 311–12, 315.

who does not yet have first-hand knowledge of the product they plan to buy has no choice but to trust that they will not receive a faulty or counterfeit item. If they are satisfied with their purchase, they might buy from the business again in future. Their decisions are facilitated by marketing that aims to build trust in and loyalty to the brand. It is in the manufacturer's best interest to not betray the trust that customers have provisionally extended and to thereby retain them in the medium and long term.

That building trust pays off is a truism in the age of accelerated capitalist growth. In the strictly regulated economy of the pre-modern period, both the number of suppliers and buyers was limited. Since the 1800s, however, rapid industrialization has vastly expanded the market and with it the scale of competition between providers. In this context, trust has become an indispensable part of economic life. Robert Bosch, who founded his global engineering and technology empire in the 1880s, explained in 1918 that he had always operated according to the principle 'better to lose money than trust': 'The inviolability of my promises, the faith in the value of my wares and my word, are more important to me that a momentary profit.'[7]

Trust has also been a watchword for the pharmaceutical giant Bayer. Since the 1930s, its logo and 'stamp of trust', which features its name in the shape of a cross, has glowed far beyond the town of Leverkusen where the company is headquartered. In 1956, its board embarked on a targeted PR campaign of 'trust advertising'. The agency commissioned came up with the tagline 'trusted by the world', seeking to draw the consumer into a 'sphere of trust' that would make them more likely to reach for the company's products.[8] Unlike Bosch, Bayer's CEOs harnessed trust as a deliberate public relations tactic with the explicit intent of making a profit. Since other people 'all over the world' had placed their trust in Bayer, it was claimed, new customers could and should do the same without hesitation.

In comparison, the pitch waged by Volkswagen was far more subtle. In 1962, Charles Wilp, the famous designer and ad man, coined the slogan: 'it runs and runs and runs', followed in 1969 by the line 'there are still some things you can rely on' in bold print. Both were referring to the Beetle, the Wolfsburg-based carmaker's first major success. The only model to perform better was the Golf, which was released in 1974; by 2019 thirty-five million units had hit the streets worldwide.[9]

---

[7] *Der Bosch-Zünder* 1, no. 2 (5 April 1919): 1.

[8] Ute Frevert, *Vertrauensfragen: Eine Obsession der Moderne* (Munich: C. H. Beck, 2013), 132–38; Ute Frevert, *The Moral Economy of Trust: Modern Trajectories* (London: German Historical Institute, 2014).

[9] Jürgen Schlegelmilch, *VW: Er läuft und läuft und läuft … Vier Jahrzehnte VW-Werbung* (Königswinter: Heel, 2006), 25; Knut Hickethier et al., eds, *Das Deutsche Auto: Volkswagenwerbung und Volkskultur* (Gießen: Anabas, 1974), 162–63, 247.

But in 2015 it seemed that customers could not rely on Volkswagen after all. The company had been systematically cheating emission tests for diesel vehicles in order to lure consumers with the false promise of 'clean diesel'. It accepted responsibility and was forced to pay billions in fines and compensation, predominantly in the US market. In large newspaper advertisements, management apologised for betraying customers' trust and vowed to win it back – which it obviously did. Volkswagen was still guilty of fraud and these adverts did little to hasten the end of the scandal. And yet, it remained in the black and continued to post healthy profits. The initial breach of trust did not cause customers to abandon the brand. Apparently, the trust relationship was too 'thin' to be permanently damaged. Moreover, there were few clean alternatives; almost all carmakers had manipulated the engine's computer software. Because Volkswagen vehicles continued to do well in price–performance comparisons, the momentary loss of trust had minimal effect. Furthermore, many buyers felt and cultivated a strong emotional attachment – called loyalty – to the brand, which outlasted the 'diesel dupe' and helped the company survive it.

Trust and Mistrust in the Weimar Republic

Trust has had political currency since the 1800s, though it surfaced with particular frequency in the 1920s. The Weimar Constitution was an act of trust in two respects: citizens pronounced their trust in the new state and its institutions by voting, and the state trusted citizens by giving them an active political role. Unlike in the German Empire, where the democratically elected parliament (albeit only by men) had no say in the formation of the government or its policies, governing in the Weimar Republic required the majority consent of the Reichstag that, since 1919, had been elected by women as well as men. If parliament refused to give it or expressed a lack of confidence, ministers had to resign. Often, they chose to resign pre-emptively.[10]

Although loss of trust had severe consequences for political order, the trust displayed or withdrawn was emotionally 'thin'. It meant little more than that MPs accepted a proposition by the government and entrusted chancellors and ministers to make the right decisions in the future. This future had a time limit: the constitution stipulated that every four years the people should return to the ballots and elect their representatives, from whom the new government would be formed. In reality, though, there were eight rather than four parliamentary elections over the fourteen years of the republic's existence. This

---

[10] Lutz Berthold, 'Das konstruktive Misstrauensvotum und seine Ursprünge in der Weimarer Staatsrechtslehre', *Der Staat* 36, no. 1 (1997): 81–94.

indicates just how difficult it was for parties to find common ground. Negative majorities were more readily achieved than positive ones; voicing mistrust was easier than building trust.

According to the liberal constitutional lawyer Hugo Preuß, this was due to the 'bitter experiences of the past'. Preuß, who became Weimar's first minister of the interior in 1919, was alluding to the parliament of the German Empire which, as a consequence of its impotence, had distrusted the government almost on principle. Under the new constitution, which had been co-drafted by Preuß, 'that mistrust felt by the masses and their representatives towards all those who govern, even towards those who have emerged from their midst and from parliamentary influence, will gradually be extinguished'. At least that was his hope.[11]

It was dashed. Mistrust reigned between the vastly polarized political camps, which fought each other bitterly in parliament and on the streets. Mistrust also made it nigh on impossible to form stable governments. At the same time, everyone knew how damaging and destructive this emotion could be. 'Mistrust', stated Social Democrat Simon Katzenstein in 1919, is 'truly no democratic virtue'. It was 'the characteristic of the slave, who is oppressed, who is incapable of deciding things independently, and whose only weapon is mistrust for the outside world and his oppressors'. Citizens in a democratic state, however, were not slaves: they had rights that they ought to safeguard and exercise. To this end, they appointed 'people of trust' to act on their behalf. Out of this relationship trust was, ideally, supposed to 'bloom like a bud', becoming a democratic virtue *sui generis*.

But trust did not come from nothing, as Katzenstein knew from experience. Parliament needed instruments and procedures to keep the executive in check and make the government accountable. In Katzenstein's view, such measures were not a sign of mistrust 'in the usual sense of the word'. Rather, they functioned as precautions that would in fact help to build trust by creating the conditions for it to take root and flourish.[12] Careful checks and balances – a concept that originated in British parliamentarianism – were the bedrock of constitutional democracy, which neither demanded unconditional trust nor could withstand profound mistrust.

The place the president occupied was up for debate. The Weimar Constitution mandated that he be directly elected by citizens; many therefore saw his role as being 'the man of trust, the tribune of the people as a whole, the

[11] Hugo Preuß, 'Das Verfassungswerk von Weimar' (1919), in Hugo Preuß, *Gesammelte Schriften*, vol. 4, ed. Detlef Lehnert (Tübingen: Mohr Siebeck, 2008), 87–93, quotes 91.
[12] Eduard Heilfron, ed., *Die deutsche Nationalversammlung im Jahre 1919*, vol. 5 (Berlin: Norddeutsche Buchdruckerei und Verlagsanstalt, 1921), 3156.

guardian of the common interest'. As a corrective to the kind of party politicking that might use parliament to advance particular interests, the 'man of trust of the nation's millions', as sociologist Max Weber called him, ought to embody the utmost legitimacy and authority. From this perspective, the duty of the president as 'the controlling organ borne by the people's trust' was not necessarily to stand up to the government but rather to what Preuß called 'parliamentary absolutism'.[13]

In 1925, the first direct presidential election took place following the death of Friedrich Ebert. Ebert had been elected by the Weimar National Assembly in 1919, before the adoption of the constitution. Several candidates vied for the powerful office. Wilhelm Marx, who had the backing of the Catholic Centre Party, the German Democratic Party and the SPD, campaigned openly on and for trust: 'millions of working people demand trust and are ready to place their trust in new leadership'. But in the second round of voting, they declined to give it to him, opting instead, in a close race, for Paul von Hindenburg, the non-partisan monarchist sixteen years his senior. In his Easter address 'to the German people', Hindenburg had not mentioned trust at all but instead emphasized his 'fidelity to the fatherland' (Figure 52).[14]

The Semantics of Fidelity

In doing so, he favoured a term with conservative connotations and free of democratic overtones. Fidelity, as Hindenburg and his generation understood it, was unconditional and eternal. It produced and reflected an enduring bond that could only be severed by death or ruined by betrayal. Fidelity or loyalty was a concept more typically associated with premodern relations: with the vassalage of medieval rulers and liegemen, with the devoted servant who would not leave his master's side, with subjects who pledged to be 'faithful, fair and abiding' to their sovereign. In the nineteenth century, 'German fidelity' was designated a national characteristic and celebrated as such in Hoffmann von Fallersleben's 1841 'The Song of the Germans', which would later become the national anthem. The founders of the German Empire, Bismarck and Wilhelm I, were posthumously styled as paragons of German

---

[13] Ibid., 3195; Friedrich Meinecke, 'Verfassung und Verwaltung der deutschen Republik [1918/19]', in Friedrich Meinecke, *Politische Schriften und Reden*, ed. Georg Kotowski (Darmstadt: Toeche-Mittler, 1958), 280–98, here 291; Max Weber, *Zur Neuordnung Deutschlands: Schriften und Reden 1918–1920* (Tübingen: Mohr Siebeck, 1988), 129; Preuß, Verfassungswerk, 91.

[14] Herbert Michaelis et al., eds, *Ursachen und Folgen*, vol. 6 (Berlin: Dokumenten-Verlag, 1961), 278–80. The German *Treue* means both fidelity and loyalty.

Figure 52 'The fatherland above all / Steadfast in fidelity': the commemorative coin for President Hindenburg's eighty-fifth birthday (Photo by ullstein bild/ullstein bild via Getty Images)

fidelity, and political parties liked to emphasize their 'unbreakable fidelity to Kaiser and Reich', as the National Liberals did in 1882.[15]

From the monarchists' point of view, the revolutionaries of 1918 had broken and betrayed this fidelity. In November of that year, the state premier of Bavaria, Kurt Eisner, received an anonymous note in the post:

> faithless perjury vaunts itself
> they plunder and they murder
> in their own country o bitter disgrace
> as if they were enemy hordes
> there is a curse to topple the king
> curse follows broken fidelity

The Berlin professor of literature Gustav Roethe also favoured the vocabularly of 'disloyalty' and was accordingly overjoyed by Hindenburg's 1925 election. The fact that the new president and former general had chosen Friedrich

---

[15] Ute Frevert and Ulrich Schreiterer, 'Treue – Ansichten des 19. Jahrhunderts', in *Der bürgerliche Wertehimmel*, ed. Manfred Hettling and Stefan-Ludwig Hoffmann (Göttingen: Vandenhoeck & Ruprecht, 2000), 217–56, esp. 243 ff.

Schlegel's 'fidelity is the mark of honour' as his motto gave rise to hopes that the 'Germany of today' might return to earlier values and traditions.[16]

The grateful and encouraging missives that Hindenburg received when he ran for office in 1925 and 1932 repeatedly evoked the wish to see a strong, reliable and, importantly, impartial man as head of state. In 1932, Christian trade unionist Hugo Dornhofer assured Hindenburg that he would show him 'the same personal courage of devotion in his heart as we showed to our army commander in the shellfire of the trenches for the protection of our ardently beloved homeland'. It was plainly unthinkable to be devoted to someone you did not trust. 'My trust in you', wrote one seventy-six-year-old widow from Leipzig, 'cannot be shaken', for she had adored him 'hand on heart' for sixteen years. Karl Geisler introduced himself as 'a poor and simple man' who confirmed that 'no one and nothing can take away my trust in you'. Annie Gerhard likewise placed her 'rock-solid trust' in Hindenburg, who 'with God's help' would 'now make everything good, just as you understood throughout the war how to find the right path'. Another clear message came from Altona: 'We do not want a braggart but a man of duty and action, and you are the only one. Take this from an unemployed man as a salutation of fidelity and trust.'[17]

Here, as in most letters, the mention of fidelity had a double function: it evoked a relationship of allegiance (often with military connotations), and it characterized Hindenburg as a person capable of fulfilling his duties out of fidelity to his fellow citizens and to his fatherland. As a 'trustee of the entire German people', Fritz Weber from Frankfurt, who had been an infantryman between 1903 and 1905 and served in the First World War, explained in 1932, Hindenburg was a 'symbol of German > honour and freedom. So loyalty begets loyalty.' Similarly steadfast was Minna Streich who praised Hindenburg as a 'great example of dutifulness and Germanic fidelity'. 'Above all party disputes, your unimpeachable heroic figure rises up for us', she exclaimed. As a 'German woman with strong national feelings' it was her 'heartfelt desire to express to you the promise of loyalty made by many women who share my fate'.

People proclaimed their loyalty to a leader who they felt was loyal to them. This held especially true for the men and women who revered Hindenburg as a heroic figure of the fallen empire. Hermann Weiß from Kiel declared that he did not bother 'in principle about politics, but with the same matter-of-factness and enthusiasm with which I went into the field in 1914 when I was

---

[16] Bavarian State Archive Munich, II, MA no. 102378: anonymous, undated; Gustav Roethe, *Deutsche Reden* (Leipzig: Quelle & Meyer, 1927), 44–45; Gustav Roethe, 'Die Hohenzollern-Bilder und die deutsche Treue', *Deutscher Volkswart* 4 (1919): 148–56.

[17] Federal Archive Berlin, R 601, no. 378: Hugo Dornhofer, 18 February 1932; B. Jost, 20 February 1932; Karl Geisler, 15 February 1932; Annie Engers, 18 February 1932; no. 380: A. Thaden, 11 March 1932.

barely 18 years old, with exactly the same matter-of-factness and enthusiasm, I will do my duty next Sunday and vote out of honest conviction for the man as president for whom loyalty is a self-evident concept'. It was no less self-evident for the 'war comrades who know what loyalty is and to whom they owe loyalty: to you, Field Marshal General, to the German people and themselves'.

Even younger people who had not fought in the trenches saw Hindenburg as a bringer of peace and unity. Women, in particular, were tired of the violence and 'party bickering' they associated with his opponents. Grete Domforde, a seamstress from Stade, expressed her thoughts on this matter with zeal and in great detail. She considered herself 'a nationally minded woman' but did not yearn 'for the old "discipline, order and cleanliness of the monarchy"'. During the 1925 elections, she had not voted for Hindenburg, because she was 'afraid of those who supported your candidacy'. 'But after your speech in parliament, where you said that you wanted to follow your predecessor, I knew I had made a mistake.' As president, Hindenburg had proven that he was 'no party man', thereby earning her 'trust in and respect for your person and politics. So fidelity is an idle delusion after all among those who still oppose you!' By 1932, she was no longer part of that camp.[18]

Paraphrasing a line from Friedrich Schiller's popular ballad 'The Pledge', Grete Domforde linked the trust that she placed in Hindenburg to the proverbial notion of covenant faithfulness. She made no secret of the fact, though, that her trust had been slow to build. After seven years as president, Hindenburg had convinced her that he was trustworthy and would not abuse her trust for partisan purposes. This type of trust clearly and vastly differed from the unconditional loyalty former and future leaders expected from their subjects.

Fidelity, Faith and Trust in the Führer

Unsurprisingly, fidelity and trust also showed up in letters to Adolf Hitler. Supporters, party comrades and entire towns assured him of their 'unswerving fidelity'. Some described feeling their loyalties torn, as did Eugen Rog from Gummersbach in 1930. He wanted to join the Nazi Party, but also to keep 'under all circumstances the loyalty I pledged to the Steel Helmet's flag'. Since the two could hardly be reconciled, his fidelity to the flag ultimately won out.[19] 'For us there is just one motto: "obedience and faith"', announced Erfurt members of the National Socialist Women's League in 1935. Hildegard

---

[18] Ibid., no. 379: Fritz Weber, 19 March 1932; Minna Streich, 7 March 1932; Grete Domforde, 6 March 1932; no. 380: Hermann Weiß, 10 March 1932.

[19] Ibid., NS 51, no. 51/1: Eugen Rog, 8 October 1930. The Steel Helmet was a right-wing veterans' organization founded in 1918 and associated with the DNVP.

Murschhauser, a kindergarten teacher from Munich, had listened to Hitler's speech from the 1936 Nuremberg Rally on the radio: 'Now everything in me has changed. A faith and trust awoke in me that I had never before felt or known. I became merry again – all fear, all doubt disappeared.' Henceforth, she passed her faith and trust on to 'the little and littlest': 'We sit in front of our decorated "Hitler Corner" and I tell them all about Hitler and his Germany! Afterwards, everyone stands to attention and we sing with raised hand German songs. To conclude we always say our little prayer, which we all recite earnestly: "Dear God, protect with a strong hand / Our Führer and the Fatherland!"'

Faith, trust, hope, fidelity: these feelings typically converged. What was novel in comparison to the period before 1933 was the emphasis on faith. The veneration for Hitler took on almost religious proportions, rendering him something like a messiah, sent and protected by God. 'Whoever believes in you, places their hope in you and trusts you completely will never perish', wrote Gerti Rehmann from Essen, the wife of a tailor, in 1938. Two years earlier, Friedel Hein, a working-class woman from Berlin, poured out her heart in a long letter:

> My husband and I have known each other since we were children. We grew up after the war, in a time that placed great political demands on us young people. Ministers changed, governments fell. We had no foothold, we believed what was promised to us, and were disappointed again and again. We became unemployed, we took what we were given, we were dulled and lost faith in everything. In the future, in Germany, in ourselves. Then you came along, my Führer, your programme. We didn't know – should there really be someone who had found a way out of the chaos? Could the cart still be moved? We waited. But when after 1933 not words but deeds spoke, then we knew that National Socialism is socialism of deeds. On Saturday evening, 7 March 1936, my husband came back from work – he has now found a job at the State Railroad Company after having worked on the autobahn for one year. With shining eyes, he spoke to me of your speech. When we read this speech together word for word in the newspaper (as we have no radio), we cried like little children. And for that my Führer, for giving us back our faith and homeland we would like to thank you.[20]

Faith, fidelity and trust played an important role in the official rhetoric of National Socialism as well. On Hitler's birthday on 20 April 1940, the party newspaper printed two articles: 'Faith in the Führer', by the regime's press chief Otto Dietrich, and 'Love, Obedience, and Trust in the Führer' by the

---

[20] Ibid.: Ortsgruppe Rosenheim, 9 July 1930; Eugen Rog, 8 October 1930; no. 75: Fanny Caspari, 19 April 1935; Hildegard Murschhauser, September 1936; no. 71: Gerti Rehmann, 27 September 1938; Friedel Hein, 12 March 1936.

minister of propaganda, Joseph Goebbels. One month later, law professor Herbert Krüger, a member of the SS and the NSDAP, delivered a matriculation speech at Heidelberg University on 'trust as the spiritual cornerstone of the *Volksgemeinschaft*'. In stark contrast to Weimar, where 'deep mistrust' was the 'foundational political mood', the 'Third Reich', according to Krüger, was based on 'the limitless trust that the people placed in their Führer'. The idea that trust could be revised or even wholly retracted did not enter the picture. As a result, this understanding of trust closely resembled fidelity, a value that occupied a privileged position in the Nazi lexicon. The motto 'My honour is loyalty' was inscribed on SS belt buckles, and lawyers spoke of the 'fiduciary duty [*Treuepflicht*] to the *Volksgemeinschaft*'. Under National Socialism, fidelity/loyalty was something unbreakable and nearly sacred. It bridged the gap to faith, as Goebbels explained on the radio on 20 April 1941: 'We do not need to know what the Führer wants to do, we have faith in him.' In his final radio address on Hitler's birthday four years later, he emphasized the 'Germanic allegiance' of his countrymen and their 'deep, unshakeable faith' in the 'man of the century'.[21]

After the collapse of the regime that had borne such unlimited trust and unconditional fidelity, the 'language of faith', as Victor Klemperer called it in 1946, lost its ability to muster strong and binding emotions almost overnight. No one wanted to hear or talk any more about loyalty 'blindly' pledged or the lure of 'allegiance' modelled on the medieval *Nibelungen* legend.[22]

The GDR: Gambling with Trust

New promises of loyalty were soon on offer, though. The GDR attached great importance to strengthening the 'trusting relationship between citizens and the democratic people's state'. What exactly the ruling SED party meant by this would become clear in 1953. On 20 June, three days after nationwide uprisings, the writer Kurt Barthel, a member of the party's central committee, accused the bricklayers, painters and carpenters who had protested against the increase in required work output of letting themselves be taken in by enemies in the West and gambling away the trust of the state's leadership. In order to be absolved of the 'disgrace' of their betrayal, they should, in the future, 'build

---

[21] Herbert Krüger, *Vertrauen als seelische Grundlage der Volksgemeinschaft* (Heidelberg: Winter, 1940), 3, 7, 13–14; Victor Klemperer, *The Language of the Third Reich: LTI – Lingua Tertii Imperii: A Philologist's Notebook,* trans. Martin Brady (London: Athlone Press, 2000), 113; *Völkischer Beobachter* (Vienna edition), 21 April 1941, 1; ibid., 20 April 1945, 1–2; Raphael Gross, '"Treue" im Nationalsozialismus', in *Treue,* ed. Nikolaus Buschmann and Karl Borromäus Murr (Göttingen: Vandenhoeck & Ruprecht, 2008), 253–73.

[22] Klemperer, *LTI*, 103–18, quotes 109, 151, 236, 240. The *Nibelungenlied* was about the unbreakable bonds of mutual fidelity between king and liegeman, among other things.

Figure 53   Proclaiming trust (*Vertrauen*) in the GDR government after the 17 June 1953 uprising (Bundesarchiv, Bild 183–20115-0002/CC-BY-SA3.0)

a lot and very well', because 'restoring damaged trust is very, very difficult' (Figure 53).

Bertolt Brecht had a famously sarcastic reaction to Barthel's comment, which he was careful not to publish at the time. In his poem 'The Solution' he wryly asked:

> After the uprising of the 17th June
> The Secretary of the Writers' Union
> Had leaflets distributed in the Stalinallee
> Stating that the people
> Had forfeited the confidence of the government
> And could win it back only
> By redoubled efforts. Would it not be easier
> In that case for the government
> To dissolve the people
> And elect another?[23]

Brecht, who in 1951 had been awarded the National Prize of the German Democratic Republic, First Class, was alluding to the economy of trust in liberal democracies: a one-time act of trust from above, the involvement of the

---

[23] *Neues Deutschland*, 20 April 1953; Bertolt Brecht, *Poems*, ed. John Willett and Ralph Manheim (London: Eyre Methuen, 1976), 440.

people in government, was matched by a periodically renewed vote of trust from below. But that was not the case in the East German state, where free elections and independent parties existed only on paper and the population lived under a tight net of mistrust and surveillance. GDR citizens could not, or could only under extremely restrictive circumstances, travel to capitalist or semi-socialist countries, such as Yugoslavia, 'for fear of a flight from the republic'. As one SED member from East Berlin put it in 1977, this gave the impression of a 'chronic mistrust of the party leadership towards our citizens, even though there is constant talk of increased trust'.[24]

The Ministry for State Security essentially embodied this mistrust. Its targeted 'decomposition work' aimed to destroy trust precisely where it was 'thickest' and most personal: in intimate and family relationships (> Hate). A letter addressed to the SED's central committee in March 1989 revealed that this work had not remained a secret from the public, despite attempts to keep it so. The pseudonymous writer urged their 'comrades' to summon the courage to 'trust the people and attach less importance to your internal security'. If those employed in the party and state apparatus were put to work in production or catering, the author predicted, 'the lost trust of the people would also return'.[25] That did not happen. When the 'comrades' falsified the results of the local elections in May 1989 so blatantly that it could not escape the attention of suspicious observers, the crisis of confidence reached its peak, sealing the downfall of the GDR only a few months later.

And yet, the regime had managed to spread something like confidence in the future among the population (> Hope). The full-throated optimism it conveyed in images, words and songs, accompanied by generous social policies, gave citizens an unswerving sense of social security. They believed that the state would look after them and shelter them from strife. With this blissful assurance, people could lead relatively carefree and calculable lives. Since 1969, the GDR consistently boasted a significantly higher birthrate than the Federal Republic and took this as proof of confidence in a system that offered women the security and material support to start a family.[26]

When the Wall came down, the birth rate in East Germany immediately started to decline, and dramatically so during the first half of the 1990s. It fell far below the Western level and only broke even again in 2015. This does indeed seem to suggest a link between people's perception of security and their readiness to bring children into the world. But it does not support the GDR's

---

[24] Gunilla Budde, *Frauen der Intelligenz* (Göttingen: Vandenhoeck & Ruprecht, 2003), quote 24.

[25] Siegfried Suckut, *Volkes Stimmen: 'Ehrlich, aber deutlich' – Privatbriefe an die DDR-Regierung* (Munich: dtv, 2015), 219, 423.

[26] Annette F. Timm, *The Politics of Fertility in Twentieth-Century Berlin* (Cambridge: Cambridge University Press, 2010), 290–91.

self-image as a warmer, more trustworthy and caring society, because the confidence that young women might have felt in the 1970s rested on false foundations. The future promised by the regime was frozen in the present, and even the present was not something the state, sinking into debt and swiftly chewing through its resources, could guarantee.

Can Trust Be Measured?

Furthermore, it is difficult to accurately gauge the effects of child-friendly social policies. Whether women decide to become pregnant or not depends only partially on their future prospects and on the extent to which the state ensures the so-called compatibility of family and career. Using higher birth rates as an indicator of civic confidence, a common practice during the Cold War, fails to account for various other influences, from individual motives to societal structures that enable, reinforce or dissuade the desire to have children.

It is equally problematic to interpret higher rates of investment, savings or consumption as proof of trust or confidence without additional evidence. In 1953, West German President Heuss considered 'the fact that savings deposits are growing and growing' as 'the most beautiful sign of national as well as individual self-confidence'.[27] Using economic metrics to capture context-laden trust processes is an inadequate approach, though. To do so is to reduce trust to a mathematical calculation of risk. Does purchasing an item really indicate that the buyer has trust or confidence in the brand or in their own future? Or might wholly different motives play a role, such as enjoyment, the desire for social prestige, the wish to be different or to conform?

It is striking that such questions are seldom raised. Instead, in the second half of the twentieth century, it has become commonplace to constantly harangue people with attitudinal surveys about their levels of trust. They are asked whether they place very much, some, not much, very little or no trust at all in the police, press, politicians. Trust in brands, companies and industries is similarly surveyed. Agencies and advisors generate 'trust indices' that companies integrate into their business and marketing strategies. Every bank and insurance firm stresses their trustworthiness – ignorant that it is all one big rhetorical loop: the declaration of trust follows the prompt about trust that follows the declaration and on it goes.

Advertising Trust in West German Politics

It is the same for politicians. They too solicit and appeal to trust and are eager to find out just how much trust they enjoy among their constituents. If

[27] Reinhard Kiehl, ed., *Alle Jahre wieder* (Düsseldorf: My favourite book, 2001), 78.

pollsters discover that their perceived trustworthiness is abating, governments and parties quickly launch new campaigns to advertise it anew.

Trust was already a campaign issue back in 1961, when Willy Brandt, the Social Democratic mayor of West Berlin, challenged incumbent Konrad Adenauer for the chancellorship. His campaign brochure was entitled *Trust* and had a print run of nearly five million copies. To foster trust in their candidate, the SPD sent him to the furthest corners of the country. Putting his telegenic face in front of the cameras forged a previously unseen form of personality campaigning. Brandt presented himself as approachable and accessible yet simultaneously statesmanlike, worldly and visionary. His campaign team was knowingly drawing on a tried-and-tested strategy from the business sector: direct addresses to the citizen-consumer would, it was thought, build trust in the brand. The brand, in this case the politician, should come across as both distinctive and capable of meeting the highest standards.[28]

Brandt was the first but hardly the last politician to campaign vigorously on trust. In 1976 and 1983, Helmut Kohl followed suit with the slogans 'The man you can trust' and 'This chancellor builds trust'. In 2002, Gerhard Schröder marketed himself as the chancellor of trust. Meanwhile in 2009, Angela Merkel campaigned on 'confidence'. She wanted to conjure a feeling that, similar to hope, is more temporal than socially determined. Unlike trust, confidence does not necessarily hinge on one person or politician but projects a generally optimistic attitude towards what is to come. In times of crisis, a campaign researcher at the time explained, voters are looking above all for security, competence and confidence; trust alone, noted the Berlin daily *Tagesspiegel*, was not enough and 'blind trust' would be downright foolish.[29]

Trust in Crisis

The twenty-first century has already provided two examples of how and whether trust actually functions in such circumstances. The first test arrived in 2008 with the global financial crisis. To prevent people from withdrawing their savings and triggering a banking collapse, the chancellor appeared before the cameras alongside her finance minister on 5 October, promising 'savers' that 'your deposits are secure'. That was not strictly true, but the direct assurance from two politicians not known for making rash bets bolstered

---

[28] Thomas Mergel, *Propaganda nach Hitler: Eine Kulturgeschichte des Wahlkampfs in der Bundesrepublik 1949–1990* (Göttingen: Wallstein, 2010), 64 ff., 72 ff., 108 ff.

[29] Frida Thurm, 'Am Busen der Kanzlerin', *Zeit online*, 10 August 2009, www.zeit.de/online/2009/33/CDU-Wahlkampf-Plakate; Antje Sirleschtov, 'Vertrauen reicht nicht', *Tagesspiegel*, 11 August 2009, http://bit.ly/3IUjyCy, both accessed 4 March 2022.

people's trust. The dreaded run on the banks never happened, and the government was able to weather the crisis with relative calm.

In 2020, civic trust was put to the test again. The situation this time was different but just as dramatic. As the COVID-19 virus began to spread through the country and infection rates started to accelerate, the German government reacted by drastically restricting the freedoms enshrined in the Basic Law: infected people had to quarantine; businesses, restaurants, schools and kindergartens were closed; people were not allowed to fraternize with anyone who was not a member of their household and were not permitted to gather outdoors. The restrictions had a tough impact on individuals' daily lives and presented numerous economic, social and psychological hurdles. And yet, the great majority of citizens trusted that the government was acting on good science, in good faith and for the benefit of the collective.

It helped that people could observe the government's deliberations and decision-making, so it seemed, up close. The ministers responsible came to their conclusions with a high degree of transparency and in continual consultation with scientific experts. The latter generously shared their knowledge with the public; at the same time, they repeatedly stressed that they were learning more day by day and revising their previous findings as a result. It was precisely this direct and open communication that convinced people to follow the guidelines. It reinforced the feeling that everyone was in the same boat and working to support the helmsman – or rather, helmswoman – to navigate the situation and carefully steer the nation forward. Trust was two-directional: the populace trusted the government and the government trusted them by loosening restrictions when the rate of infection was on the decline.

Still, there were a considerable number of citizens who did not share this trusting attitude. Some bought into conspiracy theories that preached distrust of 'elites' in science, media and politics. Others accused the government of becoming a 'dictatorship' that wanted to control people's bodies and minds (> Fear). They found support in right-wing parties that deliberately denounced policies designed to stop the virus and raised doubts about protective measures such as vaccination and mask wearing. Distrusting the government was part of an oppositional stance that became increasingly vocal and aggressive during the second year of the pandemic.

Trust as a Learning Process

Such developments show that trust is never a given and that it is based on more than one factor. Even if material evidence speaks in favour of trusting an individual or an institution, facts and the process by which they were determined might still be distrusted due to social, cultural and political cleavages.

Negotations of trust further demonstrate that trust and mistrust are by no means spontaneous affects, nor random gut feelings. Rather, they result from and mirror an emotional learning process, formed through experience and knowledge that has been accumulated and tested. They also indicate the presence or at least the possibility of alternatives. West German politicians had many opportunities to accrue both experience and knowledge. The lawmakers who drafted the Federal Republic's Basic Law in 1948 and 1949, the majority of whom were politically socialized during the Weimar era, profoundly mistrusted the citizens-to-be, scarred as they were by recent fascist history. Plebiscitary elements were therefore excluded from the constitution, as was the power of the president to bypass parliament. Even the 'votes of no confidence' so popular with the Weimar Reichstag were constructively reformed: anyone who wanted to overthrow an incumbent government required enough votes to form a new one, and a majority of parliamentarians had to express their confidence in it. This rule has proven to be of lasting value.

Citizens too have learnt from past experiences. They are less inclined to place blind trust in politicians than they once were ('Führer command us, we will follow you'). But they are similarly averse to baseless and fundamental mistrust and keep their distance from those groups and parties that actively stoke it. The vast majority of people decline to vote for them.

That does not mean, however, that people never argue or object. Trusting a person or an institution does not preclude one from evaluating them critically. This was the lesson learnt from the history of the GDR: there, the regime insisted on obtaining people's full and unlimited trust, with no criticism allowed. The rate of assent as proven by electoral turnout had to be at least 99 per cent, and if it was not, it had to be manipulated to meet official expectations. In the Federal Republic, levels of trust were not watched and monitored quite so anxiously, and citizens' trust did not have to be endlessly demonstrated and continuously proclaimed.

In this context, how trust is measured and interpreted poses questions. Does a high voter turnout really testify to people's trust in the political system? Under certain conditions and with different framings, the opposite might be true: those who do not head to the polls might feel so satisfied with how things are going that they see no reason to register a political opinion. They simply trust that things will continue as they are without their input or intervention.

Quite possibly, non-voters might not be the ideal democratic citizens dreamt of by political scientists and activists. One of the virtues of democratic societies, however, is that they do not make political participation mandatory. The reasons why someone does or does not grant a party or a person their trust may well remain as diverse and individual as the people themselves. For one person, the party platform might prove decisive, for another the character of a particular politician; someone else might vote for a party because their parents always had.

Personalizing trust has, since the 1960s, been a dominant feature of West German politics. Parties gained a reputation for being 'chancellor's election clubs' and waged campaigns with military precision to identify the 'character' of a politician and their 'selling point'. This was how Klaus Schütz framed it when he advised Willy Brandt during his candidacy for the chancellorship in 1961, using 'political advertising' strategies he had picked up in the United States.

The USA also led the way when it came to the role of the media in campaigning. Simultaneously, the media had its own requirements regarding the fit and fitness of politicians clamouring for citizens' trust. The trends towards personalization and mediatization have worked in tandem, one feeding the other: the media put individual politicians centre stage, and politicians adjusted their self-presentation to suit the media formats they made glad use of.[30]

Gerhard Schröder, SPD chancellor from 1998 to 2005, is a prime example of this symbiotic relationship. He cultivated his political persona by appearing frequently on television and proving himself to be an amusing and edgy talk-show guest. His approachability, staged by and in the media, was a necessary part of his ability to win the public's trust. It is difficult, though, to fully determine to what extent his television appearances helped him to succeed. Opinion polls are of little use since they tend to capture situational declarations of trust that are prone to change the very next day.

The only reliable indicator of political trust is elections, which give citizens the chance to vote for those they trust most to represent their individual as well as common interests over the next four or five years. In contrast to the trust invested in personal relationships, this kind of trust is emotionally 'thin'. But it is neither blind nor, like confidence, abstract or boundless. Unlike loyalty, which can only ever be betrayed, trust can be revoked without moral hesitation and handed to someone else at the next election. It has thus turned out to be the paradigm of a democratic emotion.

---

[30] Klaus Schütz, 'Politik und politische Werbung', *Die Neue Gesellschaft* 4, no. 1 (1957): 54–57; Daniela Münkel, *Willy Brandt und die "Vierte Gewalt": Politik und Massenmedien in den 50er bis 70er Jahren* (Frankfurt: Campus, 2005); Bernd Weisbrod, ed., *Die Politik der Öffentlichkeit – Die Öffentlichkeit der Politik* (Göttingen: Wallstein, 2003).

FURTHER READING

General

Katie Barclay, *The History of Emotions: A Student Guide to Methods and Sources* (London: Red Globe Press, 2020).

Rob Boddice, *The History of Emotions* (Manchester: Manchester University Press, 2018).

Lisa Feldman Barrett, *How Emotions Are Made: The Secret Life of the Brain* (Boston, MA: Houghton Mifflin Harcourt, 2017).

Ute Frevert et al., *Emotional Lexicons: Continuity and Change in the Vocabulary of Feeling 1700–2000* (Oxford: Oxford University Press, 2014).

Jan Plamper, *The History of Emotions: An Introduction* (Oxford: Oxford University Press, 2015).

Barbara H. Rosenwein and Riccardo Cristiani, *What Is the History of Emotions?* (Cambridge: Polity Press, 2018).

Robert C. Solomon, *What Is an Emotion? Classic and Contemporary Readings*, 2nd ed. (Oxford: Oxford University Press, 2003).

Anger

Martha Nussbaum, *Anger and Forgiveness: Resentment, Generosity, Justice* (New York: Oxford University Press, 2016).

Barbara H. Rosenwein, *Anger: The Conflicted History of an Emotion* (New Haven, CT: Yale University Press, 2020).

Warren D. TenHouten, *Anger: From Primordial Rage to the Politics of Hatred and Resentment* (Hauppauge, NY: Nova Science, 2020).

Belonging

Celia Applegate, *A Nation of Provincials: The German Idea of Heimat* (Berkeley: University of California Press, 1990).

Alon Confino, *The Nation as a Local Metaphor: Württemberg, Imperial Germany, and National Memory, 1871–1918* (Chapel Hill: University of North Carolina Press, 1997).

Jens Jäger, Heimat (English version), trans. David Burnett, in *Docupedia-Zeitgeschichte*, 13 August 2018, DOI: 10.14765/zzf.dok.2.1192.v1.

Jason James, *Preservation and National Belonging in Eastern Germany: Heritage Fetishism and Redeeming Germanness* (Basingstoke: Palgrave Macmillan, 2012).

Philipp Nielsen, *Between Heimat and Hatred: Jews and the Right in Germany, 1871–1935* (Oxford: Oxford University Press, 2019).

Linda Shortt, *German Narratives of Belonging: Writing Generation and Place in the Twenty-First Century* (London: Routledge, 2017).

Curiosity

Shelley Baranowski, *Strength through Joy: Consumerism and Mass Tourism in the Third Reich* (Cambridge: Cambridge University Press, 2004).

Toby E. Huff, *Intellectual Curiosity and the Scientific Revolution: A Global Perspective* (Cambridge: Cambridge University Press, 2010).

Katharina Rowold, *The Educated Women: Minds, Bodies, and Women's Higher Education in Britain, Germany, and Spain, 1865–1914* (New York: Routledge, 2010).

Kristin Semmens, *Seeing Hitler's Germany: Tourism in the Third Reich* (Basingstoke: Palgrave Macmillan, 2005).

Disgust

Sarah J. Ablett, *Dramatic Disgust: Aesthetic Theory and Practice from Sophocles to Sarah Kane* (Bielefeld: transcript, 2020).

Eleonora Joensuu, *A Politics of Disgust: Selfhood, World-Marking, and Ethics* (Abingdon: Routledge, 2019).

Daniel Kelly, *Yuck! The Nature and Moral Significance of Disgust* (Cambridge, MA: MIT Press, 2014).

Aurel Kolnai, *On Disgust*, ed. Barry Smith and Carolyn Korsmeyer (Chicago, IL: Open Court, 2004).

Michelle Mason ed., *The Moral Psychology of Contempt* (London; Rowman & Littlefield, 2018).

Winfried Menninghaus, *Disgust: The Theory and History of a Strong Sensation* (Albany: State University Press of New York, 2003).

Martha C. Nussbaum, *Hiding from Humanity: Disgust, Shame, and the Law* (Princeton, NJ: Princeton University Press, 2004).

Empathy

Aleida Assmann and Ines Detmers, eds, *Empathy and Its Limits* (Basingstoke: Palgrave Macmillan, 2016).

Thomas August Kohut, *Empathy and the Historical Understanding of the Human Past* (London: Routledge, 2020).

Susan Lanzoni, *Empathy: A History* (New Haven, CT: Yale University Press, 2018).
Heidi L. Maibom, *Empathy* (London: Routledge, 2020).

Envy

Joseph Epstein, *Envy* (Oxford: Oxford University Press, 2006).
Gwyneth H. McClendon, ed., *Envy in Politics* (Princeton, NJ: Princeton University Press, 2018).
Sara Protasi, *The Philosophy of Envy* (Cambridge: Cambridge University Press, 2021).

Fear

Frank Biess, *German Angst? Fear and Democracy in the Federal Republic of Germany* (Oxford: Oxford University Press, 2020).
Joanna Bourke, *Fear: A Cultural History* (London: Virago, 2005).
Thomas Kehoe and Michael Pickering, eds, *Fear in the German-Speaking World, 1600–2000* (London: Bloomsbury, 2020).
Michael Francis Laffan and Max Weiss, eds, *Facing Fear: The History of an Emotion in Global Perspective* (Princeton, NJ: Princeton University Press, 2012).
Jan Plamper and Benjamin Lazier, eds, *Fear Across the Disciplines* (Pittsburgh, PA: University of Pittsburgh Press, 2012).

Fondness

Andreas W. Daum, *Kennedy in Berlin*, trans. Dona Geyer (Cambridge: Cambridge University Press, 2008).
Benjamin Feyen and Ewa Krzaklewska, eds, *The ERASMUS Phenomenon – Symbol of a New European Generation?* (Frankfurt: Lang, 2013).
Kristin Haugevik, *Special Relationships in World Politics: Inter-State Friendship and Diplomacy after the Second World War* (London: Routledge, 2018).
Todd H. Hall, *Emotional Diplomacy: Official Emotion on the International Stage* (Ithaca, NY: Cornell University Press, 2015).

Grief

Carol Acton, *Grief in Wartime: Private Pain, Public Discourse* (New York: Palgrave Macmillan, 2007).
Alon Confino et al., eds, *Between Mass Death and Individual Loss: The Place of the Dead in Twentieth-Century Germany* (Oxford, NY: Berghahn, 2008).
Dorothy P. Holinger, *The Anatomy of Grief* (New Haven, CT: Yale University Press, 2020).

Hate

Richard Bessel, 'Hatred after War: Emotion and the Postwar History of Germany', *History and Memory* 17, no. 1–2 (2005): 195–216.
Berit Brogaard, *Hatred: Understanding Our Most Dangerous Emotion* (Oxford: Oxford University Press, 2020).
Melissa A. Click, *Anti-Fandom: Dislike and Hate in the Digital Age* (New York: New York University Press, 2019).
Carolin Emcke, *Against Hate* (Cambridge: Polity Press, 2019).
Teo Keipi et al., *Online Hate and Harmful Content: Cross-National Perspectives* (London: Routledge, 2017), DOI: 10.4324/9781315628370.
Aurel Kolnai, 'The Standard Modes of Aversion: Fear, Disgust and Hatred', in Aurel Kolnai, *On Disgust*, ed. Barry Smith and Carolyn Korsmeyer (Chicago, IL: Open Court, 2004), 93–109.

Honour

Kwame Anthony Appiah, *The Honor Code: How Moral Revolutions Happen* (New York: Norton & Co., 2010).
Ute Frevert, *Men of Honour: A Social and Cultural History of the Duel* (Cambridge: Polity Press, 1995).
Tamler Sommers, *Why Honor Matters* (New York: Basic Books, 2018).
Ann Goldberg, *Honor, Politics, and the Law in Imperial Germany, 1871–1914* (Cambridge: Cambridge University Press, 2010).

Hope

Ernst Bloch, *The Principle of Hope*, trans. Neville Plaice et al. (Oxford: Blackwell, 1986).
Terry Eagleton, *Hope without Optimism* (Charlottesville: University of Virginia Press, 2015).
Adrienne M. Martin, *How We Hope: A Moral Psychology* (Princeton, NJ: Princeton University Press, 2014).

Humility

Peter Bieri, *Human Dignity: A Way of Living* (Cambridge: Polity Press, 2017).
Ute Frevert, *The Politics of Humiliation* (Oxford: Oxford University Press, 2020).
Avishai Margalit, *The Decent Society* (Cambridge, MA: Harvard University Press, 1996).

Joy

Sabine Donauer, *Emotions at Work – Working on Emotions: The Production of Economic Selves in Twentieth Century Germany*, PhD thesis, Freie Universität Berlin 2013, www.diss.fu-berlin.de/diss/receive/FUDISS_thesis_000000100445.

Darrin M. MacMahon, *Happiness: A History* (New York: Atlantic Monthly Press, 2006).

Peter N. Stearns, *Happiness in World History* (New York: Routledge, 2021).

Love

Ann Brooks, *Love and Intimacy in Contemporary Society: Love in an International Context* (London: Routledge, 2020).

Dagmar Herzog, *Sexuality in Europe: A Twentieth-Century History* (Cambridge: Cambridge University Press, 2011).

Eva Illouz, *Why Love Hurts: A Sociological Explanation* (Cambridge: Polity Press, 2012).

Simon May, *Love: A History* (New Haven, CT: Yale University Press, 2011).

Josie McLellan, *Love in the Time of Communism: Intimacy and Sexuality in the GDR* (Cambridge: Cambridge University Press, 2011).

Nostalgia

Amieke Bouma, *German Post-Socialist Memory Culture: Epistemic Nostalgia* (Amsterdam: De Gruyter, 2019).

Juliane Brauer, 'Heidi's Homesickness', in Ute Frevert et al., *Learning How to Feel: Children's Literature and Emotional Socialization, 1870–1970* (Oxford: Oxford University Press, 2014), 209–27.

Thomas Dodman, *What Nostalgia Was: War, Empire, and the Time of a Deadly Emotion* (Chicago, IL: University of Chicago Press, 2018).

Rudy Koshar, *Germany's Transient Pasts: Preservation and National Memory in the Twentieth Century* (Chapel Hill: University of North Carolina Press, 1998).

Pride

Michael Eric Dyson, *Pride* (Oxford: Oxford University Press, 2006).

Gavin Brent Sullivan, ed., *Understanding Collective Pride and Group Identity: New Directions in Emotion Theory, Research and Practice* (London: Routledge, 2014).

June Price Tangney, *Self-Conscious Emotions: The Psychology of Shame, Guilt, Embarrassment, and Pride* (New York: Guilford, 1995).

Gabriele Taylor, *Pride, Shame and Guilt: Emotions of Self-Assessment* (Oxford: Oxford University Press, 1985).

Shame

Julien Deonna et al., *In Defense of Shame: The Faces of an Emotion* (Oxford: Oxford University Press, 2012).

Lina Jakob, *Echoes of Trauma and Shame in German Families: The Post–World War II Generations* (Bloomington: Indiana University Press, 2020).

Ruth Leys, *From Guilt to Shame: Auschwitz and After* (Princeton, NJ: Princeton University Press, 2007).

Sighard Neckel, 'Sociology of Shame: Basic Theoretical Considerations', in *Shame and Social Work: Theory, Reflexivity and Practice*, ed. Liz Frost et al. (Bristol: Policy Press, 2020), 39–54.

Solidarity

Kurt Bayertz, ed., *Solidarity* (Dordrecht: Kluwer, 1999).

Sabine Hake, *The Proletarian Dream, Socialism, Culture, and Emotion in Germany, 1863–1933* (Berlin: De Gruyter, 2017).

Thomas Kühne, *The Rise and Fall of Comradeship: Hitler's Soldiers, Male Bonding and Mass Violence in the Twentieth Century* (Cambridge: Cambridge University Press, 2017).

Steinar Stjernø, *Solidarity in Europe: The History of an Idea* (Cambridge: Cambridge University Press, 2005).

Trust

Ute Frevert, 'Trust as Work', in *Work in a Modern Society: The German Historical Experience in Comparative Perspective*, ed. Jürgen Kocka (New York: Berghahn, 2010), 93–108.

Geoffrey Hosking, *Trust: A History* (Oxford: Oxford University Press, 2014).

Niklas Luhmann, *Trust and Power* [1979], ed. Christian Morgner and Michael King (Cambridge: Polity Press, 2017).

Masamichi Sasaki and Robert M. March, eds, *Trust: Comparative Perspectives* (Leiden: Brill, 2012).

INDEX